SAS® ESSENTIALS

SAS® ESSENTIALS

Mastering SAS for Data Analytics

Second Edition

ALAN C. ELLIOTT and WAYNE A.WOODWARD
Department of Statistical Science
Southern Methodist University
Dallas, TX

Library of Congress Cataloging-in-Publication Data:

Elliott, Alan C., 1952-
  SAS essentials : mastering SAS for data analytics / Alan C. Elliott, Wayne A. Woodward. – Second edition.
    pages cm
  Includes bibliographical references and index.
  ISBN 978-1-119-04216-7 (pbk.)
  1. SAS (Computer file) 2. Mathematical statistics–Data processing. I. Woodward, Wayne A. II. Title.
  QA276.4.E423 2016
  005.5′5–dc23

                                                                                              2015016632

Cover credits: AUDINDesign/iStockphoto

Printed in the United States of America

Typeset in 10/12pt Times by SPi Global, Chennai, India.

V00184_051118

CONTENTS

PREFACE

SAS® Essentials: Mastering SAS for Data Analytics, Second Edition is a ground-up introduction to SAS statistical software aimed at students taking an applied statistics course as well as individuals who want to learn SAS for personal use or to supplement preparation for the SAS Base Certification Exam. Most chapters are designed so that the material can be covered in a 1-hour computer lab class. The book is sectioned into two parts. Part 1 (Chapters 1–8) covers the SAS programming language, primarily the DATA step and how to prepare data files for analysis. Part 2 (Chapters 9–19) covers commonly used SAS procedures. Many chapters are stand-alone, and readers can select to cover them in a different order or leave some out entirely. This book uses a hands-on programming approach to teaching and is filled with Hands-on Examples that will help the reader step through the learning process.

It uses the Windows version of SAS 9.4 for examples, although the vast majority of the information is applicable on any SAS platform.

Although there are millions of SAS installations around the world, there is a steep learning curve involved in mastering the program. This book is a straightforward approach developed from more than 20 years of teaching introductory SAS courses and more than 50 combined years of teaching and consulting by the authors.

Data sets and code for all of the examples can be downloaded from a web site described in Chapter 1.

ACKNOWLEDGMENTS

There is more to SAS® than a programming language and more to the output than p-values. With that in mind, this book integrates information from discussions with colleagues over several years, who contributed ideas to the selection of content for this book. Several colleagues helped by reading early versions and providing suggestions on various topics from their area of expertise. They include Terry D. Bilhartz, PhD (Sam Houston State University), Linda Hynan, PhD (UT Southwestern Medical Center, Dallas), and Cecil Hallum (Sam Houston State University).

We are also indebted to the fine editorial and production staff at Wiley and for the reviewers who provided valuable insights and suggestions. In particular, we would like to thank Susanne Steitz-Filler, Senior Editor; Sari Friedman, Senior Editorial Assistant; Dilip Kizzhakkera, Production Editor; and Lincy Priya, Project Manager for their help in getting this work into print.

We appreciate students and TAs who helped identify errors and typos in the early manuscripts. These include Chelsea Allen, Jeremy (Jiadong) Yang, Yusun Xia, Alanood Alotaibi, Daniel Ashy, Curtis Bradbury, Andrew Buck, Ashton Chmielewski, Alexandra Douglass, Robert Farrow, Benjamin Grisz, Tian Hang, Samantha Hirt, Rebin Kawani, Christina Kozell, Tony Nguyen, Morgan Slottje, Micah Thornton, Jeremy Wang, Peter Wendel, Kaitlin Willis, Xi Wu, and Yusun Xia.

Above all, we wish to thank our wives, E'Lynne and Beverly, for their patience and support through the long process of writing and rewriting the book.

Alan C. Elliott and Wayne A. Woodward
Dallas, Texas

June 2 2015

THE AUTHORS

Alan Elliott is the Director of the Statistical Consulting Center at Southern Methodist University, Dallas, Texas, within the Department of Statistical Science. Previously he served as a statistical consultant in the Department of Clinical Science at the University of Texas Southwestern Medical Center at Dallas for over 30 years. Elliott holds master's degrees in Business Administration (MBA) and Applied Statistics (MAS). He has authored or coauthored over 35 scientific articles and over 25 books including the *Directory of Microcomputer Statistical Software, Microcomputing with Applications, Using Norton Utilities, SAS Essentials, Applied Time Series Analysis*, and *IBM SPSS® by Example* (2nd Edition). Elliott has taught university-level courses in statistics, statistical consulting, and statistical computing for over 25 years.

Wayne A. Woodward, PhD, is a Professor of Statistics and chair of the Department of Statistical Science at Southern Methodist University, Dallas, Texas. In 2003, he was named a Southern Methodist University Distinguished Teaching Professor by the university's Center for Teaching Excellence, and he received the 2006–2007 Scholar/Teacher of the Year Award at SMU, an award given by the United Methodist Church. He is a Fellow of the American Statistical Association and was the 2004 recipient of the Don Owen Award for excellence in research, statistical consulting, and service to the statistical community. In 2007, he received the Outstanding Presentation Award given by the Section on Physical and Engineering Sciences at the 2007 Joint Statistical Meetings in Salt Lake City, Utah. Over the last 35 years, he has served as statistical consultant to a wide variety of clients in the scientific community and has taught statistics courses ranging from introductory undergraduate statistics courses to graduate courses within the PhD program in Statistics at Southern Methodist University. He has been funded on numerous research grants and contracts from government and industry to study such issues as global warming and nuclear monitoring. He has authored or coauthored over 70 scientific papers and four books.

PART I

DATA MANIPULATION AND THE SAS® PROGRAMMING LANGUAGE

1

GETTING STARTED

LEARNING OBJECTIVES

- To be able to use the SAS® software program in a Windows environment.
- To understand the basic information about getting data into SAS and running a SAS program.
- To be able to run a simple SAS program.

Research involves the collection and analysis of data. The SAS system is a powerful software program designed to give researchers a wide variety of both data management and data analysis capabilities. Although SAS has millions of users worldwide, it is not the simplest program to learn. With that in mind, we've created this book to provide you with a straightforward approach to learning SAS that can help you surmount the learning curve and successfully use SAS for data analysis.

Two main concepts are involved in learning SAS: (1) how to get data into SAS and ready for analysis using the SAS programming language and (2) how to perform the desired data analysis.

- Part 1 (Chapters 2–8) shows how to get data into SAS and prepare it for analysis.
- Part 2 (Chapters 9–19) shows how to use data to perform statistical analyses, create graphs, and produce reports.

This chapter introduces you to the SAS system's use in the Microsoft Windows environment and provides numerous hands-on examples of how to use SAS to analyze data.

SAS® Essentials: Mastering SAS for Data Analytics, Second Edition. Alan C. Elliott and Wayne A. Woodward.
© 2016 John Wiley & Sons, Inc. Published 2016 by John Wiley & Sons, Inc.

1.1 USING SAS IN A WINDOWS ENVIRONMENT

SAS runs on a number of computer platforms (operating systems) including mainframes and personal computers whose operating systems are UNIX, Mac OS X, Linux, or Windows. This book is based on using SAS in a Windows environment where you have the software installed on your local computer. The vast majority of the content in this book will apply to any SAS computer environment. However, we will include occasional references to differences that might be present in other operating systems. Most of the differences between versions have to do with file references. Moreover, there are multiple ways to use SAS, notably the programming or Enterprise Guide approaches. This book teaches the programming approach that offers the user the most flexibility. Before discussing the SAS program, we'll review some of the basic file-handling features of Windows.

1.1.1 Creating a Folder for Storing Your SAS Files

As there are several versions of Windows currently in use, we present general guidelines that should work in any one of them. To follow our examples, we recommend that you store the data and SAS files provided in this book in a folder named SASDATA. In fact, we recommend that you do this NOW!. The examples in this text will assume that all example files used in this book are in a folder whose file path is C:\SASDATA. You can adapt the examples by using an appropriate file path for other operating systems. Table 1.1 shows several ways to reference a file.

In your own research, you may choose to store your SAS files in a folder with a name that makes sense to you, such as C:\RESEARCH. You can also create subfolders for each analysis; for example, C:\RESEARCH\SMITH or C:\RESEARCH\JONES.

To copy the example files of this book to the C:\SASDATA folder on your own computer, perform the following:

1. Download the example files from the following Web site: http://www.alanelliott.com/sas
2. Follow the installation instructions provided on the Web site. Doing so creates the C:\SASDATA folder on your computer and copies the example files to that folder. (The Web site also includes updates concerning the information in this book.)

You can also use SAS on an Apple Mac. To do so we recommend that you install a virtual Windows environment using commercially available programs such as Bootcamp or Parallels and install SAS in the Windows environment. You can also run the SAS University Edition on Windows, Mac, or Linux environment. (Refer to the

TABLE 1.1 Accessing Files in Various Operating Systems

Operating System	Example File Reference
Windows	C:\SASATA\myfile
Windows/Cytrix	\\CLIENT\C$\SASDATA\myfile
UNIX	/home/sasdata/myfile
Open VMS	[username.sasdata]myfile
z/OS	SASDATA.myfile

www.sas.com/en_us/software/university-edition.html web address or search for "SAS University Edition" for more information.

> The examples in the book are designed to use data in the folder C:\SASDATA – in other words, in a folder on your computer's hard drive. You can also put the example files on any rewritable medium such as a flash drive or on a network drive – just remember to adjust the file names and file paths given in the examples in this book accordingly if you store your files in a location other than C:\SASDATA.

1.1.2 Beginning the SAS Program

Since there are multiple ways to use SAS, launching SAS may differ according to your installation and operating system. For a typical Windows environment, where there is a SAS icon (or tile) on your desktop, simply double-click it to launch SAS. If the SAS icon is not on your desktop, go to the Start button and select Start → Programs → SAS (English) to launch SAS. Henceforth, we will refer to this simply as the SAS icon.

(We don't recommend that you click on a .sas file to launch SAS because it may not open SAS in the way you want. Doing so may open SAS in the Enhanced Editor, Enterprise Guide, or Universal Viewer. (It depends on how SAS was installed on your computer.) This book uses the SAS Windows Enhanced Editor as the primary interface for using SAS.

1.1.3 Understanding the SAS Windows Interface

Once you begin the SAS program, you will see a screen similar to that shown in Figure 1.1. (The SAS program appearance may be slightly different depending on which versions of Windows and SAS you're using.)

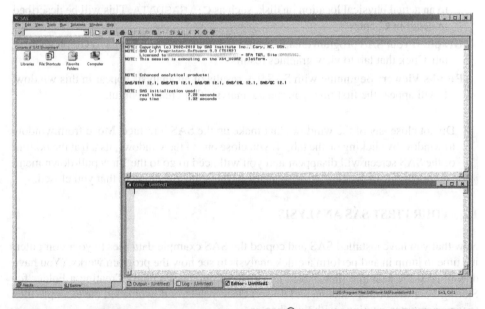

Figure 1.1 Initial SAS screen. (Source: Created with SAS® software, Version 9.4. Copyright 2012, SAS Institute Inc., Cary, NC, USA. All Rights Reserved. Reproduced with permission of SAS Institute Inc., Cary, NC)

The normal opening SAS screen is divided into three visible windows. The top right window is the **Log** Window, and at the bottom right is the **Editor**. The third window, which appears as a vertical element on the left, is called the **SAS Explorer/Results** window. There are other SAS windows that are not visible on the normal opening screen. These include the **Graph** and **Results Viewer** windows. To open a SAS window that is not currently visible, click its tab at the bottom of the screen. (The Output tab relates to a window that is not often used and we will not discuss it here.) Briefly, here are the purposes of these windows that are used in this text.

Editor: Also called the Enhanced Editor or Windows Programming Editor (WPGM), this is the area where you write SAS code. It is like a simple word processor. When you open a previously saved SAS program, its contents will appear in this window. SAS code is stored in plain ASCII text, so files saved in the ASCII format from any other editor or word processor may be easily opened in this editor. You can also copy (or cut) text from another editor or word processor and paste it into the Editor window.

Log: When you run a SAS program, a report detailing how (and if) the program ran appears in the Log Window. Typically, when you run a SAS program, you first look at the contents of the Log Window to see if any errors in the program were reported. The Log highlights errors in red. You should also look for warnings and other notes in the Log Window, which tell you that some part of your program may not have run correctly.

SAS Explorer/Results: This window appears at the left of the screen and contains two tabs (shown at the bottom of the window): The Results tab displays a tree-like listing of your output, making it easy to scroll quickly to any place in your output listing. The Explorer window (which you can display by clicking the Explorer tab) displays the available SAS libraries where SAS data files are stored. A SAS library is a nickname to an actual physical location on disk, such as C:\SASDATA. This will be described in detail in Chapter 3.

Graph: If your SAS program creates graphics output, SAS will display a Graph window tab. Click that tab to view graphics results.

Results Viewer: Beginning with SAS 9.3, results of an analysis appear in this window. It will appear the first time you run an analysis that creates output.

Do not close any of the windows that make up the SAS interface. Move from window to window by clicking on the tabs. If you close one of the windows, its tab at the bottom of the SAS screen will disappear and you will need to go to the View pull-down menu and select the appropriate window name to redisplay the element that you closed.

1.2 YOUR FIRST SAS ANALYSIS

Now that you have installed SAS and copied the SAS example data files to your computer, it's time to jump in and perform a quick analysis to see how the program works. (You have downloaded the example files, haven't you? If not, go back to the "Creating a Folder for Storing Your SAS Files" section and do so.) Once you have downloaded the example files to your computer, continue with this chapter.

The following steps show you how to open a SAS program file, perform a simple analysis using the data in the file, and create statistical output.

Our first example is a quick overview of how SAS works. You should not be concerned if you don't know much about the information in the SAS program file at this point. The remainder of the book teaches you how to create and run SAS programs.

HANDS-ON EXAMPLE

In this example, you'll run your first SAS analysis.

1. Launch SAS. SAS initially appears as shown in Figure 1.1. (If a tutorial or some other initial dialog box appears, dismiss it.)

2. Open a program file. This example uses a file named FIRST.SAS. To open this file, first make sure that your active window is the Editor Window. (Click anywhere in the Editor Window to make it the active window.) On the menu bar, select File → Open Program to open the file C:\SASDATA\FIRST.SAS. You may need to navigate to the C:\SASDATA folder to open this file.

3. Examine the opened file, the contents of which appear in the Editor Window. Maximize the Editor Window so that you can see more of the program code if necessary. Figure 1.2 shows the Editor Window maximized. We'll learn more in the latter chapters about what these lines of code mean.

Figure 1.2   The FIRST.SAS file opened.

4. Run the SAS job. There are three ways to run (sometimes called submit) your SAS code. (1) On the menu bar, select Run → Submit, (2) click the "running man" icon on the toolbar, or (3) press F8. Perform any of these to run this code. The SAS instructions in the file are carried out (or, in computer terminology, the commands

(continued)

(continued)

are executed). The SAS program creates analysis output that automatically appears in the Results Viewer.

Figure 1.3 Results for FIRST.SAS.

5. View the results shown in Figure 1.3.

   (a) The analysis requested in this SAS program is a task to calculate basic statistics (PROC MEANS) for each group (GENDER) in the data set.

   (b) Note the Results window (as opposed to the Results Viewer) on the left of the screen illustrated in Figure 1.3 – it contains a single item called **Means: The SAS System** (the full name is truncated in the image). As you perform more analyses in SAS, this list will grow. You can quickly display the results of any previous analysis by clicking the item in the list in this Results window.

6. Print the output. Make sure the Results Viewer window is active by clicking anywhere in that window. Print the contents of the window by clicking the printer icon on the toolbar or by selecting File → Print on the menu bar.

7. Save the output. To save the results shown in the Results Viewer, select File → Save As on the menu bar and enter an appropriate name for the output file, such as FIRST OUTPUT. The file will be saved as FIRST OUTPUT.MHT. (The .MHT extension refers to a single file web page file and is automatically added to the file name. If you subsequently open this file, it will open into your default web browser.)

8. Save the SAS program code (instruction file) that created the output by first going to the Editor Window that contains the FIRST.SAS program code. With the program on the screen, select File → Save As and enter a name such as MYFIRST. Make sure you are saving the code in the C:\SASDATA folder. This saves the file as MYFIRST.SAS. (The .SAS extension is automatically added to the file name.)

9. Examine the SAS Log. Click on the Log tab at the bottom of your screen and note that it contains a report on the SAS program code you just ran. It will include statements such as the following:

```
NOTE: Writing HTML Body file: sashtml.htm
NOTE: There were 18 observations read from the data set
WORK.EMPLOYEES.
```

   This indicates that the output is in an html format (web file format) and that the data set contained 18 records.

10. Clear the contents of the Log by right-clicking and selecting Edit → Clear All from the pop-up menu. In the Editor Window, right-click and select Clear All. (We'll learn a shortcut to this process later in this chapter.)

The Save As command saves the contents of whatever window is currently active. Thus, if the Results Viewer window is active, it saves the output as an *.MHT file; if the Log Window is active, it saves the contents of that window as an *.LOG file; and if the Editor Window is the active window, it saves the code as an *.SAS (SAS program code) file.

That's it! You've run your first SAS program. But wait, there's more. Now that you have one SAS job under your belt, it's time to try another one. This time, you'll make a small change to the program before you run it.

Before running each Hands-On Example, clear the Log and Editor Windows so that you will not mix up information from a previous example. To clear each window, use the right-click technique previously described, or go to the window and on the menu bar select Edit → Clear All. In the section "Using SAS Function Keys" of this chapter, we will create a way to shorten this process.

HANDS-ON EXAMPLE

In this example, you make a small change in the program and see how that change alters the output.

1. In the SAS Editor Window, open the program file SECOND.SAS. (It should be in your C:\SASDATA folder.) The SAS code looks like this:

```
* PUT YOUR TITLE ON THE NEXT LINE;
DATA EXAMPLE;
INPUT AGE @@;
DATALINES;
12 11 12 12 9 11 8 8 7 11 12 14 9 10 7 13
6 11 12 4 11 9 13 6 9 7 13 9 13 12 10 13
11 8 11 15 12 14 10 10 13 13 10 8 12 7 13
11 9 12
```

(continued)

```
(continued)
   ;
   PROC MEANS DATA=EXAMPLE;
      VAR AGE;
   RUN;
```

Run the SAS job using any of the methods described in the previous example and observe the output. Note that the title at the top of the output page is "The SAS System."

2. Under the comment line that reads

```
* PUT YOUR TITLE ON THE NEXT LINE;
```

type this new line:

```
TITLE "HELLO WORLD, MY NAME IS your name.";
```

Enter your own name instead of *your name*. Make sure you include the quotation marks and end the statement with a semicolon (;).

3. Run the SAS program, examine the output, and note how the title has changed in the output.

1.3   HOW SAS WORKS

Look at the SECOND.SAS program file to see how SAS works. It is really very simple. The lines in the file are like the items on a grocery list or a "to do" list. You create a list of things you want SAS to do and when you submit the job, SAS does its best to carry out your instructions. The basic steps are as follows:

1. Define a data set in SAS using the DATA step (which begins with the key word DATA.) In this case, the data values are a part of the code (although it is not always the case.) The data values to be used in this analysis follow the keyword DATALINES.

2. Once you have a data set of values, you can tell SAS what analysis to perform using a procedure (PROC) statement. In this case, the keywords PROC MEANS initiate the "MEANS" procedure.

3. Run the program and observe the output (in the Results Viewer).

Figure 1.4 illustrates this process.

This book teaches you how to create and use SAS by illustrating SAS techniques of data handling and analysis through a number of sample SAS programs.

To exit the SAS program, select File → Exit on the menu bar. Make sure you've saved all files you wish to save before ending the program. (The program will prompt you to save files if you have not previously done so.)

Figure 1.4   How SAS works

1.4   TIPS AND TRICKS FOR RUNNING SAS PROGRAMS

This section contains tips and tricks that can help you if something in your program goes wrong. Now that you have seen two sample SAS jobs, you should have an idea of how SAS programs are constructed. This section provides general rules for writing SAS programs.

Within a SAS program, each statement begins with an identifying keyword (DATA, PROC, INPUT, DATALINES, RUN, etc.) and ends with a semicolon (;). For example:

```
DATA TEMP;
PROC PRINT DATA=TEMP;
```

SAS statements are free-format – they do not have to begin in any particular column. Thus,

- **Statements can begin anywhere and end anywhere**. One statement can continue over several lines with a semicolon at the end of the last line signaling the end of the statement.
- **Several statements may be on the same line**, with each statement terminated with a semicolon.
- **Blanks,** as many as you want but at least one, may be used to separate the components (words) in a SAS program statement.
- Case (lower- and upper-) *doesn't* matter in most SAS statements.
- **Case *does matter* in data and quoted information.** When you enter character data values (such as M or m for "male"), case will matter when you are sorting or selecting the data. Moreover, the contents of a title or footnote are placed in quotation marks and are printed in the output using the uppercase and lowercase characters you indicate in the program code.

- **The most common error in SAS programming is a misplaced (or missing) semicolon.** Pay careful attention to the semicolons at the end of the statements; they tell SAS that the statement is completed.

- **A second common error is a missing RUN statement**. You *must* end every program with a RUN statement (in the Windows version of SAS). If you do not end the program with a RUN statement, your program may not terminate normally, and your last statement may not be completed. (For some procedures, you should also end with the QUIT; statement. Those will be discussed as they are mentioned in the text.)

- **A third common error in a SAS program is the presence of unmatched quotation marks**. If you enter a title without matching quotation marks, you will see an error message in your Log file such as "The TITLE statement is ambiguous due to . . . unquoted text." This error can cause subsequent statements in your code to be misinterpreted by SAS.

- **A search for errors in a program log should be from the top down.** It is inevitable that you will write programs that contain errors in syntax. When you get lots of errors in a SAS run, always fix the errors from the top down in your program code, because often the early errors lead to confusion that results in the latter errors.

- **If program errors cause problems that result in SAS's "freezing up" or not completing the steps in your program,** you can abort SAS's processes by pressing Ctrl-Break and selecting the "Cancel Submitted Statements" option from the dialog box that appears.

- **If you cannot resolve a problem within SAS**, *save your files*, restart SAS, and reopen the files. Try to find the code that caused the problem, and then re-run your program.

- **The structure of your SAS programs should be easy to read.** Note how the example programs in this book are structured – how some statements are indented for easy reading and how the code contains comments. (Lines that begin with an asterisk (*) are comments that are ignored when the program is run. Comments are discussed more in Chapter 5.)

Now that you've experienced running simple programs in SAS, you will want to know more about the syntax and conventions for entering and running a SAS program. The following is a brief introduction to some of the SAS program requirements you need to know.

1.4.1   Using the SAS Enhanced Editor

You may have noted that different parts of the coding in FIRST.SAS or SECOND.SAS appear in various colors and in bold font. The color coding is designed to help you clearly see step-boundaries (major SAS commands), keywords, column and table names, and constants. For example, in the SAS Enhanced Editor:

Green is used for comments.

Bold Dark Blue is used for the keyword in major SAS commands.

Blue is used for keywords that have special meaning as SAS commands.

A yellow background is used to highlight data.

A boundary line separates each step.

If you make a mistake in coding your SAS job, the appropriate colors will not appear. In fact, statements that SAS does not understand typically appear in red, which helps you locate potential problems with your code before you attempt to run the program.

TABLE 1.2   SAS Function Keys

Function Key	SAS Command	Result
F2	RESHOW	Reshows window interrupted by system command
F3	END; /*GSUBMIT BUFFER=DEFAULT*/	Submits SAS statements in clipboard
F4	RECALL	Recalls current SAS code to editor
F5	PROGRAM (PGM)	Displays Editor Window
F6	LOG	Displays Log Window
F7	OUTPUT	Displays Output Window
F8	ZOOM OFF;SUBMIT	Submits (runs) the current SAS program
F9	KEYS	Displays this Keys Window
F10	Not defined	
F11	COMMAND BAR	Moves cursor to command bar
F12	Not defined	

A boundary line separates steps (parts) of a SAS program. In the SECOND.SAS example note that a minus sign in a small box appears on the screen next to the keyword DATA (and another one next to PROC MEANS.) Clicking on this box compresses the step to its first line, and is a way to temporarily hide sections of code. When you run the code, the program still "sees and acts upon" what is in the compressed section.

1.4.2   Using SAS Function Keys

You can use keyboard function keys to move from window to window or to execute certain tasks in SAS. Some people prefer the use of function keys (rather than mouse clicks) as a quicker way of selecting program options. Table 1.2 lists some of the SAS function keys that you can use throughout this book.

You can also customize these keys. To display the full set of function key commands, on the menu bar select Tools → Options → Keys.

HANDS-ON EXAMPLE

In earlier examples, you cleared the information from the Log Windows manually. In this example, you will create a new F12 function key command that will clear the Log Window and the Results Window and return you to the Editor Window. The F12 key you're about to define uses the SAS commands:

- **CLEAR LOG** – clears the contents of the Log Window.
- **ODSRESULTS;CLEAR;** – clears the contents of the Results window (and closes that window). Note that there is no blank between ODS and RESULTS.
- **WPGM;** returns you to the WPGM (i.e. to the active window most recently edited).

Following these instructions shows how to create a new F12 function key definition.

1. Press the F9 function key to display the Keys Window. Table 1.2 shows some of the key definitions that appear on your screen.

(continued)

(continued)

2. Next to the blank F12 option, enter

```
CLEAR LOG; ODSRESULTS; CLEAR; WPGM;
```

   Press the Enter key to lock in the new command.
3. Exit the Keys Window (by clicking on the small x at the top right of the window) and try out this function key by re-running one of the previous example programs. With the output displayed on the screen, press F12. The Results Window will be cleared and closed, the Log Window information will be cleared, and the Editor Window will be displayed, still containing the current program code. Thus, this command allows you to quickly clear the Log and Results windows without deleting the program code. This new command will be used in some of our future examples. (If you press F12 and your Editor does not reappear, press it again, or press F5 to display the Editor Window.)

Use the F12 SAS function key you created to clear the contents of the Results and Log Windows between examples.

1.4.3   Using the SAS Menus

The SAS pull-down menu items differ depending on which window is currently active (Editor, Output, Log, etc.). To see the change in the menu options, click each window to make it active and note the menu choices at the top of the main SAS window, which are particular to the current window.

The SAS window you will use most is the Enhanced Editor, because that is where you will write and edit SAS code. Therefore, we'll spend a little time describing the menus for the Editor Window.

File: Used for opening and saving files, importing and exporting files, and for printing.

Edit: Used to copy, cut, and paste text, as well as to find and replace text.

View: Allows you to go back and forth between viewing the Editor Window, the Log Window, and the Output Window.

Tools: Allows you to open programs for graphics and text editing, along with other options available to customize the program to your preferences.

Run: Allows you to run (submit) a SAS program.

Solutions: Contains options to advanced procedures not discussed in this text.

Window: As in most Windows programs, allows you to choose display options for opened windows such as tile and cascade; also allows you to select (make active) a particular window, such as the Log or Output Window.

Help: Contains options for the SAS help system as well as online documentation. (See the section "Getting SAS Help" later in this chapter.)

1.4.4   Understanding Common File Extensions

Another piece of information you need to be aware of when learning and using SAS concerns the type of files used and created by SAS or mentioned in this book. Like most Windows files, they have specific file name extensions that indicate what application is associated with them (e.g., the way a *.doc or *.docx extension indicates a Microsoft Word file).

SAS Code File (*filename*.sas): This is an ACSII text file and may be edited using the SAS Editor, Notepad, or any text editor that can read an ASCII file.

SAS Log File (*filename*.log): This ASCII text file contains information such as errors, warnings, and data set details for a submitted SAS program.

SAS Results File (*filename*.mht or filename.html): This file contains the web-formatted output such as that displayed in the Results Viewer. HTML stands for Hyper-Text Markup Language and is the common language of Internet web files. MHT is short for MHTML and stands for Microsoft (or MIME) Hypertext Archive file. It is a type of HTML file that contains the entire html-coded information in a single file (whereas HTML files may access external files for some components such as graphs.)

SAS Data File (*filename*.sas7bdat): This file contains a SAS data set that includes variable names, labels, and the results of calculations you may have performed in a DATA step. You cannot open or read this file except in SAS or in a few other programs that can read SAS data files.

Raw Data Files (*filename*.dat or *filename*.txt or *filename*.csv): These ASCII (text) files contain raw data that can be imported into SAS or edited in an editor such as Notepad.

Excel File (*filename*.xls or *filename*.xlsx): The data in a Microsoft Excel file (when properly formatted into a table of columnar data) can be imported into SAS. (We'll discuss data file types that can be imported into SAS in Chapter 3.)

1.4.5   Getting SAS Help

SAS help is available from the SAS Help pull-down menu (Help → SAS Help and Documentation). When you select this option, SAS displays a help file as shown in Figure 1.5 (with the SAS Products option expanded). As with other software help systems, you can choose to search for keywords (using the Search tab), or you can scroll through the tree-like list to select topics of interest.

In Figure 1.5, note that the SAS Products section has been expanded to display links to help with a number of SAS program components. The options called Base SAS and SAS/STAT are references to the information discussed in this text. Specifically, details about the statistical procedures (PROCs) discussed in this book are documented in these two sections of the Help file.

SAS help is also available on the web in a number of forms. SAS Institute provides many of their reference manuals on the web (as pdf files), there are a number of papers presented at SAS conferences on the web, and a number of independent web sites that include SAS examples and help. A search for a particular SAS topic (i.e., "SAS ANOVA") will typically bring up a large number of links.

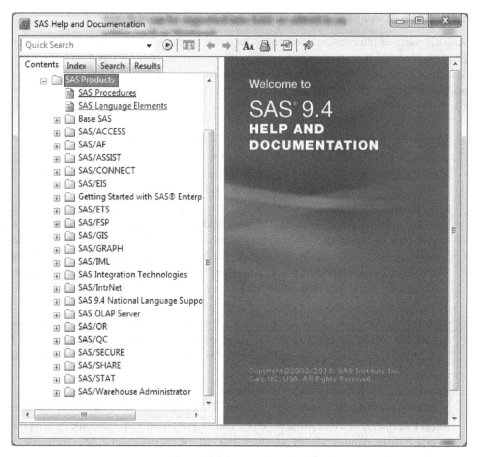

Figure 1.5   Help file display.

1.5   SUMMARY

This chapter provided an overview of SAS and examples of how to run an existing SAS program. In the following chapters, we will discuss the components of a SAS program, including how to enter data, how to request analyses, and how to format and read output.

EXERCISES

1.1   **Enter code and run a SAS program.**

Enter the following SAS code into the Editor Window and run the program. Make sure the Editor Window is clear of all other information before you begin.

```
DATA TEMP;
INPUT ID SBP DBP SEX $ AGE WT;
DATALINES;
```

```
1 120 80 M 15 115
2 130 70 F 25 180
3 140 100 M 89 170
4 120 80 F 30 150
5 125 80 F 20 110
;
RUN;
PROC PRINT DATA=TEMP;
TITLE 'Exercise 1.1 - Your Name';
RUN;
PROC MEANS;
RUN;
```

Include your name in the TITLE line. Observe the results in the Results Viewer. To save the output to a file, make sure the Results Viewer is active and select File → Save As, or you can select and copy the contents of the Results Viewer and paste the output into an e-mail or word processor document. Hints for running this program are as follows:

a. Begin SAS.

b. Enter the SAS code into the Editor Window. Pay attention to the color coding to make sure all of your code has been entered correctly.

c. Before running the program, save the SAS code under the name C:\SASDATA\ MYEXERCISE1.1.SAS.

d. Run the program. (Click the "running man" icon or select Run → Submit on the menu bar.)

e. Check the Log Window for errors.

f. If there are errors in the Log file, observe where the error occurred. SAS will usually point out the code that produced the error. If there were errors, proceed to the next step; if not, skip to step k.

g. After determining what changes should be made to your code, press F12 to clear the Log and Results Viewer if you have previously defined the F12 key. Or go to the Log Window and right-click, and choose **Edit → Clear All.** (This clears the error messages out of the log so that you won't get confused by seeing an old error.)

h. Return to the Editor Window.

i. Make corrections in the Editor Window to fix the error you discovered in step f. Re-save the code.

j. Go back to step d.

k. Examine the output in the Results Viewer.

l. You may optionally print, save, or e-mail the output as directed by your instructor.

m. Optionally end SAS.

1.2 **Change the contents of a SAS program.**

Enter the following SAS code into the Editor Window and run the program. Make sure the Editor, Log, and Results Viewer are clear of all other information before you begin. (You can clear the Log and Results Viewer by pressing F12 if you have previously defined that key.)

```
DATA RECOVERY;
INPUT LNAME $ RECTIME;
DATALINES;
JONES 3.1
SMITH 3.6
HARRIS 4.2
MCCULLEY 2.1
BROWN 2.8
CURTIS 3.8
JOHNSTON 1.8
;
RUN;
PROC PRINT DATA=RECOVERY;
Title 'Exercise 1.2 - Your Name';
RUN;
PROC MEANS DATA=RECOVERY;
RUN;
```

Include your name in the TITLE line. Observe the results in the Results Viewer. (You may optionally print, save, or e-mail the output as directed by your instructor. These instructions will be assumed from this point on and will not be included in future exercises.)

2

GETTING DATA INTO SAS®

LEARNING OBJECTIVES

- To enter data using freeform list input
- To enter data using the compact method
- To enter data using column input
- To enter data using formatted input
- To enter data using the INFILE technique
- To enter multiple-line data

Before you can perform any analysis, you must have data. SAS contains powerful tools you can use to enter, import, and manage your data. This chapter introduces the most commonly used methods for getting data into SAS. Additional techniques are covered in Chapter 3.

The main way to enter and manipulate data in SAS is by using the SAS DATA step. This DATA step creates a specially formatted type of file referred to as a "SAS data set" or "SAS data file." A SAS data set contains the raw data plus other information. It contains variable names, how data values are read and interpreted, how values are displayed in output, labels associated with the variable names, and other information.

Entering and manipulating data are the primary topics of the following several chapters. In the initial SAS examples, you may have noted that the programs begin with the keyword DATA, followed by lines of code defining the data for analysis. As noted in Chapter 1, this is

SAS® Essentials: Mastering SAS for Data Analytics, Second Edition. Alan C. Elliott and Wayne A. Woodward.
© 2016 John Wiley & Sons, Inc. Published 2016 by John Wiley & Sons, Inc.

TABLE 2.1   Overview of the SAS DATA Step

Task	How Do You Do It?
Getting data: creating a new SAS data set, either by reading a list of data or by using (importing) data that are in another file	Within the DATA step, use a SAS DATA statement as discussed in this chapter
Saving data: storing data from SAS to a permanent location on your hard drive	Within the DATA step, instruct SAS to write the created data set to a location on disk or save the data set by using a SAS library reference as discussed in Chapter 3
Preparing data for analysis: data sets must sometimes be manipulated to make the data ready for analysis – including setting missing value, rearranging data, and revising incorrect values	Within the DATA step, create variable labels, assign missing values, create new variables, and assign labels to data categories as discussed in Chapter 4

called the DATA step. Within the DATA step, data are manipulated, cleaned, and otherwise prepared for analysis. Depending on how carefully the data have been collected and entered, this process can be quick and simple or long and detailed. Either way, the DATA step is the primary way to get your data into SAS and be prepared for analysis.

Table 2.1 is an overview of how the SAS DATA step works and what will be discussed in the following few chapters.

2.1   USING SAS DATA SETS

The DATA step is the primary way in which SAS data sets are created. Therefore, it is important for you to learn how to read, manipulate, and manage SAS data sets using the DATA step. The following sections describe how to create a SAS data set, beginning with simple examples and later describing more complex data set creation techniques.

> In this book, we'll refer to a text file containing numbers and other information as a "raw data file." A "SAS data file" is a specially formatted file created and read by SAS programs containing data as well as other information about the structure of the file and the characteristics of the data values.

In the SAS language, the DATA statement signals the creation of a new SAS data set. For example, a DATA statement in SAS code may look like this:

```
DATA MYDATA;
```

The keyword DATA tells SAS to create a new SAS data set. The word MYDATA in the DATA statement is the name assigned to the new data set. (You can choose any name for a SAS data set that conforms to SAS naming conventions, as described in the section "Rules for SAS Variable Names" in this chapter.) The SAS DATA statement has two major functions, which are as follows:

- It signals the beginning of the DATA step.

- It assigns a name (of your choice) to the data set created in the DATA step. The general form of the DATA statement is as follows:

```
DATA datasetname;
```

The SAS datasetname in the DATA statement can have several forms.

- The SAS data set name can be a single name (used for **temporary data sets**, those kept only during the current SAS session). The following examples create SAS data sets that are temporary:

```
DATA EXAMPLE;
DATA OCT2016;
```

- The SAS data set name can be a two-part name. The two-part name tells SAS that this **permanent data set** will be stored on disk after the current SAS session in a SAS library indicated by the prefix name (the name preceding the dot). The following examples create permanent data sets:

```
DATA RESEARCH.JAN2016;
DATA CLASS.EX1;
DATA JONES.EXP1;
```

Thus, in the first example, the prefix RESEARCH is the name of the SAS library and JAN2016 is the name of the SAS data set. RESEARCH is a nickname for a hard disk folder. For example, RESEARCH may refer to (be a nickname for) the folder C:\SASDATA. In this case, JAN2016 is the SAS data set name, and that data set is located in the C:\SASDATA folder. Details about creating nickname references (i.e., library names) are provided in Chapter 3. Also, if you are using a Citrix Receiver version of SAS, then refer to the section titled "CITRIX Implementation of SAS" in Chapter 3 for information on how to use Windows path names in that platform. Similarly, if you are using the University Edition of SAS, refer to Appendix E for more information on how to use Windows path references for that version of SAS.

- You don't have to use a nickname to refer to a SAS data set. Another way to refer to a SAS data file that is more familiar to Windows users is to use its Windows filename. For example:

```
DATA "C:\SASDATA\CLASS";
DATA "C:\MYFILES\DECEMBER\MEASLES";
```

As in the previous example, CLASS is the name of a SAS data set, and that data set will be located in the C:\SASDATA folder. (Technically, the name of the SAS data set on disk is C:\SASDATA\CLASS.SAS7BDAT, but you do not have to include the extension .SAS7BDAT in the filename reference in the DATA statement.) This is simply a different way of referring to the same file using a different naming convention. Details of this technique are given in the following chapter.

- The SAS data set name can be omitted entirely. This technique is used for temporary data sets, which are kept only during the current SAS session. For example:

```
DATA;
```

In this case, SAS will name the data set for you. On the first occurrence of such a DATA step, SAS will name the data set DATA1, then DATA2, and so on.

The DATA statement is the usual beginning for most SAS programs. In the following sections and chapters, you will see some of the power of the DATA statement in reading and preparing data for analysis.

The general syntax for the SAS DATA statement is as follows:

```
DATA datasetname;
    <code that defines the variables in the data set>;
    <code to enter data>;
    <code to create new variables>;
    <code to assign missing values>;
    <code to output data>;
        <code to assign labels to variables>;
        <and other data tasks>;
```

Each of these components of the DATA statement will be discussed in some detail, although covering the full extent of the DATA statement's capabilities would take a book several times the length of this volume.

Technically, even data sets created with single names as in DATA EXAMPLE are also referred to in SAS as WORK.EXAMPLE. The designation WORK refers to a built-in temporary SAS library (a place that contains data files) that is deleted when you end a SAS session. In your use of temporary SAS data sets such as this, you can refer to them as either EXAMPLE or WORK.EXAMPLE.

2.2   UNDERSTANDING SAS DATA SET STRUCTURE

Once you read data into SAS, the program stores the data values in a data set (also called a data table), which is a collection of data values arranged in a rectangular table. Table 2.2 is a visual illustration of how SAS internally stores a typical data set – columns are variables (each named) and rows are subjects, observations, or records.

Although the structure of this table may look similar to the way data are stored in a Microsoft Excel spreadsheet, there are some important differences.

TABLE 2.2   SAS Data Set (Table) Structure

	ID	SBP	DBP	GENDER	AGE	WT
OBS1	001	120	80	M	15	115
OBS2	002	130	70	F	25	180
⋮	⋮	⋮	⋮	⋮	⋮	⋮
OBS100	100	120	80	F	20	110

- Each **column** represents a variable and is designated with a variable name (ID, SBP, etc.). Every SAS variable (column) must have a name, and the names must follow certain naming rules. The data in each column conform to a particular data type (numbers, text, dates, etc.).
- Each **row**, marked here as OBS1, OBS2, and so on, indicates observations or records. Each row consists of data observed from one subject or entity.

In the section "Creating a SAS Library Using a Dialog Box" in Chapter 3, you will see how to display a SAS data table in spreadsheet mode.

2.3 RULES FOR SAS VARIABLE NAMES

Each variable (column) in the SAS data set (table) must have a name, and the names must follow certain rules. This differs from Excel, which imposes no restriction on how (or if) to name columns of data. However, many of the rules for SAS are similar to those for a data table created in Microsoft Access. Each SAS variable name

- must be 1–32 characters long but must not include any blanks;
- must start with the letters A through Z (not case sensitive) or an underscore (_). A name may not include a blank;
- may include numbers (but not as the first character);
- may include upper- and lowercase characters (but variable names are case insensitive);
- should be descriptive of the variable (optional but recommended).

Here are some examples of correct SAS variable names:

```
GENDER
AGE_IN_1999 (notice underscores)
AGEin1999
_OUTCOME (notice the leading underscore)
HEIGHT_IN_CM (notice underscores)
WT_IN_LBS (notice underscores)
```

And here are some examples of incorrect SAS variable names:

```
AGE IN 2000
2000MeaslesCount
S S Number
Question 5
WEIGHT IN KG
AGE-In-2000
```

These variable names are incorrect because some include blanks (S S Number, AGE IN 2000, Question 5, WEIGHT in KG), start with something other than a letter or an underscore (2000MeaslesCount), or contain special characters other than the underscore (AGE-In-2000).

2.4   UNDERSTANDING SAS VARIABLE TYPES

SAS is designed to differentiate among three basic types of variables: numeric, text, and date.

- **Numeric Variables** (Default): A numeric variable is used to designate values that could be used in arithmetic calculations or are grouping codes for categorical variables. For example, the variables SBP (systolic blood pressure), AGE, and WEIGHT are numeric. However, an ID number, phone number, or Social Security number should not be designated as a numeric variable. For one thing, you typically would not want to use them in a calculation. Moreover, for ID numbers, if ID = 00012 were stored as a number, it would lose the zeros and become 12.

- **Character (Text, String) Variables**: Character variables are used for values that are not used in arithmetic calculations. For example, a variable that uses M and F as codes for gender would be a character variable. For character variables, case matters, because to the computer a lowercase f is a different character from an uppercase F. It is important to note that a character variable may contain numerical digits. As mentioned previously, a Social Security number (e.g., 450-67-7823) or an ID number (e.g., 043212) should be designated as a character variable because their values should never be used in mathematical calculations. When designating a character variable in SAS, you must indicate to SAS that it is of character type. This is shown in upcoming examples.

- **Date Variables**: A date value may be entered into SAS using a variety of formats, such as 10/15/09, 01/05/2010, JAN052010, and so on. As you will see in upcoming examples, dates are handled in SAS using format specifications that tell SAS how to read or display the date values. For more information about dates in SAS, see Appendix B.

2.5   METHODS OF READING DATA INTO SAS

The following few sections illustrate several techniques for entering data (creating a data set) in SAS. These are not the only ways to enter data into SAS, but they are the most common. The methods discussed are as follows:

- Reading data using freeform list input
- Reading data using the compact method
- Reading data using column input
- Reading data using formatted input.

Methods of importing data from other file formats (such as Excel) are discussed in the following chapter. Moreover, the initial examples of these data entry methods illustrate how to read data that are within the SAS code; but these methods can also be used to read in data from an external file, as will be illustrated later.

2.5.1   Reading Data Using Freeform List Input

A simple way to enter data into SAS is as freeform input. In this method, variable names in the DATA step are indicated by a list following the INPUT statement keyword. For example:

```
DATA MYDATA;
INPUT ID $ SBP DBP GENDER $ AGE WT;
```

The DATA statement gives the SAS data set the name MYDATA (as discussed earlier), and the INPUT statement tells SAS the names of the variables in the data set. Note that in the INPUT statement there is a blank and a dollar sign ($) *after* the variable names ID and GENDER. In freeform input, this notation indicates to SAS that the variables ID and GENDER are of character type. For ID, we want to preserve leading zeros in, and for GENDER the values are non-numeric M and F.

When using freeform input, the information for each subject or entity must be listed one row at a time. Each individual row of data contains all the data for that subject, and each data value is separated by at least one blank. (We intentionally put several blanks between some values in the data lines below to illustrate this point.) A DATALINES statement signals the beginning of the data values when the data values are listed within the SAS code file. For example:

```
DATALINES;
001 120 80 M      15      115
002 130 70 F 25 180
003 140 100 M 89 170
004 120 80 F 30 150
005 125 80 F 20 110
```

The first data line contains the data for a single subject. The first data value (001) in that line corresponds to the first variable (ID) in the INPUT statement. The second value (120) corresponds to SBP, and so on. Each data value on each line is separated by at least one blank.

In a SAS program, a special keyword, DATALINES, tells SAS that the upcoming lines contain data. The following code (DFREEFORM.SAS) is an example of freeform input:

```
DATA MYDATA;
INPUT ID $ SBP DBP GENDER $ AGE WT;
DATALINES;
001 120 80 M      15      115
002 130 70 F 25 180
003 140 100 M 89 170
004 120 80 F 30 150
005 125 80 F 20 110
;
PROC PRINT DATA=MYDATA;
RUN;
```

This program reads in five lines of data and creates a listing of the data (PROC PRINT) that is displayed in the Results Viewer. Here are the components of this SAS program in the order in which they should occur:

1. The DATA statement tells SAS to create a data set. In this case, the data set is named MYDATA.
2. The INPUT statement indicates the variable names (and types for character variables) for the data set.

TABLE 2.3   A Sample SAS Data Set

ID	SBP	DBP	GENDER	AGE	WT
001	120	80	M	15	115
002	130	70	F	25	180
003	140	100	M	89	170
004	120	80	F	30	150
005	125	80	F	20	110

3. The DATALINES statement tells SAS that the following lines contain data. (You may see older versions of SAS code that use the keyword CARDS instead of DATALINES. The statements are interchangeable.)

4. Each data line contains the values for one subject, and the values in the data line correspond to the variables named in the INPUT statement; and those data values must be separated on the line by at least one blank.

5. The semicolon following the data indicates the end of the data values. When SAS encounters the semicolon, it stops reading data values and creates an internal SAS data set table such as the one given in Table 2.3.

   Note that the columns of the data set table match the variable names in the INPUT statement.

6. The PROC PRINT statement tells SAS to create a listing of the data. We'll learn more about PROC PRINT in the section "Using PROC PRINT" in Chapter 5.

7. The RUN statement tells SAS to finish this section of the program. Without the RUN statement, SAS may expect that more instructions are pending, and it will not finish the procedure. Therefore, SAS programs *must* conclude with a RUN statement.

One of the most common errors in writing a SAS program is to omit the RUN; statement. Don't let this happen to you!

Advantages of Freeform List Input: Some of the advantages of freeform list input are the following:

- It's easy, with very little to specify.
- Rigid column positions are not required, making data entry easy.
- If you have a data set in which the data are separated by blanks, this is the quickest way to get your data into SAS.

Rules and Restrictions for Freeform List Input: The following rules and restrictions govern freeform list input:

- Every variable on each data line must be in the order specified by the INPUT statement.
- Data values must be separated by at least one blank. (We'll learn about data with other delimiters in the Going Deeper section "Using Advanced INFILE Statement Options" in this chapter.)

- Blank spaces representing missing variables are not allowed. Using blank spaces as missing values in the freeform data entry technique causes values to be out of sync. If there are missing values in the data, a dot (.) should be placed in the position of that variable in the data line. (We'll learn about other missing value techniques in the section "Using IF to Assign Missing Values" in Chapter 4.) For example, a data line with AGE missing might read:

```
4 120 80 F . 150
```

- Data values for character variables are restricted. In the freeform technique:
- No embedded blanks (e.g., MR ED) are allowed within the data value for a character field.
- A character field can have a maximum length of eight characters. (A later example will show how to overcome this restriction.)

HANDS-ON EXAMPLE

In this example you will enter data using the freeform data entry technique.

1. Open the program file DFREEFORM.SAS. (The code was shown above.) Run the program.
2. Observe that the output listing (shown here) illustrates the same information as in Table 2.3.

TABLE 2.4   Output from PROC PRINT for the Freeform Entry Example

Obs	ID	SBP	DBP	GENDER	AGE	WT
1	001	120	80	M	15	115
2	002	130	70	F	25	180
3	003	140	100	M	89	170
4	004	120	80	F	30	150
5	005	125	80	F	20	110

One reason to display your data using the PROC PRINT statement is to verify that SAS has properly read in your data and created a SAS data set that can now be used for further analysis.

As given in Chapter 3, some "freeform" data sets may use a delimiter other than blank. In that case, additional coding is required to properly read the data set.

2.5.2   Reading Data Using the Compact Method

A second version of freeform input allows you to have several subjects' data on a single line. This technique is often used in textbooks to save space. For example, here is SAS code using the typical way of reading freeform.

To save space, the data can be compacted using an @@ option in the INPUT statement to tell SAS to continue reading each line until it runs out of data.

```
DATA WEIGHT;
INPUT TREATMENT LOSS;
DATALINES;
1 1.0
1 3.0
1 -1.0
1 1.5
1 0.5
1 3.5
2 4.5
2 6.0
2 3.5
2 7.5
2 7.0
2 6.0
2 5.5
3 1.5
3-2.5
3-0.5
3 1.0
3  .5
;
PROC PRINT;
RUN;
```

To save space, the data can be compacted using an @@ option in the INPUT statement to tell SAS to continue reading each line until it runs out of data. For example, the save data using the compact method could look like this:

```
DATA WEIGHT;
INPUT TREATMENT LOSS @@;
DATALINES;
1 1.0 1 3.0 1 -1.0 1 1.5 1 0.5 1 3.5
2 4.5 2 6.0 2 3.5 2 7.5 2 7.0 2 6.0 2 5.5
3 1.5 3 -2.5 3 -0.5 3 1.0 3  .5
;
PROC PRINT;
RUN;
```

This second version of the input procedure takes up less space. Other than the addition of the @@ indicator, this data entry technique has the same benefits and restrictions as the previous freeform input method.

HANDS-ON EXAMPLE

In this example, you will edit a freeform data entry program to use the compact entry method.

1. Open the program file DFREEFORM.SAS, which was used in the previous example. Run the program and examine the data listing in the Results Viewer. It is the same output given in Table 2.4.

To return to the editor, and clear the Results and Log Windows, press the F12 function key. (If you have not defined the function key F12, refer to the section "Using SAS Function Keys" in Chapter 1.)

2. On the INPUT line, place a space and @@ after the WT and before the semicolon so it reads

```
INPUT ID $ SBP DBP GENDER $ AGE WT @@;
```

3. Modify the data so that there are two subjects per line. For example, the first two lines become:

```
1 120 80 M 15 115 2 130 70 F 25 180
```

4. Run the program and verify that the data are listed correctly in the Results Viewer. (The output should be the same as before.)

2.5.3   Reading Data Using Column Input

Another technique for reading data into SAS is called column input. This data entry technique should be used when your data consist of fixed columns of values that are not necessarily separated by blanks. For example, consider the following data:

```
001120 80M15115
002130 70F25180
003140100M89170
004120 80F30150
005125 80F20110
```

Because the freeform technique will not work with these data, SAS allows you to specify which columns in the raw data set contain the values for each variable. You must know the starting column and ending columns for each variable's values. The INPUT statement uses the following format:

```
INPUT variable startcol-endcol ...;
```

An example of a column data entry INPUT statement that reads data from fixed columns in the MYDATA data set is:

```
DATA MYDATA;
INPUT ID $ 1-3 SBP 4-6 DBP 7-9 GENDER $ 10 AGE 11-12 WT 13-15;
```

Note that the primary difference between this column input statement and the freeform list input statement is the inclusion of column ranges telling SAS where to find the information for each variable in the data set. (As previously, the $ *after* ID and GENDER (and before the column designations) specifies that they are character-type [text] variables.)

Here is an example program (DCOLUMN.SAS) using the column input format. This program reads in data and calculates descriptive statistics for the numeric variables using PROC MEANS (which is discussed in detail in Chapter 9).

```
DATA MYDATA;
INPUT ID $ 1-3 SBP 4-6 DBP 7-9 GENDER $ 10 AGE 11-12 WT 13-15;
DATALINES;
001120 80M15115
002130 70F25180
003140100M89170
004120 80F30150
005125 80F20110
;
RUN;
PROC PRINT DATA=MYDATA;
RUN
```

Note in the INPUT statement that each variable name is followed by a number or a range of numbers that tells SAS where to find the data values in the data set. The numbers for ID are found in columns 1–3. The values for SBP are found in the column range from 4 to 6, and so on.

Advantages of Column input: Some of the advantages of column input are as follows:
- You can input only the variables you need and skip the rest. This is handy when your data set (perhaps downloaded from a large database) contains variables you're not interested in using. Read only the variables you need.
- Data fields can be defined and read in any order in the INPUT statement.
- Blanks are not needed to separate fields.
- Character values can range from 1 to 200 characters. For example:

```
INPUT DIAGNOSE $ 1-200;
```

- For character data values, embedded blanks are no problem (e.g., John Smith).

Rules and Restrictions for Column Input: The following rules and restrictions govern column input:
- Data values must be in fixed column positions.
- Blank fields are read as missing.
- Character fields are read right justified in the field.
- Column input requires more specifications than freeform input. You must specify the column ranges for each variable.

You should also be aware of how SAS reads in and interprets column data. For example, the INPUT statement shown in the following code indicates that the character value data for GENDER appear in columns 1–3. If the value is really only one character wide, SAS reads in the value in the column and right justifies the character data. (The numbers 1234 . . . at the top of each example represent column positions.)

```
INPUT GENDER $ 1-3;
1 2 3 4 5 6 7                    1  2  3  4
    M                              M
  M                 -> All read as M
M                                  M
```

Note that all M's are stored right justified at the third column. In a similar way, numeric values can appear anywhere in the specified column range. Consider the use of the following INPUT statement to read values for the numeric variable X:

```
INPUT X 1-6;
1 2 3 4 5 6 7
      2 3 0
    2 3 . 0
  2 . 3 E 1
2 3
- 2 3
+ 2 3
```

SAS reads the information in columns 1–6 and interprets the information as a number. The above numbers are read as 230, 23, 23 (2.3E1 is a number written in scientific notation: 2.3 times 10 to the first power $= 23$), 23, -23, and 23.

HANDS-ON EXAMPLE

This example illustrates the column data input method.

1. Open the program file DCOLUMN.SAS. Run the program. The following output is given in Table 2.5.

   Note that ID and GENDER are *left* justified in the cell because they are character variables, and numbers are *right* justified.

   TABLE 2.5   Output from the Column Entry Example

Obs	ID	SBP	DBP	GENDER	AGE	WT
1	001	120	80	M	15	115
2	002	130	70	F	25	180
3	003	140	100	M	89	170
4	004	120	80	F	30	150
5	005	125	80	F	20	110

2. Suppose you are interested only in the variables ID, SBP, and AGE in this data set. Modify the INPUT statement to include only ID, SBP, and AGE:

   ```
   INPUT ID  $1-3 SBP 4-6 AGE 11-12;
   ```

3. Run the modified program. The data in the columns not specified are ignored during data input, and the listing displays only columns for ID, SBP, and AGE.

One way to tell if a variable in a SAS data set listing (PROC PRINT) is character or numeric is this: Character data are listed *left* justified in a cell and numeric data are listed *right* justified in a cell.

2.5.4 Reading Data Using Formatted Input

Another technique for reading data from specific columns is called formatted input. This technique allows you to specify information about how SAS will interpret data as they are read into the program. SAS uses the term *informat* to specify an input format specification that tells it how to read data. (A FORMAT specification tells SAS how to output data into a report. This is discussed in the section "Using FORMATs for Output" in this chapter.) Using an informat is helpful when you are reading data that might be in an otherwise hard-to-read format, such as date and dollar values. The syntax for formatted input is as follows:

```
DATA MYDATA;
INPUT @col variable1 format. @col variable2 format. ...;
```

where @col is a pointer that tells SAS from which column to *start* reading the information about a particular variable. Here is a specific example:

```
DATA MYDATA
INPUT @1 SBP 3. @4 DBP 3. @7 GENDER $1. @8 WT 3. @12 OWE COMMA9.;
```

In this example, note that the information for each variable contains three components. Thus, for the first variable, the information is the following:

1. **The pointer** (the @ sign) tells SAS to read data for this variable beginning in the indicated column (in this case column 1).
2. **The variable name** (SBP) tells SAS that the name of this first variable is SBP.
3. **The informat** (3.) tells SAS that data at this location in each row are numbers containing three digits and containing no decimal places.

Here is a brief description of how typical informat (input format) specifications are named:

Informat Type	Syntax
Character	$FORMATNAMEw.
Numeric	FORMATNAMEw.d
Date and Time	FORMATNAMEw.

- The FORMATNAME designation in the Syntax column indicates that formats will have various names
- The $ in the name always indicates a character informat.
- The w indicates the maximum data width (in number of columns) for the variable.
- The d specifies the number of digits to the right of the decimal place. (Only valid for numeric data.)
- All informats contain a decimal point (.) This allows SAS to differentiate an informat from a SAS variable.

Informats not only specify the type and width of the input data, they may "help" SAS interpret data as it is read. For example, note the informat used for the last variable (OWE) in the above example (COMMA9.). The reason this informat is used is that COMMA9. is able to interpret numbers that have dollar signs and commas and convert them into standard numbers. (Try reading data with dollar signs and commas into Excel – it's very difficult. Here is an example program that uses the example INPUT statement: (DINFORMAT.SAS).

```
DATA MYDATA;
INPUT @1 SBP 3. @4 DBP 3. @7 GENDER $1. @8 WT 3. @12 OWE COMMA9.;
DATALINES;
120 80M115 $5,431.00
130 70F180 $12,122
140100M170 7550
120 80F150 4,523.2
125 80F110 $1000.99
;
PROC PRINT DATA=MYDATA;
RUN;
```

Note that the OWE variable contains some particularly nasty-looking pieces of information that many programs would have trouble reading. With SAS it's a breeze. As you use SAS more, you will find that using informats can be a valuable time saver in getting data ready for analysis. Some common informats are listed in Table 2.6. (Additional formats are listed in Appendix A.)

TABLE 2.6   Example SAS Informats (Input Formats)

Informat	Meaning
5.	Five columns of data as numeric data
$5.	Character variable with width 5, removing leading blanks
$CHAR5.	Character variable with width 5, preserving leading blanks
COMMA7.	Seven columns of numeric data and strips out any commas or dollar signs (i.e., $40,000 is read as 40000)
COMMA10.2	Reads 10 columns of numeric data with 2 decimal places (strips commas and dollar signs). $19,020.22 is read as 19020.22
MMDDYY8.	Date as 01/12/16 (watch out for Y2K issue)
MMDDYY10.	Date as 04/07/2016
DATE7.	Date as 20JUL16
DATE9.	Date as 12JAN2016 (No Y2K issue)

If you read in data using a format such as 5. where the actual number has a decimal place in it, as in 3.4, SAS preserves the value of the number as 3.4 and does not round or truncate it into an integer.

Advantages and restrictions of formatted input: Some of the advantages and restrictions of formatted input are as follows:

- Advantages and restrictions are similar to those for column input.
- The primary difference between the column input and formatted input techniques is the ability to read in data using informat specifications.
- Formatted input is particularly handy for reading date and dollar values.

HANDS-ON EXAMPLE

In this example, you use the informat method of reading data into a SAS data set.

1. Open the program file DINFORMAT.SAS (program file shown above) and run the program. The output is given in Table 2.7.
2. Modify the INPUT statement by replacing the INFORMAT comma9. with a $9. informat specification. This tells SAS to read in the data for the variable OWE as character data rather than as numeric data.
3. Run the modified program and observe the output. How has it changed? Note that the new OWE variable read in with the $9. informat cannot be used in any calculation because it is not numeric. (Left justification tells you that the column contains a text-type variable.)

TABLE 2.7   Output from Formatted Data Entry Example

Obs	SBP	DBP	GENDER	WT	OWE
1	120	80	M	115	5431.00
2	130	70	F	180	12122.00
3	140	100	M	170	7550.00
4	120	80	F	150	4523.20
5	125	80	F	110	1000.99

2.5.5   Using FORMATs for Output

As this chapter discusses how to use informats for reading in data, it makes sense to look at their counterpart, output formats. Output formats, or simply formats, are used to tell SAS how to display data when it is listed in a procedure such as PROC PRINT. In this case, we use a SAS statement named FORMAT. For example, the statement (in a DATA step)

```
FORMAT OWE DOLLAR10.2
```

TABLE 2.8   Example SAS (Output) FORMATs

Format	Meaning
5.	Write data using five columns with no decimal points. For example, 12345
5.1	Write data using five columns with one decimal point. For example, 123.4
DOLLAR10.2	Write data with a dollar sign, commas at thousands, and with two decimal places. For example, $1,234.56
COMMA10.1	Write date with commas at thousands and with one decimal place. For example, 1,234.5
MMDDYY10.	Displays dates in common American usage as in 01/09/2016
DATE9.	Displays time using a military style format. For example, 09JAN2016
WORDDATE12.	Displays dates with abbreviated month names as in Jan 9, 2016
WORDDATE18.	Displays dates with full month names such as in January 9, 2016
WEEKDATE29.	Displays dates with day of week as in Saturday, January 9, 2016
BESTw.	Prints out numbers with maximum precision according to the designated width w

tells SAS to use the format DOLLAR10.2 when displaying the variable OWE in PROC PRINT (or any other procedure). The general syntax for the FORMAT statement is as follows:

```
FORMAT VAR1 FORMAT1. VAR2 VAR3 VAR4 FORMAT2.etc....;
```

FORMAT is the SAS keyword that begins the statement. VAR1 is a variable name to which a format is to be applied and FORMAT1. is the name of the FORMAT (3., COMMA6., DATE9., etc.) to apply to VAR1 in this case. FORMAT2. applies to VAR2, VAR3, and VAR4. You may define any number of FORMATs to variables within this statement. Some commonly used output formats are listed in Table 2.7. Note that a specification used as an informat can usually also be used as an output format, so there are some that are the same as in Table 2.8.

> If a data has a decimal such as 4.9 and you output the data using a format such as 4. that does not have a decimal place, SAS will output a rounded integer (i.e., in this case, 4.9 gets rounded to 5).

The following example illustrates how you could use both INFORMATs and FORMATs in a SAS program.

```
DATA REPORT;
INPUT @1 NAME $10. @11 SCORE 5.2 @18 BDATE DATE9.;
FORMAT BDATE WORDDATE12.;
```

This code uses the DATE9. input format to read in a data value called BDATE. The FORMAT statement tells SAS to output the same value, this time using the (output) format WORDDATE12. specification. For the SCORE value, the number is read in using a 5.2 input format. No output format is defined for this value, so it is output using the SAS default format, which in this case is called the BEST12. format, which writes out a number to the most possible decimals available. In this case, there are two decimal places read in, so two are written out.

HANDS-ON EXAMPLE

In this example, you will use informats to read in date values and formats to write out date values.

1. Open the program file DINFORMAT2.SAS. Submit the code and observe the output given in Table 2.9.

```
DATA REPORT;
INPUT @1 NAME $10. @11 SCORE 5.2 @17 BDATE DATE9.;
FORMAT BDATE WORDDATE12.;
DATALINES;
Bill      22.12 09JAN2016
Jane      33.01 02FEB2000
Clyde     15.45 23MAR1999
;
PROC PRINT DATA=REPORT;
RUN;
```

2. In the FORMAT statement, change the format for BDATE to WEEKDATE29. (Be sure to include the period at the end of the FORMAT specification.) Resubmit the program. How does that change the output? Add SCORE 5.1 to the FORMAT statement to specify an output format for the SCORE variable. Resubmit the program. How does that change the SCORE column?

3. Enter a new line of data containing your first name and your birthdate. Make sure your new data line up (i.e., are in the same columns) with the current data. Rerun the program. On what day of the week were you born?

4. Move the entire FORMAT statement (including the ;) to a line after PROC PRINT but before the last RUN statement. Rerun the program. The output should be the same in step 3. The FORMAT statement can appear either in a DATA step or in a PROC step. However, when it appears in the DATA step, it *permanently* applies that format to the designated variable. When the FORMAT statement appears in a PROC statement, it only affects the output for that PROC.

5. Put an asterisk before the FORMAT line. An asterisk changes a SAS statement into a comment that is ignored when a program is run. Rerun the edited SAS program – how does that change the output? Why? (The answer is that SAS stores dates as integers, and when there is no format assigned to a date variable, the internal representation of the date is output instead of a date value. See Appendix C for more information about dates.)

TABLE 2.9   Output from Formatted Data Entry Example Including Dates

Obs	NAME	SCORE	BDATE
1	Bill	22.12	Jan 9, 2016
2	Jane	33.01	Feb 2, 2000
3	Clyde	15.45	Mar 3, 1999

2.5.6   Using the SAS INFORMAT Statement

There is a SAS statement named INFORMAT that you could use in the freeform data entry case. For example,

```
DATA PEOPLE;
   INFORMAT LASTNAME FIRSTNAME $12. AGE 3. SCORE 4.2;
   INPUT LASTNAME FIRSTNAME AGE SCORE;
   DATALINES;
Lincoln     George      35 3.45
Ryan        Lacy        33 5.5
;
PROC PRINT DATA=PEOPLE;
RUN;
```

In this case, the INFORMAT statement can specify that a freeform input text value is longer than the default eight characters. Note that you still cannot have any blanks in the string variables (LASTNAME and FIRSTNAME). However, we will not use the INFORMAT statement in any future examples. We will prefer instead to specify informats in the INPUT statement where needed. (The code for this example is found within the program file DINFORMAT3.SAS.)

2.5.7   Reading External Data Using INFILE

In the examples used so far, the DATALINES statement has been used to tell SAS that data records follow the program statements in the DATA step. That is, the data are in the same file as your SAS code. If your data are already stored in certain types of separate computer files, you can instruct SAS to read the records from the file using the INFILE statement.

For example, in this world of data, data everywhere, data sets are available by download from a number of sources. Data are often in a text (raw data) file where the values are in fixed columns. (Typical file extensions for such files are DAT, TXT, or ASC.) In these situations, you can use either the column input or formatted input technique to read the data into SAS. In practice, because these data sets may contain hundreds or thousands of rows (thus making it difficult to embed them into your SAS code), it is usually wise to read the data from these files using the INFILE technique.

The INFILE statement is used to identify the filename of an external ASCII (text) file. When you use the INFILE statement, you do not have to also use a DATALINES statement. The INFILE statement takes the place of the DATALINES statement. The general form for the INFILE statement is as follows:

```
INFILE filespecification options;
```

For example, the file EXAMPLE.TXT contains 50 lines of data in ACSII format. (You can look at this data file using Notepad or any text editor or word processor.) The first few lines are as follows:

```
101 A  12 22.3 25.3 28.2 30.6 5 0
102 A  11 22.8 27.5 33.3 35.8 5 0
104 B  12 22.8 30.0 32.8 31.0 4 0
110 A  12 18.5 26.0 29.0 27.9 5 1
```

TABLE 2.10   Using the INFILE Statement

Variable	N	Mean	Std Dev	Minimum	Maximum
AGE	50	10.4600000	2.4261332	4.0000000	15.0000000
TIME1	50	21.2680000	1.7169551	17.0000000	24.2000000
TIME2	50	27.4400000	2.6590623	21.3000000	32.3000000
TIME3	50	30.4920000	3.0255942	22.7000000	35.9000000

Example SAS code that will read in the first six data values (columns of data each separated by blanks) of this data file is as follows:

```
DATA MYDATA;
INFILE 'C:\SASDATA\EXAMPLE.TXT';
INPUT  ID $ 1-3 GP $ 5 AGE 6-9
       TIME1 10-14 TIME2 15-19 TIME3 20-24;
```

Note the difference between the INFILE and the INPUT statements. The INPUT statement is nothing new. It uses the column entry designation discussed earlier. However, unlike before, there is no DATALINES statement as the INFILE statement takes the place of DATALINES. It tells SAS that the data are to be found in the file specified by the INFILE statement. (Note that the INFILE statement must appear in the code *before* the INPUT statement so, when the INPUT statement is read by SAS, it knows where to go to find the data.)

This output from this program uses a procedure named PROC MEANS that displays descriptive statistics for the data set. When run, this code produces the output given in Table 2.10. To summarize:

- Data are in the program code: Use a DATALINES statement.
- Data are to be read from external source: Use an INFILE statement.

A more thorough look at the INFILE statement is given later in this chapter.

HANDS-ON EXAMPLE

In this example, you will read in data from an external file and limit the number of variables read into the SAS data set.

1. Open the program file DINFILE1.SAS.

```
DATA MYDATA;
INFILE 'C:\SASDATA\EXAMPLE.TXT';
INPUT  ID $ 1-3 GP $ 5 AGE 6-9
       TIME1 10-14 TIME2 15-19 TIME3 20-24;
PROC MEANS DATA=MYDATA;
RUN;
```

Run the program and observe the output given in Table 2.10.

2. Modify the INPUT statement to read in only the variables ID, GP, AGE, and TIME3.
3. Rerun the program and observe the difference in output. Note that the new output includes statistics for AGE and TIME3. Why are statistics for ID and GP not included in the output?

2.6   GOING DEEPER: MORE TECHNIQUES FOR ENTERING DATA

SAS includes myriad ways to read in data. Techniques covered thus far are the most common methods. The following additional techniques can also be helpful when your data are listed in multiple records per subject and when your data are in comma-delimited format.

2.6.1   Reading Multiple Records per Observation

Occasionally, data will be stored in such a way that multiple lines (or records) are used to hold one subject's information. SAS is able to associate observations that span more than one line to one subject. Suppose input records are designed so that each subject's information is contained on three lines:

```
10011 M 15 115
    120 80 254
    15 65 102
10012 F 25 180
    130 70 240
    34 120 132
10013 M 89 170
    140 100 279
    19 89 111
etc.
```

One method for reading these data into a SAS data set is to have three consecutive INPUT statements. Each INPUT statement advances to the next record (but stays with the same subject). Thus, the three records in the data file combine to become one "subject" in the SAS data set:

```
INPUT ID $ SEX $ AGE WT;
INPUT SBP DBP BLDCHL;
INPUT OBS1 OBS2 OBS3;
```

Another method for reading in these data uses the / indicator in the INPUT statement to advance to the next line. Each time a / is seen in the INPUT statement, it tells SAS to go to the next physical record in the data file to find additional data for the same subject:

```
INPUT ID $ SEX $ AGE WT/ SBP DBP BLDCHL/ OBS1 OBS2 OBS3;
```

A third way to read these data is by using the #n indicator to advance to the first column of the nth record in the group. In this case, #2 instructs SAS to begin reading the second line in the data file. The highest #n used in the INPUT statement tells SAS how many lines are used for each subject:

```
INPUT ID $ SEX $ AGE WT #2 SBP DBP BLDCHL #3 OBS1 OBS2 OBS3;
```

or in another order:

```
INPUT #2 SBP DBP BLDCHL #1 ID $ SEX $ AGE WT #3 OBS1 OBS2 OBS3
```

An advantage of this technique is that you can read the data lines into SAS in any order, as specified by the #*n*. Note that all of these methods require that there be *the same number of records for each subject*. If there are differing numbers of records per subject, SAS can still read in the data, but that technique is beyond the scope of this book.

An example of a program (DMULTLINE.SAS) to read multiple-line data into SAS is the following:

```
DATA MYDATA;
INPUT ID $ SEX $ AGE WT/ SBP DBP BLDCHL/ OBS1 OBS2 OBS3;
DATALINES;
10011 M 15 115
   120 80 254
   15 65 102
10012 F 25 180
   130 70 240
   34 120 132
10013 M 89 170
   140 100 279
   19 89 111
;
PROC PRINT DATA=MYDATA;
RUN;
```

In this case, we used the / advance indicator technique to read the three data lines per person. The output for this program is given in Table 2.11. Note that how even though there are nine lines of data, the DATA step reads in the data as three records.

TABLE 2.11   Using Multiline Entry

Obs	ID	SEX	AGE	WT	SBP	DBP	BLDCHL	OBS1	OBS2	OBS3
1	10011	M	15	115	120	80	254	15	65	102
2	10012	F	25	180	130	70	240	34	120	132
3	10013	M	89	170	140	100	279	19	89	111

HANDS-ON EXAMPLE

1. Open the program file DMULTILINE.SAS. Change the INPUT line to read in data using each of the three different INPUT statements technique.
2. Change in the INPUT line to read in data using line number technique, but read in first line one #1, then line three #3, and finally line two #2. Submit the code and observe the output.

A number of examples given used INPUT column pointer control such as @5 to move the pointer to column 5. Table 2.12 lists commonly used INPUT pointer controls and arguments.

TABLE 2.12   INPUT Pointer Control Commands

INPUT Pointer Control or Arguments	Meaning
@N	Moves the pointer to the Nth column (N can be a numeric variable or a numeric expression)
+N	Moves the pointer ahead N columns (N can be a numeric variable or a numeric expression)
@	Holds the exaction of the next INPUT item and allows you to specify some conditional input criteria
@@	Must be the last item in an INPUT line. Reads data for multiple records within a single line of data
#N	Moves the pointer to record N (N can be a numeric variable or a numeric expression)
/	Advances to the next record

TABLE 2.13   INFILE Options

INFILE Option	Meaning
DLM='char'	Allows you to define a delimiter to be something other than a blank. For example, if data are separated by commas, include the option DLM= ',' in the INFILE statement
DLMSTR='string'	Allows you to define a string as a delimiter in the INFILE statement. For example, DLMSTR="~/~"
DSD	Instructs SAS to recognize two consecutive delimiters as a missing value. For example, the information M,15,, 115 would be read as M, 15, Missing, 115. Moreover, this option permits the use of a delimiter within quoted strings. For example, the data value "Robert Downey, Jr." would be read properly, meaning that SAS wouldn't interpret the comma in the name as signaling a new value
MISSOVER	Indicates to SAS that, when reading a data line, if it encounters the end of a data line without finding enough data to match all of the variables in the INPUT statement, it should continue reading data from the next input data line
TRUNCOVER	Forces the INPUT statement to stop reading data when it gets to the end of a short line
PAD and LRECL=n	This option pads short lines with extra blanks. It is used in conjunction with the LRECL= option that specifies the length of the input lines

(continued)

TABLE 2.13   (*Continued*)

INFILE Option	Meaning
FIRSTOBS=*n*	Tells SAS on what line you want it to start reading your raw data file. This is handy if your data file contains one or more header lines or if you want to skip the first portion of the data lines
OBS=*n*	Indicates which line in your raw data file should be treated as the last record to be read by SAS
FLOWOVER, STOPOVER, and SCANOVER	These commands are not discussed but may also be used to tell SAS how to read unusual input lines. See SAS documentation for more information

2.6.2   Using Advanced INFILE Statement Options

When you acquire a data set from another source that you intend to read into SAS using an INFILE statement, the data set might not be in the exact format you need. To help you read in external data, SAS includes a number of options you can use to customize your INFILE statement. Some of these INFILE options are listed in Table 2.13.

The purpose of the options in Table 2.12 is to give you more flexibility in reading data files into SAS using the INFILE statement. The following examples illustrate some of these options.

HANDS-ON EXAMPLE

1. Open the program file DINFILE2.SAS.

```
DATA MYDATA;
INFILE 'C:\SASDATA\EXAMPLE.CSV' DLM=',' FIRSTOBS=2 OBS=11;
INPUT GROUP $ AGE TIME1 TIME2 TIME3 Time4 SOCIO;
PROC PRINT DATA=MYDATA;
RUN;
```

   This code is used to import the first 10 lines of data in the raw data (comma separated) file EXAMPLE.CSV. The first few lines of this data file are as follows:

```
GROUP,AGE,TIME1,TIME2,TIME3,TIME4,SOCIO
A,12,22.3,25.3,28.2,30.6,5
A,11,22.8,27.5,33.3,35.8,5
B,12,22.8,30.0,32.8,31.0,4
A,12,18.5,26.0,29.0,27.9,5
B,9,19.5,25.0,25.3,26.6,5
B,11,23.5,28.8,34.2,35.6,5
```

   The first line in this file is a header line containing variable names. The DLM=',' option tells SAS that the data are comma delimited. The FIRSTOBS=2 option instructs SAS to start reading the data with the second line, and OBS=11 tells SAS to end with line 11, which means that it will read in the first 10 lines of data.

2. Submit this code. The PROC PRINT produces the output shown in Table 2.14.
3. Change the OBS=11 statement to read in the first 25 records of the data set and rerun the program. (Recall that the first data record is on line 2.)
4. Suppose you only want to read in records 6 through 31. Change the FIRSTOBS and OBS statements to read in only those records and rerun the program. (Recall that record 6 begins on line 7.)

TABLE 2.14   Output from Reading CSV File

Obs	GROUP	AGE	TIME1	TIME2	TIME3	Time4	SOCIO
1	A	12	22.3	25.3	28.2	30.6	5
2	A	11	22.8	27.5	33.3	35.8	5
3	B	12	22.8	30.0	32.8	31.0	4
4	A	12	18.5	26.0	29.0	27.9	5
5	B	9	19.5	25.0	25.3	26.6	5
6	B	11	23.5	28.8	34.2	35.6	5
7	C	8	22.6	26.7	28.0	33.4	3
8	B	8	21.0	26.7	27.5	29.5	5
9	B	7	20.9	28.9	29.7	25.9	2
10	A	11	22.5	29.3	32.6	33.7	2

The DLM option allows you to define the delimiter in the data. The following example illustrates how to use this option when there is an unusual delimiter.

HANDS-ON EXAMPLE

1. Open the program file DINFILE3.SAS.

```
DATA PLACES;
INFILE DATALINES DLMSTR='!~!';
INPUT CITY $ STATE $ ZIP;
DATALINES;
DALLAS!~!TEXAS!~!75208
LIHUE!~!HI!~!96766
MALIBU!~!CA!~!90265
;
PROC PRINT;
RUN;
```

The data are within this code so you can easily see the delimiter, which is !~!. The DLMSTR= options occur in the INFILE statement, and in this case the INFILE DATALINES statement tells SAS how to read the data from the DATALINES statement.

(continued)

(continued)

2. Submit this code and note that the data are read correctly into the defined variables. The output is given in Table 2.15.

3. Add a new record using the city of your choice, making sure to include the correct delimiter. Resubmit the code to make sure it works.

TABLE 2.15   Output from Reading CSV File

Obs	CITY	STATE	ZIP
1	DALLAS	TEXAS	75208
2	LIHUE	HI	96766
3	MALIBU	CA	90265

A more challenging problem is reading in a data set using INPUT where there are blank values in the data. Consider the following data set. The first three lines represent a ruler to help you see the columns where the data values are located. (It is NOT part of the data set.) That is, the last name is in column 01 through 21 (20 characters long). The maximum length of records is 45 characters.

```
0         1         2         3         4
123456789012345678901234567890123456789012345
---------------------------------------------
ABRAMS               JJ        C0001 Producer
BRISTOW              SYDNEY    C0015 Teacher
VAUGHN               MICHAEL   C0033 Agent
FLINKMAN             MARSHALL  C0123 Analyst
SLOAN                ARVIN     C0666
BRISTOW              JACK
DIXON                MARCUS    C0233 Chief
```

HANDS-ON EXAMPLE

1. Open the program file DINFILE4.SAS.

```
DATA TEST;
 INFILE "C:\SASDATA\DINFILEDAT.TXT";
 INPUT LAST $1-21 FIRST $ 22-30 ID $ 31-36 ROLE $ 37-44;
RUN;
PROC PRINT DATA=TEST;RUN;
```

2. Submit this code and observe the output. Note that the data are not correctly read. The output is shown in Table 2.16.

A check of the SAS log shows this statement:

```
The minimum record length was 25.
        The maximum record length was 44.
NOTE: SAS went to a new line when INPUT statement reached past
the end of a line.
```

TABLE 2.16   Output from Reading CSV File with Problems

Obs	LAST	FIRST	ID	ROLE
1	ABRAMS	JJ	C0001	Producer
2	BRISTOW	SYDNEY	C0015	VAUGHN
3	FLINKMAN	MARSHALL	C0123	SLOAN

This statement tells you that there are different record lengths. To solve this issue, do the following:

3. Add the option TRUNCOVER; to the end of the INFILE statement so it reads:

```
INFILE "C:\SASDATA\DINFILEDAT.txt" TRUNCOVER;
```

4. Resubmit the code and observe that the data are read in correctly. The TRUNCOVER option forces the INPUT statement to stop reading when it gets to the end of a short line. The results are shown in Table 2.17.
5. Change the input statement to

```
INFILE "C:\SASDATA\TESTDATA.TXT" LRECL=44 PAD;
```

Submit the code and observe the results. This also reads in the data correctly. The PAD option pads short lines with blanks to the length of the LRECL= option. Try running this code without PAD and observe the results.

6. Change the input statement to

```
INFILE "C:\SASDATA\TESTDATA.TXT" MISSOVER;
```

Submit the code and observe the results. The data are not read in correctly. MISSOVER prevents SAS from going to a new input line if it does not find values for all of the variables in the current line of data. Since TEACHER didn't fill out the entire space (i.e., had only 7 characters and ended on column 43), it was skipped.

TABLE 2.17   Output from Reading CSV Using TRUNCOVER

Obs	LAST	FIRST	ID	ROLE
1	ABRAMS	JJ	C0001	Producer
2	BRISTOW	SYDNEY	C0015	Teacher
3	VAUGHN	MICHAEL	C0033	Agent
4	FLINKMAN	MARSHALL	C0123	Analyst
5	SLOAN	ARVIN	C0666	
6	BRISTOW	JACK		
7	DIXON	MARCUS	C0233	Chief

(continued)

> *(continued)*
>
> This example illustrates several of the options available in the `INFILE` statement that allow you to read in data that are not easily readable using the default settings.

2.7   SUMMARY

One of the most powerful features of SAS, and a reason it is used in many research and corporate environments, is that it is very adaptable for reading in data from a number of sources. This chapter showed only the tip of the iceberg. More information about getting data into SAS is provided in the following chapter. For more advanced techniques, see the SAS documentation.

EXERCISES

2.1 **Input data into SAS.**

   a. Open the program file `EX_2.1.SAS`.

```
DATA CHILDREN;
* WT is in column 1-2, HEIGHT is in 4-5 and AGE is in 7-8;
* Create an INPUT statement that will read in this data set;
INPUT    ;
DATALINES;
64 57 8
71 59 10
53 49 6
67 62 11
55 51 8
58 50 8
77 55 10
57 48 9
56 42 10
51 42 6
76 61 12
68 57 9
;
Title "Exercise 2.1 - your name";
PROC PRINT DATA=CHILDREN;
RUN;
```

   b. Note that the `INPUT` statement is incomplete. Using one of the input techniques discussed in this chapter, complete the `INPUT` statement and run the resulting program. Verify that the `PROC PRINT` represents the data correctly.

2.2 **Complete the INPUT statement using column input.**

   The file `EX_2.2.SAS` contains a partial SAS program that includes data in the following defined columns:

Variable Name	Column	Type
ID	1-5	Text
AGE	6-7	Numeric
GENDER	8	Text (M or F)
MARRIED	9	Text (Y or N)
WEIGHT IN POUNDS	10-12	Numeric

a. Complete the SAS code snippet given below using the column input technique.

```
DATA PEOPLE;
INPUT ID $ 1-5 ; * finish INPUT statement;
DATALINES;
0000123MY201
0002143FY154
0004333FN133
0005429MN173
0013249FY114
;
Title "Exercise 2.2 - your name";
PROC PRINT DATA=PEOPLE;
RUN;
```

b. Run the program. Verify that the output lists the data correctly.

2.3 Complete the INPUT statement using formatted input.

The SAS program EX_2.3.SAS contains a data file with the following defined columns:

Variable Name	Column	Type
ID	1-5	Text
GENDER	6	Text (M or F)
MARRIED	7	Numeric 0,1
BDATE	8-16	Date

a. Complete the SAS code snippet given below using the formatted input technique. Refer to Table 2.6 to determine which date INFORMAT to use. For the output FORMAT, use the format that outputs dates in the Thursday, November 23, 2016 format.

```
DATA BIRTHDATES;
INPUT ID $ 1-5 ;            * finish INPUT statement;
FORMAT BDATE someformat.; * finish OUTPUT FORMAT statement;
DATALINES;
00001M112JAN1999
00021F003MAR1989
00043F018JUL1991
00054M022DEC1998
00132F110JUL1992
;
```

```
Title "Exercise 2.3 - your name";
PROC PRINTDATA=BIRTHDATES;
RUN;
```

2.4 **Read an external data file.**

The file BPDATA.DAT is a raw (ASCII text) data file that contains data with the following defined columns:

Variable Name	Column	Type
ID	1	Text
SBP	2-4	Numeric
DBP	5-7	Numeric
GENDER	8	Text (M or F)
AGE	9-10	Numeric
WEIGHT	11-13	Numeric

a. Complete the following SAS code snippet (EX_2.4.SAS) to read in this data set. The data are in the file named C:\SASDATA\BPDATA.DAT.

```
DATA BPDATA;
INFILE 'inputfilename'; * Finish the INFILE statement;
INPUT ID$ 1 SBP 2-4 ;    * Finish the input statement;
Title "Exercise 2.4 - your name";
PROC MEANS;
RUN;
```

b. Make sure you include your name in the title statement.

c. Run the program and observe the results.

2.5 **Going deeper: read a large external file.**

In this exercise, you will read data from an external raw data file (TRAUMA.CSV) in comma-separated-values (CSV) format that contains thousands of records. The first few records look like this:

```
SUBJECT,AGE,GENDER,PLACE,STATUS
1868,12.1,Female,Street,Alive
1931,18.7,Female,Street,Alive
1950,16.6,Female,Street,Alive
1960,8.5,Female,Street,Alive
2019,6.7,Male,Unknown,Alive
2044,7.8,Male,Street,Alive
```

Note that the first line (row) in this file contains a header with variable names.

a. Complete the SAS code snippet (EX_2.5.SAS):

```
DATA TRAUMA2;
INFILE 'filename' DLM=  FIRSTOBS= ; * Finish the INFILE state-
ment;
```

```
INPUT SUBJECT $ AGE  GENDER $ PLACE $ STATUS $;
Title "Exercise 2.5 - your name";
PROC MEANS;
RUN;
```

Finish this incomplete code by doing the following:

I. Enter the appropriate filename in the INFILE statement.

II. Place an appropriate value after the DLM = statement.

III. Place an appropriate value after the FIRSTOBS= statement to begin reading with record 2.

IV. Note that in the INPUT statement the only numeric variable is AGE.

V. Run the corrected program.

You should get the following output (with your name in the title):

Analysis Variable : AGE				
N	Mean	Std Dev	Minimum	Maximum
16242	10.6396010	5.8030633	0	21.0000000

VI. How many records are in this data set?

b. Revise the program slightly: This time include an OBS= statement so the program will read in only the first 25 records (not including the header line). Change the PROC MEANS to PROC PRINT. Run the revised program. The Results Viewer should include a listing of the first 25 records in the data set.

3

READING, WRITING, AND IMPORTING DATA

LEARNING OBJECTIVES

- To be able to work with SAS® libraries and permanent data sets
- To be able to read and write permanent SAS data sets
- To be able to interactively import data from another program
- To be able to define SAS libraries using program code
- To be able to import data using code
- To be able to discover the contents of an SAS data set
- To be able to understand how the Data Step Reads and Stores Data.

The Era of "Big Data" has arrived. Organizational data sets are growing by leaps and bounds. Institutions, government agencies, and businesses gather information from individual transactions, which can result in hundreds of thousands of data values each day. Whether the data set you are working with has millions of records or a few hundred isn't the point of this chapter. The point is that once you read in your data, you will want to store it in a way that makes it easy to retrieve for analysis. That means that you may want to store more than raw data values. You'll want your data set to include variable names, labels for your variables, manipulations you've done to get it ready for analysis, and other information.

3.1 WORKING WITH SAS LIBRARIES AND PERMANENT DATA SETS

SAS allows you to create permanent data sets that, once created, are easy to access and use. Keep in mind that an SAS data set is different from an SAS program (code) file or a raw

SAS® Essentials: Mastering SAS for Data Analytics, Second Edition. Alan C. Elliott and Wayne A. Woodward.
© 2016 John Wiley & Sons, Inc. Published 2016 by John Wiley & Sons, Inc.

data file. The SAS code files, which we used in the previous chapter, contain a listing of SAS commands and use raw data values (either within the code file or in an external file and accessed with an INFILE statement). The SAS code files and associated raw data files can be used to create an SAS data set, but the code file with raw data is not an SAS data set. Keep the following points in mind. SAS data sets

- are created by a DATA statement (there are other ways to create an SAS data set that we'll learn later in this chapter);
- are an internal representation of the data created by the DATA statement;
- contain more than the data values – they can contain variable names, labels, the results of codings, calculations, and variable formats;
- are referred to by a name that indicates whether the data set is temporary or permanent.

All of the SAS data sets created in Chapter 2 were temporary. That is, when the SAS program is exited (i.e., you exit the SAS program using File → Exit), all temporary data sets are lost. This chapter shows you how to create an SAS data set that is permanently stored in a folder on your hard disk (or flash drive, network drive, or other storage medium).

The technique for saving an SAS data set as a file in a folder location is different from what is used in most Windows applications. Instead of using the File → Save paradigm, you store an SAS data set using code in an SAS program. To illustrate how this works, you need to remember the basic differences between temporary data sets and permanent data sets:

- **A temporary SAS data set is** named with a single-level name, such as MEASLES or MAR2000. It is created in a DATA statement and is available for analysis as long as you are using the SAS software (even if you run other code files and create other SAS data sets). When you exit the SAS software program, all temporary data sets are erased.
- **A permanent SAS data set** is a file saved on your hard disk. It can be referred to with its two-part name, such as RESEARCH.DATA1 or MYSASLIB.FLU2016 or with a Windows-type specification such as "C:\SASDATA\DATA1" or "H:\NETWORK\MYFILES\FLU2016."
- Figure 3.1 provides a graphical representation of how reading data into SAS works by creating either a temporary (work) or a permanent data set.

Figure 3.1   Reading and storing data in SAS

The following few sections present information on how to create permanent SAS data sets using two techniques. The first uses Windows file specifications, and the second uses SAS libraries.

3.2   CREATING PERMANENT SAS DATA SETS USING THE WINDOWS FILE NAME TECHNIQUE

The Windows file specification technique for creating a permanent SAS data set is straightforward when using SAS in a Windows operating system. Instead of using a temporary SAS data set name such as SOMEDATA or MEASLES in the SAS DATA statement, use a Windows file name. For example, instead of using

```
DATA PEOPLE;
```

use

```
DATA "C:\SASDATA\PEOPLE";
```

How you implement this in an SAS program is illustrated in Figure 3.1.
Consider the following SAS code (WRITE.SAS):

```
DATA "C:\SASDATA\PEOPLE";
INPUT ID $ 1-3 SBP 4-6 DBP 7-9 GENDER $ 10 AGE 11-12 WT 13-15;
DATALINES;
001120 80M15115
002130 70F25180
003140100M89170
004120 80F30150
005125 80F20110
;
RUN;
PROC MEANS;
RUN;
```

This code creates a data set called PEOPLE on your hard drive in the C:\SASDATA\ folder, and the Window file name of this permanent file is PEOPLE.SAS7BDAT. To summarize:

- The statement DATA PEOPLE; creates an internal SAS data set that is *temporary*. (It vanishes when you exit the SAS program.)
- The statement DATA "C:\SASDATA\PEOPLE"; creates a *permanent* SAS data set stored on your hard drive.

In fact, you can substitute the Windows file name specification anywhere using the SAS data set name specification. This is illustrated in several of the upcoming examples.

CITRIX Implementation of SAS: If you are using a server version of SAS, the reference to the location of the file on the hard disk will be different from those shown in the examples. For example, when using a Citrix implementation of SAS on Windows, with your data stored in `C:\SASDATA`, you must use the following code rather than the `C:\SASDATA\` folder reference shown in the example:

```
DATA "\\CLIENT\C$\SASDATA\PEOPLE";
```

This code replaces the `DATA` statement in the example where the server address `\\CLIENT\C$` is used instead of `C:`. The server folder access code you use may differ depending on your server implementation of SAS. (The exact folder reference may be different for different server setups. Check your specific server implementation.)

We won't repeat this information for other examples, so you must take care to replace the C: with the appropriate code if necessary for your server installation of SAS.

HANDS-ON EXAMPLE

This example illustrates how to write data to a permanent SAS data set.

1. Open the program file `WRITE.SAS`. Note that the data statement contains a Windows file designation in quotation marks:

```
DATA "C:\SASDATA\PEOPLE";
```

2. Because the data set name in SAS is `C:\SASDATA\PEOPLE`, it follows that the data are stored in the `C:\SASDATA` folder. To verify this, open your `C:\SASDATA` folder using Windows Explorer. Verify that the `C:\SASDATA` folder contains a file named `PEOPLE.SAS7BDAT`. The .SAS7BDAT file extension indicates to the Windows operating system the type of file, and in this case, it indicates that this file is an SAS data set. (The .SAS7BDAT file extension may not be visible in Windows Explorer, depending on whether your Windows folder options include displaying file extensions.)

3.3   CREATING PERMANENT SAS DATA SETS USING AN SAS LIBRARY

In the previous section, you created an SAS data set to a Windows folder (`C:\SASDATA`) by specifying a Windows file name (`C:\SASTATA\PEOPLE`), which indicated the complete file name for the `PEOPLE.SAS7BDAT` file. That technique works only in the Windows environment.

Another technique for reading and writing SAS data sets is using the SAS Library technique. Before using an SAS Library, you have to "create" one. The following two sections provide two methods for creating a SAS Library.

Before we learn how to set up an SAS Library name, this section shows why it comes in handy. The SAS Library technique involves creating a nickname that refers to a drive location called (in SAS terminology) a library name. For example, you could create a library name such as MYWORK that refers to a simple location on your computer disk such as

C:\LOTSOFFILES

Or, you could create the MYWORK library name that refers to a complicated network folder such as

N:\MYNET\ACCOUNTING\STATMENTS\MYFOLDER\RESEARCH

Once your library "nickname" is set up, you can use the short name to refer to your disk location rather than having to use some complex Windows path name every time. With a library name, you could use the file designation:

MYWORK.JAN2016

to refer to an SAS data file named JAN2016.SAS7BDAT rather than the more complicated name:

"N:\MYNET\ACCOUNTING\STATMENTS\MYFOLDER\RESEARCH\JAN2016"

For the examples in this book, we'll create the following SAS Library nickname and use it for the upcoming exercises:

- The SAS library name: MYSASLIB
- The location of the Windows folder: C:\SASDATA

Therefore, when the library name MYSASLIB is used in a filename, it will refer to a file located in the C:\SASDATA folder. Note that if you've chosen to place the sample files for this book into a different folder than C:\SASDATA, you need to make appropriate adjustments to the library definition in the Hands-on Examples and chapter exercises.

The following two sections describe methods for creating the relationship linking a Windows folder location to an SAS Library name. Two important points to grasp are the following:

- *Every SAS library has a name* such as MYSASLIB, RESEARCH, MYDATA, and so on.
- *Every SAS library name is a nickname* that points to a specific folder such as C:\SASDATA, N:\NETWORK\DRIVE, I:\MYFLASH\DRIVE, and so on.

Within the SAS program, every SAS data set has two parts to its name. For example, the SAS data set referred to as MYSASLIB.MAY2000 consists of the following:

- the *library* named MYSASLIB;
- the *data set* named MAY2000.

Even temporary files can be referred to with a (temporary) library name, WORK. Therefore, a file named WORK.LOTSADATA consists of:

- the *library* named WORK (refers to the temporary library);
- the *data set* name is LOTSADATA.

This SAS naming convention is used for SAS data sets in all types of computers and operating systems – mainframes, Windows, Mac OS X, UNIX, and so on. Once you learn how to use SAS in Windows, you can easily transfer that skill to any other computer platform.

To summarize, once you've created an SAS library named `MYSASLIB` that points to `C:\SASDATA`, the data set you refer to as `MYSASLIB.MAY2016` is stored on your hard drive using the name `C:\SASDATA\MAY2016.SAS7BDAT`.

The following section illustrates how to create an SAS library name using two methods. The first method creates an SAS library name using a Dialog Box, and the second method creates the library name in SAS code.

3.4   CREATING A SAS LIBRARY USING A DIALOG BOX

An easy way to create an SAS library in the Windows version of SAS (with a custom name of your own choosing) is to use the New Library dialog box. To display this dialog box, make the SAS Explorer window active (click the Explorer tab at the bottom of the left window in the main SAS screen). Select File → New, click the Library option, and then click OK. The New Library dialog box is shown in Figure 3.2.

In the Name field, enter the name you want to assign to the library. In this book, the shortcut name `MYSASLIB` is used. In the Path field, enter the location of the directory. In this book, the files are assumed to be in the `C:\SASDATA` folder on the hard drive. You will typically not change anything in the Engine drop-down or the Options field. Once you've created the `MYSASLIB` library, all SAS data files in `C:\SASDATA` become a part of the library.

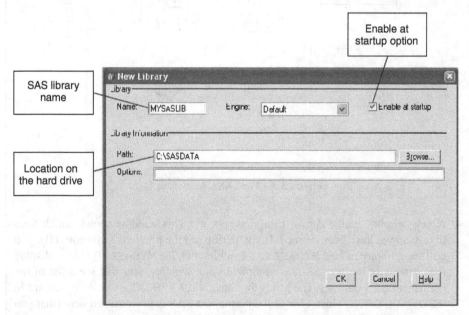

Figure 3.2   New Library dialog box. (Source: Created with SAS® software, Version 9.4. Copyright 2012, SAS Institute Inc., Cary, NC, USA. All Rights Reserved. Reproduced with permission of SAS Institute Inc., Cary, NC)

Notice the option Enable at startup. If you intend to use this library name repeatedly, you should choose this option by checking the box next to it. Choosing the Enable at startup option tells SAS to remember the library name and location and to reactivate it each time the SAS program is started.

HANDS-ON EXAMPLE

In this example, you will define an SAS library and give it a nickname.

1. Make the SAS Explorer window active. (Click the Explorer tab at the left bottom on the main SAS screen. If it is not there, click on the View menu and open Explorer.) Select File → New, select the Library option, and click OK. The dialog box shown in Figure 3.2 appears.

2. Enter MYSASLIB in the Name field and C:\SASDATA in the Path field, or you can use a path to a network or any other location where your SAS data set is stored. Check the Enable at startup option. Click OK to save the information.

3. On the left side of your SAS screen, click the Explorer tab. You should see a Libraries icon that resembles a filing cabinet, as shown in Figure 3.3. (If you don't see the Library icon, you might need to click View → Up One Level to get to this view.) Double-click the Libraries icon.

Figure 3.3 The SAS Library icon.

4. A new window called Active Libraries appears. This window shows which SAS library names have been defined. If you performed the previous steps correctly, you will see a library named MYSASLIB. Double-click the MYSASLIB icon to display the contents of the MYSASLIB window. In that window, you will see a list of the permanent SAS data sets (i.e., files that have a .SAS7BDAT extension) that are in the C:\SASDATA folder. One of the permanent SAS data sets listed here (that you downloaded from the book's web site – you did download them didn't you?) is named SOMEDATA.

5. Double-click the SOMEDATA icon. A window such as the one illustrated in Figure 3.4 is displayed.

	ID Number	Intervention Group	Age on Jan 1, 2000	Baseline	6 Months	12 Months	24 Months	Socioeconomic Status	SEX	GENDER
1	101	A	12	22.3	25.3	28.2	30.6	5		0 Female
2	102	A	11	22.8	27.5	33.3	35.8	6		0 Female
3	104	B	12	22.8	30	32.8	31	4		0 Female
4	110	A	12	18.5	26	29	27.9	5		1 Male
5	122	B	9	19.5	25	25.3	26.6	5		1 Male
6	123	B	11	23.5	28.8	34.2	35.6	6		0 Female
7	134	C	8	22.6	26.7	28	33.4	3		0 Female
8	150	B	8	21	26.7	27.5	29.5	5		0 Female
9	162	B	7	20.9	28.9	29.7	25.9	2		1 Male
10	187	A	11	22.5	29.3	32.6	33.7	2		0 Female
11	198	B	12	23.4	29.2	30.4	35.1	2		0 Female
12	201	B	14	22.5	29.3	33.4	34.8	5		0 Female
13	220	B	9	19.3	25.5	26.2	25.1	3		1 Male
14	221	B	10	18.5	24.4	26.5	26.7	4		1 Male
15	237	B	7	20.2	28.8	33.5	28.1	5		1 Male
16	282	B	13	21.3	28.7	32.3	30.3	2		0 Female
17	298	B	6	20	24.5	28.9	29.6	5		1 Male
18	307	C	11	22.6	30.1	34.4	35.2	1		0 Female
19	311	B	12	20.8	23.7	26.1	32.7	5		1 Male
20	312	A	4	17	21.3	22.7	21.2	5		1 Male
21	343	B	11	19	25.2	27.7	25.1	1		1 Male
22	376	B	9	21.1	28.1	34	31.0	5		0 Female
23	388	C	13	21	27.2	29.7	30.5	5		0 Female
24	390	A	6	21.3	30.5	30.7	30.1	4		0 Female
25	403	B	9	21.6	30.3	33.7	31.9	6		0 Female
26	404	B	7	19.2	27.6	31.5	29.3	5		1 Male
27	410	B	13	22.2	30.4	32.1	35.2	1		0 Female
28	412	C	9	19	22.5	24.9	26.6	4		1 Male
29	444	B	13	24.2	32.3	33.8	35	4		0 Female
30	445	A	12	22.1	31.3	31.6	31.6	3		1 Male
31	450	C	10	20.2	25.5	27.8	31.9	4		0 Female
32	461	B	13	21.3	27.1	31.4	32.6	5		1 Male
33	467	C	11	20.8	28.1	32.6	27.4	5		1 Male

Figure 3.4   SAS Viewtable.

6. This spreadsheet window is called the SAS Viewtable. It displays the contents of an SAS data set.

7. Close the MYSASLIB.SOMEDATA data set by selecting File → Close or by clicking the X at the top right of the window.

8. Return to the SAS Editor window (by clicking on an editor tab at the bottom of your SAS program), select File → Open Program... and open the program file LIBNAME1.SAS, which contains the following short SAS program:

```
PROC MEANS DATA=MYSASLIB.SOMEDATA;
RUN;
```

9. Run this program. In the Output window, you'll see that SAS has calculated and reported descriptive statistics for the numeric values in the MYSASLIB.SOMEDATA data set. (The results appear in the Results Viewer.)

Any SAS data file (with a .SAS7BDAT extension) that you copy into the Windows folder linked to an SAS library name automatically becomes a part of that SAS library. Thus, if you acquire a .SAS7BDAT file from some source, all you have to do to make that file available in the SAS MYSASLIB library is to copy that file (using Windows Explorer) to the C:\SASDATA folder.

3.5   CREATING A SAS LIBRARY USING CODE

Another way to create an SAS Library (nickname) is by using code. Creating a library within the code makes it active only while the SAS software is running. When you exit the SAS software program (File → Exit), the library nickname is "forgotten" by SAS, although any permanent data sets you've created are still stored in your folder referred to by the library. You may use these permanent SAS data sets again by re-creating a library nickname pointing to the Windows folder where the data file is stored.

The following SAS code creates an SAS library name called MYLIB2 at the location C:\SASDATA:

```
LIBNAME MYLIB2 "C:\SASDATA";
```

When SAS reads this code at the beginning of your SAS program, the libname (library name) MYLIB2 is created and can subsequently be used as a part of a permanent data set name. For example, suppose that you have a data set named SURVEY.SAS7BDAT in the folder C:\SASDATA. Once you define the libname MYLIB2 pointing to that folder, you can refer to that data set using the SAS data set name MYLIB2.SURVEY.

Note that for illustrative purposes we are creating the library named MYLIB2 that has a different name than MYSASLIB library previously created, but they are both nicknames to the C:\SASDATA folder. There is no conflict in creating two SAS library names that point to the same folder on your drive, although in practice, you would not normally have two such library names.

HANDS-ON EXAMPLE

In this example, you will define an SAS library in code and use the library name to read in an SAS data file.

1. In SAS Explorer, display the window named Contents of SAS Environment. Refer to previous examples if you don't remember how to display this window. Double-click the Libraries icon, shown previously in Figure 3.3.
2. A new window named Active Libraries appears. Examine the active library names. There should not be a library named MYLIB2.
3. In the Editor window, open the program file LIBNAME.SAS, which contains the following code:

```
LIBNAME MYLIB2 "C:\SASDATA";
RUN;
```

4. Run this program. The LIBNAME statement creates the SAS library nickname MYLIB2 but does not create any output. Examine the Active Libraries window in the SAS Explorer. There is now a library icon named MYLIB2. The folder represented by the filing cabinet icon indicates that SAS created the MYLIB2 library.
5. Double-click the MYLIB2 icon and verify that the library includes one or more SAS data sets (including the data sets SOMEDATA, CARS, and others). Note that this new library contains the same data sets as the MYSASLIB library because they are both defined as nicknames for "pointing to" C:\SASDATA.

In the previous example, the MYLIB2 library nickname continues to be active and available for use until you exit the SAS program. However, the library nickname MYSASLIB, created with the dialog box, using the Enable at startup option, is remembered by SAS each time you enter the SAS environment.

3.6 USING DATA IN PERMANENT SAS DATA SETS

After you have created an SAS library (either a permanent or a temporary one), you can access data in that library within SAS procedures or as input into other DATA steps. In previous examples, we created a permanent library named MYSASLIB and a temporary library named MYLIB2. They both refer to the folder location C:\SASDATA. Suppose that there is an SAS data set in that folder named SOMEDATA.SAS7BDAT. To access that data set in SAS in a PROC MEANS statement, you can use either the full Windows file path or either one of the library prefixes. For example, the following are three different statements that all access the same data set:

```
PROC MEANS DATA='C:\SASDATA\SOMEDATA';RUN;
```

Or

```
PROC MEANS DATA=MYSASLIB.SOMEDATA;RUN;
```

Or

```
PROC MEANS DATA=MYLIB2.SOMEDATA;RUN;
```

HANDS-ON EXAMPLE

In this example, you will read data from an existing SAS data set.

1. Open the program file READFILE.SAS. The entire program consists of a single line of code:

   ```
   PROC MEANS DATA='c:\sasdata\somedata';RUN;
   ```

   Note that the DATA= statement includes the information

   ```
   DATA='c:\sasdata\somedata';
   ```

2. Run this program and observe the output, a table of descriptive statistics created by the PROC MEANS statement. The data used in that procedure is from the SAS data file named SOMEDATA.SAS7BDAT. (This method of reading SAS data sets works only in the Windows environment.)
3. Change the statement in PROC MEANS to DATA=MYSASLIB.SOMEDATA. Note that you no longer put the data set designation name in quotes. Re-run the program to verify that the new data set designation works and produces the same results as those created in Step 2.
4. Change the file reference to DATA= MYLIB2.SOMEDATA and re-run the program. Again you should get the same results (as long as you do not exit SAS and lose the MYLIB2 library nickname).

3.7   IMPORTING DATA FROM ANOTHER PROGRAM

In Chapter 2, we showed how to read data from a raw (ASCII) text file using the INFILE and INPUT statements. In this section, we'll go into more detail about importing data, and we'll do it by describing three methods:

- Import data using the SAS Import Wizard.
- Import using PROC IMPORT.
- More about importing data using an INFILE statement.

3.7.1   Importing Data Using the SAS Import Wizard

The SAS Import Wizard can be used to import data from a number of formats including Microsoft Access, Microsoft Excel, Comma Separated Value files (CSV), SPSS, STATA, and others. To illustrate the wizard, we'll first look at importing a file containing comma values. Typically, this type of file has the following characteristics:

- The first row contains the names of the SAS variables, each separated by a comma, and each adhering to SAS naming conventions. (These were discussed in Chapter 2.)
- Beginning on the second line of the file, each line contains the data values for one subject, where each value is separated by a comma.
- Two commas in a row indicate a missing value. You could also designate numeric data values that are unknown or missing with a dot (.) or a missing value code (such as -99). Missing character values can be represented by a double quote such as "".

If the CSV file does not satisfy these criteria, you may need to edit the file (using a program such as Notepad) to make it conform before proceeding to import. Figure 3.5 shows the first few lines of a CSV file (CARSMPG.CSV) ready to be imported. Note that line 1 contains the 13 names of the variables separated by commas and each following line contains 13 values each separated by a comma, consistent with the data type of the variable. (Note also that in this case, it is okay that some values contain blanks, such as the blank between Civic and Hybrid because it is the comma that marks a new value, not a blank.)

To import these data, you can use the SAS Import Wizard by selecting File → Import data. The initial screen of the Import Wizard is displayed in Figure 3.6.

The Wizard prompts you to enter the following information:

- type of file to import (in this case, select the Comma Separated Values (*.csv) option.);

```
BRAND,MODEL,MINIVAN,WAGON,PICKUP,AUTOMATIC,ENGINESIZE,CYLINDERS,CITYMPG,HWYMPG,SUV,AWD,HYBRID
TOYOTA,Prius,0,0,0,1,1.5,4,60,51,0,0,1
HONDA,Civic Hybrid,0,0,0,1,1.3,4,48,47,0,0,1
HONDA,Civic Hybrid,0,0,0,1,1.3,4,47,48,0,0,1
HONDA,Civic Hybrid,0,0,0,0,1.3,4,46,51,0,0,1
HONDA,Civic Hybrid,0,0,0,0,1.3,4,45,51,0,0,1
VOLKSWAGEN,Golf,0,0,0,0,1.9,4,38,46,0,0,0
VOLKSWAGEN,Jetta,0,0,0,0,1.9,4,38,46,0,0,0
VOLKSWAGEN,New Beetle,0,0,0,0,1.9,4,38,46,0,0,0
FORD,Escape HEV 2WD,0,0,0,1,2.3,4,36,31,1,0,1
```

Figure 3.5   CSV data ready for import

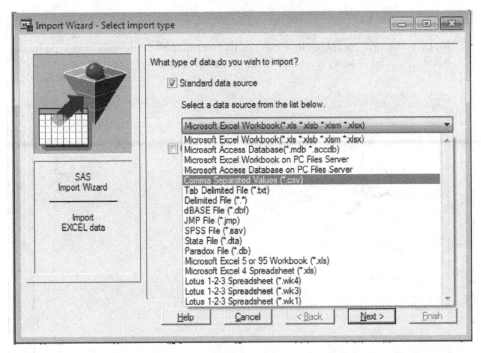

Figure 3.6   Initial screen of the SAS Import Wizard.

- the name of the Excel file to import (such as C:\SASDATA\CARSMPG.CSV);
- the SAS library where you want to store the imported data; select the WORK library to import the data into temporary storage or a library name to store the data in a permanent file.

HANDS-ON EXAMPLE

In this example, you will use the SAS import wizard to import data from a CSV file.

1. Begin the SAS Import Wizard by selecting File → Import data.
2. From the Select a data source drop-down list, select the type of file you want to import. See Figure 3.6. In this case, select Comma Separated Values (*.csv). After you've selected the type of file to import, click Next.
3. When prompted to specify "Where is the file located" either type in or browse to C:\SASDATA\CARSMPG.CSV as shown in Figure 3.7.
4. Click the Options ... button: the Options dialog box allows you to specify whether the names of the variables are on the first line of the CSV file, and on which line the data values begin. For this example, leave the "Get values from first row" checked, and first row of data set at 2. Observe that the delimiter is set as a comma. Also note that the number of rows to guess is set at the SAS default, which is 0. That is, SAS

(continued)

(continued)

looks at the first 20 values in a column to determine the column's data type (text, number, etc.). For now, accept all defaults and click OK.

Figure 3.7 Selecting a CSV file name.

5. Click Next. The Library and Member dialog boxes allow you to indicate where the imported data should be stored. As discussed earlier in this chapter, every SAS data set is stored in a location called a library. You can select either the temporary library (WORK) or a permanent library name. In this case, select the WORK library and name the data set (Member name) MPG_FOR_CARS as shown in Figure 3.8.

6. Click Next. SAS asks if you want to create an SAS program file that contains the code that could be used to create this data set. Enter C:\SASDATA\IMPORTCARS in the text field. We will use this file later. Click Finish to complete the Wizard. The data in the CARSMPG.CSV file are imported into SAS and are assigned the SAS data set name MPG_FOR_CARS in the WORK library. To verify that the SAS data set has been created:

   (a) Click the Explorer tab at the bottom left of the SAS screen. (If necessary, select View → Up one level until you are at the Contents of SAS Environment window.)

   (b) Click the Libraries icon, then the Work icon. You should see a data set (table) named MPG_FOR_CARS.

   (c) Double-click the MPG_FOR_CARS table icon, and a table appears that contains the data imported from the CARSMPG.CSV file. This data set is now ready to use in SAS. Note that because it is in the WORK library, it is a temporary data set.

Figure 3.8   Selecting the library and member name.

7. In the Editor window, enter the following code:

```
PROC PRINT DATA=MPG_FOR_CARS;RUN;
```

Run the program. The following are the first few records of the listing in the Results Viewer:

The SAS System

Obs	BRAND	MODEL	MINIVAN	WAGON	PICKUP	AUTOMATIC	ENGINESIZE	CYLINDERS	CITYMPG	HWYMPG	SUV	AWD	HYE
1	TOYOTA	Prius	0	0	0	1	1.5	4	60	51	0	0	
2	HONDA	Civic Hybrid	0	0	0	1	1.3	4	48	47	0	0	
3	HONDA	Civic Hybrid	0	0	0	1	1.3	4	47	48	0	0	
4	HONDA	Civic Hybrid	0	0	0	0	1.3	4	46	51	0	0	
5	HONDA	Civic Hybrid	0	0	0	0	1.3	4	45	51	0	0	
6	VOLKSWAGEN	Golf	0	0	0	0	1.9	4	38	46	0	0	
7	VOLKSWAGEN	Jetta	0	0	0	0	1.9	4	38	46	0	0	
8	VOLKSWAGEN	New Beetle	0	0	0	0	1.9	4	38	46	0	0	
9	FORD	Escape HEV 2WD	0	0	0	1	2.3	4	36	31	1	0	
10	HONDA	Civic	0	0	0	0	1.7	4	36	44	0	0	
11	VOLKSWAGEN	Jetta Wagon	0	1	0	0	1.9	4	36	43	0	0	
12	HONDA	Civic	0	0	0	1	1.7	4	35	40	0	0	
13	TOYOTA	Echo	0	0	0	0	1.5	4	35	42	0	0	
14	VOLKSWAGEN	Jetta	0	0	0	1	1.9	4	35	42	0	0	
15	VOLKSWAGEN	New Beetle	0	0	0	1	1.9	4	35	42	0	0	
16	FORD	Escape HEV 4WD	0	0	0	1	2.3	4	33	29	1	0	
17	TOYOTA	Echo	0	0	0	1	1.5	4	33	39	0	0	
18	HONDA	Civic	0	0	0	0	1.7	4	32	38	0	0	

(continued)

(continued)

8. Re-import this CSV data file. This time, select the library named MYSASLIB (instead of WORK) and name the SAS data set AUTOMPG. When you have imported the CSV file into an SAS data set, its name becomes MYSASLIB.AUTOMPG, and it is stored in a permanent file (on your hard drive as the file named C:\SASDATA\AUTOMPG.SAS7BDAT). (Optional: use Windows Explorer to verify that this file is on your hard drive.)

9. What is the difference between the SAS data sets MPG_FOR_CARS and MYSASLIB.AUTOMPG? (MPG_FOR_CAR is a temporary data set also known as WORK.MPG_FOR_CARS; MYSASLIB.AUTOMPG is a permanent data set.) If you didn't know the answer, go back and re-read the sections on temporary and permanent SAS data sets.

3.7.2   Importing Data Using the SAS Code

Instead of using the Import Wizard to import CSV (or other type data files), you can import data using SAS code. This technique is handy when you are importing a number of similar files. For example, suppose that your CSV data changes over time and you need to re-import it whenever it changes. When the SAS program is run, it reads the new data from the CSV file and creates an SAS data set that you can use in an analysis.

In the previous Import wizard example, we requested that SAS save the code used to import the CARSMPG data set. The wizard created PROC IMPORT code to perform the import, and because we requested it, it "wrote" that code to a file we named IMPORTCARS.SAS. The code created by the Wizard is as follows:

```
PROC IMPORT OUT= WORK.MPG_FOR_CARS
            DATAFILE= "C:\SASDATA\CARSMPG.CSV"
            DBMS=CSV REPLACE;
            GETNAMES=YES;
            DATAROW=2;
RUN;
```

(It may be slightly different depending on your version of SAS.) If you submit this code from the SAS editor, it performs the exact import performed by the wizard. A simplified syntax for PROC IMPORT is as follows:

```
PROC IMPORT OUT=dataset
            DATAFILE="filename"
            DBMS=dbmsidentifier <REPLACE>;
  <GETNAMES=YES>; *DEFAULT is YES;
            <DATAROW=n>; *DEFAULT is 2;
```

There are some advantages to using the PROC IMPORT code rather than using the wizard. Some of those will be discussed in this section. The following is an explanation of the syntax of the PROC IMPORT code used to import CARSMPG:

- PROC IMPORT is an SAS procedure you use to import data from a variety of file formats.

TABLE 3.1 SAS DBMS Data Sources

DBMS Identifier	Data Source	File Extension
XLS	Microsoft Excel 97, 2000, 2002, 2003, or 2007	.XLS
XLSX	Excel 2000 and later	.XLSX
EXCEL	Microsoft Excel 97, 2000, 2002, 2003, or 2007	.xls .xlsb .xlsm .xlsx
EXCELCS	Excel 2007 and higher (if you have the free SAS PC File Server add-on installed.)	.XLSX
DLM	Delimited file (default delimiter is a blank)	.*
CSV	Delimited file (comma-separated values)	.CSV
TAB	Delimited file (tab-delimited values)	.TXT
ACCESS	Microsoft Access database	.MDB
ACCESSCS	Access database (if you have the free SAS PC File Server add-on installed.)	.MDBX
WK1, WK3, or WK4	Lotus 1, 3 o4 4 spreadsheet	.WK1 .WK3 .WK4
DBF	dBASE file	.DBF

- The OUT= option defines the name of the SAS data set where the resulting file will be stored. In this case, because the file is WORK.MPG_FOR_CARS, it is stored in the WORK (temporary) library.
- The DATAFILE= option indicates the location of the original CSV file.
- The DBMS= option indicates the type of data source file to be imported. Table 3.1 lists the types of files SAS can import. In this case, CSV is used because the file to be imported is in CSV format.
- The REPLACE option instructs SAS to replace the old dataset with the same name.
- GETNAMES=YES indicates that the names of the variables appear on the first row of the file. (A NO option would indicate that the names are not on the first row. The GETNAMES option is not available when DBMS=EXCELCS.)
- DATAROW=2 indicates that the data values are to be imported starting with the second row.
- There are other options that are used for different DBMS specifications. Some of these will be discussed in the upcoming examples.
- Similar DBMS options are available for importing Microsoft Access files. See SAS documentation for more information.

HANDS-ON EXAMPLE

In this example, you will use an SAS code to import data into SAS.

1. Open the program file IMPORTEXAMPLE.SAS. This file contains the SAS code used to import the CARSMPG.CSV data. (This code is shown previously in the text.)
2. Change the OUT= filename to MYSASLIB.RESULTS and the DATAFILE= name to "C:\SASDATA\SURVEY.CSV".

(continued)

(continued)

3. Add a line at the bottom of the code that reads

```
PROC PRINT DATA=MYSASLIB.RESULTS;RUN;
```

4. Submit the code. It should produce a listing of the Survey data in the Results Viewer.
5. As a second example, import an Excel file (.XLS) by opening the SAS program `IMPORTEXAMPLE2.SAS`

```
PROC IMPORT OUT= WORK.FROMXL
            DATAFILE= "C:\SASDATA\EXAMPLE.XLS"
            DBMS=XLS REPLACE;
      SHEET="Database";
      GETNAMES=YES;
RUN;
PROC PRINT DATA=FROMXL;RUN;
```

6. Note the option `SHEET=`. You must know the name of the worksheet in the Excel file, and specify it in this option. The `GETNAMES=YES` indicates that the first row of the Excel file contains the names of the variables.
7. Run this code. It should produce a listing of the Example data. (Notice that because this is an XLS file, we used the `XLS DBMS` identifier. If it had been an XLSX type file, we would have used the `XLSX DBMS` identifier. An example of how to do this is in the exercises at the end of the chapter.)

3.7.3 Exporting Data Using the SAS Code

Exporting data from an SAS data file into another file type (such as a CSV file) is similar to importing. In this case, you use the `PROC EXPORT` procedure. A simplified syntax for exporting is as follows:

```
PROC EXPORT DATA=dataset
            OUTFILE='fileneme' or OUTTABLE='tablename'
            DBMS=dbmsidentifier
            <LABEL><REPLACE>;
```

The DBMS options are listed in Table 3.1.

HANDS-ON EXAMPLE

1. Open the program file `EXPORT.SAS`. This code exports the current SAS data set named `SOMEDATA` to a CSV file.

```
PROC EXPORT DATA=MYSASLIB.SOMEDATA
            OUTFILE="C:\SASDATA\EXPORTED.CSV"
            DBMS=CSV
            REPLACE;
RUN;
```

Run this code and observe (in Windows) that the file EXPORTED.CSV was created.

2. Open EXPORTED.CSV in Notepad or Word and notice that the first line in the file includes the variable names. The remainder of the file includes the data values, separated by commas.

3. Close the EXPORTED.CSV file. In your SAS code, add a LABELS statement before the REPLACE option. Run this revised code. Open EXPORTED.CSV in Excel. This time, notice that the first row contains the SAS labels for the columns rather than the variable names (Creating and using labels is introduced and discussed in Chapter 4.)

3.8   DISCOVERING THE CONTENTS OF AN SAS DATA SET

Data can come from a number of sources. A popular way to provide data, by e-mail or download, is in an SAS data set. (These data sets have a .SAS7BDAT file extension.) If you acquire an SAS data set from another source, you can find out about its contents in two ways:

- Copy the SAS7BDAT-type data file into a folder that is linked to an SAS library (such as C:\SASDATA). Use SAS Viewdata to view the contents of the data set.
- Use PROC DATASETS to list information about the variables in the data set.

We've already illustrated how to use Viewdata and PROC PRINT to see the actual contents of a data set. The PROC DATASETS technique does not show you the actual data. Instead, it provides details about the variables in the data set, including their names, formats, and labels. For example, the following SAS program (CONTENTS.SAS) displays information about the SOMEDATA data set in the MYSASLIB library:

```
PROC DATASETS;
CONTENTS DATA= 'C:\SASDATA\SOMEDATA';
RUN;
```

When you run this program, SAS produces a listing of the contents of the data set, including variable names and other information. It is a handy way to discover what information is in a particular SAS data set. This is illustrated in the following Hands-on Example.

HANDS-ON EXAMPLE

In this example, you will discover the contents of an SAS data file using PROC DATASETS.

1. Open the program file CONTENTS.SAS. Run the program.

(continued)

(continued)

2. Examine the output. The first two sections of the output contain technical information, and the third section (see Table 3.2) contains a list of variables in the data set.

   Notice that this SAS data set description contains:

   • **Variable**: Names are listed in alphabetical order.
   • **Type**: The variable type – Num (numeric), Char (Character/Text), Date, and other SAS data types.
   • **Len**: The number of characters or digits used to store the information.
   • **Label**: A description of the variable (listed only if defined).

3. Change the DATA statement to read

```
CONTENTS DATA= MYSASLIB._ALL_ ;
```

Run the revised program. The _ALL_ keyword instructs SAS to display information about all SAS data sets in the MYSASLIB library.

TABLE 3.2   Example PROC CONTENTS Output

				Alphabetic List of Variables and Attributes
#	Variable	Type	Len	Label
3	AGE	Num	8	Age on Jan 1, 2000
10	GENDER	Char	6	—
2	GP	Char	1	Intervention Group
1	ID	Num	8	ID Number
9	SEX	Num	8	—
8	STATUS	Num	8	Socioeconomic Status
4	TIME1	Num	8	Baseline
5	TIME2	Num	8	6 Months
6	TIME3	Num	8	12 Months
7	TIME4	Num	8	24 Months

3.9   GOING DEEPER: UNDERSTANDING HOW THE DATA STEP READS AND STORES DATA

To understand how SAS works, it can be helpful to "look under the hood" and see what is happening in all those bits and bytes as SAS reads and processes data. Knowing how SAS handles data is a little bit like knowing how the motor in your car works. You can usually drive around okay without knowing anything about pistons, but sometimes, it is good to know what that knocking sound means.

Having an understanding of the way the DATA step works can help you create programs that avoid problems (programming errors) and take advantage of the internal workings of the program. For example, consider the following simple program

```
DATA NEW;
INPUT ID $ AGE TEMPC;
TEMPF=TEMPC*(9/5)+32;
```

Figure 3.9   The SAS INPUT process

```
DATALINES;
0001 24 37.3
0002 35 38.2
;
RUN;
```

In this program, SAS reads in two lines of data. In addition to reading the data, it also performs a calculation. The `TEMPF=` statement calculates Fahrenheit temperature from the Celsius temperature represented by the variable `TEMPC`. To read in these data and do this calculation, SAS goes through three stages represented by the graph in Figure 3.9:

COMPILE SAS reads the syntax of the SAS program to see if there are any errors in the code. If there are no errors found, SAS "compiles" this code – that is, it transforms the SAS code into a code used internally by SAS. (You don't need to know this internal code.)

EXECUTION If the code syntax checks out, SAS begins performing the tasks specified by the code. For example, the first line of code is `DATA NEW`, so during the execution phase, SAS creates a "blank" dataset (no data in it) named `NEW` that it will use to put the data into as it is read.

OUTPUT SAS reads in each data line. It interprets this line of data into the values for each variable and stores them into the data set one line at a time until all data have been output into the specified data set.

More specifically, once SAS passes the compile phase, it creates an area of memory called the input buffer. This buffer is the location where the data values are first placed, before they are separated into values associated with a particular variable. In this instance, the first data line contains the following information:

```
0001 24 37.3
```

SAS reads this line of data and places each character into the buffer, as illustrated in the following:

1	2	3	4	5	6	7	8	9	10	11	12
0	0	0	1		2	4		3	7	.	3

SAS also creates another piece of memory called a Program Data Vector (PDV), as shown in the following:

_N_	_ERROR_	ID	AGE	TEMPC	TEMPF
1	0	.	.		.

The PDV contains the names of the variables specified in the INPUT statement, plus two temporary variables, _N_ and _ERROR_. The variable _N_ is the number of the data line being entered (set to 1 in this case for the first line) and _ERROR_ to indicate if an error in reading data has been encountered. It is initially set at 0 (which means no error detected.)

The INPUT specification tells SAS how to move the characters in the input buffer into the PDV. In this case, the freeform data entry tells SAS to read characters in the input buffer, starting with the far left and going to the right, until it sees a blank. When a blank is encountered, SAS moves the data up to that point into the first variable specified in the PDV. In this case, it moves the "0001" into the memory space in the PDV allocated for ID. When all of the information in the first line has been read, the PDV looks like the following:

_N_	_ERROR_	ID	AGE	TEMPC	TEMPF
1	0	0001	24	37.3	.

Notice that the values of each variable read from the data line are now in the PDV. However, the TEMPF variable is set at missing. SAS continues to read the code and sees that the DATA step also includes a calculation

`TEMPF=TEMPC*(9/5)+32;`

Using the data already in the PDV for TEMPC (which is 37.3), it uses that information to calculate TEMPF. Once the calculation is performed, that value is also placed in the PDV, and it looks like the following:

_N_	_ERROR_	ID	AGE	TEMPC	TEMPF
1	0	0001	24	37.3	99.14

Once all of the data for a line are read in, all of the calculations specified in the DATA step have been performed, and there are no errors detected, SAS outputs the PDV to the data set. In this case,

ID	AGE	TEMPC	TEMPF
0001	24	37.3	99.14

Notice at this stage, only the data values appear in the data set, and the two temporary variables, _N_ and _ERROR_, are not included. Therefore:

- The _N_ and _ERROR_ variables are available from one iteration of the data set to the next.

- However, they are not saved in the output data set.
- And they cannot be renamed, kept, or dropped.

The value of understanding how SAS handles data as it is read in from raw data sources is that it provides you with insight in writing code to successfully input the data in the way you want it to be read. The brief discussion here is only an introduction to this process. If you want to delve deeper into the inner workings of the DATA step, refer to SAS documentation.

3.10   SUMMARY

This chapter defined the difference between temporary and permanent data sets and illustrated several methods for importing data sets into SAS using either the SAS Wizard or PROC IMPORT. Finally, the way SAS "thinks" as it is inputting data is explained.

EXERCISES

3.1 **Create an SAS Library Reference.**

You should have already created an SAS library named MYSASLIB in the C:\SASDATA folder (or whatever is appropriate to your SAS setup). If you have not done so, use the dialog box or LIBNAME statement described in this chapter.

a. Create the following SAS libraries using the wizard technique: MYLIB1, MYLIB2, MYLIB3, MYLIB4, MYLIB5. Make all of these library definitions point to the folder C:\SASDATA (or whatever is appropriate to your SAS setup). Verify that the libraries appear in the SAS Explorer.

b. Create the following SAS libraries using the LIBNAME command in code: MYLIBA, MYLIBB, MYLIBC, MYLIBD, MYLIBE (or whatever is appropriate to your SAS setup). Verify that the libraries appear in the SAS Explorer.

3.2 **Create a permanent SAS data set.**

a. Open the program file EX_3.2.SAS.

```
DATA WEIGHT;
INPUT TREATMENT LOSS @@;
DATALINES;
1 1.0 13.0 1 -1.0 1 1.5 1 0.5 1 3.5
2 4.5 2 6.0 2 3.5 2 7.5 2 7.0 2 6.0 2 5.5
3 1.5 3 -2.5 3 -0.5 3 1.0 3 .5
;
PROC PRINT;
RUN;
```

This program creates a temporary data set called WEIGHT (or WORK.WEIGHT). Submit this code and use the SAS Explorer (WORK library) to verify that the data set was created.

b. Change the SAS program so that it creates a permanent SAS data set named WEIGHT in the C:\SASDATA folder *using the Windows folder name in the DATA statement*:

```
DATA "C:_____";
```

(or the appropriate statement for your particular SAS implantation). View the log to verify that the permanent data set was created.

c. Change the SAS program so that it creates a permanent SAS data set named MYSASLIB.WEIGHT (in the previously created SAS library MYSASLIB) using the two-level SAS data set name:

```
DATA _____._____
```

    I. To verify that the permanent data set was created, open it from the MYSASLIB library into the Viewtable.

    II. Use File → Print to print a copy of this (entire) table.

d. Using the following code:

```
PROC DATASETS;
CONTENTS DATA= MYSASLIB.WEIGHT;
RUN;
```

produce a listing of the contents of the SAS data set MYSASLIB.WEIGHT. Change the DATA= statement to

```
CONTENTS DATA=MYSASLIB._ALL_;
```

to display the contents of all data sets in the library.

3.3 **Use SAS code to import XLSX data.**

a. Write the SAS code to import data from the Excel file FAMILY2.XLSX using these criteria:

    I. Create an SAS data set named INCOME in the WORK library using the OUT= statement.

    II. Use DATAFILE= to specify the location of the original Excel file (XLSX type) on your hard disk.

    III. Use DBMS= to specify that the data source (see the chart for DBMS options earlier in the chapter for this type of file.)

    IV. Use SHEET= to designate "Data" as the name of the Excel table to import.

    V. If appropriate, use the GETNAMES= option to indicate that the variable names are on the first row of data.

b. Once the data are imported, view the contents of WORK.INCOME using Viewdata. Close the Viewdata data grid.

c. Calculate descriptive statistics for the data using this code:

```
TITLE "PUT YOUR NAME HERE";
PROC MEANS DATA=INCOME;
RUN;
```

3.4 **More about SAS libraries.**

Suppose that your SAS data sets are stored in the physical directory (folder) named
C:\RESEARCH on your hard drive.

a. If you want to create a shortcut library name in SAS named CLINICAL, what LIB-
    NAME statement would specify your data's location? (Fill in the blanks.)

    LIBNAME _____ 'C:_____';

b. If you want to use the data in a file named C:\RESEARCH\JAN2009.SAS7BDAT
    in your SAS program, fill in the blanks in the following DATA = statement:

    LIBNAME CLINICAL 'C:\RESEARCH';
    PROC MEANS DATA = _____._____;

c. Use the following information to create a LIBNAME statement:
    Hard drive location is O:\CLINICAL
    SAS library name is YOURNAME

    LIBNAME _____ '_____';

d. If you have an SAS library named CLINICAL and you want to create a permanent
    data set named MAY2007 that is stored in the C:\RESEARCH folder on your hard
    drive, what is the name of the file used in SAS code?

    _____._____

e. In step d of this exercise, what is the name of the SAS data file on your hard drive?

    _____:\RESEARCH\MAY2007._____

3.5 **Going deeper: How SAS reads data.**

In the Compile, Execution, and Output phases in the Data Step, where in the process
do these tasks take place?

a. SAS looks at the code to see if there are any errors.
    _____phase

b. SAS reads the data and performs calculations
    _____phase

c. SAS creates the data set
    _____phase

d. Identifies type and length of each variable
    _____phase

e. SAS creates the Input Buffer and puts the contents of data record one in the buffer
    _____phase

f. SAS creates the PDV
    _____phase

g. The initial values in the PDV are

```
_N_    =  ____
_ERROR_  =  ___
```

h. Once SAS has filled the PDV and there are no more lines of code in the Data Step, it sends the content of the PDV to the _____ buffer.

4

PREPARING DATA FOR ANALYSIS

LEARNING OBJECTIVES

- To be able to label variables with explanatory names
- To be able to create new variables
- To be able to use SAS® IF-THEN-ELSE statements
- To be able to use DROP and KEEP to select variables
- To be able to use the SET statement
- To be able to use PROC SORT
- To be able to append and merge data sets
- To be able to use PROC FORMAT
- Going Deeper: To be able to find first and last values in a group

You've entered your data into SAS, but before you can use them in SAS, you typically need to make corrections, perform calculations, and otherwise prepare your data for analysis. This step is sometimes overlooked in classroom settings where you often use ready-to-analyze textbook data. When you gather your own data, or even when you acquire data from a database, the data may require some changes before you can use them in an analysis.

SAS® Essentials: Mastering SAS for Data Analytics, Second Edition. Alan C. Elliott and Wayne A. Woodward.
© 2016 John Wiley & Sons, Inc. Published 2016 by John Wiley & Sons, Inc.

All of the data manipulation statements discussed in this chapter appear in your program code within the DATA step, except for PROC FORMAT. That is, they appear after the DATA statement and before the first RUN or PROC statement. Thus, all of the results of the data manipulations performed by these statements become part of the active data set.

4.1   LABELING VARIABLES WITH EXPLANATORY NAMES

SAS labels are used to provide descriptive names for variables. Data sets often contain cryptic variable names such as ID, SBP, WT, and so on. For people familiar with the data set, these make perfect sense. However, if you want to produce output that is readable by others, creating explanatory labels for variables is good practice. In SAS, this can be accomplished by using the LABEL statement. The LABEL statement uses the format:

```
LABEL    VAR1 = 'Label for VAR1'
         VAR2 = 'Label for VAR2';
```

You can use either single or double quotation marks in the LABEL statement, but you must match the type within each definition statement. When SAS prints out information for VAR1, it also includes the label, making the output more readable. The following program (DLABEL.SAS): illustrates the use of labels.

```
DATA MYDATA;
INFILE 'C:\SASDATA\BPDATA.DAT'; * READ DATA FROM FILE;
INPUT ID $ 1 SBP 2-4 DBP 5-7 GENDER $ 8 AGE 9-10 WT 11-13;
LABEL  ID = 'Identification Number'
     SBP= 'Systolic Blood Pressure'
     DBP = 'Diastolic Blood Pressure'
     AGE = 'Age on Jan 1, 2000'
     WT = 'Weight' ;
PROC MEANS;
     VAR SBP DBP AGE WT;
RUN;
```

Notice that the LABEL statement is placed within the DATA step. Also, there is only one semicolon (;) in the LABEL statement, at the very end.

The output listings in Tables 4.1 and 4.2 show how the LABEL statement adds information to the output. The first set of output shows PROC MEANS output *without* the LABEL statement. Notice that all variable names are listed just as they were created from the INPUT statement in the DATA statement.

The next set of output from PROC MEANS is from the same data, and in this case, the LABEL statement, as shown in the aforementioned example code, has been used. In this case, more informative labels are included in the output.

Follow the next Hands-on Example to add label definitions for a data set within the DATA step.

TABLE 4.1   OUTPUT without Labels

The MEANS Procedure

Variable	N	Mean	Std Dev	Minimum	Maximum
SBP	5	127.0000000	8.3666003	120.0000000	140.0000000
DBP	5	82.0000000	10.9544512	70.0000000	100.0000000
AGE	5	35.8000000	30.2605354	15.0000000	89.0000000
WT	5	145.0000000	31.6227766	110.0000000	180.0000000

TABLE 4.2   OUTPUT with Labels

The MEANS Procedure

Variable	Label	N	Mean	Std Dev	Minimum	Maximum
SBP	Systolic Blood Pressure	5	127.0000000	8.3666003	120.0000000	140.0000000
DBP	Diastolic Blood Pressure	5	82.0000000	10.9544512	70.0000000	100.0000000
AGE	Age on Jan 1, 2000	5	35.8000000	30.2605354	15.0000000	89.0000000
WT	Weight	5	145.0000000	31.6227766	110.0000000	180.0000000

HANDS-ON EXAMPLE

In this example, you will create labels for variables and learn how to output the labels using PROC PRINT.

1. Open the program file DLABEL2.SAS.

```
DATA MYDATA;
INPUT @1 FNAME $11. @12 LNAME $12. @24 BDATE DATE9.;
FORMAT BDATE WORDDATE12.;
LABEL    FNAME="First Name"; * Complete the labels;
DATALINES;
Bill       Smith       08JAN1952
Jane       Jones       02FEB1953
Clyde      York        23MAR1949
;
PROC PRINT;
RUN;
```

2. Add lines to create labels for LNAME (Last name) and BDATE (Birth date). For example, the LABEL statement could be as follows:

```
LABEL FNAME="First Name"
LNAME="Last Name"
BDATE="Birth Date";
```

Don't forget the semicolon (;) after the last label definition.

(continued)

(continued)

3. Run the program. Notice that the label information is not included in this output.

4. Most SAS PROCs output the label information automatically. However, for PROC PRINT, you must add the option LABEL to the statement. Change the PROC PRINT statement in this program to read:

PROC PRINT LABEL;

5. Run the program and observe how the labels are shown in the output. The output is shown in Table 4.3.

TABLE 4.3   Listing Formatted Dates

Obs	First Name	Last Name	Birth Date
1	Bill	Smith	Jan 8, 1952
2	Jane	Jones	Feb 2, 1953
3	Clyde	York	Mar 23, 1949

4.2   CREATING NEW VARIABLES

It is common to calculate new variables in a data set in preparation for analysis. For example, you may need to convert a temperature reading from Fahrenheit to Celsius, change a measurement from centimeters to inches, or calculate a score from a series of values. One method for creating new variables in your data set is to calculate them within the DATA step. This section describes some of the techniques you can use.

You can create new variables within an SAS DATA statement by assigning a value to a new variable name or by calculating a new variable using a mathematical or logical expression. When the SAS program is run, data values for the new variables are assigned to each of the records in the currently active data set.

> If you have experience using Microsoft Excel, you know that when you change any of the numbers that were used to calculate a value, the calculated value changes automatically. The SAS calculations in the DATA step are not like those in Excel. They are one-time calculations that take place when you run the SAS program. If you want to re-calculate the expression, you must re-run (re-submit) the SAS program.

4.2.1   Creating Numeric Variables in the DATA Step

Within the SAS DATA step, you can calculate a new variable using current variables in your data set. These calculations use standard arithmetic operators as defined in Table 4.4.

The following Hands-on Example illustrates how you could calculate a new value for each record in your data set by using a simple arithmetic expression – in this case, by multiplying two variables (WIDTH and LENGTH) that are in the data set to create a new variable (AREA).

TABLE 4.4   SAS Arithmetic Operators

Symbol	Meaning	Example
+	Addition	SUM= X+Y
−	Subtraction	DIF=X−Y;
*	Multiplication	TWICE=X*2;
/	Division	HALF=X/2;
**	Exponentiation	CUBIC=X**3;

HANDS-ON EXAMPLE

In this example, you will create a new variable by calculation from existing information in an SAS data set.

1. Open the program file DCALC.SAS. This file calculates the square footage (AREA) in various rooms of a house and adds up the total. Notice that the example defines labels for the variables, as discussed and recommended in the previous section.

```
DATA ROOMSIZE;
FORMAT ROOM $10.;
INPUT ROOM $ W L;
* The next line calculates a new variable, AREA;
AREA=L*W;
Label L="Length" W="Width" AREA="Sq. Feet";
DATALINES;
LIVING    14 22
DINING    14 12
BREAKFAST 10 12
KITCHEN 12 16
BEDROOM1 18 12
BEDROOM2 12 14
BEDROOM3 13 16
BATH1     8 12
BATH2     7 10
BATH3     6 8
GARAGE 23 24
;
RUN;
PROC PRINT Label; SUM AREA;
RUN;
```

Notice the following statement within the data step:

```
AREA = L * W;
```

This statement creates a new variable named AREA that is a result of multiplying length by width.

(continued)

(continued)

2. Run the program and observe the output in Table 4.5.

   The calculation `AREA = L * W` in the `DATA` step creates a new variable `AREA` in the data set named `ROOMSIZE`.

   - The `SUM AREA` statement in `PROC PRINT` causes SAS to report the sum of the `AREA` values.

TABLE 4.5   Output Showing Results of Calculation

Obs	ROOM	Width	Length	Sq. Feet
1	LIVING	14	22	308
2	DINING	14	12	168
3	BREAKFAS	10	12	120
4	KITCHEN	12	16	192
5	BEDROOM1	18	12	216
6	BEDROOM2	12	14	168
7	BEDROOM3	13	16	208
8	BATH1	8	12	96
9	BATH2	7	10	70
10	BATH3	6	8	48
11	GARAGE	23	24	552
				2146

3. Note the `FORMAT` statement in the code. What does it do? If you remove it, what happens to the word `BREAKFAST` in the output? Why?

SAS allows you to perform more than just simple calculations. You can perform virtually any type of algebraic calculation needed. When creating more extensive calculations, you must pay attention to the order of evaluation used in expressions. This order is similar to that used in common algebraic practice and is also commonly used in other computer programs. The priority of evaluation is as follows:

`(  )  ** *  /  +  -`

That is, when SAS evaluates an expression, it first performs calculations in parentheses, then exponentiation, then multiplication, division, addition and then subtraction. For example,

`ANSWER = A + B * C;`

results in a different answer from

`ANSWER = (A + B) * C;`

The first example multiplies B * C, then adds to the product A. The second adds A + B, then multiplies the resulting sum by C. If you are unsure about how an expression will be evaluated, use parentheses to force the evaluation to be as you intend. For example,

```
NEWVAL = (SCORE1-SCORE2)*INDEX**2;
```

gives the instruction to subtract SCORE2 from SCORE1 first, then multiply the result by $INDEX^2$.

> You may find the following mnemonic (which you may have learned in a previous math class) helpful in remembering the order of operations: "Please Excuse My Dear Aunt Sally" (**P**arentheses **E**xponents **M**ultiplication **D**ivision **A**ddition **S**ubtraction).

4.2.2   Creating New Variables as Constant Values

Sometimes, it is handy to define a new variable as a constant value. The reason for creating this type of variable is that you might want to use the value in a series of future calculations. For example, suppose that you are about to calculate new values in your data set with a formula that uses the value of *pi* (π). A statement such as the following could appear within your DATA step (before you use the variable PI in another calculation):

```
PI = 3.1415927;    *Value to be used later;
```

For example, assuming RADIUS is a variable in your data set, you could define the following expressions:

```
AREA = PI * RADIUS**2;
CIRCUM=2*PI*RADIUS;
```

to calculate the area and circumference of a circle from the measure of its radius without having to repeatedly entering 3.1415927.

> Variable names on the left side of each equation are created as a *result* of the *statement*. Variables used on the right side of any statement must already be defined in the current data set. If a variable on the right side of the statement is undefined or contains a missing value, the resulting value for the variable on the left side of the equation (the result) is set to missing.

> The SAS SUM Statement is a way to add or accumulate values over the iterations of data records read into the data set. The format is

```
ACCUM+addval
```

Note that unlike the previous examples, there is no equal (=) sign. The addval (which can be a constant, variable, or expression) is added to the variable ACCUM for each iteration data records read. The initial value of ACCUM is 0. For each iteration in the DATA step, the value addval is added (because of the + sign) to ACCUM as if the statement were ACCUM=ACCUM+addval.

4.3   USING IF-THEN-ELSE CONDITIONAL STATEMENT ASSIGNMENTS

Another way to create a new variable in the DATA step is to use the IF-THEN-ELSE conditional statement construct. (This is sometimes also referred to as an "IF statement" or an "IF-THEN statement" because you don't always have to include all three parts in a statement.) The syntax is as follows:

```
IF expression THEN statement; ELSE statement;
```

For example:

```
IF SBP GE 140 THEN HIGHBP=1; ELSE HIGHBP=0;
```

This statement tells SAS to do the following: if SBP is greater than or equal to 140 (SBP GE 140), then create a new variable named HIGHBP and set the value of that variable to 1; if SBP is less than 140 (IF SBP LT 140), set the value of the variable HIGHBP to 0. In effect, this creates a grouping variable for the data set using the variable HIGHBP with values 0 and 1. Because the first reference to HIGHBP is as a number, it is added to the list of variables in the data set as a numeric variable.

The GE operator used in this example is one of several possible conditional operators that can be used in a comparison statement. A list of common SAS comparison operators is given in Table 4.6. You can use either the symbol or the mnemonic in an SAS expression.

You can also put several conditions together in an IF statement using the AND (mnemonic &), OR (Mnemonic |), or NOT (mnemonic ^ or ~) logical operators and create expressions such as

```
IF AGE GT 19 AND GENDER="M" THEN GROUP=1;
```

or

```
IF TREATMENT EQ "A" OR GROUP >=1 THEN CATEGORY="GREEN";
```

Note, as in the aforementioned example, that you can also mix mnemonic and symbol operators in the same statement. You can also stack IF-THEN-ELSE statements by using an ELSE IF clause, as in:

```
IF TRT="A" THEN GROUP=1;
ELSE IF TRT="B" OR TRT="C" THEN GROUP=2;
ELSE GROUP=3;
```

TABLE 4.6   SAS Conditional Operators

Symbol	Mnemonic	Meaning	Example
=	EQ	Equal to	I=5
^=, or ~=	NE	Not equal to	I NE 5
<	LT	Less than	I<5
<=	LE	Less than or equal to	I<=5
>	GT	Greater than	I GT 5
>=	GE	Greater than or equal to	I >= 5
	IN	Is valued TRUE if a specified number (NUM) is in a list	NUM IN (3,4,5)

TABLE 4.7   SAS Logical Operators

Symbol	Mnemonic	Meaning	Example
&	AND	Both	I>5 AND J<3
|	OR	Either	I>5 OR J<3
^ or ~	NOT	Negate	NOT (I GT J)

The preceding lines recode the variable (TRT) into a new variable (GROUP). If TRT is equal to A, then GROUP is set to the value 1. If TRT is B or C, then GROUP is set to the value 2. Otherwise, GROUP is set to the value 3. A summary of the SAS logical operators is shown in Table 4.7.

HANDS-ON EXAMPLE

In this example, you will use an IF-THEN-ELSE conditional statement to create a new variable.

1. Open the program file DCONDITION.SAS.

```
DATA MYDATA;
INPUT ID $ SBP DBP GENDER $ AGE WT;
IF SBP GE 140 THEN STATUS="HIGH"; ELSE STATUS="OK";
DATALINES;
001 120 80 M 15 115
002 130 70 F 25 180
003 140 100 M 89 170
004 180 80 F 30 150
005 125 80 F 20 110
;
PROC PRINT;
RUN;
```

2. Notice the IF-THEN-ELSE statement. If systolic blood pressure (SBP) is greater than or equal to 140, the program assigns the value HIGH to the variable STATUS. Otherwise, it assigns the value OK to that variable.

3. Run the program and observe the results in Table 4.8.

TABLE 4.8   Results of IF-THEN-ELSE Statement

Obs	ID	SBP	DBP	GENDER	AGE	WT	STATUS
1	001	120	80	M	15	115	OK
2	002	130	70	F	25	180	OK
3	003	140	100	M	89	170	HIGH
4	004	180	80	F	30	150	HIGH
5	005	125	80	F	20	110	OK

(continued)

(continued)

Notice that the new variable STATUS is assigned either the value OK or the value HIGH depending on the value of SBP. Also notice that because the first use of the variable STATUS was as a character (text) value, it is set to an SAS character type variable.

4.3.1   Using IF-THEN to Assign Missing Values

An IF-THEN statement is a common way to specify missing values in an SAS DATA step. For example,

```
IF AGE EQ -9 then AGE = . ;
```

indicates that if the value of AGE is equal to −9, the value of AGE is set to a missing value . (dot). Because there is no ELSE clause, the value of AGE is not changed when AGE is not equal to −9. To specify a missing character value, use two quotation marks. For example,

```
IF GENDER NE "M" and GENDER NE "F" then GENDER = "";
```

specifies a missing value for GENDER (two quotation marks in a row, " ") when it is neither M nor F. A blank (two quotation marks in a row) is a common missing value for character variables.

When recoding missing values using an IF-THEN statement, you need to take care that all possibilities are accounted for. For example, suppose that you are recoding AGE into a new variable called TEEN. You could use the following code:

```
IF AGE GT 12 AND AGE LT 20 THEN TEEN=1;ELSE TEEN = 0;
IF AGE = . THEN TEEN = .;
```

The use of the IF AGE = . THEN TEEN = . guarantees that the value of TEEN is set to missing for any observation for which AGE is missing. Otherwise, any observation where AGE is less than or equal to 12 and greater than or equal to 20 is coded as TEEN = 0;.

HANDS-ON EXAMPLE

In this example, you will use IF-THEN and IF-THEN-ELSE statements in the DATA step to create a new variable and define a missing value.

1. Open the program file DMISSING.SAS.

```
DATA MYDATA;
INPUT ID $ SBP DBP GENDER $ AGE;
IF AGE GT 12 AND AGE LT 20 THEN TEEN=1;ELSE TEEN=0;
IF AGE=. THEN TEEN=.;
DATALINES;
001 120 80 M 15
002 130 70 F .
003 140 100 M 12
```

```
004 180 80 F 17
005 144 80 F 23
006 165 80 M 18
007 121 80 F 19
008 195 80 M 11
009 162 80 M 13
010 112 80 F 17
;
PROC PRINT;
RUN;
```

2. Notice the IF statements that define the new variable TEEN. They also set TEEN to missing (.) if AGE is missing. Run this program to see that the value of TEEN in the second observation is set to missing.

3. Comment the second IF AGE statement by placing an asterisk (*) before the IF. (The line should be displayed in green signifying that it is now a comment.) Submit the changed code and observe that the value of TEEN for ID 002 was incorrectly given the value 0.

4. Use the second method described previously to do the same task:

```
IF AGE=. Then TEEN=.;
ELSE IF AGE GT 12 and AGE LT 20 then TEEN=1;
ELSE TEEN=0;
```

Submit the program. Did this version work correctly?

4.3.2   Using IF and IF-THEN To Subset Data Sets

Data sets can be quite large. You may have a data set that contains some group of subjects (records) that you want to eliminate from your analysis. In that case, you can subset the data so it will contain only those records you need. For example, if your analysis concerns pregnancies, you may want to limit your data set to females.

One method of eliminating certain records from a data set is to use a subsetting IF statement in the DATA step. The syntax for this statement is as follows:

```
IF expression;
```

where the expression is some conditional statement in terms of the variables in the data set. For example, to select records containing the value F (only females) from a data set, you could use this statement within a DATA step:

```
IF GENDER EQ 'F';
```

Note that you can use single or double quotation marks ("F" or 'F') in this statement.

This subsetting IF statement is similar to a gate. It allows only records that meet a certain criterion to enter into the data set. In this case, only those records whose GENDER value is recorded as F are retained in the data set.

The opposite effect can be created by including the statement `THEN DELETE` at the end of the statement:

```
IF expression THEN DELETE;
```

For example, to get rid of certain records (all males) in a data set, you could use the code

```
IF GENDER EQ 'M' THEN DELETE;
```

When data are read into an SAS data set using this procedure and a record contains M for GENDER, then that record is *not* retained in the SAS data set. If the only values for GENDER in the data set are F and M, then these two subsetting strategies will yield the same results.

You are not limited to using the `IF` statement on character variables. An example that uses the `IF` statement on a numeric variable is as follows:

```
IF AGE GT 19;
```

You can also use combinations of conditions in any of these `IF` statements, such as

```
IF AGE GT 19 AND GENDER ="M";
```

> The statement DELETE *does not* indicate that these records are erased from the raw data file on disk. The records are only eliminated from the SAS data set created in the DATA step.

HANDS-ON EXAMPLE

In this example, you use a subsetting `IF` to select only certain records for inclusion in the MYDATA SAS data set created in the DATA step.

1. Open the program file `DSUBSET1.SAS`. In this example, subjects less than or equal to 10 years are included in the data set named MYDATA.

```
DATA MYDATA;
INFILE 'C:\SASDATA\EXAMPLE.DAT';
INPUT  ID  $ 1-3 GP $ 5 AGE 6-9 TIME1 10-14 TIME2 15-19;
IF AGE LE 10;
PROC PRINT;
RUN;
```

   Notice that the subsetting `IF` statement selects only records for which AGE is less than or equal to 10. (This does not change the contents of the file `C:\SASDATA\EXAMPLE.DAT`; it affects only the contents of the new SAS data set MYDATA.)

2. Run this program and observe the results. The data listing includes only the 22 subjects whose age is less than or equal to 10.

4.3.3 Using IF-THEN and DO for Program Control

Another use of the IF statement is to control the flow of your SAS program in conjunction with a DO statement. In this case, you can cause a group of SAS commands to be conditionally executed by using the following type of code:

```
IF expression then DO;
Code to execute;
END;
```

For example, suppose that you want to calculate BMI (Body Mass Index) for subjects in a data set, but the formula is only relevant for subjects older than 19 years. Plus, at the same time, you want to assign other values for this same group of subjects. You could use the following code:

```
IF AGE GT 19 then DO;
   BMI=(WTLBS/HTINCH**2)*703;
   ISADULT=1;
   INCLUDEINSTUDY="Yes";
END;
```

In this case, when AGE for a subject is older than 19, a series of three lines of code is processed. For other subjects in the data set where AGE is younger than or equal to 19, BMI, ISADULT, and INCLUDEINSTUDY are not assigned any values, and thus they have a missing value. (You might have a second IF-THEN-DO statement to assign other values for this case.)

4.3.4 Using @ and IF to Conditionally Read Lines in a Data Set

For big data sets, it is often the case that you don't want to read in all of the data. One method you could use to conditionally read in certain records is to set up a test condition and read in the record only if it meets that condition. To do this, you can use the @ (at) sign in your input statement to read in a portion of a record and put the input on hold while you decide whether or not to read in the complete record. This is referred to as a "trailing at." This is illustrated in the following example.

HANDS-ON EXAMPLE

This example illustrates the use of a trailing at to conditionally read in data.

1. Open the program file DSUBSET2.SAS. Note the first INPUT statement ends in a trailing at. The IF statement tests for records where group is A and age is older than or equal to 10 and reads only the records that match the condition.

```
DATA MYDATA;
INFILE 'C:\SASDATA\EXAMPLE.DAT';
INPUT GP $ 5 AGE 6-9 @;
IF GP EQ "A" and AGE GE 10 THEN
INPUT  ID  $ 1-3 GP $ 5 AGE 6-9 TIME1 10-14 TIME2 15-19;
PROC PRINT DATA=MYDATA;
RUN;
```

(continued)

(continued)

2. Change the `IF` statement to look for groups A or B using

```
IF (GP EQ "A" or GP="B") and AGE GE 10;
```

   Re-submit and observe the difference.
3. Change the program to only read records where `ID LE 100`. Re-submit to verify that your changes work.

4.4   USING DROP AND KEEP TO SELECT VARIABLES

Sometimes, you may have a data set containing *variables* you do not want to keep. The `DROP` and `KEEP` statements in the `DATA` step allow you to specify which variables to retain in a data set. The general form for these statements is as follows:

```
DROP variables;
KEEP variables;
```

   For example,

```
DATA MYDATA;
INPUT A B C D E F G;
DROP E F;
DATALINES;
...etc...
```

reads in all of the data but then drops the variables `E` and `F` so that these variables are no longer in the temporary SAS data set named `MYDATA`.

   Another way to use `DROP` and `KEEP` is as you are reading in the data. In this case, the statement is included in the `DATA` statement as an option specified in parentheses. The format for this use is (`DROP=` list of variables) or (`KEEP=` list of variables). For example,

```
DATA MYDATA (DROP=E F);
```

   The following Hands-on Example illustrates this technique.

HANDS-ON EXAMPLE

In this example, you will read in a data set but keep only a selection of the variables.

1. Open the program file `DKEEP.SAS`.

```
DATA MYDATA;
INFILE 'C:\SASDATA\EXAMPLE.CSV' DLM=',' FIRSTOBS=2 OBS=26;
INPUT  GROUP $ AGE TIME1 TIME2 TIME3 TIME4 SOCIO;
```

```
KEEP AGE TIME1 SOCIO;
PROC PRINT DATA=MYDATA;
RUN;
```

This SAS program reads the first 25 records from a file with comma-separated values. In this type of data entry, you must read in all variables. To eliminate variables you do not need, use the KEEP statement (or DROP statement).
2. Run the program. Although the program reads in seven variables, the listing from the PROC PRINT statement includes only those variables you have specified in the KEEP statement.
3. Replace the KEEP statement with the statement

```
DROP GROUP AGE SOCIO;
```

Run the program and observe the results.
4. Change the code so the DROP option appears in the DATA step instead of its own statement. Comment out the current KEEP statement and use this option instead:

```
DATA MYDATA (DROP= list variables to drop);
```

4.5   USING THE SET STATEMENT TO READ AN EXISTING DATA SET

Often, you have a "main" data set that is from some corporate, government, or organization source. If you don't want to change the original data set, you should work with a copy of it. The SET statement is what you need. The SET statement in a DATA step is used to transfer data from an existing SAS data set to a new one. When you use a SET statement, there is no need for an INPUT, INFILE, or DATALINES statement. The SET statement is often used when you want to create one or more new SAS data sets by subsetting a larger data set but preserve all data in the original data set.

The general form of the SET statement is as follows:

```
SET SASdataset;
```

For example:

```
DATA NEW; SET OLD;
```

or

```
DATA NEW; SET "C:\SASDATA\OLD";
```

In this example, the SAS data set named OLD already exists. All variables and observations in the existing SAS data set (OLD) are automatically passed through the input buffer to the new SAS data set (NEW) (unless otherwise directed with programming statements). Just as when any new data set is created, additional variables can be created with assignment statements within the SAS DATA step.

Figure 4.1   Creating a new data set using the SET statement

For example, suppose that you already have a data set named ALL. It contains several variables including the variable GENDER that is coded "M" or "F."

You want to create a subset of ALL that contains only males. The SAS code used to do this is as follows:

```
DATA MALES;
SET ALL;
IF GENDER ='M';
RUN;
```

In this code, the DATA step creates a new data set named MALES. The SET statement passes all data from the existing data set ALL into the new data set MALES. The IF statement causes the buffer to only keep the records if GENDER ="M". The result is a data set named MALES that contains only the selected records. Figure 4.1 illustrates this process.

HANDS-ON EXAMPLE

1. Open the program file DSUBSET3.SAS.

```
DATA ALL;
INPUT AGE GENDER $ FAT PROTEIN CARBO SODIUM;
DATALINES;
25      M      40      40      109      1396
26      M      47      46      125      1731
38      M      42      40      104      1431
42      M      48      46      123      1711
65      M      41      41      112      1630
68      M      34      33      96       1192
20      F      39      29      118      1454
30      F      40      40      115      1532
60      F      39      40      123      1585
;
DATA MALES;
SET ALL;
IF GENDER ='M';
RUN;
```

Notice that this code already includes one subsetting IF statement in the DATA step to create a new data set named MALES.

2. At the end of the code, add these program lines to create a FEMALES data set using the appropriate SET and IF statements.

```
DATA FEMALES;
SET ALL;
IF GENDER ='F';
RUN;
```

3. Add lines that perform a PROC PRINT for MALES and a separate PROC PRINT for females. Remember to include a RUN statement at the end of the program. The following is the statement for MALES:

```
PROC PRINT DATA=MALES;RUN;
```

Similarly, add this line to the program to print the contents for the FEMALE data set:

```
PROC PRINT DATA=FEMALES;RUN;
```

4. Run the completed program. How many data sets have been created using this program? What are their names? How are they related?

4.6 USING PROC SORT

The SORT procedure can be used in the DATA step to rearrange the observations in an SAS data set or create a new SAS data set containing the rearranged observations. With PROC SORT, you can sort on multiple sort fields and sort in ascending or descending order. The sorting sequence information for SAS data sets is shown in Table 4.9. The data are listed from the smallest to largest in terms of each character's computer index designation (ASCII code). That is, in terms of sequence, a blank is the smallest character and a ~ is the largest.

The syntax for PROC SORT is as follows:

```
PROC SORT 'options'; BY variable(s);
```

Options for PROC SORT include

```
DATA=datasetname;
OUT= outputdatasetname;
```

For example,

```
PROC SORT DATA=MYDATA OUT=MYSORT; BY RECTIME;
```

creates a new sorted SAS data set named MYSORT (and the records in the original SAS data set MYDATA remain in their original order). If you *do not include* an OUT= statement, SAS sorts the current SAS data set. In the aforementioned example, if the OUT= statement is not included, the MYDATA data set is sorted.

TABLE 4.9 SAS Sorting Sequence

Sorting sequence for **character variables**	blank!"#$%&©()*+,–./ 0123456789:;<=>?@ ABCDE- FGHIJKLMNOPQRSTUVWXYZ [\]^_abcdefghijklmnopqrstuvw xyz(l)~
Sorting sequence for **numeric variables**	Missing values first, then numeric values
Default sorting sequence	Ascending (or indicate Descending)

The BY statement in the PROC SORT paragraph must contain one or more variables and optionally the DESCENDING keyword. The BY DESCENDING statement tells SORT to arrange the values from highest to lowest instead of the default lowest to highest order. For example:

```
BY AGE;              * Sorts in ascending/alphabetical order;
BY DESCENDING AGE; * Sorts in descending order;
```

You can also sort on several variables at a time. For example,

```
PROC SORT; BY GROUP SOCIO;
```

will cause the data set to be sorted on GROUP within SOCIO.

Uppercase characters (e.g., "A") come before lowercase characters (e.g., "a"). Thus, when sorting, Z comes before a. If variables such as GENDER are entered without consistency for uppercase and lowercase (e.g., M, F, m, and f), then your sort will not properly place the records into a Male and Female grouping.

If you *do not include* an OUT= statement, SAS sorts the current SAS data set. In the aforementioned example, if the OUT= statement is not included, the MYDATA data set is sorted.

HANDS-ON EXAMPLE

In this example, you sort data in ascending and descending order.

1. Open the program file DSORT1.SAS.

```
DATA MYDATA;
INPUT GROUP RECTIME;
DATALINES;
1    4.2
2    3.6
2    3.1
1    2.1
1    2.8
```

```
2    1.5
1    1.8
;
PROC SORT DATA=MYDATA OUT=S1; BY RECTIME;
Title 'Sorting Example - Ascending';
PROC PRINT DATA=S1;
RUN;
```

Note that this program sorts the data and stores the results in an SAS data file named S1. Submit the code and observe the sorted output.

2. Write second PROC SORT and PROC PRINT statements to sort MYDATA descending and save the results in S2 by using the code

```
PROC SORT DATA=MYDATA OUT=S2; BY DESCENDING RECTIME;
```

Submit the revised program.

Notice that the two PROC SORT routines produce two different results, the data set S1 sorted ascending and data set S2 sorted descending as shown in Table 4.10.

TABLE 4.10   SAS Output Showing Sort Ascending and Descending

Sorting Example - Ascending				Sorting Example - Descending		
Obs	GROUP	RECTIME		Obs	GROUP	RECTIME
1	2	1.5		1	1	4.2
2	1	1.8		2	2	3.6
3	1	2.1		3	2	3.1
4	1	2.8		4	1	2.8
5	2	3.1		5	1	2.1
6	2	3.6		6	1	1.8
7	1	4.2		7	2	1.5

Other handy features in PROC SORT are DROP, KEEP, and RENAME. These are illustrated in the following example.

HANDS-ON EXAMPLE

Suppose that you are sorting a data set for the purpose of merging it (which is discussed in the following section) and you need to change the variable named ID to CASE.

1. Open the program file DSORT2.SAS.

```
PROC SORT DATA="C:\SASDATA\SOMEDATA"
      OUT=ANALYSIS
      (KEEP=ID GP AGE GENDER RENAME=( ID=SUBJECT AGE=DXAGE));
BY ID;
RUN;
PROC PRINT DATA=ANALYSIS;RUN;
```

(continued)

(continued)

Notice that there is a set of parentheses following the OUT= statement. Within those parentheses is a KEEP= statement that specifies which variables to keep in the output file ANALYSIS. Inside these parentheses is another statement, RENAME with its own parentheses. Inside the RENAME= parentheses are two statements that rename an old variable with a new name. The syntax of this RENAME statement is

```
RENAME =(oldname1=newname1 oldname2=newname2, etc...)
```

Therefore, this code renames two variables and saves four variables in the output. Submit this code and observe the (partial) results shown in Table 4.11.

However, note that the names to KEEP must be the original variable names, not the new names. Notice that ID and AGE are kept, but in the new data set, they are named SUBJECT and GENDER.

2. Take the variable name GENDER out of the KEEP statement. Re-run the program and see that the results no longer include the GENDER column.
3. Rename the GP variable GROUP. Re-run the code and observe the changed results.

TABLE 4.11   SAS Output Showing Sort Ascending and Descending

Obs	SUBJECT	GP	DXAGE	GENDER
1	101	A	12	Female
2	102	A	11	Female
3	104	B	12	Female
4	110	A	12	Male
5	122	B	9	Male

4.7   APPENDING AND MERGING DATA SETS

Other useful SAS data manipulation capabilities are appending and merging data sets.

- *Appending* adds new *records* to an existing data set.
- *Merging* adds *variables* to a data set through the use of a key identifier that is present in both data sets (usually an identification code).

4.7.1   Appending Two Data Sets

Appending data sets combines records from two or more data sets. (It is sometimes called a vertical merge.) For example, suppose that data are collected at two locations and you want to combine the data sets into one SAS data set for analysis. The data sets must have at least some of the same variables in common. Appending is accomplished by including multiple data set names in the SET statement. For example,

```
DATA NEW; SET OLD1 OLD2;
```

creates the data set NEW, which consists of the records in the OLD1 data set, as well as the records from the OLD2 data set.

HANDS-ON EXAMPLE

In this example, you will append one SAS data set to another, creating a larger data set.

1. Open the program file DAPPEND1.SAS.

```
DATA MYDATA;
DATA OLD1;
INPUT SUBJ $ AGE YRS_SMOKE;
DATALINES;
001 34 12
003 44 14
004 55 35
006 21 3
;
DATA OLD2;
INPUT SUBJ $ AGE YRS_SMOKE;
DATALINES;
011 33 11
012 25 19
023 65 45
032 71 55
;
RUN;
```

   This program creates two data sets, one named OLD1 and the other named OLD2. It does not create any output. Run the program and verify by looking at the contents of the Log window that the data sets have been created. Observe the following statements in the Log window:

```
NOTE: The data set WORK.OLD1 has 4 observations and 3
variables.
NOTE: The data set WORK.OLD2 has 4 observations and 3
variables.
```

2. Return to the Editor window and add the following statements to the end of this SAS program:

```
DATA NEW;SET OLD1 OLD2; RUN;
PROC PRINT DATA=NEW;RUN;
```

3. Run the SAS program and observe the results. The data from the OLD2 data set is appended to the OLD1 data set, and the combined data sets are stored in the NEW data set. The results (contents of the NEW data set) are listed using PROC PRINT.

(continued)

(continued)

4. Open the program file DAPPEND2.SAS. Notice that in this version of the program, the OLD2 data set contains an additional variable, MARRIED.

```
DATA OLD1;
... etc ...
DATA OLD2;
INPUT SUBJ $ AGE YRS_SMOKE MARRIED;
DATALINES;
011 33 11 1
012 25 19 0
023 65 45 1
032 71 55 1
;
RUN;
DATA NEW;SET OLD1 OLD2; RUN;
PROC PRINT DATA=NEW;RUN;
```

5. Run this SAS program and observe the results. Where there is no matching variable in an appended data set, the data are set to missing in the merged data set.

4.7.2   Merging Data Sets by a Key Identifier

Another way to combine data sets is to merge them by adding *new variables* from one data set to an existing data set. (It is sometimes called a horizontal merge or a many-to-many merge.) In order to accomplish this, you must have a matching identifier in each data set that can be used by SAS to match the records during the merge. For example, suppose that you have data collected on patients taken on two separate occasions, and the data for each collection time are in separate data sets. If you want to combine the data so you can compare pre- and post-treatment values, the technique for merging the data sets using some key identifier (such as patient ID) is as follows:

1. Sort each data set by the key identifier.
2. Within a DATA step, use the MERGE statement along with a BY statement to merge the data by the key identifier.

As with the SORT statement, you can RENAME, DROP, and KEEP variables during the MERGE. You can also merge many files at a time. The following shows the syntax for merging four data sets and performing a RENAME, DROP, and KEEP on the third data set.

```
DATA newdataset;
MERGE   data1
        data2
    data3   (RENAME=(oldname=newname)
             DROP=variables   or KEEP=variables))
        data4;
BY keyvar
RUN;
```

HANDS-ON EXAMPLE

In this example, you will merge data sets using a key identifier to match records. In this case, the new data set will contain more variables than either of the two original data sets.

1. Open the program file DMERGE1.SAS. The first data set created in this example is named PRE.

```
DATA PRE;
INPUT CASE $ PRETREAT;
DATALINES;
001 1.02
002 2.10
etc ...
A second data set in the program is named POST:
DATA POST;
INPUT CASE $ POSTREAT;
DATALINES;
001 1.94
002 1.63
etc ...
```

2. Note that each data set contains a variable named CASE. This is the key identifier that tells SAS which records to match when performing the merge. Before merging the data sets, you must sort them on the same identifier:

```
PROC SORT DATA=PRE; BY CASE;
PROC SORT DATA=POST; BY CASE;
```

The code you opened in SAS is not complete. You must complete the code yourself to make it run properly. For example, add the BY CASE; statement to the second PROC SORT.

Also, complete the DATA statement in the program to perform the desired merge:

```
DATA PREPOST;                    * Create new data set;
  MERGE PRE POST; BY CASE;
  DIFF=POSTREAT - PRETREAT; * Calculate DIFF in new data set;
```

The MERGE statement merges the data sets. Because you are interested in the difference between the PRE and POST values, the DATA step includes the DIFF= calculation. (Notice that the DIFF calculation is appropriate in this case because the code is within a DATA step.)

3. Run the completed program and observe the results shown in Table 4.12.

4. Make a change to the MERGE statement to rename the variable PRETREAT to BASE-LINE.

```
  MERGE PRE (RENAME=(PRETREAT = BASELINE))POST;
```

(continued)

(continued)

You will also need to change the `DIFF=` calculation to

```
DIFF=  POSTREAT-BASELINE;
```

Re-submit the code and verify that you obtain the expected results.

5. In your SAS code, delete the data line for record 2 in the `PRE` data set. Re-submit the program and observe the results. When there is no matching key value, a missing value is placed in the cell, and the calculation based on that value is a missing value.

6. Remove the `BY CASE` statement after the `MERGE` statement. Re-submit the program and observe the results. Compare the output to the original output and see that the merge no longer produces the expected results. Leaving the `BY` statement out of a `MERGE` is a common programming mistake that leads to incorrect results.

TABLE 4.12   Example Output from Merged Data Sets

Merge Example

Obs	CASE	PRETREAT	POSTREAT	DIFF
1	001	1.02	1.94	0.92
2	002	2.10	1.63	-0.47
3	003	1.88	2.73	0.85
4	004	2.20	2.18	-0.02
5	005	1.44	1.82	0.38
6	011	1.55	1.94	0.39
7	013	1.61	2.25	0.64
8	014	2.61	1.70	-0.91
9	015	1.56	1.78	0.22
10	016	0.99	1.52	0.53
11	022	1.53	1.97	0.44

4.7.3   Few-to-Many Merge

A Few-To-Many merge is used when you have records in one data set that you want to merge into some table that contains (typically) a smaller number of categories. For example, suppose that you own an auto parts store where you sell a lot of (maybe a hundred thousand) different kinds of products. You sell these products to certain types of buyers (only a few types). Each type of buyer gets a particular discount. Counter customers (the public) get no discount. Other parts stores get a discount of 40%, and auto repair shops get a discount of 30%. This discount schedule may change at any time, so you want to create a program where you can quickly merge the thousands of items to the various buyer categories – thus

TABLE 4.13   Data for a Few-to-Many Merge

Transactions (Data Set Name SALES)

ITEM	BUYERTYPE	PRICE
CARBCLEANER	REPAIR	2.30
BELT	CONSUMER	6.99
MOTOROIL	CONSUMER	14.34
CHAIN	STORE	18.99
SPARKPLUGS	REPAIR	28.99
CLEANER	CONSUMER	1.99
WRENCH	STORE	18.88

Discount types (data set name DISCOUNT)

BUYERTYPE	DISCOUNT
CONSUMER	0.00
REPAIR	0.33
STORE	0.40

a Few-to-Many (or some would call it Many-to-Few) match. Another example might be for a credit card company where there are millions of transactions each month. At the end of the month, you want to match each credit card sale (the many) to the card owner (the fewer) in order to combine those purchases by card owner to produce a monthly statement.

To continue with the auto parts example, suppose that you want to produce a report of seven transactions (to keep it simple) defined as shown in Table 4.13. The table shows the part, the type of customer, and the retail price. This is information in your "many" data set. A second table (also shown in Table 4.13) contains the current discounts offered. In this data set, there are only three records. This is your "few" dataset.

The goal is to merge the current discounts to the parts sold, allowing you to calculate the actual price you charged for the part. To perform the merge that you desire, first sort both files by the key identifier. Notice that BUYERTYPE is in both data sets. This is the key identifier by which you want to sort in preparation for the merge. The following example illustrates this merge.

Note that this merge is very similar to merging any two files by a key identifier, and it is. The difference is that in the first data set, there can be many of the same values for the key identifier (BUYERTYPE) and a list of similarly named unique categories in the second data file.

HANDS-ON EXAMPLE

1. Open the program file DMERGE2.SAS. The part of the code that performs the Few-to-Many merge is as follows:

```
PROC SORT DATA=SALES; BY BUYERTYPE;RUN;
PROC SORT DATA=DISCOUNT; BY BUYERTYPE; RUN; *COMPLETE THIS;
DATA REPORT;
   MERGE SALES DISCOUNT;BY BUYERTYPE;*COMPLETE THIS;
   FINAL = ROUND(PRICE*(1-DISCOUNT),.01);
```

(continued)

(continued)

```
RUN;
PROC PRINT DATA=REPORT;
SUM FINAL;
RUN;
```

Note that the code first sorts the data. In the DATA statement, the merge is performed, and at the same time, the final price is calculated. (The ROUND function used in the example limits the number for FINAL to two digits. See Appendix B for more explanation of how to use this function.)

2. The code in the file has some pieces missing. Complete the code as shown previously.
3. Submit the code and observe the results. The results are shown in Table 4.14. Observe the results. Notice how each ITEM is paired with a DISCOUNT according to the matching BUYERTYPE. The last column (FINAL) contains the calculated actual price charged for each item. The SUM in PROC PRINT produces a final total for all sales. For this report, the store sold $67.00 worth of merchandise.
4. The store is running a sale and is offering consumers a 15% discount. Change the consumer discount from 0 to 0.15 and re-run the program. How much less did the store make?
5. In the SALES dataset, add a line in the DATA step (before the DATALINES statement) that raises prices all by 15%. For example:

```
PRICE=PRICE*1.15;
```

TABLE 4.14   Results for the Few-to-Many Merge

Obs	ITEM	BUYERTYPE	PRICE	DISCOUNT	FINAL
1	BELT	CONSUMER	6.99	0.00	6.99
2	MOTOROIL	CONSUMER	14.34	0.00	14.34
3	CLEANER	CONSUMER	1.99	0.00	1.99
4	CARBCLEANER	REPAIR	2.30	0.33	1.54
5	SPARKPLUGS	REPAIR	28.99	0.33	19.42
6	CHAIN	STORE	18.99	0.40	11.39
7	WRENCH	STORE	18.88	0.40	11.33
					67.00

Re-submit the program. How much more money did this scenario bring the store?

There are other ways to perform appends and merges in SAS. Two other alternatives (not discussed here) are PROC APPEND and PROC SQL. Also, a version of appending called interleaving is not discussed here because it is seldom used. The SAS merge process can be tricky, and you must be careful not to violate certain rules. The following list will help you avoid common merging mistakes:

- Be careful if there are duplicate values of your KEY variable(s) in data sets to be merged. These types of merges are sometimes referred to as few-to-many, many-to-few, or many-to-many and should be avoided.
- Do not leave off the BY statement when merging data sets.
- Make sure your KEY variables in data sets to be merged are of the same data type, length, and format.
- Make sure your KEY variables uniquely identify or label the records within the data set. Beware of ambiguous KEY variables that might have been miscoded.
- Watch out for variables in data sets that have the same name but mean something different. For example, suppose that you have a variable name EX in both data sets you intend to merge. In one data set it means EXPENSE and in another EXTRA – they are two different variables with two different meanings. These are sometimes referred to as overlapping variables. When the data sets are merged, the resulting value of an overlapping variable may not be what you expect.

4.8 USING PROC FORMAT

In Chapter 3, we saw how you can use predefined SAS date formats to output dates in selected formats. For example, the format Worddate12. outputs dates in a Jan 10, 2016 format. The PROC FORMAT procedure allows you to create your own custom formats. These custom formats allow you to specify the information that will be displayed for selected values of a variable. Note that PROC FORMAT (which creates the format definition) is *not* a part of the DATA step. However, it is related to how data are displayed in the output and is therefore related to the topics of this chapter.

Once a FORMAT has been created, it must be applied within an SAS procedure in order to take effect. Thus, the steps for using formatted values are as follows:

1. Create a FORMAT definition using PROC FORMAT.
2. Apply the FORMAT to one or more variables. You can apply a format (once it is defined in PROC FORMAT) in a DATA step or in a data analysis PROC statement.

For example, suppose that your SAS data set contains a numeric variable named MARRIED coded as 0 and 1. To cause SAS to output the words Yes and No rather than 0 and 1, construct a format definition for MARRIED using the PROC FORMAT statement, as illustrated in the following:

```
PROC FORMAT;
     VALUE FMTMARRIED 0="No"
                      1="Yes";
RUN;
```

The following Hands-on Example illustrates how you would apply the FMTMARRIED format to a variable within an SAS procedure. You can choose any legitimate name for your format and define as many format names as are required for your data set. Custom formats must be defined in your code before they are used; therefore, you will usually place the PROC FORMAT early in your program listing.

Formats are not limited to numeric variables. For example, if a text variable was coded Y and N for `Yes` and `No` to survey answers, you could create the following text format (for the text variable `ANSWER`). Notice that formats for text variables begin with a dollar sign ($):

```
PROC FORMAT;
    VALUE $FMTANSWER 'Y' = 'Yes'
             'N' = 'No';
    PROC PRINT;
    FORMAT ANSWER $FMTANSWER.;
    RUN;
```

This code causes `PROC PRINT` to use the formatted values `Yes` and `No` instead of `Y` and `N` in the output. Note that the format name when specified in a `FORMAT` statement ends with a dot (.).

HANDS-ON EXAMPLE

In this example, you create a format definition (`FMTMARRIED`) for a numeric variable and apply that definition to the variable `MARRIED` in `PROC PRINT`.

1. Open the program file DFORMAT1.SAS.

```
PROC FORMAT;
    VALUE FMTMARRIED 0="No"
                    1="Yes";
RUN;
PROC PRINT DATA="C:\SASDATA\SURVEY";
    VAR SUBJECT MARRIED;
    FORMAT MARRIED FMTMARRIED.;
RUN;
```

   Make note of the following:
   - The `PROC FORMAT` statement defines a format named `FMTMARRIED`.
   - The `FORMAT` statement in `PROC PRINT` tells SAS to apply the `FMTMARRIED` format definition to the variable `MARRIED`.
   - Notice that in a `FORMAT` statement, an SAS format specification ends with a dot (.).
   - When SAS lists the data, as in a `PROC PRINT`, instead of listing data from the `MARRIED` variable as 0 or 1, it outputs the data as Yes or No.
2. Run the program and observe the output. The `MARRIED` column should contain the words Yes and No rather than 1 and 0.
3. Another variable in this data set is `GENDER`. This text variable includes the codes M for Male and F for FEMALE. Change the `PROC FORMAT` step to also include a definition for a format named $FMTGENDER by adding the VALUE statement.

```
VALUE $FMTGENDER "F" = "Female"
```

```
                    "M" = "Male";
```

Change the VAR statement to

```
VAR SUBJECT MARRIED GENDER;
```

And the FORMAT statement to

```
FORMAT MARRIED FMTMARRIED. GENDER $FMTGENDER.;
```

4. Submit the new program and observe the output. Does the MARRIED column include Male and Female instead of M and F? See the results in Table 4.15.

TABLE 4.15   Application of a FORMAT

Obs	SUBJECT	MARRIED	GENDER
1	1	Yes	Male
2	2	Yes	Male
3	3	No	Female
4	4	No	Female
5	5	Yes	Female
6	6	Yes	Female
7	7	No	Female

Notice that in the MARRIED column, the data are output as Yes and No rather than as 0 and 1 and GENDER is displayed as Male and Female.

The format name FMTGENDER is arbitrary. However, it is often a good idea to use the prefix FMT in any user-created format name to help you avoid getting format names mixed up with variable names. Format names must follow normal SAS naming conventions, but they may not end in a number.

Formats may also use ranges. For example, suppose that you want to classify your AGE data using the designations Child, Teen, Adult, and Senior. You could do this with the following format:

```
PROC FORMAT;
Value FMTAGE     LOW-12 = 'Child'
                 13,14,15,16,17,18,19 = 'Teen'
                 20-59 = 'Adult'
                 60-HIGH = 'Senior';
```

The term LOW means the lowest numeric value for this variable in the dataset; HIGH means the highest numeric value. You can also use the term OTHER= to indicate any other data not specified by the other assignments. Also, you can use lists, as in the Teen specification. (Yes, it would have been simpler to use 13−19, but we did it this way for illustrative purposes.)

You can also assign the same format to several variables. If you have questionnaire data with variables names Q1, Q5, Q7 where each question is coded as 0 and 1 for answers Yes and No, respectively, and you have a format called FMTYN, you could use that FORMAT in a procedure as in the following example:

```
PROC PRINT;
    FORMAT Q1 Q5 Q7 FMTYN.;
RUN;
```

HANDS-ON EXAMPLE

In this example, you create formats using ranges.

1. Open the program file DFORMAT2.SAS.

```
PROC FORMAT;
    VALUE FMTAGE    LOW-12 = 'Child'
                    13,14,15,16,17,18,19 = 'Teen'
                    20-59 = 'Adult'
                    60-HIGH = 'Senior';
    VALUE FMTSTAT   1='Lower Class'
                    2='Lower-Middle'
                    3='Middle Class'
                    4='Upper-Middle'
                    5='Upper';
RUN;
PROC PRINT DATA="C:\SASDATA\SOMEDATA";
VAR AGE STATUS GP;
FORMAT AGE FMTAGE. STATUS FMTSTAT.;
TITLE 'PROC FORMAT Example';
RUN;
```

2. Run the program and observe the output. Notice that values listed for AGE and STATUS are not the original values. Instead, the formatted values are listed.

3. Add the following format to the program (including changing the FORMAT statement in the PROC PRINT procedure.)

```
VALUE $FMTGP 'A'='Southern Suburbs'
             'B'='Urban'
             'C'='Northern Suburbs';
```

4. Run the revised program and observe the output.

Occasionally, there is some confusion over the difference between labels and formats. Labels provide more explanatory names to *variables* and relate to the names of *variables* only (and not to *data values*). Formats affect how actual *data values* are listed in SAS output tables.

4.8.1   Creating Permanent Formats

In all the previous examples, formats were applied in a PROC step and are considered temporary formats. You may also create permanent formats in a manner similar to that used when creating permanent data sets.

When permanent SAS formats are created, they are stored in a format catalog, either in the default SAS format catalog or in your own specified format catalog. For example, to store an SAS format in a specified permanent library location, you could use code such as

```
PROC FORMAT LIBRARY = MYSASLIB<.name>;
```

In this case, the MYSASLIB refers to an SAS library location you have previously created. (Refer to Chapter 3 for creating an SAS Library if you have not already created the MYSASLIB library.)

If you do not include a name for the format folder, the default format library name FOR-MATS is used. (In this case, it would be the MYSASLIB.FORMATS library.) That is, when you create an SAS format catalog, a folder icon appears in the designated SAS Library. In this case, it is named FORMATS and appears in the MYSASLIB library. You can verify its existence by examining the MYSASLIB library using SAS Explorer. If you double click on the FORMATS folder, you will see subfolders named with the names of the formats you have created. For example, the code

```
PROC FORMAT LIBRARY = MYSASLIB;
    VALUE FMTMARRIED 0="No"
                     1="Yes";
    VALUE $FMTGENDER "F" = "Female"
                     "M" = "Male";
RUN;
```

creates two subfolders in the MYSASLIB.FORMATS folder named FMTMARRIED and $FMTGENDER. These folders are illustrated in Figure 4.2.

To examine the contents of a particular format, double click on the format subfolder. For the FMTMARRIED folder. Table 4.16 is displayed showing the details of that format, when it was created, and what version of SAS was used.

Once you have created permanent formats, you can use them in both PROC and DATA step statements. To tell SAS the location of a particular format, use the statement

FORMATS folder

Formats

Contents
of FORMATS
folder

Fmtmarried   Fmtgender

Figure 4.2   FORMAT folders

TABLE 4.16   Contents of the FMTMARRIED Format Folder

```
                    FORMAT NAME: FMTMARRIED LENGTH: 3
      MIN LENGTH:   1  MAX LENGTH:  40  DEFAULT LENGTH:   3  FUZZ: STD

START              END                LABEL   (VER. 9.4      30SEP2014:12:52:43)

                 0               0 No
                 1               1 Yes
```

```
OPTIONS FMTSEARCH=(proclib);
```

where PROCLIB is the name of the SAS Library where your formats folder is located. For example, if you have previously created and stored the FMTMARRIED and $FMTGENDER formats in your MYSASLIB.FORMATS folder, you could use the following code to access those formats with PROC PRINT (or any PROC.)

```
OPTIONS FMTSEARCH=(MYSASLIB.FORMATS);
PROC PRINT DATA="C:\SASDATA\SURVEY";
    VAR SUBJECT MARRIED GENDER;
    FORMAT MARRIED FMTMARRIED. GENDER $FMTGENDER.;
RUN;
```

To discover what formats are in a particular format library, you can use the PROC CATALOG procedure as shown here. This code displays all of the formats stored in the MYSASLIB.FORMATS library.

```
PROC CATALOG CATALOG = MYSASLIB.FORMATS;
CONTENTS;
RUN;
QUIT;
```

HANDS-ON EXAMPLE

In this example, you explore creating and using permanent SAS formats.

1. Open the program file DFORMAT3.SAS.

```
PROC FORMAT LIBRARY = MYSASLIB.CAT1; *CREATE A FORMAT CATA-
LOG;
    VALUE FMTMARRIED 0="No"
                     1="Yes";
    VALUE $FMTGENDER "F" = "Female"
                     "M" = "Male";
RUN;
```

   Submit this code. Examine the SAS Library named MYSASLIB and note that it contains a folder named CAT1. This folder contains the two formats you just created.

2. Open the program file DFORMAT3A.SAS.

```
OPTIONS   FMTSEARCH=(_____);
PROC PRINT DATA="C:\SASDATA\SURVEY";
     VAR SUBJECT MARRIED GENDER;
     FORMAT MARRIED FMTMARRIED. GENDER $FMTGENDER.;
RUN;
```

Fill in the blank in the OPTIONS statement with MYSASLIB.CAT1 (the name of the format catalog you just created). Submit this code and verify that the output shows that the formats have been applied in the MARRIED and GENDER columns.

Suppose you have created formats in the past and somehow lost them, or someone sends you a .SASB7DAT file that uses created formats, but they did not send you that library? If you attempt to use that data set, you will get the following error message in the log.

ERROR: The format FMTMARRIED was not found or could not be loaded.

If this occurs, you must use the following OPTIONS statement (above the code where you refer to the data set) to tell SAS to access the data set, or run the procedure without using the defined formats:

OPTIONS NOFMTERR;

In this case, the output displays the raw values of the variables instead of the assigned format labels.

4.9   GOING DEEPER: FINDING FIRST AND LAST VALUES

A technique that can come in handy to understand the contents of a data set is to be able to identify the first and last values in the data set by some grouping variable. For example, in the SOMEDATA data set, the data are recorded by four Intervention Groups (GP) labeled A, B, C, and D. Suppose that you want to identify the first and last person (ID) in each of those groups. In an SAS DATA step, you identify the first and last values by FIRST.GP and LAST.GP, where GP is the name of the sorted grouping (or key) variable. The following example illustrates how that could be done.

HANDS-ON EXAMPLE

This example illustrates how to locate the first and last values in a data set that is organized by some grouping variable.

1. Open the program file DFINDFIRST.SAS. Notice the names FIRST.GP and LAST.GP used in the IF statements. Submit this code and observe the results. The first few records are shown in Table 4.17.

(continued)

(continued)

```
DATA FIRST;
SET MYSASLIB.SOMEDATA;
BY GP;
IF FIRST.GP THEN WHICHID="ISFIRST";
IF LAST.GP THEN WHICHID="ISLAST";
RUN;
PROC PRINT DATA=FIRST;
VAR ID GP WHICHID;
RUN;
```

Note that ID 101 is the first subject in group A and is now labeled ISFIRST, and ID 561 is the last subject in group A and is labeled ISLAST.

2. The IF statement created values for WHICHID, but the rest are blank. Correct this by putting the code

   WHICHID="NEITHER"; after the by GP statement. Re-submit and observe how this changes the output.

TABLE 4.17   Finding First and Last in a Group

Obs	ID	GP	WHICHID
1	101	A	ISFIRST
2	102	A	
3	110	A	
4	187	A	
5	312	A	
6	390	A	
7	445	A	
8	543	A	
9	544	A	
10	550	A	
11	561	A	ISLAST
12	104	B	ISFIRST
13	122	B	

4.10   SUMMARY

This chapter discussed several techniques for preparing your data for analysis. In the next chapter, we begin the discussion of SAS procedures that perform analyses on the data.

EXERCISES

4.1 **Sort data.**

Modify the program (EX_4.1.SAS) to sort (alphabetically) first name within last **(last first)** by adding FIRST to the BY variables in the PROC SORT statement.

```
DATA MYDATA;
INPUT @1 LAST $20. @21 FIRST $20. @45 PHONE $12.;
Label LAST = 'Last Name'
      FIRST = 'First Name'
      PHONE = 'Phone Number';
DATALINES;
Reingold            Lucius              201-876-0987
Jones               Pam                 987-998-2948
Abby                Adams               214-876-0987
Smith               Bev                 213-765-0987
Zoll                Tim Bob             303-987-2309
Baker               Crusty              222-324-3212
Smith               John                234-943-0987
Smith               Arnold              234-321-2345
Jones               Jackie              456-987-8077
;
*---- Modify to sort by first name within last (by last first);
PROC SORT; BY LAST;
PROC PRINT LABEL;
TITLE 'ABC Company';
TITLE2 'Telephone Directory';
RUN;
```

4.2 **Create subset data sets.**

Using the CARS permanent SAS dataset, write SAS code to do the following:

a. Create a subset (into an SAS data set named SMALL) consisting of all vehicles whose engine size is less than 2.0 L. On the basis of this data set, find the average city and highway miles per gallon for these vehicles.

```
DATA SMALL;SET "C:\SASDATA\CARS";
IF ENGINESIZE LT 2;
```

b. Create a subset (into an SAS data set named HYBRID) of all hybrid vehicles in the dataset. For these vehicles:

I. List the BRAND and MODEL names.

II. Find the average city and highway miles per gallon.

c. Create a subset (into an SAS data set named AWDSUV) consisting of all vehicles that are both SUVs and have all-wheel drive. For these vehicles:

I. List the BRAND and MODEL names.

II. Use PROC MEANS to find the average city and highway miles per gallon.

d. Sort the data in AWDSUV by highway miles per gallon (smallest to largest). List the BRAND, MODEL, and highway miles per gallon for this sorted data set.

4.3 **Use DROP or KEEP.**

Using the SOMEDATA permanent SAS dataset, write SAS code to do the following:

a. Calculate the changes from baseline (i.e., 6-month reading minus baseline, etc.) for 6, 12, and 24 months. Times are given as:

```
TIME1 is BASELINE
```

```
TIME2 is six months
TIME3 is twelve months
TIME4 is twenty-four months
```

To calculate the changes, use the following:

```
CHANGE6=TIME2-TIME1;
CHANGE12=TIME3-TIME1;
etc.
```

Use PROC MEANS to find the average and standard deviations for these new "change variables."

b. Create an SAS dataset that contains only the variables ID number, intervention group, age, and gender and also includes only those subjects in the intervention group A who were females. List the ID numbers for these subjects.

4.4 **Use** PROC FORMAT.

a. In the Editor window, open the program file EX_4.4.SAS.

```
PROC FORMAT;
      VALUE fmtYN     0 = 'No'
                      1 = 'Yes';
DATA QUESTIONS;
INPUT Q1 Q2 Q3 Q4 Q5;
DATALINES;
1 0 1 1 0
0 1 1 1 0
0 0 0 1 1
1 1 1 1 1
1 1 1 0 1
;
PROC PRINT;
* PUT FORMAT STATEMENT HERE;
RUN;
```

b. Run the program and observe the output. The Q1–Q5 variables are reported as 0 and 1 values.

c. In the PROC PRINT paragraph, include the statement

```
FORMAT Q1-Q5 fmtYN.;
```

d. Run the program and observe the output. How does the output differ from the version without the FORMAT statement?

4.5 **Creating and using Permanent SAS Formats.**

a. Open the program file EX_4.5.SAS. Change the FORMAT statement to create a permanent catalog named CAT2 using the statement

```
PROC FORMAT LIBRARY = MYSASLIB.CAT2;
```

b. Submit the program and verify that a catalog named CAT2 has been created in your MYSASLIB library.

c. Open the program file EX_4.5A.SAS. This program displays a listing of some of the variables in the SOMEDATA data set. Submit the code and observe that no output is created. Verify in the log that an error occurred indicating that SAS could not find the appropriate formats.

```
PROC PRINT DATA="C:\SASDATA\SOMEDATA";
VAR AGE STATUS GP;
FORMAT AGE FMTAGE. STATUS FMTSTAT.;
TITLE 'PROC FORMAT Example';
RUN;
```

d. Add an OPTIONS statement before the PROC PRINT to indicate the location of the CAT2 format catalog.

```
OPTIONS  FMTSEARCH=(MYSASLIB.CAT2);
```

e. Submit the revised code and verify that the program now runs and uses the defined formats to display the AGE and STATUS columns.

5

PREPARING TO USE SAS® PROCEDURES

LEARNING OBJECTIVES

- To be able to use SAS Support Statements
- To be able to use TITLE and FOOTNOTE
- To be able to include comments in your code
- To be able to use RUN and QUIT correctly
- To understand SAS PROC statement syntax
- To be able to use VAR statements
- To be able to use BY statements
- To be able to use ID statements
- To be able to use LABEL statements in a SAS procedure
- To be able to use WHERE statements
- To be able to use PROC PRINT
- Going Deeper: To be able to use common System Options
- Going Deeper: To be able to split column titles

This chapter illustrates a number of SAS features that allow you to make your output more readable and more organized. It also introduces you to details about SAS procedures (PROCS) that are the core of SAS analysis.

SAS® *Essentials: Mastering SAS for Data Analytics*, Second Edition. Alan C. Elliott and Wayne A. Woodward.
© 2016 John Wiley & Sons, Inc. Published 2016 by John Wiley & Sons, Inc.

5.1 UNDERSTANDING SAS SUPPORT STATEMENTS

Before using specific SAS procedures for data analysis, you should understand several basic supporting SAS options and statements that are often used in conjunction with SAS data analysis procedures. This chapter introduces you to these options and statements.

5.1.1 Using TITLE and FOOTNOTE Statements

The TITLE statement instructs SAS to place a line of text at the top of each output page or at the beginning of a procedure's output. Similarly, a FOOTNOTE statement places text lines at the bottom of each output page. Up to nine title or footnote lines can be specified. For example:

```
TITLE 'title text';
FOOTNOTE 'footnote text';
```

or

```
TITLEn 'title text';
FOOTNOTEn 'footnote text';
```

where n is a number between 2 and 9. A TITLE or FOOTNOTE statement without a number specifies an initial TITLE or FOOTNOTE line. Subsequent TITLE or FOOTNOTE lines can be defined using TITLE2, TITLE3, and so on up to TITLE9; and FOOTNOTE2, FOOT-NOTE3, and so on up to FOOTNOTE9. (There are no blanks between TITLE or FOOTNOTE and the number.) For example:

```
TITLE 'The first line of the title';
TITLE2 'The second line of the title';
TITLE5 'Several lines skipped, then this title on the fifth line';
FOOTNOTE 'This is a footnote';
FOOTNOTE3 'This is a footnote, line 3';
```

You can use either single or double quotation marks when defining a title or footnote, but you must be consistent for each definition. Once you have specified a TITLE or FOOT-NOTE, it is used in all subsequent SAS output (even when submitting new SAS program as long as you do not exit the current SAS software program) until you redefine the TITLE or FOOTNOTE lines. For example, if you include a TITLE2 statement in your code, it cancels any prior TITLE2 or higher titles. Footnotes work the same way.

You can cancel all TITLE and FOOTNOTE lines with the statement

```
TITLE; FOOTNOTE;
```

It is a good programming practice to include this line at the bottom of your SAS code file to prevent stray titles or footnotes from appearing in subsequent SAS output. We've put this code at the end of most of the SAS program example files used in this book.

HANDS-ON EXAMPLE

In this example, output is created using two SAS PROCs. A TITLE is defined for the first PROC and changed for the second.

1. Open the program file DTITLE1.SAS.

```
DATA MYDATA;
INFILE 'C:\SASDATA\EXAMPLE.DAT';
INPUT ID 1-3 GP $ 5 AGE 6-9 TIME1 10-14 TIME2 15-19
    TIME3 20-24;
RUN;
PROC PRINT;
TITLE 'Example SAS programs';
TITLE2 'These are data from the example file.';
TITLE4 'Using the EXAMPLE data set.';
FOOTNOTE 'This is a footnote';
PROC MEANS;
TITLE2 'This is output from PROC Means.';
RUN;
TITLE; FOOTNOTE;  *TURNS OFF TITLE AND FOOTNOTE;
```

2. Run the program and observe the output. A partial sample of the output for PROC PRINT is given in Table 5.1. Note that the title lines 1, 2, and 4 at the top match the titles defined in the code. The footnote appears at the bottom.

TABLE 5.1   Output Showing a Title and Footnote for PROC PRINT

Example SAS programs
These is data from the example file.

Using the EXAMPLE data set.

Obs	ID	GP	AGE	TIME1	TIME2	TIME3
1	101	A	12	22.3	25.3	28.2
2	102	A	11	22.8	27.5	33.3
3	104	B	12	22.8	30.0	32.8
4	110	A	12	18.5	26.0	29.0
5	122	B	9	19.5	25.0	25.3
47	591	B	13	23.7	32.3	34.1
48	593	B	11	18.9	23.1	27.7
49	599	B	9	20.5	24.8	30.3
50	604	B	12	22.4	27.2	31.8

This is a footnote

3. Observe the second output table for `PROC MEANS` (see Table 5.2). Note that for this output, the title in line 2 has changed according to the `TITLE2` statement before the `PROC MEANS` in the code, and all higher titles (`TITLE4`) are canceled.

TABLE 5.2   **Output Showing a Title and Footnote for PROC MEANS**

Example SAS programs
This is output from PROC Means.

The MEANS Procedure

Variable	N	Mean	Std Dev	Minimum	Maximum
ID	50	374.2200000	167.4983143	101.0000000	604.0000000
AGE	50	10.4600000	2.4261332	4.0000000	15.0000000
TIME1	50	21.2680000	1.7169551	17.0000000	24.2000000
TIME2	50	27.4400000	2.6590623	21.3000000	32.3000000
TIME3	50	30.4920000	3.0255942	22.7000000	35.9000000

This is a footnote

4. Put a `TITLE6` line in the code that reads "This is title 6" after the `TITLE2` and before the `RUN` statement for `PROC MEANS`. Submit the changed code and note where this title appears. Is the previous title at line 4 present this time? Why?

It is important to realize that `TITLE`s and `FOOTNOTE`s are remembered as long as the SAS software program is active (i.e., you have not exited the SAS software program). Therefore, if you create a title using one program, be sure to change or erase the `TITLE` when beginning a different analysis, such as starting a new procedure or performing analysis on a different set of data. Otherwise, you'll end up having an incorrect `TITLE` and/or `FOOTNOTE` on your output.

Therefore, either erase titles and footnotes at the end of the program or at the beginning of a program if there may be previous titles created in an earlier program.

Customizing Titles and Footnotes: There are a number of options that can be used with the `TITLE` or `FOOTNOTE` statements to customize the look of your title. Some of these options include specifying color with a `C=` or `COLOR=` option. For example:

```
TITLE C=BLUE "This is a title";
```

causes the title to be displayed in blue. A summary of some common options are given in Table 5.3.

HANDS-ON EXAMPLE

This example illustrates some options for the `TITLE` statement.

1. Open the program file `DTITLE2.SAS`.

```
TITLE J=RIGHT
      FONT= 'SWISS' COLOR=RED BOLD BCOLOR=YELLOW "EXAMPLE "
      C=BLACK BOLD ITALIC "TODAY IS &SYSDATE9";
TITLE2 J=CENTER C="CX3230B2" "THIS IS BRILLIANT BLUE.";
FOOTNOTE J=CENTER COLOR=PURPLE UNDERLINE=1
      HEIGHT=8PT "8 POINTS"
      HEIGHT=16PT " 16 POINTS"
      HEIGHT=24PT " 24 POINTS";
;
PROC MEANS DATA=MYSASLIB.PEOPLE;
RUN;
```

2. Note how `TITLE` and `FOOTNOTE` options are used in this program. Submit the program and observe the results as shown in Figure 5.1.

EXAMPLE *TODAY IS 05NOV2014*

THIS IS BRILLIANT BLUE.

The MEANS Procedure

Variable	N	Mean	Std Dev	Minimum	Maximum
SBP	5	127.0000000	8.3666003	120.0000000	140.0000000
DBP	5	82.0000000	10.9544512	70.0000000	100.0000000
AGE	5	35.8000000	30.2605354	15.0000000	89.0000000
WT	5	145.0000000	31.6227766	110.0000000	180.0000000

8 POINTS 16 POINTS **24 POINTS**

Figure 5.1   Illustrating options for titles and footnotes

3. Change the font specification to Times New Roman, add an underline to `TITLE2`, and change the `FOOTNOTE` to `TITLE3`. Submit the code and note the changes.

5.1.2 Including Comments in Your SAS Code

It is a good programming practice to include explanatory comments in your code. This allows you to understand what you have done when you go back into your code the next day (or the next year). Moreover, if your code is used by other SAS programmers, this will help them understand what your code does.

Comment statements can be used almost anywhere in SAS code to document the job, and you can use any number of comment statements in your code. There are two ways to

TABLE 5.3   Common Options for Titles and Footnotes

Title Option	Meaning
C=*color* or COLOR= *color*	Specifies color. See Appendix A for a summary of colors available
C="*RGBCode*"	An RGB code allows you to specify over 16 million different colors using an RGB coding system. See Appendix A for more information. For example, C="CX803009" specifies vivid reddish orange. Colors may also be defined using a Hex code. Companies often have defined colors to be used in official documents, and the RBG or Hex code is a way to match those colors
BCOLOR= *color*	Specifies background color
J=*type*	Justification. Options are left, right, or center
FONT=*fontname*	Specifies font for text. See Appendix A for more information. Example FONT= 'SWISS'
H=*n* or HEIGHT=*n*	Specifies height of text. See Appendix A for more information. Default height is 1. H=16 pt means 16 points
BOLD	Specifies bold
ITALIC	Specifies italic
UNDERLIN=*n*	0 means none, 1, 2, or 3 means underline and may specify thickness in some instances

include comments in your code. In this first example, a comment begins with an asterisk (*) and ends with a semicolon.

```
*This is a message
It can be several lines long
But it always ends with an ;
*********************************************************************
   * Boxed messages stand out more, still end in a semicolon *
********************************************************************;
DATA MYDATA; * You can put a comment on a line of code;
```

Another technique to use is to begin a comment with /* and end with */. This technique is useful when you want to include statements that contain a semicolon. For example, you can comment out several lines of code you do not want to use currently, but that you want to retain for possible future use or reference. Here are two examples of this comment technique:

```
/*This is a SAS comment*/
/* Use this comment technique to comment out lines of code
PROC PRINT;
PROC MEANS;
End of comment - the PROCS were ignored*/
```

In your own programming, it is a good idea to begin every program with a note about what it does, when it was written, and who wrote it. It may not seem important at the moment, but 6 months or a year later the note can save you valuable time.

Note that you can put a comment using either method on a line of code, but you cannot put a comment on a line of data values that follow the DATALINES statement.

- Comments are a way to cause SAS to ignore some part of your program when it is submitted. This allows you to run part of your code without having to erase code that might come in handy again, such as a format definition or the creation of a data set, but you don't want to run that code every time you run your program.
- Another way to run a partial program is to highlight the code you want and click the running man icon (or choose Run from the menu.). It's that simple. SAS will only act on the highlighted code.

5.1.3   Using RUN and QUIT Statements

The RUN statement causes previously entered SAS statements to be executed. It is called a boundary statement. For example:

```
PROC PRINT;
PROC MEANS;
RUN;
```

Include a RUN statement after major sections in your SAS code. A RUN statement *must* follow the final procedure section (e.g. PROC MEANS) in your SAS code. It is often the last statement in a Windows SAS program.

Another boundary statement is the QUIT statement. It is sometimes used in conjunction with a RUN statement to cease an active procedure. For example, you might see the following code:

```
PROC REG;
RUN;
QUIT;
```

The REG (regression) procedure, and others, needs a QUIT to instruct them to cease operation. As procedures are described in the text, those that require a QUIT statement will be noted. If you are unsure, it never hurts to include both a RUN and a QUIT at the end of any SAS job.

If you fail to include a RUN statement at the end of your SAS job (or if SAS runs into an error and never sees the RUN statement), the SAS processor may continue to run in the background. This can cause unpredictable problems. If this occurs, press Ctrl-Break. An option will appear allowing you to "Cancel Submitted Statements."

5.2   UNDERSTANDING PROC STATEMENT SYNTAX

Although there are scores of SAS PROCs (procedures), the syntax is consistent across all of them. Once you learn how SAS PROCs generally work, you should be able to use PROCs that are not covered in this book. This section discusses common syntax used in most analytical PROCs. *Options* and *statements* that are specific to a PROC are discussed in the context of that PROC. Table 5.4 lists often-used statements and options common to most SAS PROCs.

TABLE 5.4   Common Options and Statements for SAS PROCS

Common Options for SAS PROCS

PROC Option	Meaning
DATA=*datasetname*	Specifies which data set to use in the analysis
OUT=*datasetname*	Creates an output data set containing results from the procedure

Common statements for SAS PROCS

PROC statement	Meaning
VAR *variable(s)*;	Instructs SAS to use only the variables in the list for the analysis
BY *variable(s)*;	Causes SAS to repeat the procedure for each different value of the named variable(s). (The data set must first be sorted by the variables listed in the BY statement.)
ID *variable(s)*;	Instructs SAS to use the specified variable as an observation identifier in a listing of the data
LABEL var='*label*';	Assigns a descriptive label to a variable. (This statement can also appear in the DATA step.)
WHERE *condition*;	Specifies a condition for which only those records meeting the condition are used in the procedure

A simplified syntax for the SAS PROC statement is as follows:

```
PROC name <options>;
   <Statements/statementoptions;>
RUN;
```

The most commonly used *option* within the PROC statement is the DATA= option. For example:

```
PROC PRINT DATA=MYDATA;
RUN;
```

The DATA= option tells SAS which data set to use in the analysis. If there has been only one data set previously created (within a session), there is no need for this statement. However, if you've created more than one data set during a particular SAS session, it's a good idea to include a DATA= option to specify which data set SAS is to use. If you do not specify a DATA= option, SAS will use the most recently defined data set for the specified procedure.

Procedure *statements* are often required to indicate information about how an analysis is to be performed. For example, in the code

```
PROC PRINT;
VAR ID GROUP TIME1 TIME2;
RUN;
```

the VAR statement indicates that only the listed variables are to be used in the procedure. Statements can themselves have options. For example:

```
PROC FREQ;
   TABLES GROUP*SOCIO/CHISQ;
RUN;
```

In this example, the TABLES statement of the PROC FREQ (Frequencies) procedure (which is covered in detail in Chapter 10) instructs SAS to create a table based on the data from the variables GROUP and SOCIO. The statement option /CHISQ instructs SAS to calculate chi-square and other statistics on this table.

Using common SAS syntax, you can build statements to perform many types of analyses. As each PROC is described in future chapters, additional options and statements will be described that are unique to that procedure. However, some statements can be used with (almost) every SAS procedure.

5.2.1 Using the VAR Statement in a SAS Procedure

The VAR statement specifies which variables in the selected SAS data set are to be used by the procedure. The syntax of the statement is as follows:

```
VAR varlist;
```

An example is as follows:

```
PROC MEANS;
  VAR HEIGHT WEIGHT AGE;
RUN;
```

Note that variables listed in the VAR statement are separated by spaces, and not by commas. This statement tells SAS to perform PROC MEANS only on the three listed variables. If you have several variables in your data set, this is a way to limit your analysis only to those of interest.

> To save time and typing, you can use a list such as Q1-Q50 (using a single dash) to indicate 50 different sequential variable names with identical prefixes and a number suffix (Q1, Q2, Q3, etc.) in a VAR statement where the variable names are from a consecutive numerical list. SAS also understands the variable list ID -- SBP (two dashes between variable names) to indicate all variables between ID and SBP (inclusive) in the order defined in the data set.
>
> Although not discussed in detail here, you can also control elements of the variable labels including color, justification, etc. using /STYLE statementoption. This is illustrated in the Going Deeper section "Splitting Column Titles in PROC PRINT."

5.2.2 Using the BY Statement in a SAS Procedure

The BY statement is a powerful and handy method that allows you to quickly analyze subsets of your data. To use the BY statement, you must have a grouping variable such as GENDER, GROUP, RACE, and so on. Then you must sort your data (using PROC SORT) by the variable on which you wish to subset (sorting has been discussed in Chapter 4). Finally, when you add the BY statement, SAS performs the analysis separately for the groups specified in the BY statement variable. The syntax for the BY statement is as follows:

```
BY Variable list;
```

> Sort a SAS data set using PROC SORT before you perform an analysis using the BY statement.

HANDS-ON EXAMPLE

In this example, you will calculate means BY group.

1. Open the program file DSORTMEANS.SAS.

```
DATA MYDATA;
INFILE 'C:\SASDATA\EXAMPLE.DAT';
INPUT ID 1-3 GP $ 5 AGE 6-9 TIME1 10-14 TIME2 15-19
   TIME3 20-24 STATUS 31;
RUN;
* FIRST TIME ALL DATA AT ONCE;
PROC MEANS;
   VAR TIME1 TIME2;
RUN;*NOTE USES MYDATA BY DEFAULT;
* SECOND TIME MEANS BY GROUP;
PROC SORT DATA=MYDATA OUT=SORTED;BY GP; RUN;
PROC MEANS DATA=SORTED;
   VAR TIME1 TIME2;
   BY GP;
RUN;
```

2. Run the program. Observe that the first PROC MEANS statement produces the output as given in Table 5.5.

TABLE 5.5   Output from PROC MEANS

Variable	N	Mean	Std Dev	Minimum	Maximum
TIME1	50	21.2680000	1.7169551	17.0000000	24.2000000
TIME2	50	27.4400000	2.6590623	21.3000000	32.3000000

GP=A

Variable	N	Mean	Std Dev	Minimum	Maximum
TIME1	11	20.9000000	2.0813457	17.0000000	23.0000000
TIME2	11	27.0000000	2.9295051	21.3000000	31.3000000

GP=B

Variable	N	Mean	Std Dev	Minimum	Maximum
TIME1	29	21.1862069	1.5853625	18.5000000	24.2000000
TIME2	29	27.4344828	2.6357807	23.1000000	32.3000000

GP=C

Variable	N	Mean	Std Dev	Minimum	Maximum
TIME1	10	21.9100000	1.6649658	19.0000000	23.9000000
TIME2	10	27.9400000	2.6137245	22.5000000	31.1000000

This output reports means for the entire data set (50 records).

(continued)

(continued)

3. Observe that when the BY statement is used (after the data are sorted), the means are calculated separately for each value of the grouping variable GP, which has three levels (A, B, and C) as given in Table 5.5.
4. Change the grouping variable used in the SORT and PROC statements to STATUS and rerun the program. Note that the program creates five tables, one for each value of the variable STATUS.

5.3 USING THE ID STATEMENT IN A SAS PROCEDURE

The ID statement provides you with a way to increase the readability of your output. It allows you to specify a variable to be used as an observation (record, subject) identifier. For example, in a PROC PRINT procedure, you can use an ID statement that specifies a variable to be displayed at the far left of your listing.

HANDS-ON EXAMPLE

In this example, you will learn how to use the ID statement.

1. Open the program file D_ID.SAS.

```
DATA WEIGHT;
INFORMAT MDATE MMDDYY10.;
FORMAT MDATE DATE9.; *OUTPUT FORMAT;
INPUT MDATE RAT_ID $ WT_GRAMS TRT $ PINKEYE $;
DATALINES;
02/03/2009 001 093 A Y
02/04/2009 002 087 B N
02/04/2009 003 103 A Y
02/07/2009 005 099 A Y
02/08/2009 006 096 B N
02/11/2009 008 091 B Y
;
RUN;
PROC PRINT DATA=WEIGHT;
RUN;
```

This program lists information about results of an experiment involving six rats.

2. Run the program and observe the (partial) results given in Table 5.6. The first few lines of the output are as follows:

Note that the RAT_ID is the second column of the data, and the data in the Obs column are the sequential record numbers from the data set.

3. Revise the PROC PRINT line to include the following statement and then rerun the program. Observe the output in Table 5.7.

```
PROC PRINT DATA=WEIGHT;ID RAT_ID;
```

TABLE 5.6   Output before Defining ID Column

Obs	MDATE	RAT_ID	WT_GRAMS	TRT	PINKEYE
1	03FEB2009	001	93	A	Y
2	04FEB2009	002	87	B	N
3	04FEB2009	003	103	A	Y
4	07FEB2009	005	99	A	Y
5	08FEB2009	006	96	B	N
6	11FEB2009	008	91	B	Y

TABLE 5.7   Output after Defining ID Column

RAT_ID	MDATE	WT_GRAMS	TRT	PINKEYE
001	03FEB2009	93	A	Y
002	04FEB2009	87	B	N
003	04FEB2009	103	A	Y
005	07FEB2009	99	A	Y
006	08FEB2009	96	B	N
008	11FEB2009	91	B	Y

The output now places the RAT_ID variable in the leftmost column, replacing the generic Obs column.

The ID statement places a particular variable in the first column, usually to make it easier to identify your data records.

5.4   USING THE LABEL STATEMENT IN A SAS PROCEDURE

In Chapter 4, we learned how to use the LABEL statement within the DATA step to create labels for several variables. Another version of the LABEL statement allows you to create labels for variable names within a procedure. For example, suppose in the previous Hands-on Example you want the column for the variable TRT to read "Treatment." For this, include the statement

```
LABEL TRT='Treatment';
```

after the PROC PRINT statement and before the RUN statement. Moreover, you can include a LABEL option in the PROC PRINT statement to indicate that you want the printout to use defined labels.

```
PROC PRINT LABEL DATA=WEIGHT;
    ID RAT_ID;
    LABEL TRT='Treatment';
RUN;
```

In most other procedures, you can define labels in the DATA step or in the PROC and they will appear appropriately in the output. However, in the PROC PRINT procedure, you must include the LABEL option (i.e., PROC PRINT LABEL;) in order for labels to appear in the output.

HANDS-ON EXAMPLE

In this example, you will learn how to use the LABEL statement within a procedure.

1. Open the program file D_ID.SAS. Assuming that you still have the ID statement in place from the previous Hands-on Example, add a LABEL option to the PROC PRINT paragraph and a label statement specifying a label for the variable TRT.

```
PROC PRINT LABEL DATA=WEIGHT;
    ID RAT_ID;
    LABEL TRT='Treatment';
RUN;
```

2. Run the revised program. Observe the new column label for TRT in Table 5.8.
3. Remove the LABEL option in the PROC MEANS statement and rerun the program. Observe the difference in the output (the TRT column).
4. After the last RUN statement, add a PROC MEANS with LABEL statement for WT_GRAMS and MDATE:

```
PROC MEANS DATA=WEIGHT;
    LABEL WT_GRAMS="Weight in Grams"
    MDATE="MEDOBS Date";
RUN;
```

Run the revised program and observe the output given in Table 5.8. Note that labels are included for the WT_GRAMS and MDATE variables, and that you were not required to use the LABEL option when using PROC MEANS.

TABLE 5.8   Using Revised Labels in PROC PRINT

Variable	Label	N	Mean	Std Dev	Minimum	Maximum
MDATE	MEDOBS Date	6	17934.17	3.0605010	17931.00	17939.00
WT_GRAMS	Weight in Grams	6	94.8333333	5.7416606	87.0000000	103.0000000

5.5   USING THE WHERE STATEMENT IN A SAS PROCEDURE

The WHERE statement allows you to specify a conditional criterion for which output will be included in an analysis. This is different from the subsetting IF statements described in Chapter 4. In that chapter, the subsetting IF statement in the DATA step dictates which records are kept in a data set for subsequent analyses on that particular data set. The WHERE statement affects only the data used for a particular procedure. For example, in the ID example, suppose you want to output data only for treatment A in the PROC PRINT statement. Use the statement

```
WHERE TRT="A";
```

in the PROC PRINT (or any) procedure to limit the analysis to only those records that meet the criteria in the WHERE statement. Subsequent procedures within the same SAS program will *not* be subject to the WHERE restriction unless it is invoked again for that procedure.

HANDS-ON EXAMPLE

In this example, you will learn how to use the WHERE statement.

1. In the SAS file D_ID.SAS used in the previous Hands-on Example, modify the PROC PRINT statement to read:

```
PROC PRINT LABEL DATA=WEIGHT;
    ID RAT_ID;
    LABEL TRT='Treatment';
    WHERE TRT="A";
RUN;
```

2. Run the program and observe the output given in Table 5.9. Note that the WHERE statement only changed the output for the PROC PRINT (where it was used) and not the PROC MEANS procedure.

   Only the records that match the criterion specified by the WHERE statement are included in the output.

TABLE 5.9   Selection Using the Where Statement

RAT_ID	MDATE	WT_GRAMS	Treatment	PINKEYE
001	03FEB2009	93	A	Y
003	04FEB2009	103	A	Y
005	07FEB2009	99	A	Y

5.6   USING PROC PRINT

Although several previous examples have used a simple version of the PROC PRINT procedure, a number of options for this procedure have not been discussed. As demonstrated in previous examples, PROC PRINT outputs a listing of the data values in a SAS data set.

Using the options described in Table 5.10, you can enhance that listing to create a more useful report. Some of the options listed below duplicate those already discussed but are included for the sake of completeness.

Following are several examples illustrating the use of these options. For example, the N option instructs SAS to print the number of observations and allows you to specify a label to be printed:

```
N='Observations ='
```

The OBS option allows you to specify a label at the top of the Obs column in the data listing. For example:

```
OBS='Subjects'
```

The SUM statement specifies that a sum of the values for the variables listed is to be reported. For example:

```
SUM COST;
```

TABLE 5.10   Common Options and Statement for PROC PRINT

Common Options for PROC PRINT

PROC PRINT Option	Meaning
DATA=*datasetname*	Specifies which data set to use
DOUBLE	Double-spaces the output for ODS output formats such as RTF and PDF (This option has no affect in default SAS output, which is HTML.)
LABEL	Instructs SAS to use variable labels as column headings
N <= '*label*'>	Includes the number of observations in the listing and optionally specifies a label
OBS='*label*'	Specifies a label for the Obs column
NOBS	Suppresses the output column that identifies observations by number
ROUND	Rounds numbers to two decimal places unless they are otherwise formatted
SPLIT='*char*'	Defines a split character that is used to split label names for column headings. See the section "Splitting Column Titles" in this chapter
(FIRSTOBS=*n1* OBS=*n2*)	Causes PROC PRINT to only use selected records in a data set from *n*1 as specified by FIRSTOBS= to the *n*2 as specified by OBS=).

Common statements for PROC PRINT

PROC PRINT statement	Meaning
VAR *variable list;*	Specifies which variables to include in the listing and in which order
SUM *vars;*	Specifies variables to report sum
BY, ID, WHERE	See Table 5.4

The following SAS program (APRINT1.SAS) utilizes several of the PROC PRINT options and the SUM statement:

```
PROC PRINT DATA=MYSASLIB.SOMEDATA
    N= 'Number of Subjects is: '
    OBS='Subjects';
SUM TIME1 TIME2 TIME3 TIME4;
```

TABLE 5.11   PROC PRINT Using SUM, OBS, and _N_

Subjects	ID	GP	AGE	TIME1	TIME2	TIME3	TIME4	STATUS	SEX	GENDER
1	101	A	12	22.3	25.3	28.2	30.6	5	0	Female
2	102	A	11	22.8	27.5	33.3	35.8	5	0	Female
3	110	A	12	18.5	26.0	29.0	27.9	5	1	Male
4	187	A	11	22.5	29.3	32.6	33.7	2	0	Female
49	566	C	10	23.9	30.7	31.8	34.4	5	0	Female
50	578	C	12	21.6	28.1	30.9	34.1	5	0	Female
				1063.4	1372.0	1524.6	1541.9			

Number of Subjects is: 50

A partial listing of this output is displayed in Table 5.11 showing how the listing has changed because of the options included in the PROC PRINT statement

```
N = 'Number of Subjects is:'
```

produces the statement at the bottom of the printout reporting the number of subjects. Moreover, the option

```
OBS='Subjects';
```

causes the label above the record numbers to be Subjects rather than Obs. Finally, the statement

```
SUM TIME1 TIME2 TIME3 TIME4;
```

causes the totals for the four variables to be reported at the bottom of the report.

HANDS-ON EXAMPLE

1. Open the program file APRINT1.SAS.

```
PROC PRINT DATA=MYSASLIB.SOMEDATA
    N = 'Number of Subjects is:'
    Obs='Subjects';
```

(continued)

(continued)

```
    SUM TIME1 TIME2 TIME3 TIME4;
    TITLE 'PROC PRINT Example';
    RUN;
```

Note the N= and OBS= option and the SUM statement.
2. Modify the program by adding

```
PROC SORT DATA=MYSASLIB.SOMEDATA;BY GP;
```

before the PROC PRINT.
3. Modify the SUM line as

```
SUM TIME1 TIME2 TIME3 TIME4;BY GP;
```

4. Run the program. How does this change the output? In particular, note the report for the number of subjects at the end of each Intervention Group tables.

5.7 GOING DEEPER: SPLITTING COLUMN TITLES IN PROC PRINT

The statements illustrated for PROC PRINT are the most commonly used, but there are other statements available that can enhance your listing even more.

One handy statement is SPLIT= that allows you to specify how labels are split in column titles.

Normally, SAS splits titles at blanks when needed to conserve space in a report. For example, the following SAS program (APRINT2.SAS) defines labels for a number of variables. (It also uses the PROC PRINT options FIRSTOBS=11 and OBS=100 to limit the number of records listed.)

```
PROC PRINT LABEL DATA="C:\SASDATA\TRAUMA"
     (FIRSTOBS=11 OBS= 100);
VAR INC_KEY AGE GENDER ISS INJTYPE DISSTATUS;
LABEL   INC_KEY='Subject ID '
          AGE='Age in 2014 '
          GENDER='Gender '
        ISS='Injury Severity Score '
        INJTYPE='Injury Type '
        DISSTATUS='Discharge Status';
RUN;
```

When this code is run, it produces the output given in Table 5.12.

Observe how certain labels are split across two lines. SAS does this, so columns are not too wide. This is a good default feature. However, SAS allows you to be more specific. You can tell SAS where you want the labels to be split using the SPLIT= option.

TABLE 5.12   Example of Column Titles in PROC PRINT

Trauma Data Report

Obs	Subject ID	Age in 2014	Gender	Injury Severity Score	Injury Type	Discharge Status
11	603108	15.6	Female	6	Blunt	Alive
12	603110	14.3	Female	17	Blunt	Alive
13	603112	12.0	Female	5	Blunt	Alive
14	603121	13.6	Male	21	Blunt	Alive
15	603122	14.1	Male	1	Blunt	Dead
16	603129	12.7	Male	24	Blunt	Alive
17	603131	6.9	Female	1	Penetrating	Alive
18	603133	16.1	Male	5	Blunt	Alive
19	603138	14.4	Female	5	Blunt	Alive
20	603142	10.9	Male	9	Penetrating	Alive

HANDS-ON EXAMPLE

1. Open the program file APRINT3.SAS. Run this program and observe the results in Table 5.13.

TABLE 5.13   Example Revised of Column Titles in PROC PRINT

Trauma Data Report

Observation Number	Subject ID	Age in 2014	Gender	Injury Severity Score	Injury Type	Discharge Status
11	603108	15.6	Female	6	Blunt	Alive
12	603110	14.3	Female	17	Blunt	Alive
13	603112	12.0	Female	5	Blunt	Alive
14	603121	13.6	Male	21	Blunt	Alive
15	603122	14.1	Male	1	Blunt	Dead
16	603129	12.7	Male	24	Blunt	Alive
17	603131	6.9	Female	1	Penetrating	Alive
18	603133	16.1	Male	5	Blunt	Alive
19	603138	14.4	Female	5	Blunt	Alive
20	603142	10.9	Male	9	Penetrating	Alive

N = 10

```
TITLE "Trauma Data Report";
PROCPRINT DATA="C:\SASDATA\TRAUMA"
   (FIRSTOBS=11 OBS=20)
   SPLIT='*'
   N OBS='Observation*Number*===========';
```

(continued)

(continued)

```
VAR INC_KEY AGE GENDER ISS INJTYPE DISSTATUS;
LABEL INC_KEY='Subject*ID*============'
         AGE='Age in*2014*============'
         GENDER='Gender* *============'
         ISS='Injury Severity*Score*============'
         INJTYPE='Injury*Type*==========='
         DISSTATUS='Discharge*Status*==============';
RUN;
```

Note the changes. The `SPLIT="*"` statement tells SAS that the asterisk (`*`) is the delimiter that will be used to split labels into two or more lines. The double underline (created by repeated equal signs (=)) provides a break between the label and the column contents. The statement

```
N OBS = 'Observation*Number*===========';
```

tells SAS to report the total number of observations at the bottom of the listing (N) and to use the specified label for the OBS column. Note that the label contains three sections, each section splits by the delimiter *. Thus, the label displayed will be three lines long:

```
Observation
    Number
===========
```

Labels for the variables are similarly defined where the * tells SAS where to split the labels as they are used in the columns for the listing. The label Gender has a * * (note the blank between the *) indicating a skip to make the underline for Gender line up with the other labels. Compare this listing to the previous listing in Table 5.12.

Another feature to note is that labels (like the data values) are either right or left justified depending on whether the column represents numeric or text data.

2. Revise the code by changing the split character to a tilde (~) and change the underlines to single dashes. Rerun the code to make sure it works as expected.

3. GOING DEEPER: You can also control the justification and colors of the column labels with a `STYLE` option in the `VAR` statement. Change the `VAR` statement to the following by adding a STYLE statement option:

```
VAR INC_KEY AGE GENDER ISS INJTYPE DISSTATUS
/ STYLE(HEADER)={COLOR=RED background=YELLOW JUST=C};
```

Resubmit this code and observe how the `STYLE(HEADER)` option allows you to specify characteristics of the label text. In this example it sets color, background, and justification. Change the location in `STYLE()` from `HEADER` to `DATA` and resubmit again to see how to apply these options to the data portion of the output.

5.8   GOING DEEPER: COMMON SYSTEM OPTIONS

Although not a part of a PROC statement, System Options can be used to customize the way output is displayed or how data in a data set is used. System Options must be placed in the code in such a way that they are operated on before needed by any following code. Usually, this is at the top of the code file. We'll use System Options in some examples throughout the text as needed, and they will be described when used. This section introduces some commonly used options. System Options are specified using the OPTIONS statement. The syntax for the OPTIONS statement is

```
OPTIONS option1 option2 ... ;
```

Any number of options may be included in a single statement. The System Options listed in Table 5.14 are ones that are commonly used. Some of those options will be used in upcoming examples.

TABLE 5.14   Common System Options

Common System Options	Meaning
FIRSTOBS=n and OBS=n;	Specifies the first observation to be used in a data set (FIRSTOBS=) and the last observation to be used (OBS=). For example OPTIONS FIRSTOBS=2 OBS=21; causes SAS to use data records 2 through 21 in any subsequent analysis. When this option is set, it is usually a good idea to reset the values to OPTIONS FIRSTOBS=1; OBS=MAX; at the end of the program so subsequent analyses are not limited by the same options.
YEARCUTOFF=year	Specifies the cutoff year for two digit dates in a 100 year span starting with the specified date. For example if YEARCUTOFF=1920 then the data 01/15/19 would be considered 2019 while 01/15/21 would be seen as 1921. The default YEARCUTOFF is 1926. (For SAS versions 9 through 9.3, the cutoff year was 1920.)
PROBSIG=n	Specifies the number of decimals used when reporting p-values. For example PROBSIG=3 would cause p-values to be reported to three decimal places.
LINESIZE= n and PAGESIZE= n	Controls number of characters in an output line (LINESIZE) or number of lines on a page (PAGESIZE) for RTF and PDF output.
NONUMBER	Specifies no page numbers will be included in RTF or PDF output.
NODATE	Specifies no date will be included in RTF or PDF output.
ORIENTATION=option	Specifies paper orientation. Options are PORTRAIT or LANDSCAPE for RTF or PDF output.
NOCENTER	Left justifies output (default is centered)

HANDS-ON EXAMPLE

1. Open the program file `SYSOBS.SAS`.

```
OPTIONS FIRSTOBS=11 OBS=20;
PROC PRINT LABEL DATA="C:\SASDATA\SOMEDATA";
RUN;
OPTIONS FIRSTOBS=1 OBS=MAX;
```

   Run this program and observe that only the records 11 through 20 are displayed in the `PROC PRINT` listing.
2. Change `FIRSTOBS` to 5 and `OBS` to 25. Rerun and observe which records are displayed.

   Note that the last line in the code resets `FIRSTOBS` and `OBS to 1 and MAX`. It is important to reset these values; otherwise, any following SAS program may not use all of the records in a specified data set.

System Options should not be confused with similar looking options that are available as a part of a procedure. System Options affect *all* the following programs you may run, unless you reset the option. Procedure options only affect that procedure. For example, in `PROC PRINT,` you can use

```
PROC PRINT DATA=MYDATA (FIRSTOBS=11 and OBS=20);
```

to limit the number of records processed in that single procedure, but this does not affect any following procedures. On the other hand, if you use

```
OPTIONS FIRSTOBS=11 and OBS=20;
PROC PRINT DATA=MYDATA;
```

These statements limit the use of *all* the following data sets until you reset the settings with

```
OPTIONS FIRSTOBS=1 OBS=MAX;
```

or until you exit the SAS Software program.

5.9 SUMMARY

This chapter introduced you to the syntax of SAS procedures in preparation for using specific PROCs discussed in the remainder of the book. It also introduced `PROC PRINT` and illustrated some of the common options used for this procedure.

EXERCISES

5.1 **Add titles and footnotes to output.**

Open the program file `FIRST.SAS`:

a. Using the `TITLE` and `FOOTNOTE` statements, place five lines of titles at the beginning and two footnotes (i.e., footnote lines) at the end of the output.

b. Run the program and observe the output.

5.2 **Use the `ID` statement.**

Working with the `C:\SASDATA\CARS` data set, use the `ID` statement in `PROC PRINT` to create a listing where the `MODEL` variable is listed in the first column of the output.

5.3 **Use the `LABEL` statement.**

a. Open the program file `DLABEL.SAS`. Add a blank line between the `PROC MEANS` statement and the `RUN` statement. Cut and paste the `LABEL` statement (from the word LABEL to the semicolon) from its current location to just before the final `RUN` statement (this places it in the `PROC MEANS` paragraph). Run the program.

b. Do the labels appear in the output?

c. After the final `RUN` statement in the program, add a new line:

```
PROC PRINT;RUN;
```

Rerun the program. Do the labels appear in the output? Why or why not?

d. Change the `PROC PRINT` statement to

```
PROC PRINT LABEL;RUN;
```

Rerun the program. Do the labels appear? Why or why not? If you don't remember, go back to the section titled "Using the LABEL Statement in a SAS Procedure" to find out.

5.4 **Split Labels**

Open the program file APRINT1.SAS.

a. Add a `LABEL` statement to define labels for the `TIME` variables as

```
TIME1 = "Baseline Value"
TIME2 = "Observation at 60 Seconds"
TIME3 = "Observation at 120 Seconds"
TIME4 = "Observation at 5 Minutes"
```

b. Select a delimiter to use to split the labels into several lines, and alter the `LABEL` statements to include the delimiter plus an underline. For example:

```
LABEL TIME1="Baseline*Value*--------"
```

c. Using the `SPLIT=` statement, complete the changes in the code to cause the labels to be split when the listing is printed.

d. Submit the code and verify that the listing includes labels split to your specification.

6

SAS® ADVANCED PROGRAMMING TOPICS PART 1

LEARNING OBJECTIVES

- To be able to use SAS Functions
- To be able to TRANSPOSE data sets
- To be able to perform data recoding using SELECT
- To be able to use SAS programming techniques to clean up a messy data set

The SAS programming language is extensive and flexible, and there are many features of the language that were not discussed in the previous chapters of this book. The next two chapters are included for those who want to go deeper into SAS programming. This chapter introduces several topics that are commonly used in preparing data for analysis not covered in previous chapters. Additional programming topics including arrays and macros are covered in Chapter 7.

6.1 USING SAS FUNCTIONS

Sophisticated calculations can be created using SAS functions. These functions include arithmetic and text and date manipulation. The format for the use of SAS functions is

```
variable = function(argument1,argument2, etc.);
```

SAS® Essentials: Mastering SAS for Data Analytics, Second Edition. Alan C. Elliott and Wayne A. Woodward.
© 2016 John Wiley & Sons, Inc. Published 2016 by John Wiley & Sons, Inc.

Functions can require one or more arguments. Some require no arguments. For example, a few mathematical functions in SAS are as follows:

```
S = ABS(X);          Absolute value
S = FACT(X);         Factorial
S = INT(X);          Integer portion of a value
S = LOG(X);          Natural log
S = SQRT(X);         Square root
```

Some of the other functions available in SAS are SUBSTR, LAG, COS, SIN, ARCS, LOG10, UNIFORM, NORMAL, SUM, and MEAN. A list of commonly used SAS functions and additional examples can be found in Appendix B. These include functions of these types:

- Arithmetic/Mathematical
- Trigonometric
- Date and Time
- Character
- Truncation
- Special Use and Miscellaneous
- Financial
- Access Previous Observations (Lags)

Functions can also be used as a part of a more extensive calculation. For example,

```
C = MEASURE + SQRT(A**2 + B**2);
```

would calculate the square of A and then the square of B, then add those two numbers, take the square root of that value, add that number to the value of MEASURE, and assign the result to the variable named C.

As mentioned previously, functions may require no argument, one argument, or multiple arguments. A few multiargument mathematical functions in SAS are the following:

```
S = MAX(x1,x2,x3, ... );     Maximum value in the list of arguments
S = MIN(x1,x2,x3, ... );     Minimum value in the list of arguments
S = SUM(x1,x2,x3, ... );     Sum of non-missing values in a list of arguments
S = MEDIAN(x1,x2,x3, ... );  Median of a list of non-missing values
S = ROUND(value, round);     Rounds value to nearest round-off unit
```

These functions allow missing values in the list. Thus, the SUM function

```
TOTAL=SUM(TIME1,TIME2,TIME3,TIME4);
```

can create a different answer than

```
TOTAL= TIME1+TIME2+TIME3+TIME4;
```

It is important to understand that in the second instance, if the value for TIME2 were missing for a subject, the value of TOTAL would be set at missing (.). However, in the assignment using the SUM function, the value of TOTAL would contain the sum of the other time values even if TIME2 were missing.

The round-off unit in the ROUND function determines how the rounding will be performed. The default is 1. A round-off value of 0.01 means to round it off to the nearest 100th, and a round-off value of 5 means to round it off to the nearest 5. Here are a few examples:

ROUND(3.1415,.01)	Returns the value 3.14
ROUND(107,5)	Returns the value 105
ROUND(3.6234)	Returns the value 4

A function that takes no argument is TODAY(). For example, the code

```
NOW=TODAY();
```

puts the current date value from the computer's clock into the variable named NOW.

When arguments are a list of values, such as in MAX or MIN, you can specify the list as variables separated by commas, or as a range preceded by the word OF. For example, if these variables have the following values:

```
X1 = 1;   X2 = 2;   X3 = 13;   X4=10;
```

Then

MAX(1,2,3,4,5)	Returns the value 5
MAX(X1,X2,X3,X4)	Returns the value 13
MAX(OF X1-X4)	Returns the value 13

Note that the designation OF X1-X4 is interpreted by SAS as all same-named consecutively numbered variables from X1 to X4 in the MAX() function example above. If there are missing values in the list, they are ignored. Other similar functions are illustrated here:

MIN(OF X1-X4)	Returns the value 1
SUM(OF X1-X4)	Returns the value 26
MEDIAN(OF X1-X4)	Returns the value 6 (the average of 2 and 10)
NMISS(OF X1-X4)	Returns 0 (number of missing values)
N(OF X1-X4)	Returns 4 (number of non-missing values)

There is also an extensive collection of functions available to allow you to manipulate text and date values. As an example of a date function, the INTCK function counts the number of intervals (INTerval Count) between two dates or times. The result is an integer value. The format for this function is

```
INTCK('interval',from,to)
```

The `from` and `to` variables are SAS date values. The `'interval'` argument can be one of the following lengths of time:

```
DAY
WEEKDAY
WEEK
TENDAY
SEMIMONTH
MONTH
QTR
SEMIYEAR
YEAR
```

Thus, the following function counts the number of years between the date variables BEGDATE and ENDDATE because the date interval indicated is `'YEAR'`.

```
INTCK('YEAR',BEGDATE,ENDDATE)
```

The following code counts the number of months between these two dates because the date interval indicated is `'MONTH'`.

```
INTCK('MONTH',BEGDATE,ENDDATE)
```

Another handy date function is the MDY function. This allows you to convert numbers into a SAS date value. For example,

```
BDATE = MDY(10,12,1989);
```

converts the date October 12, 1989, into a SAS date value. Dates must be in SAS date format in order for you to use other SAS date functions or to output dates using SAS format specifications. Or if in a data set you have these values

```
    MTH=5;      DAY=9;      YR=2016;
```

the MDY function

```
    VISITDATE = MDY(MTH,DAY,YR);
```

creates a SAS date variable named VISITDATE with the value May 9, 2016. For a more comprehensive list of functions, refer to Appendix B in this book.

HANDS-ON EXAMPLE

This example illustrates a method for calculating the difference between two dates (AGE) using the INTCK function. The procedure uses these steps:

1. Read in BDATE as a SAS date value using the INFORMAT MMYYDD8. specification in the INPUT statement.

(continued)

(continued)

2. Convert the target date 08/25/2016 into a variable named TARGET using the MDY function.

3. Use the INTCK function to count the number of years between each date (BDATE) in the data set and the TARGET date and assign this value to the variable AGE.

4. Assign the count of years to the variable named AGE.

Here are the steps:

1. Open the program file DDATES.SAS.

```
DATA DATES;
INPUT @1 BDATE MMDDYY8.;
TARGET=MDY(08,25,2009);          * Uses MDY() function;
AGE=INTCK('YEAR',BDATE,TARGET);  *  INTCK function;
DATALINES;
07101952
07041776
01011900

;
PROC PRINT DATA=DATES;
FORMAT BDATE WEEKDATE. TARGET MMDDYY8.;
RUN;
```

2. Note the statement.

```
INPUT @1 BDATE MMDDYY8.;
```

This statement reads in a variable named BDATE as a SAS date value starting in column 1 (specified by the pointer @1) using the format MMDDYY8. The SAS date variable TARGET is created with the MDY function, using constant values for month, day, and year. To display the dates in a readable manner, a FORMAT statement is included in the PROC PRINT paragraph.

3. Run the program and observe the output in Table 6.1.

Note that the program calculates AGE as the difference in years (the count of the "year" intervals) between the TARGET date and the date value for each record in the SAS data set.

TABLE 6.1 Results of the INTCK Function
Calculation

Obs	BDATE	TARGET	AGE
1	Thursday, July 10, 1952	08/25/16	64
2	Thursday, July 4, 1776	08/25/16	240
3	Monday, January 1, 1900	08/25/16	116

4. To illustrate the `TODAY()` function, change the `TARGET` date to today's date using the code

```
TARGET=TODAY();
```

   Resubmit the code and observe the results.
5. Another function you can use to find the difference between two dates is `YRDIF`. Change the `AGE=INTCK` statement to the following:

```
AGE=YRDIF(BDATE,TARGET,'ACT/365');
```

   This function finds the difference in two dates using the method of dividing the number of days by 365. Run the program. See Appendix B for more information about this and other functions.
6. For you history buffs: If you include the date

```
09041752
```

   (September 4, 1752) into the list of data values and run the program, it indicates that this date fell on a Monday (in the current Gregorian calendar). However, this date did not exist. When Britain adopted the Gregorian calendar, the day after September 2, 1752, was September 14, 1752. Thus, if SAS is used to calculate dates before September 2, 1752, care must be taken because SAS does not convert dates to the older Julian calendar designation.

6.2   USING PROC TRANSPOSE

`PROC TRANSPOSE` allows you to restructure the values in your data set by transposing (or reorienting) the data. This is typically performed when your data are not in the structure required for an analysis. For example, if your data are listed with subjects as columns, you can transpose the data so the subjects represent rows. The simplified syntax for `PROC TRANSPOSE` is:

```
PROC TRANSPOSE DATA=input-data OUT=output-data;
<PREFIX=prefix>;
<BY <variables>
VAR variables;
```

- The input data set is the data set to be transposed.
- The output data set is the resulting data set.
- `PREFIX` specifies a prefix to the names of variables created in the transposition. The default names are `COL1`, `COL2`, and so on.
- The `BY` variable, when specified, causes the transpose to be performed once per category specified by the `BY` group's categorical variable.
- The `VAR` statement specifies which variables are to be transposed.

HANDS-ON EXAMPLE

Suppose you have been given a data set in which each line represents a variable and each subject's data are in a single column. This example illustrates how to use PROC TRANSPOSE to restructure this data set. Note that because some of the data are text, you must indicate that with a $ after each variable name in the INPUT statement.

1. Open the program file DTRANSPOSE1.SAS.

```
DATA SUBJECTS;
INPUT SUB1 $ SUB2 $ SUB3 $ SUB4 $;
DATALINES;
12 21 13 14
13 21 12 14
15 31 23 23
15 33 21 32
 M  F  F  M
;
PROC TRANSPOSE DATA=SUBJECTS OUT=TRANSPOSED;
   VAR SUB1 SUB2 SUB3 SUB4;
RUN;
PROC PRINT DATA=TRANSPOSED;
RUN;
```

2. Run the program. The OUT=TRANSPOSED statement creates a data set named OBS_TRANSPOSED from the procedure. The resulting data set is given in Table 6.2.

TABLE 6.2   Example of Transposed Data

PROC TRANSPOSE EXAMPLE

Obs	_NAME_	COL1	COL2	COL3	COL4	COL5
1	SUB1	12	13	15	15	M
2	SUB2	21	21	31	33	F
3	SUB3	13	12	23	21	F
4	SUB4	14	14	23	32	M

3. You can control the names of the columns with a PREFIX statement. Change the PROC TRANSPOSE statement to

```
PROC TRANSPOSE DATA=SUBJECTS OUT=TRANSPOSED PREFIX=INFO;
```

   Rerun the program and observe the names of the columns.

4. The solution isn't exactly what you want. One way you could fix that is to use the RENAME statement to give each column a new name. Enter the following code. Note how each variable is renamed to a better name, particularly GENDER:

```
DATA NEW;SET TRANSPOSED;
RENAME  INFO1=T1 INFO2=T2 INFO3=T3 INFO4=T4 INFO5=GENDER;
RUN;
PROC PRINT DATA=NEW;
RUN;
```

Submit this code and verify that it provides better names for the data set.

Another possibility when transposing data is to use an available label to name new variables. Consider the following code (DTRANSPOSE1A.SAS):

```
DATA SUBJECTS;
INPUT LAB $ SUB1 $ SUB2 $ SUB3 $ SUB4 $;
DATALINES;
BASELINE 12 21 13 14
TIME1 13 21 12 14
TIME2 15 31 23 23
TIME3 15 33 21 32
GENDER   M  F  F  M
;
PROC TRANSPOSE DATA=SUBJECTS OUT=TRANSPOSED;
  ID LAB;
  VAR SUB1 SUB2 SUB3 SUB4;
RUN;
PROC PRINT DATA=TRANSPOSED;
RUN;
```

In this version of the program, there is a variable called LAB that provides a label for columns. The ID statement in PROC TRANSPOSE allows you to specify LAB for the new variable names.

HANDS-ON EXAMPLE

1. Open the file DTRANSPOSE1A.SAS. Submit the code and observe the output given in Table 6.3.

```
PROC TRANSPOSE DATA=SUBJECTS OUT=TRANSPOSED;
  ID LAB;
  VAR SUB1 SUB2 SUB3 SUB4;
RUN;
```

Because of the ID statement in PROC TRANSPOSE, the values for ID become the column names.
2. Change the values in the data set from BASELINE, TIME1, and so on to READ1 through READ4. Leave GENDER as is. Resubmit the code and note the changed variable names.

(continued)

(continued)

TABLE 6.3   Transposed Data with ID

Obs	_NAME_	BASELINE	TIME1	TIME2	TIME3	GENDER
1	SUB1	12	13	15	15	M
2	SUB2	21	21	31	33	F
3	SUB3	13	12	23	21	F
4	SUB4	14	14	23	32	M

TABLE 6.4   Data from the COMPLICATIONS Data Set

Obs	SUBJECT	COMPLICATION
1	1001	Heart Attack
2	1033	Heart Attack
3	1048	Heart Attack
4	1054	Heart Attack
5	1073	Heart Attack
6	1135	Wound Infection
7	1149	Compartment Syndrome
8	1368	Pneumonia
9	1379	Heart Attack
10	1536	Heart Attack
11	1545	Heart Attack
12	1615	Heart Attack
13	1643	Pancreatitis
14	1645	Pneumonia
15	1796	Coagulopathy
16	1859	Pneumonia
17	1921	Pneumonia
18	1921	Renal Failure
19	2023	Pneumonia
20	2039	Coagulopathy
21	2074	Coagulopathy
22	2076	Pneumonia
23	2076	Heart Attack
24	2076	Renal Failure

6.2.1 Using TRANSPOSE to Deal with Multiple Records per Subject

As a second example using `PROC TRANSPOSE`, suppose you have data that have several (and possibly differing numbers of) observations per subject, but you want to analyze the data by observation (a set of observations per row). You can use `PROC TRANSPOSE` to transpose the data by a key variable. For example, Table 6.4 is a partial list of records in a simulated SAS data set named `COMPLICATIONS`. These are observed complications for accident victims. Note that some subjects have more than one complication (subject 1921, for example).

HANDS-ON EXAMPLE

This example uses `PROC TRANSPOSE` to rearrange the `COMPLICATIONS` data set so that there is only one subject per row and to output a data set for subjects with three or more complications. Notice that data are already sorted by `SUBJECT`, but if this was not the case, you would need to do a `PROC SORT` by `SUBJECT` before doing `PROC TRANSPOSE`.

1. Open the program file `DTRANSPOSE2.SAS`.

```
PROC TRANSPOSE DATA=MYSASLIB.COMPLICATIONS
     OUT=COMP_OUT PREFIX=COMP;
(Continued)
     BY SUBJECT;
     VAR COMPLICATION;
RUN;
DATA MULTIPLE;SET COMP_OUT;
DROP _NAME_ ;
IF COMP3 NE '';
RUN;
PROC PRINT DATA=MULTIPLE; VAR SUBJECT COMP1-COMP4;
FORMAT SUBJECT 10. COMP1-COMP4 $10.;
RUN;
```

   The `PROC TRANSPOSE` step outputs a data set named `COMP_OUT`. The `BY` statement indicates that the transpose is by subject, so there will be one subject per row. The `PREFIX=` option specifies the prefix for the new variables created for complications. That is, the first complication for a subject is named `COMP1`, the second `COMP2`, and so on. The `VAR` statement indicates which variable (`COMPLICATION`) will be used as the output variable (named with the `COMP` prefix).

   A second data set is created (`MULTIPLE`) that contains only records where the value for `COMP3` is not blank. Thus, only subjects that have three or more complications are retained in the `MULTIPLE` data set. For example, subject 1921 has only two complications, so this subject is not included in the `MULTIPLE` data set, but subject 2076 does appear. The results are reported using a `PROC PRINT` statement.

2. Run this program. The abbreviated output given in Table 6.5 presents the first few records. Note that each of subjects listed has at least three complications.

3. Change the code to select only subjects with four or more complications, that is, change the IF statement and change `COMP4` to `COMP5` in two places. Resubmit and confirm that the change worked.

(continued)

(continued)

TABLE 6.5   Output from PROC TRANSPOSE

Illustrates PROC TRANSPOSE, compressing
multiple subject records to a single record.
Reports subjects having 3 or more complications.

Obs	SUBJECT	COMP1	COMP2	COMP3	COMP4
1	2076	Pneumonia	Heart Atta	Renal Fail	
2	3585	DVT (Lower	Pneumonia	Renal Fail	
3	3630	DVT (Lower	Heart Atta	Pancreatit	Pneumonia
4	4585	Compartmen	Pneumonia	Skin Break	
5	4599	Aspiration	Pneumonia	Renal Fail	
6	4760	Acute Resp	Pneumonia	Renal Fail	

6.3   THE SELECT STATEMENT

The IF statement allows you to conditionally perform certain SAS calculations and assignments and is handy for recoding a small number of values. For more complex recoding, or recoding with more categories, the SELECT statement is often easier and more efficient to use. The SELECT statement evaluates the value of a variable and creates new assignments based on those values. Syntax (simplified) is as follows:

```
SELECT <(select-expression)> ;
     WHEN-1  statement;
     ...  WHEN-n  statement;
     < OTHERWISE statement;>
```

For example, suppose you want to calculate NEWVAL according to some specific values of the variable OBSERVED. That is, if OBSERVED=1, you want to set NEWVAL=AGE+2. If OBSERVED=2 or 3, you want to set NEWVAL=AGE+10, and so on. A SELECT statement to perform this recoding would be as follows:

```
SELECT (OBSERVED);
   WHEN (1) NEWVAL=AGE+2;
   WHEN (2, 3) NEWVAL=AGE+10;
   WHEN (4,5,6) NEWVAL=AGE+20;
OTHERWISE NEWVAL=0;
END;
```

Another way to use SELECT is without a specific select-expression. In this case, the WHEN statements include conditional expressions that should be in parentheses. For example:

```
SELECT;
   WHEN (GP='A') STATUS2=1;
```

```
WHEN (GP='B' and SEX=1) STATUS2=2;
WHEN (GP='C' and SEX=0)  STATUS2=3;
OTHERWISE  STATUS2=0;
END;
```

HANDS-ON EXAMPLE

As an example of using the `SELECT` statement, suppose you want to recode the numeric variable `STATUS` into a text variable called `ECONOMIC`, and combine some of the groups.

1. Open the program file `DSELECT.SAS`. Note the `SELECT` statement. Submit the code and verify that it creates a new variable named `ECONOMIC`. Partial output is given in Table 6.6.

```
DATA MYDATA;SET "C:\SASDATA\SOMEDATA";
FORMAT ECONOMIC $7.;
SELECT(STATUS);
    WHEN (1,2) ECONOMIC="LOW";
    WHEN (3) ECONOMIC="MIDDLE";
    WHEN (4,5) ECONOMIC="HIGH";
    OTHERWISE ECONOMIC="MISSING";
END;
PROC PRINT DATA=MYDATA;
RUN;
```

TABLE 6.6   Example of SELECT Statement

This example illustrates the Select Statement

Obs	ID	GP	AGE	TIME1	TIME2	TIME3	TIME4	STATUS	SEX	GENDER	ECONOMIC
1	101	A	12	22.3	25.3	28.2	30.6	5	0	Female	HIGH
2	102	A	11	22.8	27.5	33.3	35.8	5	0	Female	HIGH
3	110	A	12	18.5	26.0	29.0	27.9	5	1	Male	HIGH
4	187	A	11	22.5	29.3	32.6	33.7	2	0	Female	LOW
5	312	A	4	17.0	21.3	22.7	21.2	5	1	Male	HIGH
6	390	A	6	21.3	30.5	30.7	30.1	4	0	Female	HIGH

2. Using another `SELECT` statement without a select expression, add new code to the DATA step that does the following recode:
   - For ages 12 and under set `AGEGROUP="CHILD"`.
   - For ages 13 to 19 set `AGEGROUP="TEEN"`.
   - For ages 20 and above set `AGEGROUP="ADULT"`.
   - `OTHERWISE` set `AGEGROUP="NA"`.

   Here is partial code:

```
SELECT;
WHEN (AGE LE 12) AGEGROUP="CHILD";
WHEN (AGE GT 12 AND AGE LE 19) AGEGROUP="TEEN";
FINISH THE CODE;
```

(continued)

> *(continued)*
>
> 3. Submit the code and verify that your new SELECT statement works. Note that although both STATUS and AGE are numeric, STATUS is categorical and lends itself to using SELECT with a select expression, whereas AGE is a continuous numeric variable that lends itself to using a SELECT statement without a select expression.

6.4   GOING DEEPER: CLEANING A MESSY DATA SET

Many of the features in the SAS language are helpful in cleaning up messy data. By messy we mean data sets that are not quite ready for analysis. Most data analysts experience problems dealing with files that contain data that have coding problems and must be fixed before a proper analysis is possible. This section walks you through a case study of a data set with problems and illustrates how they might be corrected.

The data set in question is named MESSYDATA and represents an actual data set (with some information changed to protect the innocent) that was created from a survey taken at a clinic. Originally entered into an Excel spreadsheet, it was imported into SAS using PROC IMPORT. Information about this process has been discussed in Chapter 3. In this case study, we start with the MESSYDATA.SA7BDAT file, which contains a number of problems that should be fixed before performing any type of analysis.

We use this case study to provide a series of actions you can take to correct some errors in the data. Of course, if you do not first clean up your data set, any analysis may be wrong, may reach incorrect conclusions, and may cost you time and money if you have to make the corrections later.

A portion of the original MESSYDATA data set is displayed in Table 6.7.

A few of the problems you might quickly note include the following:

- Line 17 is blank.
- There are non-date values in the "DateLeft" column.
- There is a non-number in the "Age" column (>29).
- Values of Gender are mixed upper and lower cases.
- There are multiple answers in columns that should have only one answer.

It is easy to see that some of these errors should have been dealt with in the design of the survey or in the data entry process. Nevertheless, this data set represents an accurate view of typical problems an analyst will see.

You can correct these issues by using SAS code. One reason this is a good idea is that it leaves an audit trail of changes. You should always make changes in a copy of the original data set so that the original data will not be changed in any way. Again, this is a good practice. If you alter the original data file, and accidently change something that should not have been changed, it might be difficult to get the original data set back.

6.4.1   Fix Labels, Rename Variables

The first step in creating a clean data set is to attach labels to the variables. This helps create more understandable output. Of course, you need to know what each variable means

TABLE 6.7 A Messy Data Set

#	SUBJECT	DateArrived	Time/Arrive	DateLeft	TimeLeft	Married	Single	Age	Gender	Education	Race	How Arrived	Top Reason	Arrival	Satisfaction
1	00001	2/7/2005	11:18:00 A	2/7/2005	2:15:00 PM	1	0	29	M	12	H	Bus	1	101.5	84.7
2	00002	3/10/2005	1:23:00 PM	3/11/2005	12:40:00 AM	1	0	21	M	12	AA	Car	1	98.6	82.8
3	00003	3/2/2005	1:08:00 PM	3/2/2005	5:07:00 PM	0	1	21	F	12	AA	Car	1	98.2	68.2
4	00004	5/2/2005	11:46:00 A	5/2/2005	9:45:00 PM	1	0	29	F	11	AA	Car	2	100	70
5	00005	1/31/2005	12:09:00 P	2/1/2005	1:30:00 AM	0	0	47	F	12	NA	Car	1	101	81.4
6	00006	2/1/2005	2:27:00 PM	2/1/2005	2:40:00 PM	0	0	45	F	12	H	Car	3	37.2	87.7
7	00007	2/3/2005	11:50:00 A	2/3/2005	9:08:00 PM	1	0	21	F	10	AA	Car	1,3	99.8	68.7
8	00008	2/4/2005	10:47:00 A	#VALUE!	11:50:00 PM	0	0	46	M	12	H	Bus	1	99.5	89.2
9	00009	2/5/2005	11:42:00 A	2/5/2005	12:51:00 PM	0	1	28	F	14	MEX	Car	2	97.1	88.7
10	00010	1/30/2005	12:53:00 P	1/30/2005	11:40:00 PM	0	1	28	M	14	AA	Car	1	36.7	85.6
11	00011	2/6/2005	9:22:00 AM	2/6/2005	2:40:00 PM	0	0	34	M	12	C	Car	3	101	73.6
12	00012	1/30/2005	2:30:00 AM	Missing	8:00:00 PM	0	1	20	F	9	H	Car	1	37.2	79.4
13	00013	2/6/2005	7:10:00 AM	2/7/2006	12:20:00 AM	1	0	35	M	11	H	Bus	1	97.8	86.9
14	00014	2/6/2005	9:35:00 AM	2/6/2005	7:25:00 PM	1	0	33	F	16	AA	Walk	1	37.5	87.6
15	00015	2/7/2005	9:50:00 AM	2/7/2005	8:30:00 AM	1	0	27	F	12	H	Car	1	101.8	79.1
16	00016	2/7/2005	10:55:00 A	2/7/2005	11:20:00 AM	0	0		F	12	AA	Car	3	100.2	81
17															-99
18	00017	2/7/2005	12:40:00 P	2/7/2005	3:15:00 PM	1	1	36		12	H	Bus, Walk	1	97.1	81
19	00018	5/9/2005	1:20:00 PM	5/9/2005	7:20:00 PM	0	1	34	F	12	AA	Car	1	38	86.3
20	00019	2/7/2005	2:40:00 PM	2/8/2005	2:00:00 AM	1	0	26	M	12	X	Car	1,5	97.8	87
21	00020	2/9/2005	12:00:00 A	2/9/2005	7:45:00 PM	0	0	44	M	9	H	Car	2	99.2	86.8
22	00021	3/21/2005	4:35:00 PM	3/21/2005	1:36:00 PM	0	1	>29	F	16		Car	1	36.8	84.8
23	00022	1/31/2005	8:20:00 AM	2/1/2005	1:50:00 AM	1	0	53	M	7	C	Car	3	37.6	85.4
24	00023	1/26/2005	10:25:00 A	10/28/2001	12:00:00 AM	1	1	45	F	12	A	Car	3	99.8	85.4
25	00024	1/25/2007	12:10:00 P	1/25/2005	7:45:00 PM	1	0	22	F	10	M	Car	3	97.4	84.6
26	00025	1/25/2005	2:44:00 PM	1/25/2005	3:25:00 PM	11	0	22	F	9	C	Car	3	98.6	86.1
27	00026	1/25/2005	10:29:00 A	1/25/2005	11:30:00 PM	1	0	42	M	10	H	UKN	1	99.2	86.1
28	00027	1/25/2005	2:52:00 PM	1/26/2005	12:30:00 AM	0	0	39	F	8	H	Bus	3	98.8	72
29	00028	1/25/2005	12:30:00 P	1/26/2005	3:20:00 PM	1	1	48	M	9	AA	Car	2	99.7	83.5
30	00029	1/25/2005	2:25:00 PM	1/26/2005	2:25:00 AM	1	0	39	M	13	AA	Car	1	98.3	86
31	00030	1/25/2005	11:00:00 A	1/26/2005	12:45:00 AM	0	0	28	f	12	H	Car	2	37.8	74
32	00031	1/25/2005	2:20:00 PM	1/25/2005	2:45:00 AM	0	1	21	M	10	AA	Cra	1	101.9	

147

in order to assign the variables labels, and this should be provided in the form of some type of data dictionary, as illustrated in Table 6.8.

TABLE 6.8   Data Dictionary for Messy Data Set

Variable	Name	Type	Label
1	Subject	Char	Subject ID
2	DateArrived	Date	Date Arrived
3	TimeArrive	Time	Time Arrived
4	DateLeft	Date	Date Left
5	TimeLeft	Time	Time Left
6	Married	Num	Married?
7	Single	Num	Single?
8	Age	Num	Age Jan 1, 2014
9	Gender	Char	Gender
10	Education	Num	Years of Schooling
11	Race	Char	Race
12	How_Arrived	Char	How Arrived at Clinic
13	Top_Reason	Num	Top Reason for Coming
14	Arrival	Num	Temperature
15	Satisfaction	Num	Satisfaction Score

You may note in Table 6.7 that there are some variables whose values are suspect, and some that are not of the right data type. That will be fixed later. In this example, the program assumes that you have a SAS library named MYSASLIB. (A LIBNAME statement is included in the code to help you set up this library if needed.) The PROC PRINT statement lists the first 10 observations to make it easy to verify that the changes made took place.

HANDS-ON EXAMPLE

1. Open the program file MESSY1.SAS (Only a portion of the code for this exercise is shown here.). In this program, only some of the labels have been assigned. The variable ARRIVAL is replaced with TEMP to avoid confusion with other variables. Submit this code and observe the results given in Table 6.9.

```
DATA MYSASLIB.CLEANED;SET MYSASLIB.MESSYDATA;
LABEL
      EDUCATION='Years of Schooling'
      HOW_ARRIVED='How Arrived at Clinic'
      TOP_REASON='Top Reason for Coming'
      SATISFACTION='Satisfaction Score'
TEMP=ARRIVAL;
DROP ARRIVAL;
LABEL TEMP='Arrival Temperature';
RUN;
PROC PRINT LABEL
    DATA=MYSASLIB.CLEANED
```

```
        (firstobs=1 obs=10);
    VAR   SUBJECT EDUCATION ARRIVAL
          TOP_REASON SATISFACTION;
RUN;
```

TABLE 6.9   First Pass to Fix Messy Data

Obs	SUBJECT	Years of Schooling	Arrival Temperature	Top Reason for Coming	Satisfaction Score
1	00001	12	101.5	1	84.7
2	00002	12	98.6	1	82.8
3	00003	12	98.2	1	68.2
4	00004	11	100.0	2	70
5	00005	12	101.0	1	81.4
6	00006	12	37.2	3	87.7
7	00007	10	99.8	1,3	68.7
8	00008	12	99.5	1	89.2
9	00009	14	97.1	2	88.7
10	00010	14	36.7	1	85.6

9. Enter the remainder of the Labels (see Table 6.8) and submit the program. Note that the resulting program is stored in the file `MYSASLIB.CLEANED`.

Note: It is possible to rename the `ARRIVAL` variable using the code.

```
RENAME ARRIVAL=TEMP;
```

However, as we will use `TEMP` in some later calculations within the same data set, it is easier in this case to create a new variable because if `RENAME` is used, the variable `TEMP` can't be used in latter calculations within the same `DATA` step.

6.4.2   Fix Case Problems, Allowed Categories, and Delete Unneeded Lines

A second common fix to apply to data values is to make sure that case is consistent within a variable. For example, if Gender is recorded as F and f, the computer sees that as two separate categories and any summary by gender will not be correct. To correct case problems, you can use the `UPCASE()` or `LOWCASE()` function to convert data values to all upper or all lower case.

A second common fix is to verify that all items in a categorical variable are allowable. For example, in the `HOW_ARRIVED` variable, only `CAR`, `BUS`, or `WALK` is acceptable. If data values do not equal any of the allowed values, we'll set the value to missing. In the case of `HOW_ARRIVED` missing is a blank value, represented by " ". The `IN` function can check to see if a variable contains one of the values in a set of specified values. For example:

```
IF HOW_ARRIVED NOT IN ('CAR','BUS','WALK') THEN HOW_ARRIVED="";
```

A third easy-to-perform check is to delete irrelevant records. In this data set, if a line does not contain a Subject ID, we want to eliminate that record. This is done with an IF statement.

```
IF SUBJECT ="" THEN DELETE;
```

These fixes are illustrated in the next example.

HANDS-ON EXAMPLE

1. Open the program file MESSY2.SAS. Note the code marked as Step 2 in a comment line. This code was added on to the end of the changes from MESSY1.SAS. Only the new code is listed here. Submit the code and observe the results. A portion of the resulting data set (with selected variables) is shown in Table 6.10. You should note that all of the text variables are in upper case, and some of the HOW_ARRIVED values have been set to blank.

```
* FIX 1 - Convert text values to all uppercase;
gender=upcase(gender);
race=upcase(race);
HOW_ARRIVED=upcase(HOW_ARRIVED);
* FIX 2 SET BAD UNKNOWN VALUES TO MISSING;
IF HOW_ARRIVED NOT IN ('CAR','BUS','WALK') THEN HOW_ARRIVED="";
* FIX 2 - GET RID OF EMPTY ROWS;
IF SUBJECT="" THEN DELETE;
```

TABLE 6.10   Some Corrected Variables in the Messy Data Set

Obs	Subject ID	Gender	Race	How Arrived at Clinic
1	00001	M	H	BUS
2	00002	M	AA	CAR
3	00003	F	AA	CAR
4	00004	F	AA	CAR
5	00005	F	NA	CAR
6	00006	F	H	CAR
7	00007	F	AA	CAR
8	00008	M	H	BUS

2. Add new lines using the IN() function to check for correct values in GENDER (M or F) and in RACE (H, AA, and C). For example,

```
IF GENDER NOT IN('M','F') THEN GENDER="";
```

Submit the new code and observe the results.

3. Upon further examination, you verify with the survey coordinator that an answer of "MEX" or "M" for race should be corrected to "H," "W" should be corrected to "C," and "A" should be corrected to "AA". If RACE is "X," "NA" or "." then set it to blank (missing). The code to correct two of these items (which must appear after the UPCASE fixes and before the IN() function fixes) is

```
IF RACE="MEX" OR RACE="M" then RACE="H";
IF RACE="X" OR RACE="NA" then RACE="";
```

   Enter these fixes. Submit the code and verify that the fixes work (including checking the log for error messages).

6.4.3   Check and Fix Incorrect Categories, Fix duplicated Variables

Two troubling variables are MARRIED and SINGLE. The survey asked respondents their marital status, and the information was recorded in the data set where 1 means yes and 0 means no. Technically, these two variables should be the opposite of each other, and you should only require one of them in the data set. However, if you look at the frequencies of each using PROC FREQ, you discover that they are not telling you the same thing. To check these and other categorical variables, use the PROC FREQ procedure. This is illustrated in the next example.

HANDS-ON EXAMPLE

This example checks for incorrect entries using PROC FREQ and fixes the problems.

1. Open the program file DISCOVER1.SAS.

```
PROC FREQ data=MYSASLIB.cleaned;
TABLES MARRIED SINGLE TOP_REASON RACE GENDER HOW_ARRIVED;
run;
```

   Submit the code and observe the results in Table 6.11. (Only some of the output is shown here.) Note what you discover:
   - There are codes for MARRIED that are incorrect.
   - The two tables MARRIED and SINGLE are not the opposite of one another as you would expect. Typically, you'd only need one table or the other. In this case, the researcher chooses to use the SINGLE table, so the MARRIED variable can be deleted.

   - Several values for TOP_REASON are incorrect.
   - RACE still contains some incorrect values. (The previous fix didn't correct all the problems.)

(continued)

(continued)

TABLE 6.11 **Frequencies for Several Categorical Variables**

		Married?		
Married	**Frequency**	**Percent**	**Cumulative Frequency**	**Cumulative Percent**
0	38	48.10	38	48.10
1	39	49.37	77	97.47
9	1	1.27	78	98.73
11	1	1.27	79	100.00

		Single?		
Single	**Frequency**	**Percent**	**Cumulative Frequency**	**Cumulative Percent**
0	43	54.43	43	54.43
1	36	45.57	79	100.00

		Top Reason for Coming		
Top_Reason	**Frequency**	**Percent**	**Cumulative Frequency**	**Cumulative Percent**
1	44	55.70	44	55.70
1,2,3	1	1.27	45	56.96
1,3	1	1.27	46	58.23
1.5	1	1.27	47	59.49
2	19	24.05	66	83.54
3	12	15.19	78	98.73
3&1	1	1.27	79	100.00

		Race		
Race	**Frequency**	**Percent**	**Cumulative Frequency**	**Cumulative Percent**
A	1	1.32	1	1.32
AA	37	48.68	38	50.00
C	5	6.58	43	56.58
H	32	42.11	75	98.68
W	1	1.32	76	100.00
Frequency Missing = 3				

- GENDER appears to be okay now. Note that it contains two missing values as a result of the fixes in the previous example. (This table is not shown here.)
- All categories in HOW_ARRIVED are okay. (This table is not shown here.)

With this information, you can continue cleaning the data set.

2. Open the program file MESSY3.SAS. Observe the code listed under the Step 3 comment lines. The code already includes the following fixes:
   - The MARRIED variables are eliminated.
   - Additional RACE fixes are included.

```
DROP MARRIED;
IF RACE NOT IN ('AA','H','C') THEN RACE="";
To fix the TOP_REASON problems, use an IF statement as shown in
this code (note that TOP_REASON) is a character variable.
IF TOP_REASON NE "1" And
   TOP_REASON NE "2" and
   TOP_REASON NE "3" then TOP_REASON="";
```

   Submit the updated code and observe the results.

3. Go back to DISCOVER1.SAS, take out the MARRIED variable from the TABLE statement and resubmit it to verify that all changes have been made. Note that for character variables the missing values are noted at the bottom of the table, and for the numeric variable (TOP_REASON) the missing values category (.) is listed in the table.

6.4.4 Check and Fix Out-of-Range Numeric Variables

Now that categorical variables have been cleaned, it is time to turn attention to the numeric measurement variables: AGE, ARRIVAL (Temperature), EDUCATION, and SATISFACTION. One way to take an initial look at numeric variables is with PROC MEANS. In particular, you are looking for unusual minimum and maximum values. The following example illustrates how to find problem values using PROC MEANS and how to correct them.

HANDS-ON EXAMPLE

This example corrects problems associated with numeric variables.

1. Open the program file DISCOVER2.SAS and submit it to create the table of means shown in Table 6.12. (The output depends on you doing the previous exercises correctly, so if you have not done them your answer may differ.)

```
PROC MEANS MAXDEC=2 DATA=CLEAN.CLEANED;RUN;
```

   When you run PROC MEANS, it displays means of all numeric variables. Note in this case that AGE is not included in the output. On further inspection, you see that AGE is a character-type variable in the data set. (A common problem when importing data from Excel or CSV files.) One way to convert this variable to numeric is with the INPUT() function (see Appendix B). You also note problems with some minimum

(continued)

(continued)

and maximum values. On further inspection, you decide these are the items that need to be fixed:

- Set the value 99 for Education as a missing value.
- Some temperatures were taken as Celsius and some as Fahrenheit. They should all be Fahrenheit. In consultation with the physician in the clinic, you decide that any temperature under 45 should be considered Celsius and should be converted.
- By looking at records you find that the temperature coded as 1018 should have been 101.8.
- Set the value −99 for SATISFACTION as a missing value.
- Ignore the Subject ID variable for now.

TABLE 6.12   Checking Means for Several Variables

Variable	Label	N	Mean	Std Dev	Minimum	Maximum
Subject	Subject ID	79	39.99	22.96	1.00	79.00
Single	Single?	79	0.46	0.50	0.00	1.00
Education	Years of Schooling	78	14.64	17.16	6.00	99.00
Satisfaction	Satisfaction Score	79	77.92	21.70	-99.00	94.10
TEMP	Arrival Temperature	79	96.04	108.39	36.30	1018.00

Convert AGE to numeric. Give it the new name AGEN and assign a label. Note that changes need be made to SINGLE.

2. To fix those problems, open the program file MESSY4.SAS. Observe the code listed under Part 4 in the code, where each of the identified fixes is made. Submit the code and observe the output.

```
IF EDUCATION=99 then EDUCATION=.;
IF TEMP LT 45 THEN TEMP=(9/5)*TEMP+32;
IF TEMP=1018 then TEMP=101.8;
IF SATISFACTION=-99 THEN SATISFACTION=.;
* Convert AGE from character to numeric;
AGEN=INPUT(AGE,5.);
DROP AGE;
LABEL AGEN="Age Jan 1, 2014";
```

3. To verify that the changes have been made, rerun the code in DISCOVER2.SAS. Now that AGEN is a numeric variable, you note that the minimum and maximum is 0 and 220. In checking with the researcher, you conclude that ages should be between 10 and 99.

4. Go back to MESSY4.SAS and make this additional fix. Note that you are now using the numeric variable AGEN rather than the previous character variable AGE.

```
IF AGEN LT 10 or AGEN GT 99 THEN AGEN=.
```

Run the MESSY4.SAS code, then run the DISCOVER2.SAS code to make sure the correction took place.

> When you convert character data to numeric, as in the case of AGE to AGEN, any values that cannot be converted to numeric are made missing (.). Therefore, the entries for AGE such as >29 are recoded as missing values as a result of this conversion.

6.4.5 Correct Date and Time Values

The date and time the subject arrived and left the clinic are needed to calculate how long it took to serve each patient. However, these values are currently of character type. The following example illustrates how to convert the character variables to SAS date and time values, and how to combine them in a single datetime value.

This conversion uses the INPUT() function to convert from character to date and time format. For example, to convert the DATEARRIVED variable:

```
DATEARRIVED2=INPUT(TRIM(DATEARRIVED),MMDDYY10.);
```

The new (converted) variable must have a new name. In this case DATEARRIVED2 as you cannot convert a variable to a different type and keep the same name. In this conversion, the DATEARRIVED text value is first trimmed using the TRIM() function. The resulting trimmed text value is then converted in the INPUT) () function using the informat MMDDYY10. and stored in the new variable named DATEARRIVED2.

The TIME value is a little trickier. Because the text value for TIME includes AM or PM, this information must be stripped off before it can be converted. To do this, the blank before the AM or PM is located using the FIND() function:

```
I= FIND(TIMEARRIVE," ");
```

However, you want to know if TIME was PM or AM because that information is needed to convert TIME to 24-h style (military-type) time. Therefore, perform a second FIND and look for P as that will uniquely indicate PM. Use this code:

```
P= FIND(TIMEARRIVE,"P");
```

If P is greater than 0, then a P is present in the statement, and you know that the time represents a time value after noon. Otherwise, the time represents a time before noon (AM).

The result of these two FIND() functions is a value for I representing the location of the blank before AM or PM and P representing whether the time is before or after noon.

The I value is used with a SUBSTR() function to extract a sub-string that contains only the time information:

```
TIMEARRIVE=SUBSTR(TIMEARRIVE,1,I-1);
```

Use an INPUT() function converting the resulting text value for TIMEARRIVE to a new DATE-type variable called TIMEARRIVET by applying the time format TIME8.

```
TIMEARRIVET=INPUT(TRIM(TIMEARRIVE),TIME8.);
```

You're not finished yet! Because time is recorded as AM or PM, you may need to adjust the time. If the time is in the afternoon (if P=1), you want to add 12 hours to the recorded time value. Because the time value is in seconds, you calculate that the number of seconds in 12 hours is $12 \times 60 \times 60 = 43,200$, so the conversion statement is

```
IF P>0 THEN TIMELEFTT=TIMELEFTT+43200;
```

Finally, the DHMS() function is used to combine the date and time values using the code:

```
ARRIVEDT=DHMS(DATEARRIVED2,0,0,TIMEARRIVET)
```

The arguments for the DHMS() function are DATE, HOUR, MINUTE, and SECONDS. In this case, we use

- DATEARRIVED2 as the DATE value
- TIMEARRIVET as the SECONDS value
- Because the seconds incorporate hours and minutes, we enter 0 for the HOUR and 0 for the MINUTE arguments.

Appropriate formats are also used so that date and time values are displayed appropriately. Unneeded variables are dropped. The following example illustrates how this is done.

HANDS-ON EXAMPLE

This example corrects problems associated with numeric variables.

1. Open the program file MESSY5.SAS and observe the code after the Part 5 comment.

```
FORMAT ARRIVEDT DATETIME18.;
DATEARRIVED2=INPUT(TRIM(DATEARRIVED),MMDDYY10.);
I= FIND(TIMEARRIVE," ");
P=FIND(TIMEARRIVE,"P");
TIMEARRIVE=SUBSTR(TIMEARRIVE,1,I-1);
TIMEARRIVET=INPUT(TRIM(TIMEARRIVE),TIME8.);
IF P>0 AND TIMEARRIVET LT 43200 THEN TIMEARRIVET=TIMEARRIVET
+43200;
ARRIVEDT=DHMS(DATEARRIVED2,0,0,TIMEARRIVET) ;
Label ARRIVEDT="Date & Time Arrived";
```

   Submit this code and observe the output in Table 6.13.
   Table 6.13 shows relevant variables for the first few converted records. Note that the original values are left justified in the cell, indicating text values and the converted values are right justified indicating numbers/dates. The ARRIVALDT (Date & Time Arrived) value includes the combined date and time values. Also note that the time arrived for the second observation, which was 1:23 PM was converted to the 24-h time 13:23.

TABLE 6.13   Converting Date and Time Values

Obs	Subject ID	Date Arrived	Time Arrived	DATEARRIVED2	TIMEARRIVET	Date & Time Arrived
1	00001	2/7/2005	11:18:00 A	07FEB2005	11:18:00	07FEB05:11:18:00
2	00002	3/10/2005	1:23:00 PM	10MAR2005	13:23:00	10MAR05:13:23:00
3	00003	3/2/2005	1:08:00 PM	02MAR2005	13:08:00	02MAR05:13:08:00
4	00004	5/2/2005	11:46:00 A	02MAY2005	11:46:00	02MAY05:11:46:00
5	00005	1/31/2005	12:09:00 P	31JAN2005	24:09:00	01FEB05:00:09:00
6	00006	2/1/2005	2:27:00 PM	01FEB2005	14:27:00	01FEB05:14:27:00
7	00007	2/3/2005	11:50:00 A	03FEB2005	11:50:00	03FEB05:11:50:00
8	00008	2/4/2005	10:47:00 A	04FEB2005	10:47:00	04FEB05:10:47:00
9	00009	2/5/2005	11:42:00 A	05FEB2005	11:42:00	05FEB05:11:42:00

2. Using the conversion code used to convert DATEARRIVED and TIMEARRIVE, perform a similar conversion for DATELEFT and TIMELEFT. Name the final variable LEFTDT and add a LABEL statement to label the new value "Date & Time Left." Submit the code and verify that the correct changes have been made.

3. Once you have times for arrival and departure, you can calculate how long a subject stayed in the clinic. Enter this code, using the INTCK function with a "MINUTES" argument

```
STAYMINUTES=INTCK( 'MIN', ARRIVEDT, LEFTDT );
```

And then divide by 60 and round it off to get the number of hours stayed in the clinic:

```
STAYHOURS=ROUND(STAYMINUTES/60,.1);
```

4. Add STAYHOURS to the PROC PRINT VAR list. Submit the code and observe the results in Table 6.14.

TABLE 6.14   Calculating Time Stayed in Clinic

Obs	Subject ID	Date Arrived	Time Arrived	DATEARRIVED2	TIMEARRIVET	Date & Time Arrived	Date & Time Left
1	00001	2/7/2005	11:18:00	07FEB2005	11:18:00	07FEB05:11:18:00	07FEB05:14:15:00
2	00002	3/10/2005	1:23:00	10MAR2005	13:23:00	10MAR05:13:23:00	11MAR05:12:40:00
3	00003	3/2/2005	1:08:00	02MAR2005	13:08:00	02MAR05:13:08:00	02MAR05:17:07:00
4	00004	5/2/2005	11:46:00	02MAY2005	11:46:00	02MAY05:11:46:00	02MAY05:21:45:00
5	00005	1/31/2005	12:09:00	31JAN2005	12:09:00	01FEB05:00:09:00	01FEB05:01:30:00
6	00006	2/1/2005	2:27:00	01FEB2005	14:27:00	01FEB05:14:27:00	01FEB05:14:40:00
7	00007	2/3/2005	11:50:00	03FEB2005	11:50:00	03FEB05:11:50:00	03FEB05:21:08:00
8	00008	2/4/2005	10:47:00	04FEB2005	10:47:00	04FEB05:10:47:00	.
9	00009	2/5/2005	11:42:00	05FEB2005	11:42:00	05FEB05:11:42:00	06FEB05:00:51:00
10	00010	1/30/2005	12:53:00	30JAN2005	12:53:00	31JAN05:00:53:00	30JAN05:23:40:00
11	00011	2/6/2005	9:22:00	06FEB2005	9:22:00	06FEB05:09:22:00	06FEB05:14:40:00
12	00012	1/30/2005	2:30:00	30JAN2005	2:30:00	30JAN05:02:30:00	.
13	00013	2/6/2005	7:10:00	06FEB2005	7:10:00	06FEB05:07:10:00	07FEB06:12:20:00
14	00014	2/6/2005	9:35:00	06FEB2005	9:35:00	06FEB05:09:35:00	06FEB05:19:25:00

(continued)

(continued)

Note that some STAYHOURS are negative and (if you look at more of the output) some values are very large – both positive and negative. It is obvious that some of the dates and times were entered incorrectly. For example, in observation 13, the time left is more than a year after arrival.

If possible you could check original records to reconcile the values. For this exercise, set any negative STAYHOURS or any values greater than 48-h to missing using this code:

```
IF STAYHOURS<0 or STAYHOURS>48 then STAYHOURS=.;
```

Resubmit the program and observe the results.

6.4.6   Looking for Duplicate Records

A final check for this data set is to determine if there are duplicate records. Typically, this is accomplished by looking for duplicate IDs. A simple way to do this is with PROC FREQ. This final example for this section illustrates this process.

HANDS-ON EXAMPLE

This example shows how to find and correct duplicate records.

1. Open the program file DISCOVER3.SAS and observe the code. A PROC FREQ is performed on the ID (in this case, the variable SUBJECT). The results are stored in a file named FREQCNT (using the statement OUT=FREQCNT). The NOPRINT tells SAS not to display the frequency table, which might be very large. Finally, the PROC PRINT displays only records where COUNT is 2 or more.

```
PROC FREQ data=MYSASLIB.cleaned NOPRINT;
    TABLES SUBJECT / OUT=FREQCNT;
RUN;
PROC PRINT DATA=FREQCNT;
WHERE COUNT>1;
RUN;
```

Submit this code and observe the results in Table 6.15. Subject ID=26 is used for two records.

TABLE 6.15   Discovering Duplicate IDs

Obs	SUBJECT	COUNT	PERCENT
26	00026	2	2.53165

2. Add this code to DISCOVER3.SAS to list only records were SUBJECT=26.

```
PROC PRINT DATA=MYSASLIB.CLEANED;
    WHERE FIND(SUBJECT,"0026");
RUN;
```

```
An alternative method that accomplishes the same thing is
PROC PRINT DATA=MYSASLIB.CLEANED;
   WHERE COMPRESS(SUBJECT)='00026';
RUN;
```

The first method uses the FIND function to locate the string '0026' in the SUBJECT variable. The second method removes all blanks from SUBJECT using the COMPESS() function and then looks for an exact matches to '00026'. Choose one of these options, enter it into the code, submit the updated code, and observe the results in Table 6.16. (Partial results are shown.) Note that the SUBJECT records 26 are together. Using this Information you may be able to refer to original records to find that the second observation should be SUBJECT=27.

To correct the problem, add this code to the end of your edited MESSY5.SAS that changes the value of SUBJECT to 27 on record number _N_=27.

```
IF _N_=27 THEN SUBJECT=27;
```

Run the code to complete the exercise.

TABLE 6.16   Discovering Observation Number for Supplicate IDs

Obs	SUBJECT	DateArrived	TimeArrive	DateLeft	TimeLeft	Single	Gender
26	00026	1/25/2005	10:29:00 A	1/25/2005	11:30:00 PM	0	M
27	00026	1/25/2005	2:52:00 PM	1/26/2005	12:30:00 AM	0	F

A final version of the code is in the file MESSY_ALL.SAS. When working with a new data set, this type of code is a typical example of what you will need to do before you use the data to create any reports or perform any statistical analysis.

6.4.7   Cleaning a Data Set: Summary

This case study illustrated typical steps for correcting problems in a messy data set. (And almost every real-world data set is messy.) Every data set is different, and there are multiple ways to perform each of the tasks shown in this example, so don't limit yourself to these procedures only.

Although this process of cleaning a data set can be tedious and time consuming, spending some time cleaning your data can increase your chances of getting more reliable and meaningful results. In summary, use these steps as a guideline whenever you get a data set to analyze:

1. After importing or receiving a data set, create an initial report and visually inspect the data set for obvious problems. Correct any obvious problems using the procedures listed below (but they do not have to be in this order).
2. Rename variables that have strange or unclear names.

3. Label your variables. This will help prevent confusion and will result in more readable output.

4. Fix case problems by converting case in all text categories to all upper case (or all lower case).

5. Delete any unneeded records.

6. Use PROC FREQ to discover if there are inappropriate values present in categorical variables. Either fix or replace the inappropriate values or set these values as missing values.

7. Check for and correct any duplicated variables.

8. Use PROC MEANS (or PROC UNIVARIATE) to check for unusual minimum or maximum values in numeric variables. Either fix/replace any incorrect values or set the values to missing.

9. For all variables with known missing value codes, set those missing value codes to SAS missing dot (.) or blank.

10. Convert any variables that are not in a correct format to an appropriate format.

11. Separate information that is initially contained in a single variable (i.e., convert 120/80 blood pressure to two separate variables) or combine variables that need to be combined (i.e., date and time to datetime).

12. Search for and reconcile any duplicate records.

Although these steps do not cover all problems concerning messy data set, they go a long way to cleaning up messy information to make your data more accurate and (hopefully) more reliable.

6.5 SUMMARY

This chapter provides additional information on common programming topics for the SAS language. The subjects covered are not exhaustive but were selected because they are often used for preparing data for analysis. Many more topics could have been covered, and readers are encouraged to refer to the SAS documentation for additional information.

EXERCISES

6.1 Using PROC TRANSPOSE.

Use PROC TRANSPOSE to summarize multiple records.

Using DTRANSPOSE2.SAS as an example, complete the program below (EX_6.1.SAS). The purpose of this program is to expand the AMOUNTOWED values onto one line for each ID, then to sum the rows and display the results. Use the following guidelines:

- Name the output file created by PROC TRANSPOSE as EXPANDED.
- Use AMT as the prefix to the expanded variable.
- Expand on the variable AMOUNTOWED.
- Expand by ID.

```
DATA OWED;
INPUT ID $3. AMOUNTOWED DOLLAR9.;
DATALINES;
001 $3,209
002 $29
002 $34.95
003 2,012
003 312.45
003 34.23
004 2,312
004 $3.92
005 .98
;
RUN;
PROC TRANSPOSE DATA=OWED OUT=_____ PREFIX=____;
    BY ___;
    VAR _____;
RUN;
DATA SUMMARIZE;SET EXPANDED;
TOTAL=SUM(of AMT1-AMT3);
DROP _NAME_;
RUN;
PROC PRINT DATA=SUMMARIZE;
RUN;
```

Your output should look like Table 6.17.

a. In the DATA SUMMARIZE data step, include the statement

```
FORMAT TOTAL DOLLAR9.2;
```

Rerun the program. How does that change the results?

b. Note that SUM (of list of variables) summed the data and ignored missing values. Change the TOTAL= statement to

```
TOTAL = AMT1+AMT2+AMT3;
```

Rerun the program. What are the differences in the answers?

TABLE 6.17   Listing of Transposed Data

Obs	ID	AMT1	AMT2	AMT3	TOTAL
1	001	3209.00	.	.	3209.00
2	002	29.00	34.95	.	63.95
3	003	2012.00	312.45	34.23	2358.68
4	004	2312.00	3.92	.	2315.92
5	005	0.98	.	.	0.98

6.2 **Using SELECT.**

Using the WOUND data set, recode the variable AGE to a new variable named AGEGP using the SELECT statement and the following criteria:

```
Age LE 4 - Toddler
Age GT 4 and LE 12 - Child
Age GT 12 and LE 18 - Teen
Age GT 18 - Adult
```

Here is a start to the SAS program to do this:

```
DATA NEW; SET MYSASLIB.WOUND;
    SELECT  ;
*recode AGE to AGEGP in code here;
    END;
RUN;
```

6.3 **Cleaning a messy data set.**

Using the SAS data file SOMEMISS, do the following to correct some problems and save the results in a SAS data file named FIXMISS:

a. Discover problems with GENDER and fix them. Replace any obvious bad data with missing data values.

b. Discover problems with AGE and replace any obvious bad data with missing values, and create a numeric variable named AGEN.

7

SAS® ADVANCED PROGRAMMING TOPICS PART 2

LEARNING OBJECTIVES

- To be able to create and use arrays
- To be able to use DO loops
- To be able to use the RETAIN statement
- To be able to create and use SAS macro variables
- To be able to create and use SAS macro routines

This chapter continues with the presentation of topics that are useful in preparing a data set for analysis. The topics here are designed to provide greater flexibility in constructing SAS programs. Using these techniques can simplify coding for tasks that involve repeated or related observations.

7.1 USING SAS ARRAYS

A SAS ARRAY statement provides a method for placing a series of observations into a single variable called an array. Often these variables are referenced as part of a DO loop, which is a technique for iterating through a set of data. (DO loops are presented in the following section of this chapter.) A simplified syntax for SAS arrays is the following:

```
ARRAY ARRAY-NAME(SUBSCRIPT) <$> ARRAY-VALUES
```

SAS® *Essentials: Mastering SAS for Data Analytics*, Second Edition. Alan C. Elliott and Wayne A. Woodward.
© 2016 John Wiley & Sons, Inc. Published 2016 by John Wiley & Sons, Inc.

One-dimensional arrays are specified with an `ARRAY` statement, such as

```
ARRAY TIME(1:6) TIME1-TIME6;
```

This `ARRAY` statement creates a one-dimensional array called `TIME1` with an index value indicated in a parenthesis so `TIME(1)=TIME1, TIME(2)=TIME2`, and so on. In this case, six values are assigned to the values `TIME(1)` through `TIME(6)`. Here are some more ways to create an `ARRAY`:

```
ARRAY TIME(6) TIME1-TIME6;
```

The result is the same as the previous example.

```
ARRAY TIME(0:5) A B C D E F;
```

`TIME(0)=A, TIME(1)=B`, and so on. Note that in this case, the index begins with a 0 instead of 1, because the initial definition of the array size in the parentheses (0:5) specified a beginning and end for the index values.

```
ARRAY ANSWER(*) Q1-Q50;
```

`ANSWER(1)=Q1, ANSWER(2)=Q2`, and so on. In this example, the size of the array is not specified. Instead it is indicated as (*). SAS figures out how many items are being assigned to the array and makes it the required size.

```
ARRAY ANSWER(1:5) $ Q1-Q5;
```

where Q1–Q5 are text values. Text arrays are created in the same way as numeric arrays but with text values. The $ after the array definition indicates to SAS that the array is of character type.

```
ARRAY VALUE[5] (2 4 6 8 10);
```

Specifies actual values for the array where `VALUE(1)=2, VALUE(2)=4`, and so on. Note the difference here is that the values are within parentheses (you can use [], {}, or () for brackets in the `ARRAY` statement); similarly, the expression

```
ARRAY ABC[5];
```

When no values or variables are given, SAS creates the variables based on the array name: `ABC1, ABC2`, and so on, and their initial values are missing values.

```
ARRAY FRUIT[3] $10 ("apple" "orange" "lemon");
```

Specifies actual character values of the `FRUIT` array as text values. The $10 specifies that the items in the array are character, and that the maximum number of characters for each item in the array is 10.

```
ARRAY DRINKSIZE[*] SMALL REGULAR LARGE MEGA (8, 16, 24, 32);
Or
ARRAY CUPSIZE[*] CUP1-CUP4 (8, 16, 24, 32);
```

Specifies initial values for the items in an array. In the first example, DRINKSIZE(1) equals SMALL equals 8. In the second example, CUPSIZE(1) is equal to CUP1 is equal to 8.

7.1.1   Referring to Values in an Array

Once an array is created (such as TIME[1:6]), you can refer to a value in the array by specifying an index value, and use that value in any common SAS statement. For example,

```
NEWVAL=(TIME[5]/365);
```

This expression uses the value of TIME at index 5 in the calculation.

When using (*) in a array specification, as in

```
ARRAY TIME(*) TIME1-TIME6;
```

you may not know the value of the largest index. You can access these values using SAS functions. In this case, the upper bound is set to the value DIM(arrayname) or DIM(TIME), which is 6. Moreover, the function LBOUND(arrayname) represents the lowest index in the specified array and HBOUND(arrayname) represents the highest index.

Once you create an array, you'll want to access the values in the array. It should be clear in the above example that to refer to TIME1, you could use TIME(1) and to refer to TIME4 you could use TIME(4). In other words, use the original variable name or the corresponding indexed array value. The following example illustrates how to refer to values of an array when using a SAS function.

HANDS-ON EXAMPLE

1. Open the program file DARRAY1.SAS.

```
DATA A;
INPUT ONE TWO THREE FOUR;
ARRAY T(4) ONE TWO THREE FOUR;
TSUM1=SUM(OF ONE TWO THREE FOUR);
TSUM2=SUM(OF T(1) T(2) T(3) T(4));
TSUM3=SUM(OF T(*));
DATALINES;
1 2 3 4
5 6 7 8
;
RUN;
PROC PRINT DATA=A;RUN;
```

(continued)

(continued)

2. Submit this code and observe the results in Table 7.1.

TABLE 7.1   Values in an Array

Example of using an ARRAY

Obs	ONE	TWO	THREE	FOUR	TSUM1	TSUM2	TSUM3
1	1	2	3	4	10	10	10
2	5	6	7	8	26	26	26

Note that all three versions of the SUM() function yield the same answer. They calculate the sum of the values in the T() array. Look at the three references to SUM. This code illustrates that when referring to values in an array, you can use the variable's original (ONE TWO THREE FOUR) or the indexed array names (T(1) T(2) t(3) T(4)) to mean the same thing. The T(*) reference is a shortcut way to represent all of the T() array elements.

3. Change the functions in the code from SUM to MEDIAN and the variable names from TSUM1-TSUM3 to MED1-MED3. Resubmit and observe the results. You should get the same answers for all three versions of the MEDIAN() function.

4. Another interesting function to try is the CAT function, which concatenates values. (See Appendix B for more information about this function.) Change the function in the example from MEDIAN to CAT and the variable names to CAT1-CAT3. Resubmit and observe the results. Note that in this case, the resulting values CAT1-CAT3 are character variables.

There are a number of tasks that are made easier when using arrays. One example is searching the contents of an array for a specific number or text value. This is accomplished with an IN statement. For example, the statement

```
IF 3 IN MYARRAY THEN some expression;
```

performs the expression when there is a 3 somewhere in the array named MYARRAY.

HANDS-ON EXAMPLE

As an example illustrating the use of the IN statement, do the following example.

1. Open the program file DARRAY2.SAS.

```
DATA B;
FORMAT ONE TWO THREE FOUR $10.;
INPUT ONE $ TWO $ THREE $ FOUR $;
ARRAY FRUIT(4) ONE TWO THREE FOUR;
IF "ORANGE" IN FRUIT THEN ISORANGE=1;ELSE ISORANGE=0;
```

```
DATALINES;
APPLE ORANGE PINEAPPLE APRICOT
LEMON APPLE KIWI STRAWBERRY
;
RUN;
PROC PRINT DATA=B;
RUN;
```

2. Submit the code and observe the results in Table 7.2.

   Note that the array FRUIT contains the word ORANGE in observation 1, so the variable ISORANGE takes on the value 1. If there is no ORANGE fruit in the list, ISORANGE=0;

3. Change the IF statement to

```
IF "ORA" IN FRUIT then ISORANGE1;ELSE ISORANGE=0;
```

   How does that change the answer? Does the IN statement find a partial word?

TABLE 7.2   Example Using the IN Statement with an Array

Example of using an ARRAY

Obs	ONE	TWO	THREE	FOUR	ISORANGE
1	APPLE	ORANGE	PINEAPPLE	APRICOT	1
2	LEMON	APPLE	KIWI	STRAWBERRY	0

7.2   USING DO LOOPS

The DO statement is a way to control the flow of your program. These are the varieties of DO loops available in SAS:

1. IF and DO: Use a DO in an IF statement to cause a group of statements to be conditionally executed.
2. Iterative DO loop: Iterate through a series of statements based on some incremental index.
3. DO UNTIL: Execute a group of statements until some condition is met.
4. DO WHILE: Execute a group of statements as long as specified condition is true.

The IF and DO combination statement has been briefly discussed in Chapter 4. The primary DO statement discussed in this chapter is the iterative DO loop. An iterative DO loop is a way of incrementing through series of statements based on some index. A simplified syntax of an iterative DO loop is as follows:

```
DO indexvariable=initialvalue to endvalue <by incrementvalue>;
. . . SAS statements . . .
END;
```

For example, consider the SAS code that follows. In this case, the index variable is ILOOP (choose any legitimate SAS variable name that is not being used for another purpose within your SAS program), and the initial value of ILOOP is 1. The last referenced value is 4, and the implied increment value is 1. (You can optionally specify a different increment value.)

```
SUM=0;
DO ILOOP=1 to 4;
   SUM=SUM+ILOOP;
END;
```

Here is how to follow the action of this code: The value of SUM is initially set to 0. In the DO loop, the index ILOOP is first set to the initial value 1. The following code is executed:

```
SUM=0+1;
```

When the code encounters the END statement, ILOOP is incremented by 1 (the increment value) and the flow of the program goes back to the DO statement. As long as the index is not greater than the end value, another pass through the loop is performed. Once ILOOP is greater than 4, the loop stops. In that case, the process yields the following statements:

```
SUM=0;
SUM=0+1;
SUM=1+2;
SUM=3+3;
SUM=6+4;
```

The final value of SUM at the end of the loop is 10.

In a DO UNTIL loop, the increment is replaced with an UNTIL clause with (ILOOP GT 4) in parentheses. For example,

```
ILOOP=1;
SUM=0;
DO UNTIL (ILOOP GT 4);
     SUM=SUM+ILOOP;
ILOOP+1;
END;
```

This code is similar to the previous example except the user now has direct control of the variable ILOOP. It is initially set to one and then incremented by 1 (ILOOP+1) during the loop. The loop continues until ILOOP is greater than 4. The results are the same as in the previous example.

In DO WHILE, the loop continues until the condition is no longer true. Once it is false, the loop stops. For example, the following code results in the same loop as the two previous examples.

```
ILOOP=1;
SUM=0;
DO WHILE(ILOOP LT 5);
      SUM=SUM+ILOOP;
ILOOP+1;
END;
```

HANDS-ON EXAMPLE

This program illustrates the uses of the DO WHILE loop.

1. Open the program file DWHILE.SAS.

```
DATA TMP;
N=0;
SQUARESUM=0;
DO WHILE(N<5);
   SQUARESUM=SQUARESUM+N**2; OUTPUT;
   N+1;
END;
RUN;
PROC PRINT;
RUN;
```

   The OUTPUT statement in the code causes SAS to save each SQUARESUM as a record in the data set TMP so you'll see the values at each iteration.
2. Run the program and observe the output data set given in Table 7.3. Why do the values of N range from 0 to 4?
3. Change the code to use a DO UNTIL to get the same results.
4. Change the code to use an iterative DO loop to get the same results.

TABLE 7.3   Example of Using
the DO WHILE Statement

Obs	N	SQUARESUM
1	0	0
2	1	1
3	2	5
4	3	14
5	4	30

   One of the most powerful uses of the DO loop is realized when it is used in conjunction with an array. For example, suppose you take five systolic blood pressure readings on each subject. Suppose that if any of these readings is above 140, you want to classify the subject with the value HIGHBP=1, or else the subject will have the value HIGHBP=0. The following code could perform that task:

```
DATA PRESSURE;SET MEDDATA;
ARRAY SBP(5) READING1-READING5;
HIGHBP=0;
DO I=1 TO 5;
     IF SBP(I) GT 140 THEN HIGHBP=1;
END;
```

- The ARRAY statement sets up an array named SBP that contains the values of the variables READING1 through READING5.
- In the DO statement, the variable I iteratively takes on the values from 1 to 5.
- Within the DO loop, if any of the five readings is greater than (GT) 140, the variable HIGHBP is set to 1. Otherwise, the value of HIGHBP for that subject remains at 0.

Once the value of HIGHB takes on the value 1, there is no way for it to be set back to 0 within the same loop. Therefore, for each record HIGHBP starts out at 0 and when changed within the loop, it doesn't get reset to 0 until the next record in the data set it read.

For another example, suppose you have a questionnaire in which the variables (answers) are named Q1 to Q50 and the answers recorded are YES, NO. Missing answers were originally coded in the data set as NA. Suppose you want to change these values to the value " " (two quote marks together representing a blank, which is typically a missing value for a character variable). Using an array and a DO loop, you can quickly perform this task within a DATA step.

```
DATA NEW;SET OLD;
ARRAY ANSWER(1:50) $ Q1-Q50;
DO I=1 TO 50;
     IF ANSWER(I)="NA" then ANSWER(I)="";
END;
```

- The ARRAY statement sets up an array named ANSWER that contains the text values of the variables Q1–Q50.
- The DO statement begins a loop wherein the variable I iteratively takes on the values from 1 to 50. The DO loop ends with the END statement.
- Within the DO loop, the IF statement is performed 50 times, each time with a different value of ANSWER(I) representing the different values of Q1, Q2, and so on.
- Thus, for the first subject, each of the 50 questions is examined. If an answer is "NA" it is recoded with value " ".

```
IF ANSWER(1)="NA" THEN ANSWER(1)="";
```

which can be interpreted as

  IF Q1 has an answer NA, then recode Q1 as " ".

In a similar way, if your answers are numeric, 1=Yes, 0=No, and −9=Missing, then you could use the following code to set all −9 missing values to the standard SAS missing value code dot (.). In this case, note that the variables Q1-Q50 are numeric.

```
DATA NEW;SET OLD;
ARRAY ANSWER(1:50)Q1-Q50;
```

```
DO I=1 to 50;
     IF ANSWER(I)= -9 then ANSWER(I)=.;
END;
```

HANDS-ON EXAMPLE

This example illustrates how to use ARRAYs and DO loops in a SAS program. Suppose you have a record of a measure taken on subjects who repeatedly came to a clinic. However, the number of times they came was not the same for each patient. You want to know the value of the measurement (any non-missing value) observed the last time a subject was in the office.

1. Open the program file DDOLOOP.SAS.

```
DATA CLINIC;
INPUT @1 ID $3. @4 VISIT1 4. @7 VISIT2 4.
      @10 VISIT3 4. @13 VISIT4 4. @16 VISIT5 4.;
ARRAY TIME (5) VISIT1-VISIT5;
LAST=VISIT1;
DO I=1 TO 5;
   IF TIME(I) > 0 THEN LAST=TIME(I);
END;
DROP I;
DATALINES;
001 34 54 34 54 65
002 23 43 54 34
003 23 43 .  43
004 45 55 21 43 23
005 54
;
PROC PRINT DATA=CLINIC; RUN;
```

2. Run this program and observe the output in Table 7.4. Note that the variable LAST contains the value of the observation for the last "good" value from the list of visits.

3. If you also want to know the number of times a value was recorded for each subject, then put the following statement, using the N() function, in the DATA step to get that value. Resubmit the code. You should have a new column containing the number of visits.

```
NUMVISITS=N(OF TIME(*));
```

4. In the same way, use the MAX function to find the maximum value for each subject. Resubmit the code and observe the results.

```
MAXVISITS=MAX(OF TIME(*));
```

(continued)

(continued)

TABLE 7.4 Example of ARRAYs and DO Loops

Illustrates the use of DO LOOPS and ARRAYS

Obs	ID	VISIT1	VISIT2	VISIT3	VISIT4	VISIT5	LAST
1	001	34	54	34	54	65	65
2	002	23	43	54	34	.	34
3	003	23	43	.	43	.	43
4	004	45	55	21	43	23	23
5	005	54	.	.	.	.	54

HANDS-ON EXAMPLE

This example illustrates the use of a DO loop when you don't know the lower and upper bounds of an array. The data set used is a report of crimes in Washington, DC, between the years 1978 and 2007. The code converts the raw incident values into a percentage (incident/population × 100.)

1. Open the program file DARRAY3.SAS.

```
DATA CRIME;SET MYSASLIB.DC_CRIME78_07;
FORMAT TOTAL 6.;
ARRAY INCIDENTS(*) VIOLENT-CARTHEFT;
DO I= LBOUND(INCIDENTS) to HBOUND(INCIDENTS);
      TOTAL=SUM(of TOTAL,INCIDENTS(i));
END;
DROP I;
RUN;
PROC PRINT DATA=CRIME;
VAR YEAR POP-CARTHEFT TOTAL;
RUN;
```

Note in this code that the array named INCIDENTS uses (*) instead of a fixed number of elements. That is, we don't specify in the code how many variables are included in the list VIOLENT – CARTHEFT. Even though we don't know the bounds of the INCIDENTS array, we can still increment over the entire list by using the LBOUND and HBOUND functions in the DO loop.

Submit this code and observe the results. Notice in the displayed results that the large numbers are shown without commas.

2. You want to also find the total number of crimes per year, and the percentage of crimes by population.

```
TOTALCRIMES=SUM(of INCIDENTS(*));
PCTTOTAL=TOTALCRIMES/POP*100;
```

TABLE 7.5   Results of Using LBOUND and HBOUND in a DO Loop

Obs	Year	POP	Index	Violent	Property	Murder	Rape	Robbery	Assault	Burglary	Larceny	CarTheft	TOTALCRIMES	PCTTOTAL
1	1978	674000	50950	9515	41435	189	447	6333	2546	12497	25744	3194	101,900	15.1187
2	1979	656000	56430	10553	45877	180	489	6920	2964	13452	28819	3606	112,860	17.2043
3	1980	635233	63668	12772	50896	200	439	8897	3236	16260	31068	3568	127,336	20.0456
4	1981	636000	67910	14468	53442	223	414	10399	3432	16832	32845	3765	135,820	21.3553
5	1982	631000	65692	13397	52295	194	421	9137	3645	14774	33435	4086	131,384	20.8216
6	1983	623000	57776	11933	45843	183	406	7698	3646	12483	29405	3955	115,552	18.5477
7	1984	623000	63624	10726	42799	175	366	6087	4097	10954	27471	4374	107,048	17.1827
8	1985	626000	50075	10171	39904	147	337	5230	4457	10005	24874	5025	100,150	15.9984
9	1986	626000	52204	9423	42781	194	328	4720	4181	10815	25861	6105	104,408	16.6786
10	1987	622000	52569	10016	42553	225	245	4462	5084	11244	25012	6297	105,138	16.9032
11	1988	620000	61471	11914	49557	369	165	5690	5690	12300	28624	8633	122,942	19.8294
12	1989	604000	62172	12937	49235	434	186	6542	5775	11780	29164	8291	124,344	20.5868

Add these statements to the code. The trick is where to put these statements. As they use the array INCIDENTS, they must come *after* the ARRAY statement. However, they do not need to be within the DO loop. Put these lines in the proper location in the code. Moreover, add TOTALCRIMES and PCTTOTAL to the VAR statement. Submit the code and observe the results.

3. Change TOTALCRIMES format so that it includes commas by including the statement

```
FORMAT TOTALCRIMES COMMA10.;
```

on a program line before you do the TOTALCRIMES calculation. Change the PROC PRINT code in the VAR statement to

```
VAR YEAR POP--CARTHEFT TOTALCRIMES PCTTOTAL;
```

Submit the code and observe the results in Table 7.5. You should see that the TOTALCRIMES column values are now formatted with commas.

7.3   USING THE RETAIN STATEMENT

The RETAIN statement, used in a DATA step, allows you to retain values of a variable across iterations as data records are read into the data set. The basic syntax for RETAIN is as follows:

```
RETAIN <var <initial-value(s) > var2 <initial-values(s) > and so on;
```

For example, to instruct SAS to remember the value of the variable SCORE, you would use the statement

```
RETAIN SCORE;
```

A statement that retains the values of several variables could be

```
RETAIN TIME1-TIME10 SCORE VISITDATE;
```

By default, the initial value of retained variables is missing. A statement to retain the value of SCORE, with an initial value of 1, is

```
RETAIN SCORE 1;
```

In the following instance, CATEGORY has an initial value of NONE and variables TIME1-TIME10 have initial values of 0.

```
RETAIN CATEGORY "NONE" TIME1-TIME10 0;
```

To set the values of a list, use this format:

```
RETAIN TIME1-TIME4   (1 2 3 4);
```

or

```
RETAIN TIME1-TIME4   (1, 2, 3, 4);
```

or

```
RETAIN TIME1-TIME4   (1:4);
```

To retain the values of all variables, use

```
RETAIN _ALL_;
```

You may also set a value of a variable before you initiate the RETAIN, then the initial value becomes the current value of that variable.

For example, suppose you have a sequence of observations that includes a date variable and you want to calculate the number of days since the first date. One way to do that is with the RETAIN statement. Assuming the data are sorted by date, consider the following code:

```
DATA DAYS;SET MYDATA;
IF _N_=1 THEN FIRST=VISIT_DATE;
RETAIN FIRST;
DAYS=VISIT_DATE-FIRST;
```

- The IF _N_=1 statement creates a new variable called FIRST and sets the initial value of FIRST to the value of VISIT_DATE in the first record.
- The RETAIN statement tells SAS to keep the value of FIRST as it was read from the previous record (otherwise it will be missing).
- The DAYS= statement uses the FIRST variable to calculate a difference between the current record's VISIT_DATE value and FIRST, giving you the number of days since the first visit.

HANDS-ON EXAMPLE

This example calculates the number of days since the first visit.

1. Open the program file DRETAIN1.SAS.

```
DATA MYDATA;
INPUT VISIT_DATE ANYDTDTE10.;
DATALINES;
01/04/2015
01/29/2015
03/07/2015
04/25/2015
07/06/2015
08/30/2015
;
DATA DAYS;SET MYDATA;
IF _N_=1 THEN FIRST=VISIT_DATE;
RETAIN FIRST;
DAYS=VISIT_DATE-FIRST;
RUN;
PROC PRINT DATA=DAYS;
Title 'These are the contents of the dataset DAYS';
FORMAT VISIT_DATE FIRST DATE10.;
RUN;
```

2. Run this example and observe the output in Table 7.6.
3. Remove the RETAIN statement and rerun the program. Note that the variable FIRST loses its value after the first iteration, and the variable DAYS has a missing value for all records after the first record.

TABLE 7.6   Results of Calculation Using the RETAIN Statement

These are the contents of the dataset DAYS

Obs	VISIT_DATE	FIRST	DAYS
1	04JAN2015	04JAN2015	0
2	29JAN2015	04JAN2015	25
3	07MAR2015	04JAN2015	62
4	25APR2015	04JAN2015	111
5	06JUL2015	04JAN2015	183
6	30AUG2015	04JAN2015	238

As a second example of the use of the RETAIN statement, suppose you have a lemonade kiosk at an outdoor mall. You have data for the first 7 days of sales, and you want to create a report that provides the accumulated sales and also keeps track of the maximum sales you've had. The following example illustrates how you could do this using the RETAIN statement. The following code contains the sales data for the lemonade kiosk and a code to calculate the desired values.

```
DATA LEMON;
INPUT DAY SALES;
IF _N_=1 then DO; TOTAL=0; END;
RETAIN TOTAL MAX;
TOTAL=SALES+TOTAL;
IF SALES>MAX then MAX=SALES;
```

Examine this code and note the statement that accumulates the sum:

```
TOTAL=SALES+TOTAL;
```

and the statement that sets MAX to the largest observed values.

```
IF SALES>MAX then MAX=SALES;
```

To illustrate how this program is using the RETAIN statement, do the following example:

HANDS-ON EXAMPLE

This example illustrates the RETAIN statement for accumulating data and identifying minimum and maximum.

1. Open the program file DRETAIN2.SAS.

```
DATA LEMON;
INPUT DAY SALES;
IF _N_=1 THEN TOTAL=0;
RETAIN TOTAL MAX;
TOTAL=SALES+TOTAL;
IF SALES>MAX then MAX=SALES;
DATALINES;
1 23.40
2 32.50
3 19.80
4 55.55
5 34.90
6 65.30
7 33.40
;
RUN;
PROC PRINT DATA=LEMON;RUN;
```

Submit the code and verify that you get the output given in Table 7.7.

2. Comment out the RETAIN statement and resubmit the program. How does this change the output and why?

TABLE 7.7   Using RETAIN to Accumulate TOTAL and Find MAX

Obs	DAY	SALES	TOTAL	MAX
1	1	23.40	23.40	23.40
2	2	32.50	55.90	32.50
3	3	19.80	75.70	32.50
4	4	55.55	131.25	55.55
5	5	34.90	166.15	55.55
6	6	65.30	231.45	65.30
7	7	33.40	264.85	65.30

3. Take the comment off of the `RETAIN` statement, comment out the `IF _N_=1` statement

```
/*IF _N_=1 then DO; TOTAL=0; END;*/
```

Resubmit the program. How does this change the output and why? (Hint: Since an accumulation using + is set to missing if any variable is missing, then the first

```
TOTAL=SALES+TOTAL;
```

is set to missing, as are all the rest.) On the other hand, the `IF SALES>MAX` works correctly because a positive number is greater than a missing value.
4. Change `TOTAL=SALES+TOTAL` to

```
TOTAL=SUM(SALES,TOTAL);
```

Resubmit the code. Does this version work correctly?
5. The current code finds the `MAX` sales amount. Add code to find the `MIN` sales amount.

7.4   USING SAS MACROS

Macros, a powerful programming tool within SAS, allow you to

- set aside repetitive sections of code and to use them again and again when needed,
- create dynamic variables (macro variables) within the code that can take on specified values.

The following brief and limited introduction to this topic illustrates some common ways to use SAS macros. For more information about macros, refer to the SAS documentation.

7.4.1 Creating and Using SAS Macro Variables

A SAS macro variable is a powerful programming concept that allows you to write code that can be easily changed to reflect new values for selected variables or code. This is accomplished with a SAS macro. A SAS macro variable is the symbolic name that stores information that can be used to dynamically modify SAS code through symbolic substitution.

You can think of this substitution in a way that is similar to a "replace" in a word processor. SAS can dynamically (during the process of running a program) replace the value of a specified macro variable with another value you specify throughout your program code.

For example, suppose you have written a SAS program that uses the year value 2016 repeatedly in your code. Later on you want to update the program to use 2017 instead. But if you attempt to manually change the entire 2016 year references in the program, you might miss one. Moreover, in a program of hundreds of lines of code, this task could take a long time. If you need to make many code changes such as this in a long SAS program, the task becomes daunting.

A better programming technique is to use a macro variable rather than fixed code in places where you know you'll need to make changes in the future. That's one setting in which macro variables come in handy.

For example, suppose you have a program that calculates values based on a given year and a comparison based on the value DEPT. You can create macro variables called YEAR and DEPT using the statements

```
%LET YEAR=2015;
%LET DEPT=ENGINEERING;
```

The SAS %LET statement allows you assign a value to a SAS macro variable. Note the % prefix to the %LET statement. Also note that these are not typical assignment statements like you would use in a DATA step. In fact, %LET statements do not have to appear in a DAT step. This type of statement typically appears at the beginning of your program before any DATA step or PROC.

The general format for creating a macro variable is as follows:

```
%LET macrovariablename = text;
```

The value assigned to the macro variable is always a text value, even if (as in the above example) the assigned value is 2015.

Once you have created the macro variable, you refer to it in your SAS program by placing an & (ampersand) as a prefix to the variable name. Thus, once you define YEAR as a macro variable, you use it in a statement in the following way:

```
IND_DAY=MDY(7,4,&YEAR);
```

In this example, &YEAR is replaced by the value of the macro variable, 2015, before SAS executes the code. Thus, SAS "sees" the replaced code

```
IND_DAY=MDY(7,4,2015)
```

and executes that statement. In the case of the macro variable DEPT, the statement

```
GROUP = "&DEPT";
```

is "seen" by SAS as the code

```
GROUP = "ENGINEERING";
```

The &DEPT macro variable is replaced with its value ENGINEERING. The quotations were required in the statement to make the completed statement resolve into acceptable SAS code.

The following code uses these two macro variables within a TITLE statement:

```
TITLE "Analysis for &DEPT for the year &YEAR";
```

If there is no text provided in a %LET statement, the contents of the macro variable is a null value (0 characters). For example,

```
%LET ISNULL=;
```

It is important to understand that any leading or trailing blanks in the macrotext value are ignored. For example,

```
%LET CITY=DALLAS;
```

produces the same result as code that has several blanks around the name:

```
%LET CITY =      DALLAS      ;
```

The blanks in front of or after the text are ignored.

HANDS-ON EXAMPLE

This example illustrates the use of macro variables.

Open the program file DMACRO1.SAS. Note the two macro variables assigned in the %LET statement and their inclusion in the PROC MEANS statement. The DNAME macro variable is used for the name of the data set to use, and the VARIABLES macro variable provides a list of variables to be analyzed.

```
%LET DNAME=C:\SASDATA\SUBJECTS;
%LET VARIABLES = AGE TIME_EXPOSED;
PROC MEANS DATA="&DNAME";
VAR &VARIABLES;
RUN;
```

Submit the code and observe the results given in Table 7.8. The code produces descriptive statistics for the specified list of variables.

Change the data set named from DOSUBJECTS to SOMEDATA and the list of variables to TIME1-TIME4. Resubmit the program and observe the results.

(continued)

(continued)

TABLE 7.8   Using the %LET Statement to Create Macro Variables

Variable	Label	N	Mean	Std Dev	Minimum	Maximum
AGE	AGE	50	10.4600000	2.4261332	4.0000000	15.0000000
TIME_EXPOSED	TIME_EXPOSED	50	21.6744000	1.7464894	17.7900000	25.1200000

This exercise illustrates how to define macro variables at the beginning of your program and use them throughout your code. If you make any changes in the value of the text in the %LET statement, they are changed in the entire program at the time SAS compiles the SAS code.

7.4.2   Combining Macro Variables

Sometimes you want to combine macro variables together or with some other text. This may allow you to create code that is more generalizable and reuse the code again and again by only changing the values of the macro variables. For example, consider the following macro variable assignments:

```
%LET PATH=C:\SASDATA\;
%LET DSN=SOMEDATA;
%LET CLASS=GP;
%LET SELECTVAR=AGE TIME1-TIME4;
```

The macro variable PATH is the Windows location of data files, the DSN is the data set name, CLASS is a grouping variable, and SELECTVAR is a list of variables for some analysis. An example of how these could be used in a PROC MEANS statement is given here:

```
PROC MEANS DATA="&PATH&DSN" MAXDEC=2;
    CLASS &CLASS;
    VAR &SELECTVAR;
RUN;
```

Note how &PATH&DSN are placed together. When the names are resolved, the results are C:\SASDATA\SOMEDATA, which is the reference to the data file needed for PROC MEANS. The CLASS and SELECTVAR macro variables provide additional information for the procedure. By separating PATH and DSN, it makes it simpler to change the value of one or the other. If there is ambiguity in how two items are concatenated, you can use a dot (.) as a separator. For example, suppose you have

```
%LET STATUS=PRE;
```

If you want to combine &PRE with the word PRODUCTION, and if you used "&PRE-PRODUCTION", SAS could not resolve the macro variable correctly. Using the code "&PRE.PRODUCTION" works.

HANDS-ON EXAMPLE

This example illustrates combining macro variables.

1. Open the program file DMACRO2.SAS. Note the four macro variable assignments and how they are used in PROC MEANS. In particular, note how PATH and LET are concatenated.

```
%LET PATH=C:\SASDATA\;
%LET DSN=SOMEDATA;
%LET CLASS=GP;
%LET SELECTVAR=AGE TIME1-TIME4;
TITLE "Descriptive Statistics";
PROC MEANS DATA="&PATH&DSN" MAXDEC=2;
    CLASS &CLASS;
    VAR &SELECTVAR;
RUN;
```

2. Submit this code and observe the results given in Table 7.9.

TABLE 7.9 Output Created Using Macro Variables

Intervention Group	N Obs	Variable	Label	N	Mean	Std Dev	Minimum	Maximum
A	11	AGE	Age on Jan 1, 2000	11	10.36	2.87	4.00	13.00
		TIME1	Baseline	11	20.90	2.08	17.00	23.00
		TIME2	6 Months	11	27.00	2.93	21.30	31.30
		TIME3	12 Months	11	30.35	3.20	22.70	34.20
		TIME4	24 Months	11	30.44	3.96	21.20	35.80
B	29	AGE	Age on Jan 1, 2000	29	10.31	2.48	6.00	15.00
		TIME1	Baseline	29	21.19	1.59	18.50	24.20
		TIME2	6 Months	29	27.43	2.64	23.10	32.30
		TIME3	12 Months	29	30.33	2.87	25.30	34.20
		TIME4	24 Months	29	30.51	3.47	25.10	35.60
C	10	AGE	Age on Jan 1, 2000	10	11.00	1.83	8.00	14.00
		TIME1	Baseline	10	21.91	1.66	19.00	23.90
		TIME2	6 Months	10	27.94	2.61	22.50	31.10
		TIME3	12 Months	10	31.12	3.52	24.90	35.90
		TIME4	24 Months	10	32.24	3.19	26.60	36.10

3. Add a new macro variable assignment statement

```
%LET STATUS=Pre;
```

and change the TITLE to

```
TITLE "Descriptive Statistics for &STATUS.Production";
```

(continued)

(continued)

4. Submit the code and note the title in the output that reads "Descriptive Statistics for PreProduction." Take the dot out from between &STATUS and Production. Rerun the code and note how the concatenation is no longer correctly resolved.

The use of macro variables can become quite complex, and there are a number of capabilities and uses that are not covered in this discussion. However, the following section does include information on how to create and use macro variables as a part of a macro routine. For more information on macro variables refer to SAS Documentation.

7.4.3   Creating Callable Macro Routines

A SAS macro is a series of SAS statements that performs a general task, such as creating a report. Instead of "hard coding" this routine with fixed values, you write your code so that certain portions of the code can be altered using macro variables.

Once a macro routine is defined properly, you can use it again and again in your program. This is referred to as "calling" the macro.

When you call a SAS macro routine, you typically "send" it a series of macro variables and these variables contain information that is substituted into portions of the macro routine code to customize it dynamically as the program is run. The simplified syntax of a SAS macro is

```
%MACRO macroname <(parameter-list)></ option-1 <...option-n>>;
     SAS code that optionally contains macro variables;
%MEND macroname;
```

Here is a brief explanation of how this macro code works:

- The information between the %MACRO statement and the %MEND statement is a SAS macro routine consisting of SAS code.
- The *macroname* is the name you give to the macro that obeys standard SAS naming conventions.
- The parameter list indicates a way to "send" information into the macro routine (illustrated in an upcoming example).
- Within the SAS macro (between %MACRO to %MEND), the variables referenced in the parameter list become macro variables within the macro and may be referred to with the standard macro variable syntax and variablename.

For example, the following program code, which contains a macro routine named REPORT, prints out a short report on a requested subject, specified by the macro variable SUBJECTS, from a data set, specified by the macro variable name DSN. Because you may want to create these reports for a number of people, you can use a macro and call it as many times as needed. Within the macro report code, the dynamic variable that is replaced by a subject name is &SUBJ and the dynamic variable replaced by a data set name is &DSN.

```
%MACRO REPORT(SUBJ, DSN);
    DATA REPORT;SET "&DSN";
    IF SUBJ=&SUBJ;
    TITLE "REPORT ON SUBJECT # &SUBJ";
     PROC PRINT NOOBS DATA=REPORT;
         VAR GENDER TIME_EXPOSED DIAGNOSED;
     RUN;
%MEND REPORT;
```

The first line of the macro routine

```
%MACRO REPORT(SUBJ, DSN);
```

specifies the name of the macro (REPORT) and the two macro variables that are used to send information into the macro routine (SUBJ and DSN).

The macro is typically placed at the beginning of your SAS code file so that when you submit the code, SAS sees and compiles the macro first. Once the macro is defined, you can "call" it using a macro call command. The call for any macro is a % followed by the macro routine name. In this case, the routine name is REPORT so an example call to the routine is

```
%REPORT(SUBJ=001, DSN=C:\SASDATA\SUBJECTS)
```

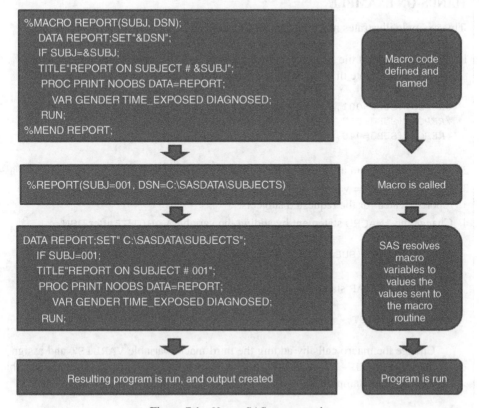

Figure 7.1 How a SAS macro works

Note that for the call, certain values are assigned to the macro variables. For this example, SUBJ is assigned the value 001, and the value of DSN is a path to a SAS data set named SUBJECTS. (There are no quotation marks around either value.)

Once the macro routine REPORT is compiled by SAS, a call to it using the example information does the following:

1. The values assigned to SUBJ and DSN are sent to the macro routine.
2. Within the routine wherever &SUBJ is found, it is substituted for the value of SUBJ. Wherever &DSN is found, it is substituted for the value of DSN.
3. For this example, the SAS code after the substitutions becomes

```
DATA REPORT;SET "C:\SASDATA\SUBJECTS";
IF SUBJ=001;
TITLE "REPORT ON SUBJECT # 001";
 PROC PRINT NOOBS DATA=REPORT;
     VAR GENDER TIME_EXPOSED DIAGNOSED;
 RUN;
```

4. The revised code is run by SAS, and a report is created by the PROC PRINT statement. This process is illustrated in Figure 7.1.

HANDS-ON EXAMPLE

This example illustrates how to use a SAS macro routine.

1. Open the program file DMACRO3.SAS. This is the same code illustrated previously in this section. Note that following the macro routine code is a series of macro calls

```
%REPORT(SUBJ=001, DSN=C:\SASDATA\SUBJECTS)
%REPORT(SUBJ=017, DSN=C:\SASDATA\SUBJECTS)
%REPORT(SUBJ=040, DSN=C:\SASDATA\SUBJECTS)
```

2. Submit the program and observe the output given in Table 7.10.
3. Change the SUBJ= values to 002, 010, and 020. Submit the program and observe the reports created for the requested subjects.
4. Change the %MACRO statement by adding the variable VARLIST after DSN.

```
%MACRO REPORT(SUBJ, DSN, VARLIST);
```

Replace the VAR statement in the PROC PRINT with this statement

```
VAR &VARLIST;
```

Change the macro calls by adding the third macro variable VARLIST and assign it the value GROUP--DIAGNOSED. (Note that it is a double dash between the variable names.) For example,

```
%REPORT(SUBJ=002, DSN=C:\SASDATA\SUBJECTS,
    VARLIST=GROUP--DIAGNOSED)
```

Comment out the other two calls. Resubmit the program to see how this has changed the reports.

TABLE 7.10   Output from Macro Program

REPORT ON SUBJECT # 001

GENDER	TIME_EXPOSED	DIAGNOSED
M	23.31	1

REPORT ON SUBJECT # 017

GENDER	TIME_EXPOSED	DIAGNOSED
F	20.95	1

REPORT ON SUBJECT # 040

GENDER	TIME_EXPOSED	DIAGNOSED
F	18.1	0

7.4.4   Using a Macro with No Parameters

A simple macro is one that contains no parameters. In this case, the macro routine is defined as

```
%MACRO macroname;
    SAS code;
%MEND macroname;
```

This could be used to call a set of standard code within a larger program so you don't have to rewrite the same code again and again. It could be used to display a title, run a series of interim reports that change when a data set is updated, run a standard report, and so on. For example, suppose you have a standard disclaimer that you use when you create reports. The following macro routine contains code that outputs a message using PROC GSLIDE. (Options for the output, such as J for justification and H for height, are similar to the options previously discussed for titles and footnotes.) This code is in DMACDISCLAIM.SAS.

```
%MACRO DISCLAIM;
proc gslide;
NOTE J=C H=1
```

```
"Data provided by ACME Company exchanges may be delayed";
NOTE J=C H=1
"as specified by financial exchanges or our data providers. ";
NOTE J=C H=1
"ACME does not verify any data and disclaims any obligation to
    do so.";
run;
quit;
%MEND DISCLAIM;
```

Once this macro is defined, it can be called whenever you want that disclaimer to appear in your output.

```
%DISCLAIM
```

This is illustrated in an upcoming example.

7.4.5   Including SAS Macro Code

You may create a number of SAS macro routines that you want to use again and again. Instead of including the macro code in the program where you are going to call it, you may want to include the macro code dynamically in your program. For example, the file that contains the DISCLAIM macro is DMACRODISCLAIM.SAS. By placing a %INCLUDE command, given here, at the top of your code, you can make this macro available for use in a program.

```
%INCLUDE "C:\SASDATA\DMACRODISCLAIM.SAS";
```

HANDS-ON EXAMPLE

This example illustrates how to include external SAS code in a program.

1. Open the program file FIRST.SAS. This was the first SAS program we used. On the line before the DATA statement enter

```
%INCLUDE "C:\SASDATA\DMACRODISCLAIM.SAS";
```

And on the line after the last RUN statement enter

```
%DISCLAIM;
```

(You are not required to put a semicolon after a macro call, but sometimes it helps if you have other code following.)

When you run this program, SAS includes the code from the file DMACDIS-CLAIM.SAS in the program stream (because of the %INCLUDE statement) causing that macro code to be compiled at the beginning of the FIRST program. Therefore,

it is ready to be called when the code sees the %DISCLAIM statement at the end of the program.
2. Submit the code and observe the output given in Table 7.11. It contains the disclaimer from the macro routine. This illustrates that you can keep certain macros in files, include them in any program you want to use them in, and call them at locations in your program where you want the macro to run.

TABLE 7.11   Output Showing GSLIDE Results

The MEANS Procedure

			Analysis Variable : AGE			
GENDER	N Obs	N	Mean	Std Dev	Minimum	Maximum
FEMALE	9	9	40.8888889	14.2954927	24.0000000	72.0000000
MALE	9	9	38.7777778	15.1226467	18.0000000	64.0000000

```
Data provided by ACME Company exchanges may be delayed as
specified by financial exchanges or our data providers.
@@ACME does not verify any data and disclaims any obliga-
tion to do so.
```

7.4.6   Using The SAS Macro %DO Loop

The SAS %DO loop statement is similar to the previously discussed DO loop, but in this macro version (note the percentage sign before the DO), you are able to define increment macro variables that take on dynamic values. The %DO loop statement must appear inside a SAS macro routine, but unlike the standard DO loop, it does not have to appear within a DATA step. A simplified syntax is as follows:

```
%DO macrovariable=start %TO stop <%BY increment>;
 SAS statements
%END;
```

Note that one of the big differences in this %DO loop is the variable being incremented, called *macrovariable* here. That is, this variable is like a macro variable created in a %LET statement, but you have the ability to make it increment over a selected range in the loop. For example, the following %DO loop iterates from the variable I (which we refer to as &I, a macro variable) to 5 and assigns the name of a DATA file based on the value of &I.

```
%do i=1 %to 5;
    data gp&i;
        set mysaslib.somedata;
        where status=&i;
    run;
%end;
```

The code GP&I resolves to the data set names GP1, GP2, GP3, and so on within the loop as I increments from 1 to 5.

HANDS-ON EXAMPLE

This example illustrates how to use a %DO loop in a SAS macro.

1. Open the program file DMACRO4.SAS. This routine contains a macro named GROUPS that creates SAS data sets from the SOMEDATA data set based on the value of the variable STATUS. Submit this code and examine the log. Verify that five data sets GP1, GP2, GP3, GP4, and GP5 were created.

```
%MACRO GROUPS(COUNT);
    %DO I=1 %TO &COUNT;
        DATA GP&I;
            SET MYSASLIB.SOMEDATA;
            WHERE STATUS=&I;
        RUN;
    %END;
%MEND GROUPS;
%GROUPS(COUNT=5);
TITLE "LISTING FOR STATUS=1";
PROC PRINT DATA=GP1;RUN;
TITLE "LISTING FOR STATUS=2";
PROC PRINT DATA=GP2;RUN;
```

Note that the call to the macro program (%GROUPS(COUNT=5);) sends the macro variable named COUNT the value 5, which was used in the DO loop at the %TO value. The data set names are created by concatenating GP with the increment variable &I and they are GP1, GP2, and so on. The PROC PRINT statements list the contents of the first two data sets created. Submit this code and observe the results in Table 7.12.

TABLE 7.12   Output Showing Results of %DO Loop

Listing for STATUS=1

Obs	ID	GP	AGE	TIME1	TIME2	TIME3	TIME4	STATUS	SEX	GENDER
1	343	B	11	19.0	25.2	27.7	25.1	1	1	Male
2	410	B	13	22.2	30.4	32.1	35.2	1	0	Female
3	307	C	11	22.6	30.1	34.4	35.2	1	0	Female

Listing for STATUS=2

Obs	ID	GP	AGE	TIME1	TIME2	TIME3	TIME4	STATUS	SEX	GENDER
1	187	A	11	22.5	29.3	32.6	33.7	2	0	Female
2	162	B	7	20.9	28.9	29.7	25.9	2	1	Male
3	198	B	12	23.4	29.2	30.4	35.1	2	0	Female
4	282	B	13	21.3	28.7	32.3	30.3	2	0	Female
5	575	B	8	21.2	25.7	28.9	31.6	2	0	Female
6	589	B	7	22.0	25.5	28.2	30.9	2	0	Female
7	593	B	11	18.9	23.1	27.7	25.6	2	1	Male

2. Change the macro call to

```
%GROUPS(5)
```

Resubmit and see that the call still works. As long as there is no ambiguity in the call, you do not have to include a specific assignment such as COUNT=5.

7.4.7   Using CALL SYMPUT to Create a Macro Variable

The SAS CALL SYMPUT routine assigns a value to a macro variable within a DATA step. The call does not have to be within a macro routine, although it can be. The syntax of the call is as follows:

```
CALL SYMPUT('macrovariablename', value);
```

The *macrovariablename* is the name you want to assign a value (similar to how the %LET statement assigns a value). However, in this case, the value in the routine can be an expression, and the name itself can be created using SAS text operators. This is illustrated in the following example:

HANDS-ON EXAMPLE

This example illustrates how to use CALL SYMPUT.

1. Open the program file DMACRO5.SAS. The data set CARS contains two MPG variables CITYMPG and HYWMPG. This macro allows you to specify which version of MPG to use in a procedure (PROC MEANS in this case). Submit this code and observe the output. The DATA _NULL_ statement is used to allow you to do procedures that must take place in a DATA step, but you do not want to save any data values to a SAS data set.

```
%MACRO CARINFO(WHICHPLACE);
DATA _NULL_;
CALL SYMPUT('TIMEVAR', CATT('&WHICHPLACE.','MPG' ));
RUN;
TITLE "THE VALUE OF THE MACRO VARIABLE TIMEVAR IS &TIMEVAR ";
PROC MEANS MAXDEC=2 DATA=MYSASLIB.CARS;
VAR &TIMEVAR;
RUN;
%MEND CARINFO;
%CARINFO(WHICHPLACE=CITY);
```

(continued)

(continued)

> ### THE VALUE OF THE MACRO VARIABLE TIMEVAR IS CITYMPG
>
> The MEANS Procedure
>
> | Analysis Variable : CityMPG | | | | |
> |---|---|---|---|---|
> | N | Mean | Std Dev | Minimum | Maximum |
> | 1081 | 19.29 | 4.60 | 10.00 | 60.00 |

Note that the macro variable sent to the macro, WHICHPLACE has the value CITY. The SYMPUT call concatenates '&WHICHPLACE.' with 'MPG' to create the string CITYMPG. The dot (.) after &WHICHPLACE is a macro variable delimiter required to avoid ambiguity when there is some character following the macro variable. In this case, the quote character follows the macro variable name, so the dot separates the two.

2. Take out the dot after the 'WHICHPLACE' in the CALL SYMPUT statement and resubmit the code. You get an output message 'The value of the macro variable is &WHICHNAMEMPG' that is not what you want. Put the dot back, rerun, and verify that it works again.

3. An important SAS concept is that a macro variable created in a DATA step cannot be used in that same data step. That is why a RUN ends the DATA step before the TITLE statement is given. To test this, put the RUN statement after the TITLE statement instead of before it. Resubmit the code and verify that you do not get the desired output. Fix these lines and verify that the code now works again. (This might seem to be a trivial situation until you spend hours trying to figure out why your code doesn't work.)

7.5   SUMMARY

This chapter provides information on two topics that allow you to write SAS code that can simplify complex procedures: mainly arrays and macros. Arrays can simplify creating and using large data constructs that must be manipulated by code. Macro variables allow you to create generalized programs, and macro routines allow you to create code that can be used over and over again.

EXERCISES

7.1 **Creating and using array and a DO loop.**

You want to create a program that calculates an average grade based on the best 4 of 5 recorded grades. Open the program file EX_7.1.SAS, a partial SAS program to perform this task:

```
DATA GRADES;
INPUT IDNO GRADE1 GRADE2 GRADE3 GRADE4 GRADE5;
ARRAY G(5) ; *FINISH THE STATEMENT;
* FIND LOWEST GRADE;
LOW=100;
DO ; * FINISH THE STATEMENT;
   if G(I)<LOW then LOW=G(I);
END;
TOTAL=; * FINISH THE STATEMENT;
AVERAGE=TOTAL/4;
DATALINES;
001 90 34 88 79 88
002 99 69 87 86 98
003 91 75 85 94 100
004 88 57 68 74 89
;
RUN;
PROC PRINT DATA=GRADES;RUN;
```

a. Complete the missing statements.
   - For the array statement, specify the range GRADE1-GRADE5.
   - For the DO statement, increment from 1 to 5.
   - For the TOTAL statement, use the SUM(of variables) statement and subtract the value LOW from the result.
   - For the AVERAGE statement, divide the TOTAL result by 4.
   - Submit the code and verify that the result in AVERAGE is the average grade for each student, leaving out the lowest grade for each average.

b. Examine how LOW is calculated as the lowest grade for each student. Answer the following questions:
   Why is LOW initially set to 100?
   In the DO loop, when is LOW assigned a new value?
   At the end of the DO loop, what is the value of LOW and why?
   Why subtract LOW from the SUM(Of GRADE1-GRADE5) in the TOTAL= statement?

7.2 **Use a SAS macro.**

Using the SAS code in DMACRO3.SAS as an example, complete the program below to create a report using the CARS data set. This code is in EX_7.2.SAS. Use this information:

- The name of the macro is GETCARS.
- The name of the SAS data set is "C:\SASDATA\CARS". Use this in the SET statement.
- For the second and third reports, use FORD and TOYOTA. Note that the name must be in all caps.
- Place the macro variable named &CHOICE in the title.

```
%MACRO _____(CHOICE=);
   DATA TEMP; SET "C:_____";
   IF BRAND="&CHOICE";
```

```
      TITLE "CAR SELECTION FOR _____ ";
      PROC PRINT; VAR BRAND MODEL CITYMPG;
      RUN;
%MEND GETCARS;
ODS HTML;
%GETCARS(CHOICE=SCION)
%GETCARS(CHOICE=_____)
%GETCARS(CHOICE=_____)
```

a. Run the program and observe the results. It should create three reports, one for each brand of car.

b. Create a new call using VOLKSWAGEN.

c. To verify that case matters, perform the following call:

```
%GETCARS(CHOICE=Honda)
```

Why didn't it produce a report?

d. Change the IF statement to

```
IF BRAND=UPCASE("&CHOICE");
```

Perform a call using

```
%GETCARS(CHOICE=Honda)
```

Why does it now work?

7.3 Using RETAIN.

You are a football fan and are keeping up with the number of yards gained by your favorite running back. Using DRETAIN1.SAS as an example, write a SAS program that calculates the accumulated yards gained and finds the maximum and minimum yards gained in any one game.

Game	Yards Gained
1	55
2	105
3	110
4	153
5	99
6	69
7	34
8	101
9	110
10	120

8

CONTROLLING OUTPUT USING ODS

LEARNING OBJECTIVES

- To be able to specify ODS output format and destination
- To be able to specify ODS style
- To be able to select specific tables for output
- To be able to capture information from ODS tables
- To be able to use ODS graphics from SAS® procedures
- To be able to use Traffic Lighting to highlight selected values

ODS, or Output Delivery System, is a method for controlling the output from SAS procedures. ODS began with version 8 and continues with added enhancements in more recent versions.

8.1 SPECIFYING THE ODS OUTPUT FORMAT AND DESTINATION

The SAS ODS is set up so that you "turn on" or initiate output into a designated output format. Once the output format has been initiated, SAS procedures send information to that output format. You can send output from one or more procedures to the output stream. Following the procedures for which you want the ODS output, you "turn off" or end the output. To initiate output using ODS, use the following statement:

```
ODS OUTPUT-FORMAT <OPTIONS>;
```

SAS® Essentials: Mastering SAS for Data Analytics, Second Edition. Alan C. Elliott and Wayne A. Woodward.
© 2016 John Wiley & Sons, Inc. Published 2016 by John Wiley & Sons, Inc.

To end the ODS output, use the CLOSE statement:

```
ODS OUTPUT-FORMAT CLOSE;
```

Here are several ODS output formats:

```
ODS LISTING <FILE='file-specification'>;
ODS HTML <BODY='HTML-FILE-PATHNAME.HTML>';
ODS PDF <FILE='PDF-FILE-PATHNAME.PDF'>;
ODS RTF <FILE='RTF-FILE-PATHNAME.RTF'>;
ODS PS <FILE='PS-FILE-PATHNAME.PS'>;
ODS PLC <FILE='PCL-FILE-PATHNAME.PCL'>;
```

Note that most of the output formats include the option to specify a filename with a FILE= option. The HTML format uses BODY= rather than FILE= since that is the terminology used by HTML to describe a displayed page of information. These output formats are described more fully as follows:

HyperText Markup Language (HTML): HTML is the current standard (default) output format used in Windows SAS versions. This HTML format is the same used for displaying Web pages on the Internet and is also recognized by most word processors such as Microsoft Word. To reset SAS to this default (if it becomes turned off, use the statement ODS PREFERENCES;)

LISTING: This "old-style" SAS output format was the default output location used in SAS Windows versions prior to 9.1. It is sometimes called "typewriter output" and is based on a monospaced font.

Portable Document Format (PDF): PDF is widely used to distribute documents by e-mail or via Internet downloads. Use of a PDF document requires that the (free) Adobe Reader or a similar program be installed on your computer. One of the benefits of the PDF format is that the contents of your document will appear the same when viewed under many types of computer operating systems, such as Windows, Mac OS X, and UNIX and its Linux derivations.

Rich Text Format (RTF): RTF is a common language for word processors. When you capture information in this format, it can be opened and edited by most word processors such as Microsoft Word or even Wordpad.

Postscript (PS): PS is a printer language, and the output captured in this format is usually designed to be printed on a PS printer.

Print Command Language (PCL): PCL is a printer language, and the output captured in this format is usually designed to be printed on a PCL printer.

Extensible Markup Language (XML): XML is a plain text data interchangeable format that can be read using a normal text editor but is in a standard machine readable format.

Tagsets.ExcelXP: The Tagsets.ExcelXP option allows you to output XML tables that can be read by Microsoft version 2002 or later.

Other specialty output formats are DOCUMENT, MARKUP, and WML (Wireless Markup Language).

The file names following the ODS output format are optional, but SAS may prompt you for a file name if it is omitted. Note that when you specify a file name in Windows, it must include the correct extension if Windows is to recognize the output file type. For example, to send data to a PDF file, you could use the following syntax:

```
ODS PDF file='WINDOWS-PATH\Filename.PDF';
```

or, as a specific example:

```
ODS PDF FILE='C:\SASDATA\MYOUTPUT.PDF';
```

If you leave off the destination, as in

```
ODS PDF;
... some procedures
ODS PDF CLOSE;
```

SAS will send the output to the SAS Results Viewer window without prompting you for a file name. For output formats such as PDF and RTF, if you do not indicate a file name, you may be prompted to enter one (or you may choose to have the results go into the SAS Results Viewer). When you use the default HTML output format, you are not prompted for a file name.

It is important to remember that after you specify an ODS output, you also need to close it to tell SAS to finish sending the output to that location. If you do not close the location, you may not be able to see the results. For example, if you use ODS RTF; to open the RTF (Word) output, then you must at some point close with the statement ODS RTF CLOSE;. Thus, the statements would be

```
ODS RTF;
SAS code that produces output...;
ODS RTF CLOSE;
```

Beginning with SAS 9.2 the default output location became HTML. (Previously it was LISTING.) Beginning with SAS Version 9.4, the output defaults are as follows:

- Default output is HTML and the default style is HTMLBlue
- ODS Graphics is on
- Listing is closed

However, if you use the ODS statement to close the HTML location (ODS HTML CLOSE;), SAS may not produce any output. This will cause an error message in the log that indicates that there is no output destination open. If this happens, you should reset the HTML default option in SAS. Use this statement:

```
ODS PREFERENCES;
```

to restore the default HTML output settings.

TABLE 8.1   ODS Styles for SAS 9.4

Analysis	GrayscalePrinter	MeadowPrinter	PowerPointLight
BarrettsBlue	HTMLBlue	Minimal	Printer
BlockPrint	Harvest	MonochromePrinter	Raven
Daisy	HighContrast	Monospace	Rtf
Default	Journal	Netdraw	Sapphire
Dove	Journal1a	NoFontDefault	SasDocPrinter
Dtree	Journal2	Normal	SasWeb
EGDefault	Journal2a	NormalPrinter	Seaside
FancyPrinter	Journal3	Ocean	SeasidePrinter
Festival	Journal3a	Pearl	StatDoc
FestivalPrinter	Listing	Plateau	Statistical
Gantt	Meadow	PowerPointDark	

8.2 SPECIFYING ODS OUTPUT STYLE

When you output information to a SAS ODS format, the tables, graphs, and text are defined with default colors and fonts. You can select from several built-in ODS styles. Each style is based on some theme or a format appropriate for a specific purpose. For example, the JOURNAL style formats your output in black and white that is appropriate for inclusion in a journal article. The option to specify a style is

```
STYLE=styletype;
```

This option appears in the ODS statement. For example,

```
ODS RTF STYLE=JOURNAL;
... some procedures
ODS RTF CLOSE;
```

To see a listing of the available SAS styles, use the code:

```
PROC TEMPLATE; LIST STYLES; RUN;
```

The default style is Styles.Default. The SAS format styles for version 9.4 as reported by PROC TEMPLATE are given in Table 8.1 (with the prefix "Styles." removed to make it easier to read the table).

HANDS-ON EXAMPLE

This example illustrates outputting information to a specific HTML file.

1. Open the program file ODS1.SAS.

```
DATA TEST; SET "C:\SASDATA\SOMEDATA";
* DEFINE WHERE HTML LISTING WILL GO;
ODS HTML BODY='C:\SASDATA\ODS.HTML';
```

```
PROC MEANS MAXDEC=2; VAR AGE TIME1-TIME4;
TITLE 'ODS HTML Example';
RUN;
* CLOSE THE HTML OUTPUT;
ODS HTML CLOSE;
RUN;
ODS PREFERENCES;
```

As discussed earlier, the ODS HTML BODY= statement specifies the file name where the HTML output is stored on disk.

2. Submit the program. Observe the HTML output in the Results Viewer.
3. Go to Windows and open Windows Explorer (or click on My Computer Icon on your desktop). Drill down to the C:\SASDATA folder. You should see a file named ODS.HTML. Double click on this file name, and then the contents of the file will be displayed in your default browser (see Table 8.2). Thus, the SAS output from this program has been saved locally in the HTML format, viewable in a Web browser. (It could also be uploaded to a remote server and made available on the Internet, and it can also be opened in most word processors, including Microsoft Word, that "understand" the HTML language.)

TABLE 8.2 HTML Output Using SAS ODS

ODS HTML Example

The MEANS Procedure

Variable	Label	N	Mean	Std Dev	Minimum	Maximum
AGE	Age on Jan 1, 2000	50	10.46	2.43	4.00	15.00
TIME1	Baseline	50	21.27	1.72	17.00	24.20
TIME2	6 Months	50	27.44	2.66	21.30	32.30
TIME3	12 Months	50	30.49	3.03	22.70	35.90
TIME4	24 Months	50	30.84	3.53	21.20	36.10

4. Return to SAS and note that the same output is displayed in the SAS Results Viewer (which is similar to a web browser).
5. Close the Results Viewer, return to the Editor window, and add a STYLE option to the ODS statement:

```
ODS HTML BODY='C:\SASDATA\ODS.HTML' STYLE=JOURNAL;
```

Change the title to "HTML Output Example Using Journal Style".

6. Resubmit the program and observe the output. Note that the new program produces output based on this black-and-white "journal" style (see Table 8.3).
7. To cause the output to be sent to a PDF file, change the ODS statement to

```
ODS PDF FILE='C:\SASDATA\ODS.PDF' STYLE=STATISTICAL;
```

(continued)

(continued)

TABLE 8.3   ODS HTML Output Using JOURNAL Style

ODS HTML Example Using Journal Style

The MEANS Procedure

Variable	Label	N	Mean	Std Dev	Minimum	Maximum
AGE	Age on Jan 1, 2000	50	10.46	2.43	4.00	15.00
TIME1	Baseline	50	21.27	1.72	17.00	24.20
TIME2	6 Months	50	27.44	2.66	21.30	32.30
TIME3	12 Months	50	30.49	3.03	22.70	35.90
TIME4	24 Months	50	30.84	3.53	21.20	36.10

TABLE 8.4   Output in PDF Format with the Statistical Style

ODS PDF Example

The MEANS Procedure

Variable	Label	N	Mean	Std Dev	Minimum	Maximum
AGE	Age on Jan 1, 2000	50	10.46	2.43	4.00	15.00
TIME1	Baseline	50	21.27	1.72	17.00	24.20
TIME2	6 Months	50	27.44	2.66	21.30	32.30
TIME3	12 Months	50	30.49	3.03	22.70	35.90
TIME4	24 Months	50	30.84	3.53	21.20	36.10

Change the ODS HTML CLOSE statement to

```
ODS PDF CLOSE;
```

(See ODS2.SAS.) The results will appear in the Results Viewer. Depending on your particular computer setup, the Adobe Reader program may start up and display the ODS.PDF file. The results are given in Table 8.4. This output is created in the STATISTICAL style format as specified in the ODS statement FILE= statement. Similar results can be observed by outputting information in other ODS formats.

8.3   USING ODS TO SELECT SPECIFIC OUTPUT TABLES FOR SAS PROCEDURES

SAS procedures often output a lot of information you don't want or need. In ODS output, each part of the output is contained in a table. Using ODS options, you can customize which tables you want SAS to output to the ODS destination. For example, suppose you are calculating a number of 2×2 cross-tabulations in a chi-square analysis. SAS automatically includes the Fisher's Exact test results in the output. If you do not want that part of the output displayed (maybe you want to save paper when you print results), you can use an ODS statement to instruct SAS to exclude the Fisher table (or any table) from the output.

To include or exclude a table from the output, you first need to know the table's name. You can discover this information by using the ODS TRACE command in the following way:

```
ODS TRACE ON;
    procedure specifications;
ODS TRACE OFF;
```

This ODS option outputs information in the Log window that indicates the name of each output table. Once you've discovered the name of one or more tables you want to include (in this example) in the output, you can use the following code to make that request:

```
ODS SELECT tables-to-include;
PROC FREQ CODE;
```

When you run the program, only the tables requested in the SELECT statement are included in the output. Similarly, you can use an ODS EXCLUDE statement to exclude tables from output.

HANDS-ON EXAMPLE

This example illustrates how to use ODS to limit output from a SAS analysis.

1. Open the program file ODS3.SAS. This program performs a chi-square analysis on a 2×2 contingency table.

```
DATA TABLE;
INPUT A B COUNT;
DATALINES;
0 0 12
0 1 15
1 0 18
1 1 3
;
ODS TRACE ON;
PROC FREQ;WEIGHT COUNT;
    TABLES A*B /CHISQ;
    TITLE 'CHI-SQUARE ANALYSIS FOR A 2X2 TABLE';
RUN;
ODS TRACE OFF;
```

(continued)

(continued)

2. Run the program and observe the results. Note that the results consist of the following tables (not shown here):

   (a) The A by B cross-tabulation table

   (b) Statistics for the A by B analysis

   (c) Fisher's Exact test.

   Examine the information in the Log window. The portion of the Log file shown in Figure 8.1 is the information created as a result of the ODS TRACE ON and ODS TRACE OFF statements.

```
Output Added:
-------------
Name:        CrossTabFreqs
Label:       Cross-Tabular Freq Table
Template:    Base.Freq.CrossTabFreqs
Path:        Freq.Table1.CrossTabFreqs
-------------

Output Added:
-------------
Name:        ChiSq
Label:       Chi-Square Tests
Template:    Base.Freq.ChiSq
Path:        Freq.Table1.ChiSq
-------------

Output Added:
-------------
Name:        FishersExact
Label:       Fisher's Exact Test
Template:    Base.Freq.ChisqExactFactoid
Path:        Freq.Table1.FishersExact
-------------
```

Figure 8.1   ODS TRACE output

Note the names of the tables:

- CrossTabFreqs
- ChiSq
- FishersExact

Knowing these names (they are not case sensitive), you can, for example, limit your output to only the CrossTabFreqs and ChiSq tables.

3. Open the program file ODS4.SAS. Note the statement beginning with ODS SELECT. It is the statement that specifies what tables to include in the output.

```
DATA TABLE;
INPUT A B COUNT;
DATALINES;

0 0 12
0 1 15
1 0 18
1 1 3
;
ODS SELECT CROSSTABFREQS CHISQ;
PROC FREQ;WEIGHT COUNT;
    TABLES A*B /CHISQ;
    TITLE 'CHI-SQUARE ANALYSIS FOR A 2X2 TABLE';
RUN;
```

4. Submit this program. Note that it produces (almost) the same output as the previous code, but without the Fisher's table. You would get the same results by using the EXCLUDE option as in the following code:

```
ODS EXCLUDE FISHERSEXACT;
```

8.4   GOING DEEPER: CAPTURING INFORMATION FROM ODS TABLES

Another way to use the information from ODS TRACE is to capture output from procedures and save that information in a SAS output file. Once you know the name of the output table, you can use ODS to output the table as a SAS data file using the command

```
ODS OUTPUT NAMEOFTABLE=OUTPUTDATASET;
```

After outputting the information to a new data set, you can merge that information into the current SAS data set using the following code:

```
DATA NEW; SET ORIGINAL;
IF _N_=1 THEN SET OUTPUTDATASET;
```

The _N_ is a special variable whose value is a sequential number of a record as a SAS data set is read into the memory buffer. Thus, the statement

```
IF _N_=1 then SET OUTPUTDATASET;
```

tells SAS to merge the information from record 1 of OUTPUTDATASET into the NEW data set (along with the information from ORIGINAL). This is illustrated in the following Hands-on Example.

HANDS-ON EXAMPLE

This example illustrates how to capture a specific statistic from the output of a procedure and save that information in a SAS data set.

1. Open the program file ODS5.SAS.

```
DATA WT;
INPUT WEIGHT @@;
DATALINES;
64 71 53 67 55 58
77 57 56 51 76 68
;
ODS TRACE ON;
PROC MEANS DATA=WT;
RUN;
ODS TRACE OFF;RUN;
QUIT;
```

2. Run this program. It uses the TRACE option to display the names of the output tables for PROC MEANS in the Log Window, as shown in Figure 8.2. Note that the name of the output table is "Summary."

```
Output Added:
--------------
Name:       Summary
Label:      Summary statistics
Template:   base.summary
Path:       Means.Summary
```

Figure 8.2 Trace output from a PROC MEANS

3. Close the Results Viewer and clear the output and log files. Open the program ODS6.SAS. Note that the SAS code has been modified by the removal of the TRACE ON and TRACE OFF commands and the addition of the following statement just before the PROC MEANS statement, as shown here:

```
ODS OUTPUT SUMMARY=STATS;
PROC MEANS;
```

SUMMARY in the ODS OUTPUT statement is the name of the table, and STATS is the name of the output data set you are creating.

4. Run the edited SAS program (ODS6.SAS). Look in the Log window and see the following statement, which tells you that SAS created the requested data set.

```
NOTE: The data set WORK.STATS has 1 observation and 5
variables.
```

5. Examine the Results Viewer window to see the contents of the new data set created, as given in Table 8.5. This information can now be used in other calculations, as illustrated in the next step.

TABLE 8.5   The SAS Data Set Created Using ODS Output

Output statistics to a data set					
Obs	WEIGHT_N	WEIGHT_Mean	WEIGHT_StdDev	WEIGHT_Min	WEIGHT_Max
1	12	62.75	8.9861003778	51	77

The `WEIGHT_MEAN` and `WEIGHT_STDDEV` values calculated and stored in the STATS data set can be used to calculate a Z-value for the weights of subject in the WT data set. The following two lines of code can be used to calculate the Z-statistic for each `WEIGHT` value:

```
DIFF=WEIGHT-WEIGHT_MEAN;
Z=DIFF/WEIGHT_STDDEV;
```

However, in order to do this calculation, you must merge the WT data set with the statistics in the STAT data set. The next step shows how this is accomplished.

6. Open the program file ODS7.SAS. The purpose of this code is to use the information created by PROC MEANS and saved in the STATS data set as information used to calculate the DIFF and Z values in a new data set.

```
DATA WT;
INPUT WEIGHT @@;
DATALINES;
64 71 53 67 55 58
77 57 56 51 76 68
;
DATA WTDIFF;SET WT;
IF _N_=1 THEN SET STATS;
DIFF=WEIGHT-WEIGHT_MEAN;
Z=DIFF/WEIGHT_STDDEV; * CREATES STANDARDIZED SCORE (Z-SCORE);
RUN;
PROC PRINT DATA= WTDIFF;VAR WEIGHT DIFF Z;
RUN;
```

This program creates a new data set called WTDIFF that consists of the original data set WT merged with the first (and only) row of the new STATS data set. This merge is accomplished with the statement

```
IF _N_=1 THEN SET STATS;
```

The statement merges in the needed variables `WEIGHT_MEAN` and `WEIGHT_STDDEV`, from the STAT data set, making them available for the Z calculation. A calculation is then made to create the Z variable.

(continued)

(continued)

7. Run this program and observe the output, which contains Z-scores for each record, as given in Table 8.6. Using this technique, you can capture any statistic from a SAS output table, merge it into another data set, and use that information to calculate new variables.

TABLE 8.6   Results of Calculating Z-Score

Output statistics to a data set

Obs	WEIGHT	DIFF	Z
1	64	1.25	0.13910
2	71	8.25	0.91808
3	53	-9.75	-1.08501
4	67	4.25	0.47295
5	55	-7.75	-0.86244
6	58	-4.75	-0.52859
7	77	14.25	1.58578
8	57	-5.75	-0.63988
9	56	-6.75	-0.75116
10	51	-11.75	-1.30757
11	76	13.25	1.47450
12	68	5.25	0.58424

8.4.1   Using ODS Graphics from SAS Procedures

ODS graphics refers to graphs that are created from SAS procedures. Although ODS graphics have been around for several SAS versions, the graphics only recently began appearing automatically when you run a SAS PROC (at least in the Windows edition of SAS).

SAS offers ways to customize the automatically created graphs using PROC TEMPLATE and the Graph Template Language (GTL). However, this feature is not covered in this book. Refer to SAS documentation for more about the GTL programming features. The creation of custom graphs using SAS/GRAPH is covered in Chapter 18.

Sometimes, the automatic creation of ODS graphics takes a while, and if you are doing a lot of analyses and only want the tabled output, you might be interested in shutting off ODS graphics for a while. You can do this (temporarily) using the command

```
ODS GRAPHICS CLOSE;
```

Figure 8.3   Preferences/results dialog box

To turn ODS graphics back on use

```
ODS GRAPHICS ON;
```

You can also turn off ODS graphics by selecting (in SAS) the menu options Tools → Options → Preferences, and select the Results Tab. The dialog box shown in Figure 8.3 is displayed. Note the option Use ODS Graphics. If you want to turn off graphics, uncheck this box.

Although SAS automatically produces plots for numerous procedures, there may be additional plots you want to display that are not automatically created. In this case, many procedures have added PLOT options that allow you to make these types of requests. As an example, consider the following example:

HANDS-ON EXAMPLE

1. Open the program file ODS8.SAS. This example creates a table of frequencies for the variable STATUS in the data set SOMEDATA. Run this code and observe the output. There is no graph created with the tabled output (see Table 8.7).

```
PROC FREQ DATA="C:\SASDATA\SOMEDATA";
     TABLES STATUS;
TITLE 'Simple Example of PROC FREQ';
RUN;
```

(continued)

(continued)

TABLE 8.7   Frequency Output from PROC FREQ

		Socioeconomic Status		
STATUS	Frequency	Percent	Cumulative Frequency	Cumulative Percent
1	3	6.00	3	6.00
2	7	14.00	10	20.00
3	6	12.00	16	32.00
4	8	16.00	24	48.00
5	26	52.00	50	100.00

2. Make a small change in the code by adding an option to the `TABLES` statement

```
TABLES STATUS/ plots=freqplot;
```

Submit this code and observe the results. A graph is included in the output, as shown in Figure 8.4.

Figure 8.4   Requested ODS graph from PROC FREQ

As procedures are discussed in future chapters, `ODS PLOT` options will be introduced to show how to create graphs for procedures when they are not automatically generated.

8.5   GOING DEEPER: USING TRAFFIC LIGHTING TO HIGHLIGHT SELECTED VALUES

There may be an instance when you are creating a report using PROC PRINT that you want to highlight certain values according to some criteria. (This feature only works in PROC PRINT, TABULATE, and REPORT. This example only discusses its use in PROC PRINT.) For example, if a value is importantly high or low, you might want to highlight the value with a color. Traffic Lighting is a way to do that. Using Traffic lighting is a two-step procedure:

1. Create a format that indicates colors for certain values. For example, suppose you want to highlight values of ISS, the Injury Severity Score according to severity. A format to do that could be created using this code:

```
PROC FORMAT;
VALUE FMTSEVERE
        LOW-<10="GREEN"
        10-<20="BLUE"
        20-HIGH="RED";
RUN;
```

2. In PROC PRINT, you tell SAS which variable to assign this formatting for using the VAR statement. For example,

```
VAR ISS/STYLE={FOREGROUND=FMTSEVERE.};
```

The following example illustrates Traffic Lighting.

HANDS-ON EXAMPLE

1. Open the program file ODS9.SAS. This example lists the first 10 records in the TRAUMA data set. Note the three VAR statements. They specify the order of variables for the listing. For the ISS variable, the STYLE is set to the format FMTSEVERE. Submit the code and observe the results, which are given below; see Table 8.8.

```
PROC FORMAT;
VALUE FMTSEVERE
        LOW-<0="BLACK"
        0-<10="GREEN"
        10-<20="BLUE"
        20-HIGH="RED";
RUN;
TITLE "Trauma Data Report";
PROC PRINT LABEL DATA=MYSASLIB.TRAUMA   (FIRSTOBS=1 OBS=20);
ID INC_KEY;
```

(continued)

(continued)

```
    VAR AGE GENDER INJTYPE DISSTATUS;
    VAR ISS/STYLE={FOREGROUND=FMTSEVERE.};
    LABEL   INC_KEY='Subject ID '
              AGE='Age in 2014 '
              GENDER='Gender '
          ISS='Injury Severity Score '
          INJTYPE='Injury Type '
          DISSTATUS='Discharge Status';
RUN;
```

Note the on-screen color coding in the ISS column.

TABLE 8.8   Traffic Light Example

Trauma Data Report					
Subject ID	Age in 2014	Gender	Injury Severity Score	Injury Type	Discharge Status
468879	9.1	Female	1	Blunt	Alive
468942	17.7	Female	20	Blunt	Alive
468961	16.6	Female	5	Blunt	Alive
468971	6.5	Female	5	Blunt	Alive
469030	6.7	Male	-81		Alive
469055	10.8	Male	1		Alive
487580	17.7	Male	25	Penetrating	Alive
597075	14.6	Male	9	Blunt	Alive
603091	5.1	Female	17	Blunt	Alive
603104	8.3	Male	5	Blunt	Alive

2. Create a second format for AGE where <13 is displayed as RED and 13 or older is displayed as black.

3. Create the following format:

```
VALUE FMTISS
        LOW-<0="MISSING"
        0-<10="OKAY"
        10-<20="CONCERN"
        20-HIGH="SEVERE";
```

Apply it to the ISS variable. Submit the code and observe that the ISS column is now displayed as different color words for each category of injury.

4. Add the following attributes by changing the VAR statement for ISS to

```
VAR ISS/STYLE={FOREGROUND=FMTSEVERE.
               BACKGROUND=LIGHTYELLOW
               FONT_WEIGHT=BOLD
               FONT_FACE=SCRIPT
               FLYOVER='Severity Rating'};
```

Run this new code and observe how the additional attributes change the output. Put your cursor over one of the cells and see that a pop-up appears that says "Severity Rating." This was set up with the FLYOVER attribute. Other ODS style attributes, colors, and fonts are listed in Appendix A.

8.6   EXTENDED ODS FEATURES

This chapter has introduced a number of features available in SAS ODS. However, there are many features not covered here. For example, every ODS table output by a SAS procedure uses a template to control the way it is created. Using PROC TEMPLATE, you can modify these templates to customize the content and look of each output table.

You can store the components of any ODS report in order to modify and replay them using PROC DOCUMENT. These tasks are beyond the scope of this book, and we refer you to the SAS documentation if you want to learn more about these topics.

8.7   SUMMARY

The SAS ODS provides a number of ways to manipulate output from SAS procedures. Many examples in the book have used ODS to output results from procedures into HTML and other formats. This chapter introduced other ways to use ODS, including additional options for outputting results from SAS procedures, outputting SAS data sets, and using ODS to enhance graphic output.

EXERCISES

8.1 **Using ODS PDF.**

Using the FIRST.SAS program file, include output to the ODS PDF format using the STATISTICAL style.

8.2 **Using ODS TRACE.**

Open the program file EX_8.2.SAS. Note the TRACE ON and TRACE OFF commands. Run this program to discover the names of the output tables (in the Log window). They are as follows:

a. Statistics

b. Conflimits

c. _____

d. _____

e. _____

f. _____

Use this information in an ODS SELECT statement to limit output of the procedure to the tables for statistics and *t*-tests only.

8.3 **Use** ODS SELECT.

Open the program file EX_8.3.SAS

```
DATA TABLE;
INPUT EXPOSURE DISEASE COUNT;
DATALINES;
0 0 24
0 1 8
1 0 9
1 1 19
;
PROC FREQ DATA=TABLE; WEIGHT COUNT;
TABLES EXPOSURE*DISEASE/CHISQ;
RUN;
```

This file contains the code to analyze the 2×2 information in this table.

		DISEASED	
		YES	NO
EXPOSED	YES	24	8
	NO	9	19

The output of this program consists of three tables: a cross-tabulation, chi-square results, and Fisher's Exact test results. Using TRACE and SELECT, modify this code so that it will display only the cross-tabulation and the Fisher's Exact test (and not display the chi-square table).

8.4 **Use** ODS **to extract table statistics.**

Using information from Exercise 8.3, write a program that will save the contents of the Fisher's Exact test to a SAS data file. Use the command

```
ODS OUTPUT nameoftable=STATSOUT;
```

where *nameoftable* is the name of the Fisher's Exact test you discovered using the TRACE commands in Exercise 8.3.

a. Use Viewtable to examine the output SAS data set named STATSOUT (or use a PROC PRINT).

b. Note the name of the variable that contains the value of XP2_FISH. The value is

_____.

c. Note the name of the variable that contains the *p*-value for XP2_FISH. The value is _____.

8.5 **Use ODS to select a specific value in a table.**

In order to minimize the amount of output for the test, suppose you want to see only the *p*-value for the two-sided Fisher's Exact test. You can do this by capturing specific values from the STATSOUT data set.

a. Use the following code to print out the *p*-value from the Fisher's Exact test. (This program uses several features that were discussed in previous chapters.)

```
PROC PRINT LABEL DATA=STATSOUT;
LABEL CVALUE1='P-VALUE' NAME1='TEST';
WHERE NAME1="XP2_FISH";
VAR NAME1 CVALUE1;
ID TABLE;
RUN;
```

b. Why is the LABEL option included in the PROC PRINT statement? (See Chapter 4, the section "Labeling Variables with Explanatory Names.")

c. What does the WHERE statement do?

d. What does the ID statement do?

Hint: To figure out what each statement does, comment out the statement and rerun the program to see what happens.

PART II

STATISTICAL ANALYSIS USING SAS® PROCEDURES

9

EVALUATING QUANTITATIVE DATA

LEARNING OBJECTIVES

- To be able to calculate basic descriptive statistics using PROC MEANS
- To be able to produce graphs using PROC MEANS
- To be able to create output from PROC MEANS
- To be able to calculate basic and advanced descriptive statistics and analyze the characteristics of a set of data using PROC UNIVARIATE
- To be able to create graphs using PROC UNIVARIATE

The ancient Greek philosopher Socrates had a saying: "Know thyself." In statistics, it's important to know thy data. You need to have knowledge of the distribution and characteristics of your data before you can successfully perform other analyses. If your data are quantitative in nature (e.g., a measure such as height or the volume of liquid in a bottle), the SAS® procedures in this chapter can help you glean a lot of information from the numbers.

9.1 USING PROC MEANS

PROC MEANS is useful for evaluating quantitative data in your data set and for creating a simple summary report. Using this procedure, you can calculate simple statistics that

SAS® *Essentials: Mastering SAS for Data Analytics*, Second Edition. Alan C. Elliott and Wayne A. Woodward.
© 2016 John Wiley & Sons, Inc. Published 2016 by John Wiley & Sons, Inc.

include the mean and standard deviation, plus the minimum and maximum, all of which allow you to see quickly whether data values fall within allowed limits for each variable. If a data value is smaller or larger than expected, check your data to determine if the value has been miscoded. PROC MEANS can be used for the following:

- Describing quantitative data (numerical data on which it makes sense to perform arithmetic calculations)
- Describing means by group
- Searching for possible outliers (unusually small or large values) or incorrectly coded values
- Creating a simple report showing summary statistics.

The following section includes a list of commonly used options and statements illustrated in this chapter along with a few options that might be helpful when you use this procedure. For more information, refer to the SAS documentation.

9.1.1 PROC MEANS Statement Syntax and Options

The syntax of the PROC MEANS statement is as follows:

```
PROC MEANS <options> <statistics keywords>; <statements>;
```

The items listed in angle brackets (< >) are optional. The most commonly used options are listed in Table 9.1.

TABLE 9.1 Common Options for PROC MEANS

Option	Meaning
DATA=*dataname*	Specifies data set to use
MAXDEC=n	Uses *n* decimal places to print output
NOPRINT	Suppresses output of descriptive statistics
ALPHA=*p*	Sets the level for confidence limits (default 0.05)

Statistics keywords for PROC MEANS are listed in Table 9.2. In the table, the options in bold are the default statistics reported by SAS if no statistics keywords are listed. On the other hand, you can select your own list of statistics to report. For example, the statement

```
PROC MEANS DATA=RESEARCH MEAN MEDIAN STD;RUN;
```

instructs SAS to calculate the mean, median, and standard deviation on the quantitative data in the RESEARCH data set. The confidence interval settings are based on a default Alpha = 0.05. This can be changed using the ALPHA= option as shown here:

```
PROC MEANS DATA=RESEARCH ALPHA=.10 MEAN MEDIAN STD CLM;RUN;
```

TABLE 9.2   Statistics Keywords for PROC MEANS

Option	Meaning
CLM	Two-sided confidence interval
CSS	Corrected sum of squares
CV	Coefficient of variation
KURTOSIS	Kurtosis
LCLM	Lower confidence limit
MAX	Maximum (largest)
MEAN	Arithmetic average
MEDIAN (P50)	50th percentile
MIN	Minimum (smallest)
MODE	Mode
N	Number of observations
NMISS	Number of missing observations
P1	1st percentile
P5	5th percentile
P10	10th percentile
P90	90th percentile
P95	95th percentile
P99	99th percentile
PROBT	p-Value associated with t-test requested by the option T
Q1 (P25)	1st quartile
Q3 (P75)	3rd quartile
QRANGE	Quartile range
RANGE	Range
SKEWNESS (SKEW)	Skewness
STDDEV (STD)	Standard deviation
STDERR	Standard error
SUM	Sum of observations
SUMWGT	Sum of the WEIGHT variable values
T	Student's t-value
UCLM	Upper confidence limit
USS	Uncorrected sum of squares
VAR	Variance

9.1.2   Commonly Used Statements for PROC MEANS

Statements related to PROC MEANS appear after the semicolon in the initial PROC MEANS statement. Table 9.3 lists commonly used statements for PROC MEANS. For more information, consult the SAS documentation. The following examples illustrate the use of PROC MEANS options and statements:

```
* Simplest invocation - on all numeric variables *;
PROC MEANS;

*Specified statistics and variables *;
PROC MEANS N MEAN STD;
VAR SODIUM CARBO;
```

TABLE 9.3   Common Statements for PROC MEANS

Statement	Meaning
VAR *variable(s)*;	Identifies one or more variables to analyze. This can be any standard SAS variable list such as AGE SBP GENDER, or a range such as TIME1-TIME10
CLASS *variable(s)*;	Specifies variables that the procedure uses to group the data into classification levels
OUTPUT OUT=*dataname*;	Specifies a SAS output data set that will contain statistics calculated in PROC MEANS. For example, OUTPUT OUT=*SAS-data-set*; To specify names of specific variables' output, use the following format: OUTPUT <OUT=*SAS-data-set*> *statistic-keyword-1=name(s)* <... *statistic-keyword-n-name(s)*> <*percentiles-specification*> ;
FREQ *weight* variable;	Specifies a variable that represents a count of observations
BY, FORMAT, LABEL, WHERE	These statements are common to most procedures and may be used here

```
* Subgroup descriptive statistics in separate table
  using the BY statement*;
PROC SORT; BY GENDER;RUN;
PROC MEANS; BY GENDER;
  VAR FAT PROTEIN SODIUM;


* Subgroup descriptive statistics in the same table
  using the CLASS statement*;
PROC MEANS; CLASS GENDER;
  VAR FAT PROTEIN SODIUM;
```

HANDS-ON EXAMPLE

In this example, you will learn how to use some of the basic options in PROC MEANS. Suppose you have a data set of measurements (weight, height, and age) from several children. You will perform the following tasks using PROC MEANS:

- Report simple descriptive statistics.
- Limit the output to two decimal places.
- Request a selected list of statistics.

1. Open the program file AMEANS1.SAS.

```
DATA CHILDREN;
INPUT WEIGHT HEIGHT AGE;
DATALINES;
```

```
64  57  8
71  59  10
53  49  6
67  62  11
55  51  8
58  50  8
77  55  10
57  48  9
56  42  10
51  42  6
76  61  12
68  57  9
;
PROC MEANS DATA=CHILDREN;
TITLE 'PROC MEANS, simplest use';
RUN;
PROC MEANS MAXDEC=2; VAR WEIGHT HEIGHT;
TITLE 'PROC MEANS, limit decimals, specify variables';
RUN;
PROC MEANS MAXDEC=2 N MEAN STDERR MEDIAN; VAR WEIGHT HEIGHT;
TITLE 'PROC MEANS, specify statistics to report';
RUN;
```

TABLE 9.4   Output for PROC MEANS

PROC MEANS, simplest use

The MEANS Procedure

Variable	N	Mean	Std Dev	Minimum	Maximum
WEIGHT	12	62.7500000	8.9861004	51.0000000	77.0000000
HEIGHT	12	52.7500000	6.8240884	42.0000000	62.0000000
AGE	12	8.9166667	1.8319554	6.0000000	12.0000000

PROC MEANS, limit decimals, specify variables

The MEANS Procedure

Variable	N	Mean	Std Dev	Minimum	Maximum
WEIGHT	12	62.75	8.99	51.00	77.00
HEIGHT	12	52.75	6.82	42.00	62.00

PROC MEANS, specify statistics to report

The MEANS Procedure

Variable	N	Mean	Std Error	Median
WEIGHT	12	62.75	2.59	61.00
HEIGHT	12	52.75	1.97	53.00

(continued)

(continued)

2. Run the program and observe the output in Table 9.4. Note the following:
   - In the first output table, statistics are reported to seven decimal points in the first PROC MEANS output and are limited to two decimal points for the other two calls to PROC MEANS, as controlled by the MAXDEC=2 option.
   - In the second table, descriptive statistics are reported only for the two variables specified in the VAR statement.
   - In the third table, only the statistics selected in the PROC statement are reported.

9.1.3   Using PROC MEANS with BY Group and CLASS Statements

It is common to compare means across the levels of some grouping factor that, for example, specifies treatment times. The following Hands-on Example shows you how to use PROC MEANS to calculate weight gain in chickens by the type of feed. This example uses two methods for producing the desired calculations:

- Results reported for each group in separate tables using the BY group option (following a call to PROC SORT).
- Results reported for each group in a single table using the CLASS option.

HANDS-ON EXAMPLE

In this example, you will learn how to display basic statistics by groups using two techniques.

1. Open the program file AMEANS2.SAS.

```
DATA FERTILIZER;
INPUT FEEDTYPE WEIGHTGAIN;
DATALINES;
1 46.20
1 55.60
1 53.30
1 44.80
1 55.40
1 56.00
1 48.90
2 51.30
2 52.40
2 54.60
2 52.20
2 64.30
2 55.00
;
```

```
PROC SORT DATA=FERTILIZER;BY FEEDTYPE;
PROC MEANS; VAR WEIGHTGAIN; BY FEEDTYPE;
TITLE 'Summary statistics by group';
RUN;
PROC MEANS; VAR WEIGHTGAIN; CLASS FEEDTYPE;
TITLE 'Summary statistics USING CLASS';
```

2. Examine the SAS code. Note that the data must be sorted before you can use a BY group option in a PROC MEANS statement. In the second PROC MEANS, where you are using the CLASS option, sorting is not necessary (even if the data are not already sorted).
3. Run the program. Examine the output from the first PROC MEANS, which uses the BY option (Table 9.5). The output contains two separate tables, one for each value of FEEDTYPE.
4. Examine the output given in Table 9.6 for the second PROC MEANS. In this instance, which uses the CLASS option, the output for both variables appears in a single table, broken down by FEEDTYPE. (Note the N Obs and N columns. If there are missing values, the N column will be less than the N Obs column.)
5. Modify the second call to PROC MEANS (using the CLASS statement) to output the following statistics:

N MEAN MEDIAN MIN MAX

and use MAXDEC=2 to limit number of decimals in output. Run the edited program and observe the output.

TABLE 9.5   PROC MEANS Output Using the BY Option

Summary statistics by group

The MEANS Procedure

FEEDTYPE=1

Analysis Variable : WEIGHTGAIN			
N	Mean	Std Dev	Minimum	Maximum
7	51.4571429	4.7475808	44.8000000	56.0000000

FEEDTYPE=2

Analysis Variable : WEIGHTGAIN			
N	Mean	Std Dev	Minimum	Maximum
6	54.9666667	4.7944412	51.3000000	64.3000000

(continued)

(continued)

TABLE 9.6   PROC MEANS Output Using the CLASS Option

Summary statistics USING CLASS

The MEANS Procedure

Analysis Variable : WEIGHTGAIN						
FEEDTYPE	N Obs	N	Mean	Std Dev	Minimum	Maximum
1	7	7	51.4571429	4.7475808	44.8000000	56.0000000
2	6	6	54.9666667	4.7944412	51.3000000	64.3000000

9.1.4   Output Statistics from PROC MEANS

PROC MEANS allows you to capture statistics into a new SAS Data file that you could then use in another DATA step or procedure. The OUTPUT statement is used to specify the name of the output data set. The syntax for this statement is

```
OUTPUT OUT=filename statisticname=<varname>;
```

You can specify a number of statistics and names, or leave off the name such as MEAN= . The output will include all of the variables in the VAR list, or all numeric variables if no VAR list is specified. For example,

```
PROC MEANS DATA="C:\SASDATA\SOMEDATA";
OUTPUT OUT=TIME1MEAN MEAN=T1;
VAR TIME1;
RUN;
```

outputs the means of TIME1 to a data SAS set named TIME1MEAN and gives it the SAS variable name T1.

HANDS-ON EXAMPLE

In this example, you will learn how to output statistics into a new SAS data file using PROC MEANS.

1. Open the program file AMEANS3.SAS. Note the OUTPUT statement including OUT=TIME1MEAN and MEANS=T1. This names the output file TIME1MEAN and names the mean of TIME1 as T1. Submit this program and observe the output given in Table 9.7.

```
PROC MEANS DATA="C:\SASDATA\SOMEDATA";
OUTPUT OUT=TIME1MEAN MEAN=T1;
VAR TIME1;
RUN;
PROC PRINT DATA=TIME1MEAN;RUN;
```

TABLE 9.7   PROC MEANS Using OUTPUT Statement

Analysis Variable : TIME1 Baseline				
N	Mean	Std Dev	Minimum	Maximum
50	21.2680000	1.7169551	17.0000000	24.2000000

Obs	_TYPE_	_FREQ_	T1
1	0	50	21.268

2. Take off the `T1` from the `MEAN=` statement (keep it as `MEAN=`) and resubmit. The only change is that the variable name reported in the `PROC PRINT` is now `TIME1` instead of `T1` since the name was no longer in the `OUTPUT` statement.

3. Change the `OUTPUT` statement to

```
OUTPUT OUT=TIME1MEAN MEAN=T1MEAN STD=T1STD;
```

Resubmit and observe the resulting variables listed in the `TIME1MEAN` data set.

4. To use the output from `PROC MEANS` to calculate a z-score for `TIME1`, add the following `DATA` step at the end of the code:

```
DATA ZSCORE;SET "C:\SASDATA\SOMEDATA";
IF _N_=1 then SET TIME1MEAN;
ZSCORE=(TIME1-T1MEAN)/T1STD;
DROP _TYPE_ _FREQ_;
RUN;
PROC PRINT DATA=ZSCORE;RUN;
```

The IF statement where `_N_=1` includes the first observation from the data set `TIME1MEAN` in the new `ZSCORE` dataset, making the information shown in Table 9.7 available for the subsequent `ZSCORE` calculation.

Resubmit and observe the output. A portion of the output is given in Table 9.8. Note the columns containing the mean and standard deviation of `TIME1` plus the calculated column named `ZSCORE`. This illustrates how you can use calculated values from `PROC MEANS` output as import into another data set calculation.

(continued)

(continued)

TABLE 9.8   Output Includes Calculated ZSCORE

Obs	ID	GP	AGE	TIME1	TIME2	TIME3	TIME4	STATUS	SEX	GENDER	T1MEAN	T1STD	ZSCORE
1	101	A	12	22.3	25.3	28.2	30.6	5	0	Female	21.268	1.71696	0.60106
2	102	A	11	22.8	27.5	33.3	35.8	5	0	Female	21.268	1.71696	0.89228
3	110	A	12	18.5	26.0	29.0	27.9	5	1	Male	21.268	1.71696	-1.61216
4	187	A	11	22.5	29.3	32.6	33.7	2	0	Female	21.268	1.71696	0.71755
5	312	A	4	17.0	21.3	22.7	21.2	5	1	Male	21.268	1.71696	-2.48580
6	390	A	6	21.3	30.5	30.7	30.1	4	0	Female	21.268	1.71696	0.01864

9.2   USING PROC UNIVARIATE

The earlier section described how to use the PROC MEANS statement to calculate basic statistics for a quantitative variable. PROC UNIVARIATE provides a wider variety of statistics and graphs and is better suited to helping you discover important information about the distribution of each variable, such as whether

- the data are approximately normally distributed.
- there are outliers in the data (if so, where?)
- data distributions for variables differ by group.

With this information in hand, you can make informed decisions about how best to present and analyze your data. The syntax of the PROC UNIVARIATE statement is as follows:

```
PROC UNIVARIATE <options>; <statements>;
```

Common options and statements for PROC UNIVARIATE are listed in Tables 9.9 and 9.10, respectively.

Histogram Options: Table 9.11 lists options for the HISTOGRAM statement. These provide a number of ways you can enhance the basic histogram. These options appear after a slash / in the HISTOGRAM option. For example,

```
HISTOGRAM  var/options;
```

or more specifically

```
HISTOGRAM AGE/NORMAL;
```

Color Options: Color options for PROC UNIVARIATE are shown in Table 9.12. They specify color for various parts of the histogram. These options appear after a slash / in the HISTOGRAM option and typically relate to a displayed NORMAL curve. For example,

```
HISTOGRAM AGE/ NORMAL (COLOR=RED);
```

TABLE 9.9   Common Options for PROC UNIVARIATE

Option	Meaning
DATA=dataname	Specifies data set to use
CIBASIC	Requests confidence limits for the mean, standard deviation, and variance based on normally distributed data
ALPHA=p	Specifies the level for the confidence limits
MU0=n	Specifies the value of the location parameter for the one-sample t-test, sign test, and signed rank test (MU stands for the Greek letter μ, which symbolizes the population mean)
NORMAL	Requests tests for normality
PLOTS	Requests stem-and-leaf, box, and probability plots Request a series of explanatory plots to be created. These include a horizontal histogram, a box plot, and a normal probability plot.
NOPRINT	Suppresses the output of descriptive statistics (primarily used in conjunction with the OUTPUT statement)
TRIMMED=value	Trims the top and bottom proportion of the data before calculating the mean; this can be used to eliminate outliers from the calculation (e.g., TRIMMED=0.1)

TABLE 9.10   Common Statements for PROC UNIVARIATE

Option	Meaning
VAR variable(s);	Identifies one or more variables to analyze
OUTPUT	Identifies output data set and statistics to include in the data set; the syntax for this statement is OUTPUT <OUT=SAS-data-set> statistic-keyword-1=name(s) < ... statistic-keyword-n=name(s)> <percentiles-specification>;
HISTOGRAM	Produces a histogram of one or more specified variables; the syntax is HISTOGRAM <variable(s)> </ option(s)>; A simple program that creates a histogram using the variable AGE in the SOMEDATA data set is PROC UNIVARIATE DATA="C:\SASDATA\SOMEDATA"; VAR AGE; HISTOGRAM AGE; RUN; See options for this statement below
INSET	Puts a box containing summary statistics in a graph associated with CDFPLOT, HISTOGRAM, PPPLOT, PROBPLOT, or QQPLOT statements
BY,CLASS,WHERE	Statements common to most PROCS.

(Apart from HISTOGRAM, these options also work with CDFPLOT, PPPLOT, PROBPLOT, and QQPLOT.)

A listing of SAS colors can be found in Appendix A. Note: For recent versions of SAS, you may have to "turn off" ODS graphics for these to work. Do this with the code

TABLE 9.11   Common OPTIONS for the PROC UNIVARIATE HISTOGRAM Statement

Option	Meaning

Density curves such as NORMAL	Overlays a density curve on the histogram. Common options would be NORMAL or KERNEL. NORMAL displays a Gaussian (bell-shaped) curve over the histogram. KERNEL displays a smoothed nonparametric density curve. Specifies characteristics of the curve in parentheses. For example,
	`HISTOGRAM AGE/NORMAL (COLOR=GREEN W=5);`
	specifies a green normal curve with width 5 (1 is default). Another example:
	`HISTOGRAM AGE/NORMAL (COLOR=green W=5)`
	`CFILL=YELLOW;`
	fills under the curve with the color specified by the CFILL option. You could also use PFILL to indicate a pattern.
	Note: Some color options may not work in some versions of SAS unless you turn off ODS graphics using code such as
	`ODS GRAPHICS OFF;`

MIDPOINTS	This option allows you to specify the intervals for the histogram bars MIDPOINTS = min to max by units For example, MIDPOINTS =**0** to **40** by **2** specifies that the horizontal axis will have a minimum of 0, a maximum of 40, and increment of two units. The midpoints of the intervals would be 0, 2, 4, ... , 40
VSCALE	This option specifies the scale of the vertical axis VSCALE=type scale (count, proportion, or percent) For example, VSCALE=COUNT specifies that the scale of the vertical axis will be the number of observations per bin (count). You can alternately request that the scale be proportion or percent
WAXIS=*width*	This option specifies the width of the histogram bars For example, WAXIS= 3 specifies that the axis width be three units wide (1 is the default)
WBARLINE=*width*	This option specifies the width of the line around the bar `WBARLINE= width-scale (1 is the default)` For example, WBARLINE= 3 specifies that the lines around the histogram bars be three units wide

NROWS=*n*
 	
NCOLS=*n*
	Specifies the number of rows or columns in a matrix of histograms specified when a CLASS statement is used to produce multiple histograms. For example,
	`PROC UNIVARIATE;`
	`CLASS GENDER;`
	`VAR AGE;`
	`HISTOGRAM AGE/NROWS=2;`
	produces two histograms one over the other (two rows)

TABLE 9.12   Common OPTIONS for the COLOR Statement (in a Univariate Graph)

Option	Meaning
(COLOR=color)	Specifies the color of the density line. Put the COLOR option in parentheses. For example, HISTOGRAM AGE/ NORMAL (COLOR=RED);
CAXIS=color	Specifies the color of axes. After a density curve request (such as HISTOGRAM), this option does not appear in parentheses. For example, HISTOGRAM AGE/ NORMAL (COLOR=BLUE) CAXIS=RED; Color choices are described in Appendix A
CBARLINE=color	Specifies the color of the line around the bars. For example, HISTOGRAM AGE/ NORMAL CAXIS=RED CBARLINES=GREEN;
CFILL=color	Specifies the color of the bars. For example, HISTOGRAM AGE/ NORMAL CAXIS=RED CFILL=GREEN;
CFRAME=color	Specifies the background color within the frame. For example, HISTOGRAM AGE/ NORMAL CAXIS=RED CFRAME=YELLOW;
CTEXT=color	Specifies the color of tick mark values and labels For example, HISTOGRAM AGE/CTEXT=GREEN; specifies that the borders around the histogram bars will be green

```
ODS GRAPHICS OFF:
```

You can subsequently turn ODS graphics back on with

```
ODS GRAPHCIS ON;
```

Bar Characteristics: Use the statements in Table 9.13 to specify bar characteristics in the */options* section of the HISTOGRAM statement. A listing of SAS pattern codes can be found in Appendix A.

TABLE 9.13   Common OPTIONS for the PROC UNIVARIATE BAR Statement (Related to a Histogram)

Option	Meaning
BARWIDTH=n	Specifies bar width where *n* is the percent of the screen. For example, HISTOGRAM AGE/BARWIDTH=10;
PFILL=patterncode	Indicates which fill pattern to use in the histogram bars For example, HISTOGRAM AGE/PFILL=R4; specifies that right 45° stripes will fill the boxes. The 4 specifies the width of the stripes. See also CBARLINE and WBARLINE above. Fill options are described in Appendix A
BARLABEL	Places a label above the bar. Options include COUNT, PERCENT, and PROPORTION. For example, HISTOGRAM AGE/normal kernel BARLABEL=COUNT;

Inset Statement: The INSET statement puts a box containing summary statistics in a graph associated with CDFPLOT, HISTOGRAM, PPPLOT, PROBPLOT, or QQPLOT statements. Commonly used INSET options are listed in Table 9.14. For example, the code

```
HISTOGRAM AGE/NORMAL;
INSET MEAN STD ;
```

creates a plot with mean and standard deviation listed in an inset box within the graph frame.

For additional options see the SAS documentation.

TABLE 9.14   Common OPTIONS for the PROC UNIVARIATE INSET Statement

Option	Meaning
Display statistics	Indicates which statistics to report in the inset box. The list is the same as the statistics used in PROC MEANS. Commonly used statistics include N, NOBS, MEAN, STD, SUM, MIN, MAX, MEDIAN, and so on. For example, PROC UNIVARIATE; VAR AGE HISTOGRAM AGE/NORMAL; INSET MEAN STD MIN MAX;
Format values	Allows you to specify labels and formats for displayed statistics. For example, PROC UNIVARIATE; VAR AGE HISTOGRAM AGE/NORMAL; INSET MEAN="Mean" (5.2) STD ='St. Dev." (5.2); where the item in parentheses is a format applied to the displayed statistics
NORMALTEST	Displays a test for normality. To use, place a NORMALTEST option in the PROC UNIVARIATE statement and NORMALTEST and PNORMAL INSET option. For example,
PNORMAL	PROC UNIVARIATE NORMALTEST; VAR AGE; HISTOGRAM AGE; INSET NORMALTEST PNORMAL; displays results of Shapiro–Wilk test for normality
Inset position	Positions the inset box inside the graph frame using map-type specifications such as NE (northeast – upper right), NW, SE, SW, N (top middle), S (bottom middle). You may also position the box outside the frame using TM (top middle), BM, RM, or LM
Inset box title	Includes a title for the inset box by indicating it after a slash in the INSET statement using HEADER=, FORMAT=, and POSITION=. For example, HISTOGRAM AGE; INSET NORMALTEST PNORMAL/HEADER="Key Title" POSITION=RM FORMAT=5.2; places the box outside the frame at the right middle (RM) and formats all statistics using 5.2
NOFRAME	Does not display a box around the inset
HEIGHT=	Height of characters in the inset box. The default is 1

PROC MEANS is useful for calculating descriptive statistics for many variables at a time, whereas PROC UNIVARIATE is best for the case in which you want to analyze only one or a few variables in depth and create detailed histograms. The following Hands-on Example illustrates some of these commonly used options and statements.

HANDS-ON EXAMPLE

In this example, you will learn how to use PROC UNIVARIATE.

1. Open the program file AUNI1.SAS.

```
DATA EXAMPLE;
INPUT AGE @@;
DATALINES;
12 11 12 12 9 11 8 8 7 11 12 14 9 10 7 13
6 11 12 4 11 9 13 6 9 7 13 9 13 12 10 13
11 8 11 15 12 14 10 10 13 13 10 8 12 7 13
11 9 12
;
PROC UNIVARIATE DATA=EXAMPLE;
     VAR AGE;
RUN;
```

2. Run this program and observe that this procedure produces several tables of output, and that the output in the Results Viewer is in HTML format. Below is a description of the statistics reported in these tables.

9.2.1   Understanding PROC UNIVARIATE Output

The output from the Hands-on Example is given in several tables, and we describe the contents in each table below:

Moments Output: The first table (Moments; Table 9.15) provides a list of descriptive statistics for the variable AGE.

N is the sample size.

Sum Weights is the same as the sample size unless a WEIGHT statement is used to identify a separate variable that contains counts for each observation.

Mean is the arithmetic mean (also known as the average).

Sum Observations is the total (sum) of all the data values.

Std Deviation is the standard deviation.

Variance is a measure of the spread of the distribution (and is the square of the standard deviation).

Skewness is a measure of the symmetry of the data. For normally distributed data, skewness should be close to 0. A positive value indicates that the skew is to the right (long right tail), and a negative value indicates a skew to the left (long left tail).

TABLE 9.15   Moments Output for PROC UNIVARIATE

Moments			
N	50	Sum Weights	50
Mean	10.46	Sum Observations	523
Std Deviation	2.42613323	Variance	5.88612245
Skewness	-0.5119219	Kurtosis	-0.2610615
Uncorrected SS	5759	Corrected SS	288.42
Coeff Variation	23.1943903	Std Error Mean	0.34310705

Kurtosis measures the shape of the distribution (0 indicates normality), where a positive value indicates a distribution that is more peaked with heavier tails than a normal distribution and a negative value indicates a flatter distribution with lighter tails.

Uncorrected SS is the sum of the squared data values.

Corrected SS is the sum of the squared deviations from the mean, a quantity that is used in the calculation of the standard deviation and other statistics.

Coef Variation is the coefficient of variation, which is a unitless measure of variability. It is usually expressed as a percentage and is helpful in comparing the variability between two measures that may have differing units of measurement.

Std Err Mean is the standard error of the mean. This is calculated as the standard deviation divided by $\sqrt{N}$, and it provides a measure of the variability of the sample mean. That is, if we were to take similar samples over and over again, the standard error of the mean would approximate the standard deviation of the sample means.

Basic Statistical Measures: The second table from PROC UNIVARIATE (Table 9.16) provides several measures of the central tendency and spread of the data. Some values are repeated from the previous table.

Median is the centermost value of the ranked data.

Mode is the most frequent value in the data.

Range is the maximum value minus the minimum value, which is a measure of the spread of the data.

Interquartile Range (IQR) is the difference between the 25th and 75th percentiles of the data and is a measure of spread of the data.

TABLE 9.16   Basic Statistical Measures from PROC UNIVARIATE

Basic Statistical Measures			
Location		Variability	
Mean	10.46000	Std Deviation	2.42613
Median	11.00000	Variance	5.88612
Mode	12.00000	Range	11.00000
		Interquartile Range	3.00000

TABLE 9.17   Tests for Location from PROC UNIVARIATE

Tests for Location: Mu0=0				
Test		Statistic	p Value	
Student's t	t	30.48611	Pr > |t|	<.0001
Sign	M	25	Pr >= |M|	<.0001
Signed Rank	S	637.5	Pr >= |S|	<.0001

Tests for Location: The tests for location given in Table 9.17 are used to determine whether the mean (or central tendency) of the data is significantly different from 0 (or another hypothesized value). These tests are discussed more thoroughly in upcoming chapters and are only briefly described here.

Student's *t*-Test is a single sample *t*-test of the null hypothesis that the mean of the data is equal to the hypothesized value (in this case 0 by default). When $p < 0.05$, you would typically reject this hypothesis.

Sign Test is a test of the null hypothesis that the probability of obtaining a positive value (often these values are differences) is the same as that for a negative value.

Signed Rank Test is a nonparametric test often used instead of the Student's *t*-test when the data are not normally distributed and the sample sizes are small.

Quantiles: Table 9.18 provides a listing of commonly used quantiles of the data including the median (listed as the 50th quantile). To interpret the values in the quantile table, note that the *k*th quantile is the value below which *k*% of the values in the data fall. ("Definition 5" in the table refers to the specific method used to calculate the quantiles using an empirical distribution with averaging; see Frigge, Hoaglin, and Iglewicz, 1989).

TABLE 9.18   Quantiles from PROC UNIVARIATE

Quantiles (Definition 5)	
Quantile	Estimate
100% Max	15
99%	15
95%	14
90%	13
75% Q3	12
50% Median	11
25% Q1	9
10%	7
5%	6
1%	4
0% Min	4

Extreme Observations: The Extreme Observations table (Table 9.19) provides a listing of the largest and smallest values in the data set. This is useful for locating outliers in your data. Note that with each extreme value listed in the table, the observation number is also provided. This helps you to be able to go back to locate these extreme observations in your data set.

TABLE 9.19   Extreme Values Output from PROC UNIVARIATE

Extreme Observations			
Lowest		Highest	
Value	Obs	Value	Obs
4	20	13	42
6	24	13	47
6	17	14	12
7	46	14	38
7	26	15	36

9.2.2   Using PROC UNIVARIATE to Assess the Normality of the Data

When you select certain options in the PROC UNIVARIATE statement, SAS produces information helpful in assessing the normality of your data. This is important information because a number of statistical tests are based on an assumption of normality. For example, consider the following SAS code that can be used to assess normality:

```
PROC UNIVARIATE NORMAL PLOT DATA=EXAMPLE; VAR AGE;
    HISTOGRAM AGE/NORMAL;
```

The NORMAL and PLOT options produce the following output:

- Tests for normality
- Stem-and-leaf plot (for some SAS versions)
- Box plot
- Normal probability plot.

The HISTOGRAM statement with the NORMAL option in addition produces a

- histogram
- superimposed normal distribution curve.

HANDS-ON EXAMPLE

In this example, you will learn how to request options to assess normality using PROC UNIVARIATE.

1. Open the program file AUNI2.SAS.

```
DATA EXAMPLE;
INPUT AGE @@;
DATALINES;
12 11 12 12 9 11 8 8 7 11 12 14 9 10 7 13
6 11 12 4 11 9 13 6 9 7 13 9 13 12 10 13
11 8 11 15 12 14 10 10 13 13 10 8 12 7 13
11 9 12
;
PROC UNIVARIATE NORMAL PLOT DATA=EXAMPLE; VAR AGE;
TITLE 'PROC UNIVARIATE EXAMPLE';
RUN;
```

2. Run this program and observe the output, which is described below. PROC UNI-VARIATE provides several tests and graphical methods useful in assessing normality. Observe the graphs shown in Figure 9.1. These are the default graphs produced by PROC UNIVARIATE.

Figure 9.1   Default plots to assess normality from PROC UNIVARIATE

(continued)

(continued)

Using Graphs as a Visual Check for Normality: The graphics shown in Figure 9.1 may differ for different versions of SAS. They include a distribution plot (horizontal histogram) with a box-and-whiskers plot and a normal probability plot. Here are brief explanations of each plot:

- The **horizontal histogram** (top left) is a visual representation of the distribution of the values of AGE. To assess normality, you want the histogram to have a peak in the middle with equal tails trailing off on either side. (In some versions of SAS, this plot is a stem-and-leaf plot.)

- The **box-and-whiskers plot** or boxplot (top right) is a graphical representation of the quartiles of the data with 50% (the middle) of the data represented by the box and the whiskers representing 25% of the data on each side. The center line represents the median (50th percentile) and the diamond (◊) indicates the mean. The "o" that stands alone at the bottom of the box-and-whiskers plot indicates an extreme value or outlier. If the data are normally distributed, the box-and-whiskers plot is approximately symmetric with similar values for the mean and median.

- The **normal probability plot** (bottom) provides a graphic that (if the data are normally distributed) is a plot of points (shown as dots) that lie in a tight random scatter around the reference (diagonal) line. (In this case, the fact that AGE is recorded in whole numbers causes a sequence on the horizontal line that may make the plot confusing to interpret.)

3. Because the NORMAL option is included in PROC UNIVARIATE, tests for normality are displayed. These are shown in Table 9.20, labeled goodness-of-fit for normal distribution.

TABLE 9.20   Test for Normality from PROC UNIVARIATE

Goodness-of-Fit Tests for Normal Distribution				
Test		Statistic	p Value	
Kolmogorov-Smirnov	D	0.14806740	Pr > D	<0.010
Cramer-von Mises	W-Sq	0.14576151	Pr > W-Sq	0.026
Anderson-Darling	A-Sq	0.83498886	Pr > A-Sq	0.030

Tests for Normality: Tests for normality given in Table 9.20 are one way to assess whether the data appear normally distributed. Three tests for normality are provided: Kolmogorov–Smirnov, Cramer–von Mises, and Anderson–Darling. Some versions of SAS also include a Shapiro–Wilk test. The *p*-values in this table are for testing the null hypothesis that the AGE variable is normally distributed. In this case, all three tests indicate an issue with normality since the *p*-values for all three tests are all <0.05.

The three tests for normality represent differing statistical approaches for answering the same question. Frankly, many statisticians believe that these tests are helpful tools but should not be used as the only basis for assessing normality. Moreover, some references indicate that these tests are helpful only when the size of the data set is less than 50.

9.2.3 Creating a Histogram Using PROC UNIVARIATE

A histogram is a commonly used plot for visually examining the distribution of a set of data. You can produce a histogram in PROC UNIVARIATE with the following statement:

```
HISTOGRAM AGE;
```

The statement HISTOGRAM AGE produces a histogram for the variable AGE. If you use the code

```
HISTOGRAM AGE/NORMAL;
```

then the NORMAL option produces a superimposed normal curve. The command including the NORMAL option produces the plot shown in Figure 9.2.

HANDS-ON EXAMPLE

1. As a continuation of the previous example using the program file AUNI2.SAS, add the statement

```
HISTOGRAM AGE/NORMAL;
```

after the PROC UNIVARIATE statement and before the TITLE statement. Run the revised program and observe the new histogram with superimposed normal curve included in the output, as shown in Figure 9.2.

Figure 9.2   Histogram with normal curve superimposed

The superimposed normal curve on the histogram allows you not only to assess whether the data are approximately normally distributed but also to visualize the apparent departure from normality. If the data are normally distributed, you will expect the peak of the histogram bars to approximately coincide with the peak of the normal curve. In this case, the data again appear to be skewed to the left.

These options provide several methods for you to assess the normality of your data. No plot or test by itself is definitive. They should be taken as a whole.

9.3 GOING DEEPER: ADVANCED PROC UNIVARIATE OPTIONS

With a few additional commands using PROC UNIVARIATE, it is relatively easy to create a series of histograms that allow you to compare subgroups of your data. In this Going Deeper section, we show how to display the distributions of a variable at each of several levels of a grouping variable using data in a simulated data set. The following Hands-on Example illustrates how you could create histograms for systolic blood pressure by RACE using PROC UNIVARIATE.

HANDS-ON EXAMPLE

In this example, you will learn how to create multiple histograms using a grouping (CLASS) variable.

1. Open the program file AUNI3.SAS. The variables in the WOUND data set include AGE, GENDER, RACE_CAT, ISS (Injury Severity Score), DISSTATUS (Discharge Status), WOUND (Wound type), SBP, and TEMP_C (Temperature in Celsius).

```
PROC UNIVARIATE DATA="C:\SASDATA\WOUND" NOPRINT;
   CLASS RACE_CAT;
   LABEL RACE_CAT="RACE";
   VAR SBP;
   HISTOGRAM /NORMAL (COLOR=GREEN W=5) NROWS=3;
RUN;
```

The new statements used in this example include the following:
- The NOPRINT statement suppresses most output except the graph because we're interested only in producing the graph.
- The CLASS RACE statement indicates that the data are to be examined for each category (classification) of the RACE variable.
- LABEL creates an output label for RACE_CAT as RACE.
- NROWS=3 indicates that three graphs (three rows) will appear on each output page. Because there are three RACE groups, all graphs will appear together. Similarly, you can use NCOLS=3 to place all three graphs on the same page in three columns.
- The COLOR=GREEN and W=5 statements in parentheses refer to the NORMAL option and tell SAS to display the fitted normal curve with a green line and with a width of 5.
- The DATA= statement accesses the data from the file WOUND.SAS7BDAT. You could also use the statement DATA=MYSASLIB.WOUND to access the data if the MYSASLIB library is defined.

2. Run the program and observe the output in the Results Viewer (see Figure 9.3). Note that the three histograms are for the variable SBP separately for three values of RACE_CAT. In this case, there is a visual agreement that SBP is similarly distributed for all races, and the assumption of normality for each race appears plausible. (Note: If you do not get this plot, place the command ODS GRAPHICS OFF; at the beginning of your code. This is needed for some versions of SAS.)

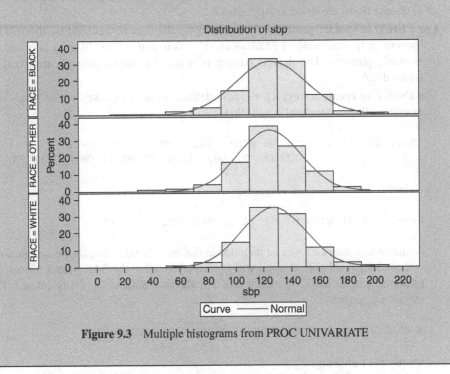

Figure 9.3   Multiple histograms from PROC UNIVARIATE

There are a number of formatting options you can apply to histograms to customize their appearance. Briefly, here are common ways to enhance a histogram:

Use PROC FORMAT: Prepare your categorial variables with formats that allow you to display names of categories in the histogram. Use this, for example, in the WOUND SAS data set, so that you could use the following code to assign names to the two categories. Using this format allows you to display names of the group categories causing the PENETRATE and NONPENETRATE to appear in the graph rather than with the 0, 1 data codes.

```
PROC FORMAT;
VALUE FMTWOUND 0="NONPENETRATE"
               1="PENETRATE";
RUN;
```

Include a CLASS statement: Including a CLASS statement allows you to display comparative histograms by grouping factors such as (in the case of the WOUND data set) by WOUND type and GENDER.

Include HISTOGRAM Options: The options within the `HISTOGRAM` statement define how the graph will appear. The statements `NROWS=2 NCOLS=2` produce two histograms per row (for `WOUND`, the first item in the `CLASS` statement) and two histograms per column (for `GENDER` or the second item in the `CLASS` statement).

Use CFILL to specify color fill: The bar colors are specified by the `CFILL` (color fill) statement: `CFILL=BLUE`. Some of the colors available in SAS (there are thousands to choose from) are listed in Appendix A.

Use PFILL to specify patterns: The pattern for the bars is specified by the `PFILL` (pattern fill) statement: `PFILL=M3N45`. You can select from a number of available patterns. The default pattern is solid. Additional patterns are listed in Appendix A.

Use INSET to create a key: This option defines an inset or a key to the graph. An example `INSET` statement is as follows:

```
INSET N='N:' (4.0) MIN='MIN:' (4.1) MAX='MAX:' (4.1)
            / HEADER="My Key" NOFRAME POSITION=NE HEIGHT=2;
```

In this code

```
N='N:' (4.0) MIN='MIN:' (4.1) MAX='MAX:' (4.1)
```

defines which statistics will be included in the inset. In this case, `N` (the sample size) will be designated with `N:` and will be displayed using the SAS output format 4.0 (designated in the code in parentheses). The `MIN` and `MAX` are similarly defined. The remaining options

```
/ HEADER="My Key" NOFRAME POSITION=NE HEIGHT=2;
```

specify the following:
- A header will be included for the box titled My Key.
- No frame will be printed around the inset.
- The inset box position will be in the `NE` (northeast) corner of the graph.
- The height of the characters will be set at 2 units.

The following example makes use of these `PROC UNIVARIATE` options when creating a custom `HISTOGRAM`.

HANDS-ON EXAMPLE

1. Open the program file `AUNI4.SAS`.

```
PROC FORMAT;
VALUE FMTWOUND 0="NONPENETRATE"
               1="PENETRATE";
RUN;
```

```
TITLE 'HISTOGRAMS of SBP by GENDER and WOUND TYPE';
PROC UNIVARIATE DATA="C:\SASDATA\WOUND" NOPRINT;
  CLASS WOUND GENDER;
  VAR SBP;
  HISTOGRAM / NROWS=2 NCOLS=2 CFILL=BLUE PFILL=M3N45;
  INSET N='N:' (4.0) MIN='MIN:' (4.1) MAX='MAX:' (4.1)
               / NOFRAME POSITION=NE HEIGHT=2;
  FORMAT WOUND FMTWOUND.;
RUN;
```

2. Observe the statements in this program. In this example, you are telling SAS to display histograms by two grouping variables, WOUND and GENDER:

3. Run this SAS code and observe the output, as shown in Figure 9.4.

Figure 9.4   PROC UNIVARIATE histogram output using two grouping variables

4. Change the program using the following items:

   (a) Make the histogram color green.

   (b) Add the option MEAN='MEAN:' (4.1) to the INSET option. For example,

```
      N='N:' (4.0) MIN='MIN:' (4.1) MAX='MAX:' (4.1)
MEAN='MEAN:' (4.1)
```

(continued)

(continued)

(c) After `HISTOGRAM/`, add the option

```
NORMAL (COLOR=BROWN W=3)
```

   to superimpose a normal plot on each histogram.

(d) Run the revised program and observe the results.

9.4   SUMMARY

In this chapter, you learned how to use `PROC MEANS` and `PROC UNIVARIATE` to calculate basic statistics and graphics for describing the characteristics of a set of data.

EXERCISES

9.1 **Create histograms.**

   Use the `WOUND` data set (`C:\SASDATA\WOUND`) as in this chapter's Hands-on Examples and create the following histograms:

   a. Create a matrix of histograms with `RACE_CAT` (three categories) using the pattern `M3XO` and `CFILL=RED`.

   b. Place the key on the upper left corner (`NW`).

   c. Add mean (`MEAN='MEAN:' (4.1)`) to the list of statistics reported and standard deviation.

   d. Put your name in a `TITLE` statement.

   e. Redo the plot using solid blue bars.

   f. For this exercise, capture the output using `ODS RTF`.

   (Note: If color options do not work in this exercise, place the command `ODS GRAPHICS OFF;` at the beginning of your code. This is needed for some versions of SAS.)

9.2 **Produce normal probability plots using** `PROC UNIVARIATE`.

   Using the `WOUND` data set from Exercise 9.1, use `PROC UNIVARIATE` with the statement

```
PROBPLOT SBP/NORMAL (COLOR=BLUE W=5) NROWS=3;
```

   to produce a normal probability plot by `RACE_CATEGORY`.

9.3 **Assess normality using a Q–Q plot.**

   Open the file `AUNI1.SAS`. After `VAR AGE;` and before the `RUN;` command, enter the statement

```
QQPLOT AGE;
```

to request a Q–Q plot, which can be used to assess normality. Run the program. If the data are normal, the plot will show a tight cluster of points around a straight line. Do you think this plot suggests that the data are normally distributed?

9.4 **Display multiple histograms.**

Open the program file AUNI5.SAS and complete the code to create two columns and two rows of histograms from the CARS data set showing a comparison of city MPG for vehicles that are SUVs or not and for vehicles that have automatic transmissions or not. Missing information in the code is indicated as ???.

a. Complete the PROC FORMAT statement to define values for the 0/1 codes for the SUB and AUTOMATIC variables where 1 means "SUV" for the SUV variables and 0 means "Standard" for the AUTOMATIC variable.

b. Because there are two values for each CLASS variable, indicate NROWS=2 and NCOLS=2.

c. Indicate that the format for the MEAN should be (4.1).

d. Place the inset in the northeast corner of the graph.

e. In the FORMAT statement, indicate the name of the defined format for the AUTO-MATIC variable as FMTAUTO. (Don't forget the dot at the end of the definition.)

```
PROC FORMAT;
VALUE FMTSUV 0="NOT SUV"
             1="???";
VALUE FMTAUTO 0="???"
              1="Automatic";
RUN;
TITLE 'HISTOGRAMS of CITY MPG by SUV and AUTOMATIC';
PROC UNIVARIATE DATA="C:\SASDATA\CARS" NOPRINT;
  CLASS AUTOMATIC SUV;
  VAR CITYMPG;
  HISTOGRAM / NROWS=??? NCOLS=??? CFILL=BLUE
  PFILL=M3N45;
  INSET N='N:' (4.0) MIN='MIN:' (4.1) MAX='MAX:' (4.1)
MEAN='MEAN' (???)
               / NOFRAME POSITION=??? HEIGHT=2;
  FORMAT AUTOMATIC ??? SUV FMTSUV.;
RUN;
```

Run the program. Your results should look like the histograms in Figure 9.5.

(Note: If color options do not work in this exercise, place the command ODS GRAPHICS OFF; at the beginning of your code. This is needed for some versions of SAS.)

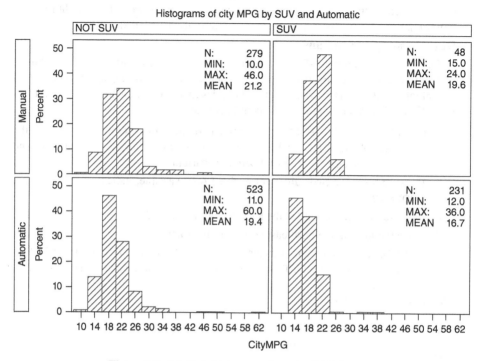

Figure 9.5   Multiple histograms from the **CAR** data set

10

ANALYZING COUNTS AND TABLES

LEARNING OBJECTIVES

- To be able to use PROC FREQ to create one-way frequency tables
- To be able to use PROC FREQ to create two-way (cross-tabulation) tables
- To be able to use two-by-two contingency tables to calculate relative risk measures
- To be able to use Cohen's kappa to calculate inter-rater reliability

Data that are collected as counts require a specific type of treatment. It doesn't make sense to calculate means and standard deviations on this type of data. Instead, categorical data (also called qualitative data) are often analyzed using frequency and cross-tabulation tables. The primary procedure within SAS® for this type of analysis is PROC FREQ.

10.1 USING PROC FREQ

PROC FREQ is a multipurpose SAS procedure for analyzing count data. It can be used to obtain frequency counts for one or more individual variables or to create two-way tables (cross-tabulations) from two variables. (Tables using three variables are discussed later in the chapter.)

PROC FREQ can also be used to perform statistical tests on count data. The syntax for PROC FREQ and commonly used options and statements that are discussed in this chapter is as follows:

SAS® Essentials: Mastering SAS for Data Analytics, Second Edition. Alan C. Elliott and Wayne A. Woodward.
© 2016 John Wiley & Sons, Inc. Published 2016 by John Wiley & Sons, Inc.

`PROC FREQ` <*options(s)*>; <*statements*> `TABLES` *requests* </*options*> ;

Some common options for `PROC FREQ` are listed in Table 10.1.
Some common statements for `PROC FREQ` are listed in Table 10.2.

TABLE 10.1   Common Options for PROC FREQ

Option	Meaning
`DATA=`*dataname*	Specifies which data set to use
`ORDER=`*option*	Specifies the order in which results are listed in the output table Options are `DATA`, `FORMATTED`, `FREQ`, and `INTERNAL`. This is illustrated in an upcoming example
`PAGE`	Specifies that only one table will appear per page (not applicable to `HTML` output)
`ALPHA=`*n*	Sets the level for confidence limits (default 0.05)
`COMPRESS`	Begins the next table on the same page when possible (not applicable to `HTML` output)
`NOPRINT`	Used when you want to capture output but not display tables

TABLE 10.2   Common Statements for PROC FREQ

Option	Meaning
`EXACT`	Produces exact *p*-values for tests. Fisher's Exact test automatically calculated for a 2×2 table
`OUTPUT=`*dataname*	Creates an output data set containing statistics from an analysis
`WEIGHT` *variable*	Identifies a weight variable that contains summarized counts
`TABLES` <*variable-combinations/options*>;	Specifies which tables will be displayed. More information about this statement is given below (Required)
`TEST`	Specifies which statistical tests will be performed (requires a `TABLES` statement)
`BY`, `FORMAT`, `LABEL`, `WHERE`	These statements are common to most procedures and may be used here

10.1.1   The TABLES Statement

The `TABLES` statement is required for all of the examples in this chapter. Its format is as follows:

`TABLES` <*variable-combinations/options*>;

where *variable-combinations* specifies frequency or cross-tabulation tables.
    For examples, see Table 10.3.
    Options for the `TABLE` statement follow a slash (/). For example,

`TABLES A*B / CHISQ;`

requests that the chi-square and related statistics will be reported for the cross-tabulation
A*B. Commonly used `TABLE` options following a / are listed in Table 10.4.

For example, in a simple use of PROC FREQ, to obtain counts of the number of subjects observed in each category of group (GP), use the following:

```
PROC FREQ; TABLES GP; RUN;
```

To produce a cross-tabulation table of GENDER by treatment GP, use

```
PROC FREQ; TABLES GENDER*GP;RUN;
```

The variables specified in the TABLES statement can be either of type categorical/character or numeric (where numeric values represent discrete categories). To request chi-square

TABLE 10.3   Sample TABLES Statements

Table Specification	Description
TABLES A;	Specifies frequencies for a single variable
TABLES A*B;	Specifies a cross-tabulation between two variables
TABLES A*B B*C X*Y; Also, TABLES A*(B C D); is the same as TABLES A*B A*C A*D;	Specifies several cross-tabulation tables
TABLES (A -- C)*X; is the same as TABLES A*X B*X C*X;	Uses a range of variables in a TABLES statement

TABLE 10.4   Options for the TABLE Statement

Option	Description
AGREE	Requests kappa statistic (inter-rater reliability). To include significance tests for kappa, add a TEST statement. For example, TABLES A*B /AGREE; TEST KAPPA;
RELRISK	Requests relative risk calculations
FISHER	Requests Fisher's Exact test for tables greater than 2×2
SPARSE	Requests all possible combinations of variable levels even when a particular combination never occurs
MISSING	Requests that missing values be treated as nonmissing
CELLCHI2	Displays the contribution to chi-square for each cell
NOCOL	Suppresses column percentages for each cell
NOCUM	Suppresses cumulative frequencies and cumulative percentages in one-way frequency tables and in list format
NOFREQ	Suppresses frequency count for each cell
NOPERCENT	Suppresses row percentage and column percentage in cross-tabulation tables, or percentages and cumulative percentages in one-way frequency tables and in list format
NOPRINT	Suppresses tables but displays statistics
NOROW	Suppresses row percentage for each cell
TESTP=(list)	Specifies a test based on percentages for the chi-square test (see the goodness-of-fit example)

statistics for a table, include the option /CHISQ at the end of the TABLES statement. For example,

```
PROC FREQ; TABLES GENDER*GP/CHISQ;
```

The following sections describe in more detail how to use PROC FREQ to create and analyze tables of counts.

10.2 ANALYZING ONE-WAY FREQUENCY TABLES

When count data are collected, you can use PROC FREQ to produce tables of the counts by category as well as to perform statistical analyses on the counts. This section describes how to create tables of counts by category and how to perform a goodness-of-fit test.

The number and type of tables produced by the PROC FREQ procedure are specified with a TABLES statement. When individual variables are used in the TABLES statement, PROC FREQ produces a frequency table. The following Hands-on Example illustrates how to create a frequency table for a single variable.

> Recall that sample data sets are in the C:\SASDATA folder and the SOMEDATA data set contains a sample data set of 50 records. In the following Hands-on Example, note that the DATA= statement could also be DATA=MYSASLIB.SOMEDATA if you have the MYSASLIB library defined.

HANDS-ON EXAMPLE

In this example, you will learn how to use PROC FREQ to display frequency information for a qualitative (categorical) data variable.

1. Open the program file AFREQ1.SAS.

```
PROC FREQ DATA="C:\SASDATA\SOMEDATA";
     TABLES STATUS;
TITLE 'Simple Example of PROC FREQ';
RUN;
PROC FREQ DATA="C:\SASDATA\SOMEDATA" ORDER=FREQ;
     TABLES STATUS;
TITLE 'Example of PROC FREQ Using ORDER= Option';
RUN;
```

This SAS code includes two PROC FREQ statements. In the first example, a table is requested for the variable STATUS. The second example is similar, but an additional option, ORDER=FREQ, is used to request that the table to be sorted by the descending order of the frequency count.

Following are some of the PROC FREQ ORDER= options.

DATA

Orders values by their order in the data set.

FORMATTED

Orders values by ascending values determined by a FORMAT statement (see PROC FORMAT in Chapter 4).

FREQ

Orders values by descending frequency count.

ORDER

Orders values by order in data set.

2. Run this program and observe the output (Table 10.3) from the first PROC FREQ.

The "Frequency" column gives the count of the number of times the STATUS variable takes on the value in the STATUS column. The "Percent" column is the percent of total (50). The "Cumulative Frequency" and "Percent" columns report an increasing count and percent for values of STATUS. You use this type of analysis to learn about the distribution of the categories in your data set. For example, in these data, more than half of the subjects are in the STATUS=5 category. If you had planned to have approximately the same number of observations in each category, this table would indicate that that criterion had not been met.

Run this code and observe the output in Table 10.5. Note that the order of categories in the table is based on ascending values of STATUS.

TABLE 10.5   Simple Output for PROC FREQ

Simple Example of PROC FREQ				
The FREQ Procedure				
Socioeconomic Status				
STATUS	Frequency	Percent	Cumulative Frequency	Cumulative Percent
1	3	6.00	3	6.00
2	7	14.00	10	20.00
3	6	12.00	16	32.00
4	8	16.00	24	48.00
5	26	52.00	50	100.00

3. The second PROC FREQ in the code includes the ORDER=FREQ option. The output from this version of PROC FREQ is given in Table 10.6. In this table, the order of categories is based on frequencies (as requested by the ORDER=FREQ option). Using the ORDER=FREQ option helps you quickly identify which categories have the most and fewest counts.

(continued)

(continued)

TABLE 10.6   PROC FREQ Output Using the ORDER = FREQ Option

Example of PROC FREQ Using ORDER= Option

The FREQ Procedure

Socioeconomic Status				
STATUS	Frequency	Percent	Cumulative Frequency	Cumulative Percent
5	26	52.00	26	52.00
4	8	16.00	34	68.00
2	7	14.00	41	82.00
3	6	12.00	47	94.00
1	3	6.00	50	100.00

The following example illustrates another way to change the order in which the categories are displayed. This example uses the ORDER=FORMATTED option for PROC FREQ. In this case, you must first create a custom format in a PROC FORMAT command to define the order that you want to be used in your output table.

HANDS-ON EXAMPLE

1. Open the program file AFREQ2.SAS.

```
PROC FORMAT;
VALUE $FMTRACE  "AA"="African American"
                "H"="Hispanic"
                "OTH"="Other"
                "C"="White";
RUN;


PROC FREQ ORDER=FORMATTED DATA="C:\SASDATA\SURVEY";
    TABLES RACE;
    TITLE 'Example of PROC FREQ using OPTION=Formatted';
    FORMAT RACE $FMTRACE.;
RUN;
```

This program uses the ORDER=FORMATTED option to control the order in which the categories will be displayed in the table. To use this option, you must define a format where the labels are in an ascending order you want to use. In this program, a format named $FMTRACE is created in a PROC FORMAT statement. To apply this order to the categories, use the ORDER=*option*:

```
ORDER=FORMATTED
```

This specifies that the table is to be sorted in ascending order by the formatted values for RACE based on the $FMTRACE format. To let SAS know to apply the format $FMTRACE. to the RACE variables, include the statement

```
FORMAT RACE $FMTRACE.;
```

which applies the $FMTRACE. format to the RACE variable.

2. Submit this program and observe the results given in Table 10.7. Note that it is the assigned label that is used to specify the order, and not the original values of RACE.

TABLE 10.7   Output from PROC FREQ Using the
ORDER=FORMATTED Option

Example of PROC FREQ using OPTION=Formatted

The FREQ Procedure

RACE				
RACE	Frequency	Percent	Cumulative Frequency	Cumulative Percent
African American	37	46.84	37	46.84
Hispanic	30	37.97	67	84.81
Other	4	5.06	71	89.87
White	8	10.13	79	100.00

3. To emphasize the effect of this format statement, place an asterisk at the beginning of the SAS statement containing the FORMAT statement:

```
*     FORMAT RACE $FMTRACE.;
```

This turns the statement into a comment. Rerun the program and observe how the table has changed. Because no format is associated with RACE, the frequencies are displayed in the table based on the alphabetical order of the category values AA, C, H, and OTH.

10.3   CREATING ONE-WAY FREQUENCY TABLES FROM SUMMARIZED DATA

Suppose you broke into your piggy bank and made stacks of the coins you found. In this case, your data are already summarized into counts. To analyze this type of data using SAS, use the WEIGHT statement to indicate the variable that represents the counts.

HANDS-ON EXAMPLE

This example illustrates how to summarize counts from a data set into a frequency table.

1. Open the program file AFREQ3.SAS.

```
DATA COINS;
     INPUT @1 CATEGORY $9. @11 NUMBER 3.;
DATALINES;
CENTS     152
CENTS     100
NICKELS   49
DIMES     59
QUARTERS  21
HALF      44
DOLLARS   21
;
PROC FREQ; WEIGHT NUMBER;
  TITLE 'Reading Summarized Count data';
  TABLES CATEGORY;
RUN;
```

Note that the data are already in counts. The statement

```
WEIGHT NUMBER;
```

tells PROC FREQ that the data for the variable NUMBER are counts. Even though there are two records for CENTS, the program is able to combine the WEIGHT (counts) into a single CENTS category (252 CENTS).

2. Run the program and observe the output, as given in Table 10.8.

TABLE 10.8 Simple Output for PROC FREQ

Reading Summarized Count data

The FREQ Procedure

CATEGORY	Frequency	Percent	Cumulative Frequency	Cumulative Percent
CENTS	252	56.50	252	56.50
DIMES	59	13.23	311	69.73
DOLLARS	21	4.71	332	74.44
HALF	44	9.87	376	84.30
NICKELS	49	10.99	425	95.29
QUARTERS	21	4.71	446	100.00

3. To tell SAS to reorder this table in the order in which you specified the categories in the data set (which makes more sense in this example), use the ORDER=DATA option in the statement:

PROC FREQ ORDER=DATA;

Rerun the analysis and observe the new frequency table.

10.3.1   Testing Goodness of Fit in a One-Way Table

A goodness-of-fit test of a single population is a test to determine if the distribution of observed frequencies in the sample data closely matches with the expected number of occurrences under a hypothetical distribution for the population. The observations are assumed to be independent, and each data value can be counted in one and only one category. It is also assumed that the number of observations is fixed. The hypotheses being tested are as follows:

H_0: The population follows the hypothesized distribution.

H_a: The population does not follow the hypothesized distribution.

A chi-square statistic is calculated, and a decision can be made based on the p-value associated with that statistic. A low p-value indicates that the data do not follow the hypothesized, or theoretical, distribution. If the p-value is sufficiently low (usually <0.05), you will reject the null hypothesis. The syntax to perform a goodness-of-fit test is as follows:

PROC FREQ; TABLES *variable* / CHISQ TESTP=(*list of ratios*);

As an example, we will use data from an experiment conducted by the nineteenth-century monk Gregor Mendel. According to a genetic theory, crossbred pea plants show a 9:3:3:1 ratio of yellow smooth, yellow wrinkled, green smooth, and green wrinkled offspring. Out of the 556 plants, under the theoretical ratio (distribution) of 9:3:3:1, you would expect about

$(9/16) \times 556 = 312.75$ yellow smooth peas (56.25%)
$(3/16) \times 556 = 104.25$ yellow wrinkled peas (18.75%)
$(3/16) \times 556 = 104.25$ green smooth peas (18.75%)
$(1/16) \times 556 = 34.75$ green wrinkled peas (6.25%)

After growing 556 of these pea plants, Mendel observed the following:

315 have yellow smooth peas
108 have yellow wrinkled peas
101 have green smooth peas
32 have green wrinkled peas

Do these offspring support the hypothesized ratios? The following Hands-on Example illustrates the use of SAS PROC FREQ to run a goodness-of-fit test to assess whether the observed frequencies seem to support the theory.

HANDS-ON EXAMPLE

This example illustrates how to perform a goodness-of-fit-test.

1. Open the program file AFREQ4.SAS.

```
DATA GENE;
      INPUT @1 COLORTYPE $13. @15 NUMBER 3.;
DATALINES;
YELLOWSMOOTH   315
YELLOWWRINKLE  108
GREENSMOOTH    101
GREENWRINKLE    32
;
* HYPOTHESIZING A 9:3:3:1 RATIO;
PROC FREQ ORDER=DATA ; WEIGHT NUMBER;
   TITLE 'GOODNESS OF FIT ANALYSIS';
   TABLES COLORTYPE / NOCUM CHISQ
          TESTP=(0.5625 0.1875 0.1875 0.0625);
RUN;
```

Note the following components of this SAS program:

- The data are summarized as indicated by the WEIGHT NUMBER statement in PROC FREQ.
- The ORDER=DATA option causes the output frequencies to be ordered as they were input into the data set.
- Frequencies are based on the variable COLORTYPE.
- The /NOCUM CHISQ and TESTP= statements request the goodness-of-fit test. The test ratios are based on the percent progeny expected from each of the four categories. The NOCUM option requests a table without the cumulative column.
- The NOCUM option instructs SAS not to include the "Cumulative Frequency" column in the table.

Note that you must use the ORDER=DATA option to ensure that the hypothesized ratios listed in the TESTP= statement match up correctly with the categories in the table.

2. Run the program and observe the output, as given in Table 10.9. A graph showing deviations is also included in the output (in the latest versions of SAS), but not shown here.

It is a good idea to make sure the "Test Percent" column matches the hypothesized percentages for the categories of the tested variable.

Note that in this case, the p-value for the chi-square test is >0.05 ($p = 0.9254$), which leads us not to reject the null hypothesis and conclude that the evidence indicates support for the theory that the population exhibits the 9:3:3:1 phenotypic ratios.

TABLE 10.9   Goodness-of-Fit Test Using PROC FREQ

COLORTYPE	Frequency	Percent	Test Percent
YELLOWSMOOTH	315	56.65	56.25
YELLOWWRINKLE	108	19.42	18.75
GREENSMOOTH	101	18.17	18.75
GREENWRINKLE	32	5.76	6.25

Chi-Square Test for Specified Proportions	
Chi-Square	0.4700
DF	3
Pr > ChiSq	0.9254

10.4   ANALYZING TWO-WAY TABLES

To create a cross-tabulation table using PROC FREQ for relating two variables, use the TABLES statement with both variables listed and separated by an asterisk (*), (e.g., A*B). A cross-tabulation table is formed by counting the number of occurrences in a sample across two grouping variables. The number of columns in a table is usually denoted by c and the number of rows by r. Thus, a table is said to be an $r \times c$ table, that is, it has $r \times c$ cells. For example, in a dominant-hand (left–right) by hair color table (with five hair colors used), the table would be referred to as a 2×5 table.

The hypotheses associated with a test of independence are as follows:

H_0: The variables are independent (no association between them).

H_a: The variables are not independent.

Thus, in the "dominant-hand/hair color" example, the null hypothesis is that there is no association between dominant hand and hair color (each hand-dominance category has the same distribution of hair color). The alternative hypothesis is that left- and right-handed people have different distributions of hair color – perhaps left-handed people are more likely to be brown-haired.

Another test that can be performed on a cross-tabulation table is a test of homogeneity. In this case, the table is built of independent samples from two or more populations, and the null hypothesis is that the populations have the same distribution (they are homogeneous). In this case, the hypotheses are as follows:

H_0: The populations are homogeneous.

H_a: The populations are not homogeneous.

Rows (or columns) represent data from different populations (e.g., treated and not treated), and the other variable represents categorized data observed on the population.

The chi-square test of independence or homogeneity is reported by PROC FREQ (the tests are mathematically equivalent) by the use of the /CHISQ option in the TABLES statement. For example,

```
PROC FREQ; TABLES GENDER*GP/CHISQ;
```

will create a two-way cross-tabulation table and statistics associated with the table. Also included in the output are the likelihood ratio chi-square, Mantel–Haenszel chi-square, phi, contingency coefficient, and Cramer's V. For a 2×2 table, a Fisher's Exact test is also performed.

HANDS-ON EXAMPLE

Data for this example come from a study performed by Karl Pearson in 1909 involving the relationship between criminal behaviors and drinking alcoholic beverages. The category "Coining" refers to counterfeiting. For the DRINKER variable, 1 means yes and 0 means no.

1. In the Editor window, open the program AFREQ5.SAS.

```
DATA DRINKERS;
INPUT CRIME $ DRINKER COUNT;
DATALINES;
Arson      1    50
Arson      0    43
Rape       1    88
Rape       0    62
Violence   1    155
Violence   0    110
Stealing   1    379
Stealing   0    300
Coining    1    18
Coining    0    14
Fraud      1    63
Fraud      0    144
;
PROC FREQ DATA=DRINKERS;WEIGHT COUNT;
     TABLES CRIME*DRINKER/CHISQ;
TITLE 'Chi Square Analysis of a Contingency Table';
RUN;
```

2. Run the program and observe the cross-tabulation table given in Table 10.10. The four numbers in each cell are the overall frequency, the overall percent, the row percent, and the column percent. The cells in the margins show total frequencies and percentages for columns and rows.

TABLE 10.10   Cross-Tabulation from PROC FREQ

Frequency Percent Row Pct Col Pct	Table of CRIME by DRINKER		
		DRINKER	
CRIME	0	1	Total
Arson	43 3.02 46.24 6.39	50 3.51 53.76 6.64	93 6.52
Coining	14 0.98 43.75 2.08	18 1.26 56.25 2.39	32 2.24
Fraud	144 10.10 69.57 21.40	63 4.42 30.43 8.37	207 14.52
Rape	62 4.35 41.33 9.21	88 6.17 58.67 11.69	150 10.52
Stealing	300 21.04 44.18 44.58	379 26.58 55.82 50.33	679 47.62
Violence	110 7.71 41.51 16.34	155 10.87 58.49 20.58	265 18.58
Total	673 47.19	753 52.81	1426 100.00

3. Observe the statistics table given in Table 10.11. The chi-square value is 49.7 and $p < 0.0001$. Thus, you reject the null hypothesis of no association (independence) and conclude that there is evidence of a relationship between drinking status and type of crime committed.

   Note that the likelihood ratio statistic given in Table 10.9 is an alternative to the chi-square. While the results are usually similar, many practitioners prefer to report the chi-square statistic. The other statistics reported in this table are for special settings and are not discussed here.

(continued)

(continued)

TABLE 10.11   Statistics for Drinking and Crime Cross-Tabulation

Statistic	DF	Value	Prob
Chi-Square	5	49.7306	<.0001
Likelihood Ratio Chi-Square	5	50.5173	<.0001
Mantel-Haenszel Chi-Square	1	13.0253	0.0003
Phi Coefficient		0.1867	
Contingency Coefficient		0.1836	
Cramer's V		0.1867	

4. To discover the nature of the relationship suggested by the significant chi-square test, alter the program by changing the TABLES statement to the following:

```
TABLES CRIME*DRINKER/CHISQ EXPECTED NOROW NOCOL NOPERCENT;
```

EXPECTED specifies that expected values are to be included in the table, and NOROW, NOCOL, and NOPERCENT tell SAS to exclude these values from the table. The results are given in Table 10.12.

TABLE 10.12   Expected Values for Drinking and Crime Data

Frequency Expected	Table of CRIME by DRINKER		
		DRINKER	
	CRIME	0	1	Total
	Arson	43 43.891	50 49.109	93
	Coining	14 15.102	18 16.898	32
	Fraud	144 97.694	63 109.31	207
	Rape	62 70.792	88 79.208	150
	Stealing	300 320.45	379 358.55	679
	Violence	110 125.07	155 139.93	265
	Total	673	753	1426

Run the revised program and note that while most of the expected values are close to the observed values, those for Fraud are very different from what was expected. This information leads to the conclusion that those involved in Fraud as a crime are less likely to drink alcoholic beverages than those involved in other crimes.

10.4.1 Creating a Contingency Table from Raw Data, the 2 × 2 Case

If your data are stored as individual observations in a SAS data set, you can use the PROC FREQ procedure to create a table of counts and analyze the results. The following Hands-on Example illustrates this.

HANDS-ON EXAMPLE

In this example, we consider a data set collected for the purpose of studying the relationship between two commercial floor cleaners and the presence or absence of the appearance of a skin rash on the hands of the users. The data for 40 subjects are in a SAS data set named RASH.SAS7BDAT. A few of the records are shown in Figure 10.1. The floor cleaner brands are coded 1 or 2, and the presence of a rash is coded Y or N.

1. Open the program file AFREQ6.SAS.

```
PROC FREQ DATA="C:\SASDATA\RASH";
   TABLES CLEANER*RASH /CHISQ;
   TITLE 'CHI-SQUARE ANALYSIS FOR A 2X2 TABLE';
RUN;
```

	Subject	Cleaner	Rash
1	001	1	N
2	002	1	Y
3	003	1	Y
4	004	1	Y
5	005	1	N
6	006	1	Y
7	007	1	Y
8	008	1	Y
9	009	1	Y
10	010	1	N
11	011	1	Y
12	012	1	Y
13	013	1	Y
14	014	1	Y

Figure 10.1 Partial viewtable for the RASH data set

2. Run the program and observe the output. The cross-tabulation table is given in Table 10.13, which contains the cell count for each combination of cleaner type and observed rash.
3. Observe the statistics tables as given in Table 10.14. Statistics for a 2×2 cross-tabulation are reported in two tables. The first table is similar to the one

(continued)

(continued)

TABLE 10.13   Cross-Tabulation of Cleaner By Rash

Frequency Percent Row Pct Col Pct	Table of Cleaner by Rash		
		Rash(Rash)	
Cleaner(Cleaner)	N	Y	Total
1	7 17.50 35.00 30.43	13 32.50 65.00 76.47	20 50.00
2	16 40.00 80.00 69.57	4 10.00 20.00 23.53	20 50.00
Total	23 57.50	17 42.50	40 100.00

TABLE 10.14   Statistics Tables for a 2 × 2 Analysis

Statistic	DF	Value	Prob
Chi-Square	1	8.2864	0.0040
Likelihood Ratio Chi-Square	1	8.6344	0.0033
Continuity Adj. Chi-Square	1	6.5473	0.0105
Mantel-Haenszel Chi-Square	1	8.0793	0.0045
Phi Coefficient		-0.4551	
Contingency Coefficient		0.4143	
Cramer's V		-0.4551	

Fisher's Exact Test	
Cell (1,1) Frequency (F)	7
Left-sided Pr <= F	0.0048
Right-sided Pr >= F	0.9995
Table Probability (P)	0.0042
Two-sided Pr <= P	0.0095

reported for the crime data, while the second reports the results of a Fisher's Exact test. In this case, the chi-square statistic, 8.29, $p = 0.004$, indicates an association between CLEANER and RASH (rejects the null hypothesis that the proportion of rash for the two cleaners is the same). The continuity adj. chi-square (sometimes called Yates's chi-square) is an adjustment that some statisticians use to improve the chi-square approximation in the case of a 2×2 table. The p-value for the adjusted chi-square is also <0.05. The second table of statistics reports the Fisher's Exact test. This test is based on all possible 2×2 tables that have the same marginal counts as those observed. This test is often reported instead of the chi-square when counts in the table are small. Typically, the two-sided p-value $\Pr \le P$ value is the correct value to report except in specialized cases. For this example, the Fisher's p-value is $p < 0.0095$.

10.4.2 Tables with Small Counts in Cells

When you summarize counts in tables, and there are small numbers in one or more cells, a typical chi-square statistical analysis may not be valid. For example, suppose you have sampled freshmen and sophomores at a college to see if they took advantage of the Learning Enhancement Center (LEC) tutorials and you want to know if the proportion using the center differs by class. The following example illustrates how this example (with a small sample size) can lead to interpretation problems.

HANDS-ON EXAMPLE

This example creates a 2×2 table from count data, but the sample size is small enough that there are interpretation problems.

1. Open the program file AFREQ7.SAS.

```
DATA LEARN;
INPUT CLASS $ LEC $ COUNT;
DATALINES;
S Y 4
S N 11
F Y 5
F N 3
;
PROC FREQ DATA=LEARN;WEIGHT COUNT;
     TABLES CLASS*LEC/CHISQ;
TITLE 'Chi Square Analysis of a Contingency Table';
RUN;
```

This program analyzes a 2×2 table from summary data. Submit the program and observe the results. Partial results are given in Table 10.15.

In the chi-square table, observe the warning message "WARNING: 50% of the cells have expected counts <5. Chi-square may not be a valid test."

2. Change the TABLE statement to

```
TABLES CLASS*LEC/CHISQ EXPECTED NOPERCENT NOCOL NOROW;
```

(continued)

(continued)

Resubmit the program and observe the cross-tabulation table, given in Table 10.16. Because this uses the EXPECTED option the output displays expected frequencies in each cell. Observe that the expected values for Female for both No and Yes (LEC) are <5. This indicates that the chi-square test may not be valid. In this case, the Fisher's Exact test (given in Table 10.13) is more reliable. Usually, the Two-sided p-value ($p = 0.1793$) would be the correct value to report for this analysis.

TABLE 10.15 Cross-Tabulation of a 2 × 2 Table with Small Cell Sizes

Statistic	DF	Value	Prob
Chi-Square	1	2.8126	0.0935
Likelihood Ratio Chi-Square	1	2.8066	0.0939
Continuity Adj. Chi-Square	1	1.5094	0.2192
Mantel-Haenszel Chi-Square	1	2.6903	0.1010
Phi Coefficient		-0.3497	
Contingency Coefficient		0.3301	
Cramer's V		-0.3497	

WARNING: 50% of the cells have expected counts less than 5. Chi-Square may not be a valid test.

Fisher's Exact Test	
Cell (1,1) Frequency (F)	3
Left-sided Pr <= F	0.1102
Right-sided Pr >= F	0.9834
Table Probability (P)	0.0935
Two-sided Pr <= P	0.1793

TABLE 10.16 Cross-Tabulation of a 2 × 2 Table Showing Expected Values

Frequency Expected	Table of CLASS by LEC		
		LEC	
CLASS	N	Y	Total
F	3	5	8
	4.8696	3.1304	
S	11	4	15
	9.1304	5.8696	
Total	14	9	23

10.5   GOING DEEPER: CALCULATING RELATIVE RISK MEASURES

Two-by-two contingency tables are often used when examining a measure of risk. In a medical setting, these tables are often constructed when one variable represents the presence or absence of a disease and the other is some risk factor. A measure of this risk in a retrospective (case–control) study is called the odds ratio (OR). In a case–control study, a researcher takes a sample of subjects and looks back in time for exposure (or nonexposure). If the data are collected prospectively, where subjects are selected by presence or absence of a risk and then observed over time to see if they develop an outcome, the measure of risk is called relative risk (RR).

In either case, a risk measure (OR or RR) equal to 1 indicates no risk. A risk measure different from 1 represents a risk. Assuming the outcome studied is undesirable, a risk measure >1 indicates that exposure is harmful and a risk measure <1 implies that exposure is a benefit.

In PROC FREQ, the option to calculate the values for OR or RR is RELRISK and appears as an option to the TABLES statement as shown here:

```
TABLES CLEANER*RASH /RELRISK;
```

The following Hands-on Example illustrates how to calculate OR for the cleaner/rash data described previously.

HANDS-ON EXAMPLE

This example uses the RASH data in the previous Hands-on Example. Here we assume that the data were collected in a retrospective (case–control) study.

1. Open the program file AFREQ6.SAS (used in a previous example) and change the TABLES statement to read

```
TABLES CLEANER*RASH /RELRISK;
```

2. Run the revised program and observe the output as given in Table 10.17. In this table, the OR=0.1346 specifies the odds of Row1/Row2 – that is, for cleaner 1 versus cleaner 2. Because OR is <1, this is interpreted to mean that the odds of a person's having a rash who is using cleaner 1 is less than they are when the person is using cleaner 2.

TABLE 10.17   Relative Risk Measures for the Floor
Cleaner Data

Estimates of the Relative Risk (Row1/Row2)		
Type of Study	Value	95% Confidence Limits
Case-Control (Odds Ratio)	0.1346	0.0322	0.5625
Cohort (Col1 Risk)	0.4375	0.2316	0.8265
Cohort (Col2 Risk)	3.2500	1.2776	8.2673

(continued)

(continued)

It is helpful to note that the inverse of this OR (1/0.1346=7.49) indicates that the odds of a person using cleaner 2 getting a rash is 7.49 times greater than that of a person using cleaner 1. A method for altering this program to report the odds of cleaner 2 versus cleaner 1 is given in the chapter exercises.

10.6   GOING DEEPER: INTER-RATER RELIABILITY (KAPPA)

A method for assessing the degree of agreement between two raters is Cohen's kappa coefficient. For example, kappa is useful for analyzing the consistency of two raters who evaluate subjects on the basis of a categorical measurement.

Using an example from Fleiss (1981, p. 213), suppose you have 100 subjects rated by two raters on a psychological scale that consists of three categories. The data are given in Table 10.18.

TABLE 10.18   Data for Inter-Rater Reliability Analysis

		RATER A			
		Psyc.	**Neuro.**	**Organic**	
	Psych.	75	1	4	80
Rater B	Neuro.	5	4	1	10
	Organic.	0	0	10	10
		80	5	15	100

Source: Fliess (1981, Table 13.1, p. 213). Reproduced with permission from Wiley.

HANDS-ON EXAMPLE

This example illustrates how to calculate the kappa statistic in an inter-rater reliability analysis.

1. Open the program file
   AKAPPA1.SAS.

```
DATA KAPPA;
INPUT RATER1 RATER2 WT;
DATALINES;
1     1     75
1     2     1
1     3     4
2     1     5
2     2     4
```

```
2       3       1
3       1       0
3       2       0
3       3       10
;
PROC FREQ ;
   WEIGHT WT;
   TABLE  RATER1*RATER2 / AGREE ; TEST KAPPA;
   TITLE 'KAPPA EXAMPLE FROM FLEISS';
RUN;
```

This SAS command is similar to that used for a chi-square analysis except with a /AGREE option to request the kappa statistic and a TEST KAPPA statement to request a kappa analysis.

2. Run this program and observe the tables of output. Partial results are given in Table 10.19.

TABLE 10.19   Results for Kappa Analysis

Test of Symmetry	
Statistic (S)	7.6667
DF	3
Pr > S	0.0534

Simple Kappa Coefficient	
Kappa	0.6765
ASE	0.0877
95% Lower Conf Limit	0.5046
95% Upper Conf Limit	0.8484

Test of H0: Kappa = 0	
ASE under H0	0.0762
Z	8.8791
One-sided Pr > Z	<.0001
Two-sided Pr > |Z|	<.0001

The "Test of Symmetry" table provides a Bowker's test of marginal homogeneity. A nonsignificant result (which is usually what you want) indicates that there is no evidence that the two raters have differing tendencies to select categories. In this case, the results are marginally nonsignificant ($p = 0.053$).

The "Simple Kappa Coefficient" table reports the kappa statistic and related measures. In this case, kappa = 0.6765. ASE is the asymptotic standard error. A 95% confidence interval is also reported. A large value of kappa (many would say 0.61

(continued)

(continued)

or higher) indicates a moderate to substantial level of agreement. This is based on a widely referenced interpretation of kappa suggested by Landis and Koch (1977) and given in Table 10.20.

TABLE 10.20   Interpretation of Kappa Statistic

Kappa Value	Interpretation
< 0	No agreement
0.0 - 0.20	Poor agreement
0.21 - 0.40	Fair agreement
0.41 - 0.60	Moderate agreement
0.61 - 0.80	Substantial agreement
0.81 - 1.00	Almost perfect agreement

The test of hypothesis "Test of H_0:" table in Table 10.19 provides a test of the null hypothesis that kappa = 0. In this case, the test indicates you would reject the null hypothesis ($p < 0.0001$).

The "Weighted Kappa Coefficient," table (not shown here) is *not* the appropriate statistic to report for these data because the rater categories are not ordinal.

3. Observe the graphical output as shown in Figure 10.2. (This may not appear if you are using an older version of SAS.) This graph provides a visual inspection of how well raters agreed on the three categories. The larger squares indicate larger samples sizes in the cell. The inner square indicates exact agreement and the outer square is partial agreement. The larger the area represented with the dark, the larger the kappa will be.

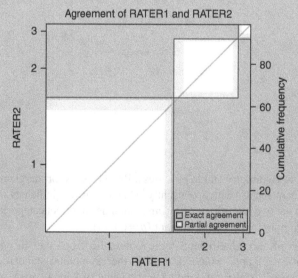

Figure 10.2   Example graphical output from a kappa test

10.6.1   Calculating Weighted Kappa

For the case in which rated categories are ordinal, it is appropriate to use the weighted kappa statistic, because it is designed to give partial credit to ratings that are close to but not on the diagonal.

For example, in a test of recognition of potentially dangerous airline passengers, suppose a procedure is devised that classifies passengers into three categories: 1 = No threat/Pass, 2 = Concern/Recheck, and 3 = Potential threat/Detain. To assess the reliability of this measure, suppose two security officers are trained in the procedure, and they rate 99 passengers. A partial listing of the data is given in Table 10.21. Note that the categories are ordinal, so weighted kappa is an appropriate analysis.

TABLE 10.21   Partial SECURITY Data

RATER1	RATER2
1	1
1	1
1	1
1	1
1	3
3	2
2	2
etc.	etc.

HANDS-ON EXAMPLE

This example uses the hypothetical security office training data set to illustrate how to calculate the kappa statistic in an inter-rater reliability analysis when categories are ordinal. Unlike the previous example, in which the data are summarized in the data set, in this example the data are listed by subject (see Table 10.21), and the PROC FREQ procedure creates the appropriate cross-tabulation of counts for the analysis.

1. Open the program file AKAPPA2.SAS.

```
PROC FREQ data="C:\SASDATA\SECURITY";
   TABLE  RATER1*RATER2 / AGREE ; TEST WTKAP;
   TITLE 'Security Data';
RUN;
```

2. Run the program and observe the cross-tabulation table given in Table 10.22.
3. The AGREE option specifies the kappa statistic, and the TEST WTKAP produces tests for the weighted statistic. The kappa and weighted kappa results are given in Table 10.23.

The test of symmetry is nonsignificant ($p = 0.84$) and suggests there is no evidence that the two raters have differing tendencies to select categories. Note that both the simple and weighted kappa statistics and confidence limits are calculated by SAS. Because the data are ordinal, the appropriate statistic for this analysis is the weighted kappa. The

(continued)

(continued)

test of hypothesis "Test of H_0:" table indicates that you would reject the hypothesis that kappa $= 0$ ($p < 0.0001$) indicating agreement.

Weighted kappa $= 0.74$ in this example statistic can be interpreted as suggesting a "substantial agreement" between the two raters using the criteria of Landis and Koch. The researcher involved in this experiment must determine, in relation to the importance of the decision involving the lives of passengers, if this result indicates sufficient agreement to adopt the classification method.

TABLE 10.22   Cross-Tabulation of Security Data

Frequency Percent Row Pct Col Pct	Table of RATER1 by RATER2			
		RATER2(RATER2)		
RATER1(RATER1)	1	2	3	Total
1	58	3	1	62
	58.59	3.03	1.01	62.63
	93.55	4.84	1.61	
	90.63	10.71	14.29	
2	5	24	2	31
	5.05	24.24	2.02	31.31
	16.13	77.42	6.45	
	7.81	85.71	28.57	
3	1	1	4	6
	1.01	1.01	4.04	6.06
	16.67	16.67	66.67	
	1.56	3.57	57.14	
Total	64	28	7	99
	64.65	28.28	7.07	100.00

TABLE 10.23   Kappa Results for Security Data

Test of Symmetry	
Statistic (S)	0.8333
DF	3
Pr > S	0.8415

Simple Kappa Coefficient	
Kappa	0.7386
ASE	0.0654
95% Lower Conf Limit	0.6104
95% Upper Conf Limit	0.8667

TABLE 10.23   (Continued)

Weighted Kappa Coefficient	
Weighted Kappa	0.7413
ASE	0.0674
95% Lower Conf Limit	0.6092
95% Upper Conf Limit	0.8735

Test of H0: Weighted Kappa = 0	
ASE under H0	0.0845
Z	8.7682
One-sided Pr > Z	<.0001
Two-sided Pr > |Z|	<.0001

10.7   SUMMARY

This chapter discusses the capabilities of PROC FREQ for creating one- and two-way frequency tables, analyzing contingency tables, calculating measures of risk, and measuring inter-rater reliability (using KAPPA).

EXERCISES

10.1 **Perform a goodness-of-fit analysis.**

Suppose you conduct a marketing survey in a city where you hypothesize that people frequent restaurants at lunchtime in the following proportions: Mexican food (40%), home cooking (20%), Italian food (20%), and Chinese food (20%). The results of a random sample from the population are given below in which subjects were asked to specify the type of restaurant at which they most recently ate lunch.

Mexican: 66

Home cooking: 25

Italian: 33

Chinese: 38

The DATA statement to read in this information is in EX_10.1.SAS:

```
DATA FOOD;
INPUT @1 CATEGORY $13. @14 NUMBER 3.;
DATALINES;
Mexican      66
Home cooking 25
```

```
Italian        33
Chinese        38
;
RUN;
```

Using this as a starting point, perform a goodness-of-fit test using PROC FREQ. Hint: Use the coins Hands-on Example discussed earlier in this chapter as a template for the analysis. Use the statements:

```
PROC FREQ ORDER=DATA; WEIGHT NUMBER;
```

and

```
TESTP=(.4,.2,.2,.2);
```

in your SAS program to perform the appropriate goodness-of-fit test.

10.2 **Perform a contingency table analysis.**

Historical data used to research the relationship between smoking and cancer yields the following data.

Smoking Habit/Cancer	Cancer	No Cancer	Total
None to slight	56	956	1012
Moderate to excessive	269	1646	1915
Total	325	2602	2927

a. Using the cleaner/rash SAS program example as a template for your SAS program code (AFREQ6.SAS), perform a chi-square test on these data using PROC FREQ and state your conclusions.

b. What is the hypothesis tested in this example?

10.3 **Going deeper: calculate risk.**

a. Using the code in AFREQ6.SAS, change the TABLES statement to

```
TABLES CLEANER*RASH /RELRISK;
```

Run the program and observe that the OR = 0.1346 representing the risk of getting a rash when using Cleaner 1 versus Cleaner 2.

b. Change the table to calculate the risk of Cleaner 2 versus Cleaner 1. To do this, you must change the order of the cleaner categories. By default, SAS orders them in numerical order (1 and 2). To change this order, create a formatted value for CLEANER and use the ORDER=FORMATTED option to put the categories in the desired order. Enter this code at the top of the program:

```
PROC FORMAT;
VALUE $FMTYN "Y"="1 YES"
```

```
    "N"="2 NO";
RUN;
```

Moreover, change the PROC FREQ statement to read

```
PROC FREQ DATA="C:\SASDATA\RASH" ORDER=FORMATTED;
```

and add a FORMAT statement after the TITLE statement and before RUN.

```
FORMAT RASH $FMTYN.;
```

Run the revised program. The order of CLEANER should be changed according to the formatted values, and the OR reported is the reciprocal of 0.1346, or 7.429.

c. What does OR = 7.429 mean?

10.4 Going deeper: calculate kappa.

Suppose a researcher is examining the reliability of a method for interpreting X-rays displayed on photographic film. Two raters examine a series of images and classify the severity of a bone break using a 1, 2, 3 system with 1 indicating a minor break and 3 indicating a severe break. The data are as follows:

		Rater 1		
		1	2	3
	1	43	7	1
Rater 2	2	9	24	5
	3	4	8	19

a. Which is the appropriate kappa statistic to use for this analysis (kappa or weighted kappa)? Do the rates seem to be in agreement? (Assess the agreement visually before calculating any statistics.)

b. Write a SAS program to read the data and calculate the appropriate kappa statistic.

c. What is the value of the kappa statistic?

According to the Landis and Koch criteria, how would you characterize the strength of this result?

11

COMPARING MEANS USING *T*-TESTS

LEARNING OBJECTIVES

- To understand the use of the one-sample *t*-test using PROC UNIVARIATE and PROC TTEST
- To understand the use of the two-sample *t*-test using PROC TTEST
- To understand the use of the paired *t*-test using PROC MEANS and PROC TTEST

Experiments whose outcome measures are quantitative variables are often analyzed by comparing means. The Student's *t*-test is the most commonly used statistical test for comparing two means or for comparing an observed mean with a known value. If more than two groups are observed, an analysis of variance (ANOVA) is used to compare means across groups (discussed in Chapter 13).

11.1 PERFORMING A ONE-SAMPLE *T*-TEST

A one-sample *t*-test is often used to compare an observed mean with a known or "gold standard" value. For example, in a quality control setting, you may be interested in comparing a sample of data to an expected outcome, such as the observed calories of liquid in cans of baby formula against the claim on the label. The purpose of the one-sample *t*-test, in this case, is to determine if there is enough evidence to dispute the claim. In general, for a one-sample *t*-test you obtain a random sample from some population and then compare the

SAS® *Essentials: Mastering SAS for Data Analytics*, Second Edition. Alan C. Elliott and Wayne A. Woodward.
© 2016 John Wiley & Sons, Inc. Published 2016 by John Wiley & Sons, Inc.

observed sample mean to some fixed value. The typical hypotheses for a one-sample *t*-test are as follows:

$H_0 : \mu = \mu_0$: The population mean is equal to a hypothesized value, μ_0.

$H_a : \mu \neq \mu_0$: The population mean is not equal to μ_0.

The key assumption underlying the one-sample *t*-test is that the population from which the random sample is selected is normal. If the data are non-normal, then nonparametric tests such as the sign test and the signed rank test are available (see Chapter 15). However, because of the central limit theorem, whenever the sample size is sufficiently large, the distribution of the sample mean is approximately normal even when the population is non-normal. A variety of rules of thumb have been recommended to help you determine whether to go ahead and trust the results of a one-sample *t*-test even when your data are non-normal. The following are general guidelines (see Moore, McCabe, and Craig, 2014).

- Small sample size ($N < 15$): You should not use the one-sample *t*-test if the data are clearly skewed or if outliers are present.
- Moderate sample size ($N > 15$): The one-sample *t*-test can be safely used except when there are severe outliers.
- Large sample size ($N > 40$): The one-sample *t*-test can be safely used without regard to skewness or outliers.

11.1.1 Running the One-Sample *t*-Test in SAS®

In SAS there are (at least) two ways to perform a one-sample *t*-test. Using PROC UNIVARIATE, you can specify the value of μ_0 for the test reported in the "Tests for Location" table given in Table 11.1 using the option MU0=*value*. For example,

```
PROC UNIVARIATE MU0=4;VAR LENGTH ;RUN;
```

would request a one-sample *t*-test of the null hypothesis that $\mu_0 = 4$.

A second method in SAS for performing this one-sample *t*-test is to use the PROC TTEST procedure. For this procedure, the corresponding SAS code is

```
PROC TTEST H0=4;VAR LENGTH; RUN;
```

The upcoming Hands-on Example illustrates these two techniques.

TABLE 11.1   *t*-Test Results Using PROC UNIVARIATE

Tests for Location: Mu0=4				
Test		Statistic	p Value	
Student's t	t	-1.40593	Pr > |t|	0.1759
Sign	M	-1.5	Pr >= |M|	0.6291
Signed Rank	S	-26.5	Pr >= |S|	0.2240

HANDS-ON EXAMPLE

In this example, you will learn how to perform a one-sample *t*-test using SAS commands. A certain medical implant component is reported to be 4 cm in length by its manufacturer. Precision of the component length is of the utmost importance. To test the reliability of the manufacturer's claim, a random sample of 20 of the components is collected, and the following SAS code is used to test $\mu_0 = 4$.

1. Open the program file ATTEST1.SAS.

```
DATA ONESAMPLE;
INPUT LENGTH @@;
DATALINES;
4     3.95  4.01  3.95  4.00
3.98  3.97  3.97  4.01  3.98
3.99  4.01  4.02  4.02  3.98
4.01  3.99  4.03  4.00  3.99
;
Title 'Single sample t-test, using PROC UNIVARIATE';
PROC UNIVARIATE DATA=ONESAMPLE MU0=4;VAR LENGTH ;RUN;
Title 'Single sample t-test using PROC TTEST';
PROC TTEST DATA=ONESAMPLE H0=4;var LENGTH;
RUN;
```

   Note that the *t*-test is performed twice: once using PROC UNIVARIATE and again using PROC TTEST.

   Note that depending on which version of SAS you are running (older versions), you may need to add the statement

```
ODS GRAPHICS ON;
```

   at the first of your code to get the graphs mentioned in this example.

2. Run this program and observe the "Test for Location" table from PROC UNIVARIATE given in Table 11.1. The row titled "Student's *t*" includes the information for the test: $t = -1.40$ and $p = 0.1759$. This *p*-value indicates that you would not reject $H_0 : \mu = 4$ at the $a = 0.05$ level of significance. PROC UNIVARIATE also reports that the sample mean is 3.993 and the sample standard deviation is 0.022 (not shown here). Two nonparametric tests are also performed: the sign and signed rank tests. These tests are discussed in Chapter 15. Because the sample size is small, normality is an issue that needs to be addressed. The results of these tests show that we make the same decision (i.e., not to reject the null hypothesis) whether or not normality is assumed. A more direct assessment of the normality of the data is discussed in step 5.

3. Observe the results from PROC TTEST, given in Table 11.2. Note that the *t*-statistic is the same as with PROC UNIVARIATE, and the sample mean and standard deviation are 3.993 and 0.022, respectively, as before. This table also reports the Degrees of freedom (DF). The results of this analysis are that the *t*-statistic (which has 19 DF) is equal to -1.41 and the *p*-value is 0.1759. The "*t*(19)" shows the number of degree

of freedom (19 in this case), which should be included when you report these results. The TTEST output also gives you a 95% confidence interval of the mean under the 95% CL mean heading (3.9826, 4.0034). Both the *p*-value and the fact that the confidence interval contains the hypothesized value 4 indicate that $H_0 : \mu = 4$ would not be rejected at the 0.05 level of significance.

TABLE 11.2   *t*-Test results using PROC TTEST

N	Mean	Std Dev	Std Err	Minimum	Maximum
20	3.9930	0.0223	0.00498	3.9500	4.0300

Mean	95% CL Mean		Std Dev	95% CL Std Dev	
3.9930	3.9826	4.0034	0.0223	0.0169	0.0325

DF	t Value	Pr > |t|
19	-1.41	0.1759

4. Although the statistical test did not reject the null hypothesis, the researcher should also consider the minimum and maximum values in the table to determine if, in a clinical setting, either of these lengths would present a detrimental clinical issue.

5. Observe the plots in Figure 11.1. The blue (or solid curve in some SAS versions) is a normal curve based on the mean (3.993) and standard deviation (0.022) estimated from the data. The red (or dashed in some SAS versions) curve is a kernel density

Figure 11.1   Histogram and normal curve output for single same *t*-test

(continued)

(continued)

estimator, which is a smoothed version of the histogram. If dramatic skewness were evident in the data, then the skewness would also be displayed in the kernel density estimator. Another plot (a q–q plot) that can help you assess normality is also displayed in the output (although not shown here.) This is the same type of plot discussed earlier in the section on PROC UNIVARIATE in Chapter 9.

These plots provide information about the normality assumption. There does not appear to be a dramatic departure from normality because the kernel density estimator is fairly bell-shaped. At the bottom of the histogram is a boxplot that plots the minimum, 25th, 50th, and 75th percentiles along with the maximum of the data. The boxplot is fairly symmetrical in shape.

SAS always reports two-tailed *p*-values for this statistical test. If you are interested only in rejecting the null hypothesis if the population mean differs from the hypothesized value in a particular direction of interest, you may want to use a one-tailed (sometimes called a one-sided) test. For example, if you want to reject the null hypothesis only if there is sufficient evidence that the mean is smaller than the hypothesized value, the hypotheses become as follows:

$H_0: \mu = \mu_0$: The population mean is equal to a hypothesized value, μ_0.
$H_a: \mu < \mu_0$: The population mean is less than μ_0.

Because SAS always reports a two-tailed *p*-value, so you need to modify the reported *p*-value to fit a one-tailed test by dividing it by 2 if your results are consistent with the direction specified in the alternative hypothesis. These comments also apply to the two-sample and paired *t*-tests discussed in this chapter.

11.2 PERFORMING A TWO-SAMPLE *T*-TEST

The SAS PROC TTEST procedure is used to test for the equality of means for a two-sample (independent group) *t*-test. For example, you might want to compare males and females regarding their reaction to a certain drug. The purpose of the two-sample *t*-test is to determine whether your data provide you with enough evidence to conclude that there is a difference in mean reaction levels. In general, for a two-sample *t*-test you obtain independent random samples of size N_1 and N_2 from the two populations of interest, and then you compare the observed sample means. The typical hypotheses for a two-sample *t*-test are as follows:

$H_0: \mu_1 = \mu_2$: The population means of the two groups are equal.
$H_a: \mu_1 \neq \mu_2$: The population means are not equal.

As in the case of the one-sample *t*-test, SAS provides *p*-values for a two-tailed test. If you have a one-tailed alternative, the *p*-values will need to be modified as mentioned in the section on one-sample *t*-tests (i.e., divide the *p*-value by 2 if the results are consistent with the alternative hypothesis). Key assumptions underlying the two-sample *t*-test are that the random samples are independent and that the populations are normally distributed with equal variances. If the data are non-normal, then nonparametric tests such as the Mann–Whitney U are available (see Chapter 15: Nonparametric Statistics).

The following are guidelines regarding normality and equal variance assumptions:

Normality: As in the one-sample case, rules of thumb are available to help you determine whether to go ahead and trust the results of a two-sample *t*-test even when your data are non-normal. The sample size guidelines given earlier in this chapter for the one-sample test can be used in the two-sample case by replacing N with $N_1 + N_2$ (see Moore, McCabe, and Craig, 2014).

Equal variances: There are two *t*-tests reported by SAS in this setting: one based on the assumption that the variances of the two groups are equal (and thus using a pooled estimate of the common variance) and one (Satterthwaite) not making that assumption. Both methods make the same assumptions about normality. There is no universal agreement concerning which *t*-test to use.

A conservative approach suggested by some statisticians (see Moore, McCabe, and Craig, 2014) is to always use the version of the *t*-test (Satterthwaite) that does not assume equal variances. The classical approach to deciding which version of the *t*-test to use is to formally test the equal variance assumption using an *F*-test that SAS gives in the *t*-test output. The typical decision criterion using this approach is that if the *p*-value for the *F*-test test is less than α (say 0.05), then you conclude that the variances are unequal and use the Satterthwaite *t*-test. If the *p*-value for the *F*-test is greater than α, you use the *t*-test based on a pooled estimate of the variances. At least one of the reasons for the recommendation to always use the Satterthwaite test is that studies have shown that the *F*-test for assessing whether the variances are equal is unreliable.

> If your observations are related across "groups" as paired or repeated measurements, the two-sample *t*-test is an *incorrect* version of the *t*-test. For that case, see the section on the paired *t*-test that follows.

11.2.1 Running the Two-Sample *t*-Test in SAS

Two sample *t*-tests can be obtained using the PROC TTEST procedure which was previously introduced in the context of a one-sample test. In this section, we'll describe PROC TTEST more completely. The syntax for the TTEST procedure is as follows:

```
PROC TTEST <options>; CLASS variable; <statements>;
```

Table 11.3 lists common options and statements used with PROC TTEST.

Other options and statements exist for PROC TTEST concerning analyses not discussed in this text. Consult the SAS documentation for more information .

TABLE 11.3   Common Options for PROC TTEST

Option	Explanation
`DATA = datasetname`	Specifies which data set to use
`COCHRAN`	Specifies that the Cochran and Cox probability approximation is to be used for unequal variances. (The Satterthwaite test is another approximation used for unequal variances. It is the default.)
`H0=n`	Specifies the hypothesized value under H_0 (null hypothesis) in a one-sample *t*-test
`WEIGHT var;`	Specifies that an observation is to be counted a number of times according to the value of the `WEIGHT` variable. This is the same usage as discussed for `PROC FREQ` in Chapter 10: Analyzing Counts and Tables

Common statements for **PROC TTEST**

`CLASS variables;`	The `CLASS` statement is required for a two-sample *t*-test, and it specifies the grouping variable for the analysis. The data for this grouping variable must contain two and only two values. An example `PROC TTEST` command is `PROC TTEST; CLASS GROUP; VAR SCORE;` In this example, where `GROUP` contains two values, say 1 or 2, a *t*-test will be performed on the variable `SCORE`
`VAR variables;`	Specifies which variables will be used in the analysis. For example, `PROC TTEST; CLASS GROUP; VAR SCORE WEIGHT HEIGHT;` would produce three *t*-tests, one for each variable in the VAR statement
`PAIRED x*y;`	Specifies that a paired *t*-test is to be performed and which variables to use. For example, `PROC TTEST; PAIRED BEFORE*AFTER;`
`BY, FORMAT, LABEL, WHERE`	These statements are common to most procedures, and may be used here

---

HANDS-ON EXAMPLE

In this example, a biologist experimenting with plant growth designs an experiment in which 15 seeds are randomly assigned to one of two fertilizers and the height of the resulting plant is measured after 2 weeks. She wants to know if one of the fertilizers provides more vertical growth than the other.

1. Open the program file `ATTEST2.SAS`.

```
DATA GROW;
INPUT BRAND $ HEIGHT;
DATALINES;
```

```
A    20.00
A    23.00
A    32.00
A    24.00
A    25.00
A    28.00
A    27.50
B    25.00
B    46.00
B    56.00
B    45.00
B    46.00
B    51.00
B    34.00
B    47.50
;
PROC TTEST;
    CLASS BRAND;
    VAR HEIGHT;
    Title 'Independent Group t-Test Example';
RUN;
```

2. Run this program and observe the output for PROC TTEST, given in Table 11.4.

TABLE 11.4   Two-Sample *t*-Test Output from PROC TTEST

BRAND	N	Mean	Std Dev	Std Err	Minimum	Maximum
A	7	25.6429	3.9021	1.4748	20.0000	32.0000
B	8	43.8125	9.8196	3.4717	25.0000	56.0000
Diff (1-2)		-18.1696	7.6778	3.9736		

BRAND	Method	Mean	95% CL Mean		Std Dev	95% CL Std Dev	
A		25.6429	22.0340	29.2517	3.9021	2.5145	8.5926
B		43.8125	35.6031	52.0219	9.8196	6.4925	19.9855
Diff (1-2)	Pooled	-18.1696	-26.7541	-9.5852	7.6778	5.5660	12.3692
Diff (1-2)	Satterthwaite	-18.1696	-26.6479	-9.6914			

Method	Variances	DF	t Value	Pr > |t|
Pooled	Equal	13	-4.57	0.0005
Satterthwaite	Unequal	9.3974	-4.82	0.0008

Equality of Variances				
Method	Num DF	Den DF	F Value	Pr > F
Folded F	7	6	6.33	0.0388

(continued)

(continued)

- There is a lot of output, so you have to be careful about what you are reading. Note that there are actually four tables. The first table gives you the sample mean, standard deviation, standard error of the mean, and the minimum and maximum for each value of BRAND (A and B). The last line includes similar information for the mean difference.

- The second table gives the mean and standard deviations again along with 95% confidence intervals for the means and standard deviations in each group along with 95% confidence intervals for the difference in the group means using a pooled estimate of the variance (if you believe the variances are equal) and based on the Satterthwaite method that does not make an assumption of equal variances.

- The third table gives the results of the two *t*-tests. The *t*-test based on a pooled estimate of the variance has a *p*-value of 0.0005 while for the Satterthwaite version, $p = 0.0008$. Note that the Satterthwaite version generally reports fractional DF. In this case, that value is 9.4. Note also that the decision regarding which *t*-test to use is not crucial here because both suggest rejecting the null hypothesis. This agreement will often be the situation.

- The fourth table gives the results of the *F*-test for deciding whether the variances can be considered equal. The *p*-value for this test is 0.0388, so at the 0.05 level we would conclude that the variances are not equal, and it appears that the variance for BRAND B is larger than that for BRAND A. Thus, the classical approach would lead us to use the Satterthwaite *t*-test.

3. Observe the graphical information shown in Figure 11.2. This figure is similar to Figure 11.1, but it shows histograms, normal curves, kernel density estimators, and boxplots for HEIGHT separately for BRAND A and BRAND B. In both cases,

Figure 11.2   Plots produced by PROC TTEST

normality looks like a fairly good assumption, but there seems to be evidence that the variance for BRAND B is larger than that for A. Q–Q plots are also included in the output (not shown here). The information in the plots is consistent with the conclusions of the *F*-test given in Table 11.3.

11.2.2 Using PROC BOXPLOT

A complementary graphical procedure that can be used to compare means visually is PROC BOXPLOT. Although boxplots are produced by default as shown in the preceding example, you might want to create a plot that includes only the side-by-side boxplots. You can use PROC BOXPLOT to create this type of graph (see Chapter 18).

11.3 PERFORMING A PAIRED *T*-TEST

To perform a paired *t*-test to compare two repeated measures (such as in a before–after situation), where both observations are taken from the same or matched subjects, use PROC TTEST with the PAIRED statement. Suppose your data contain the variables WBEFORE and WAFTER (before and after weight on a diet) for eight subjects, the hypotheses for this test are as follows:

$H_0: \mu_{\text{Loss}} = 0$: The population average weight loss is zero.

$H_a: \mu_{\text{Loss}} \neq 0$: The population average weight loss is not zero.

HANDS-ON EXAMPLE

In this example, you will learn how to perform a paired *t*-test using PROC TTEST.

1. Open the program file ATTEST3.SAS.

```
DATA WEIGHT;
INPUT WBEFORE WAFTER;
DATALINES;
200 185
175 154
188 176
198 193
197 198
310 275
245 224
202 188
;
PROC TTEST;
PAIRED WBEFORE*WAFTER;
TITLE 'Paired t-test example';
RUN;
```

(continued)

(continued)

2. Run the program and observe the output in Table 11.5. The mean of the difference is 15.25. The *t*-statistic used to test the null hypothesis is 3.94, and the *p*-value for this paired *t*-test is $p = 0.0056$, which provides evidence to reject the null hypothesis. The output also provides a 95% confidence interval on the difference (7.23, 22.26), which indicates that the population's mean weight loss could plausibly have been as little as 7.23 lb and as much as 22.26 lb. In either case, it appears that the mean weight loss is greater than zero. A one-sided test might have been used here because the goal of the study (before any data were collected) was to produce a positive weight loss.

TABLE 11.5   Paired *t*-Test Output

Difference: WBEFORE - WAFTER

N	Mean	Std Dev	Std Err	Minimum	Maximum
8	15.2500	10.9381	3.8672	-1.0000	35.0000

Mean	95% CL Mean		Std Dev	95% CL Std Dev	
15.2500	6.1055	24.3945	10.9381	7.2320	22.2621

DF	t Value	Pr > |t|
7	3.94	0.0056

2. Observe the graphic illustrating the distribution of the difference in Figure 11.3. In this graph, the histogram, the kernel density estimator, and the boxplot all suggest that

Figure 11.3   Plots produced by PROC TTEST using the PAIRED option

the differences are reasonably normally distributed. Thus, even though the sample size is quite small, it seems reasonable to use the paired t-test. The PAIRED option produces several other plots that are not shown here.

The paired t-test is actually a one-sample t-test computed on the differenced data. That is, if we computed a new variable DIF=WBEFORE-WAFTER and ran a one-sample t-test on the variable DIF testing $H_0: \mu_{DIF} = 0$, we would get identical results. The normality assumption in this case applies to the differenced data.

11.4 SUMMARY

This chapter illustrated how to perform tests on one or two means using PROC MEANS. In particular, the chapter emphasizes the fact that it is important to keep in mind the distinction between an independent group's comparison and a repeated (paired) observation's comparison.

EXERCISES

11.1 **Perform a t-test.**

Suppose you are interested in knowing if comprehension of certain medical instructions is dependent on the time of day when the instructions are given. In a school setting, you randomize members of a 12th-grade class into two groups. In the morning at 8:30, Group A is shown a video describing how to use an infant forehead thermometer. The same video is shown to Group B at 3:00 on the same day. The next day all students are given a test over the material. The following scores were observed.

Group A Subjects	Test Score	Group B Subjects	Test Score
1	88	1	87
2	89	2	69
3	79	3	78
4	100	4	79
5	98	5	83
6	89	6	90
7	94	7	85
8	95		

a. Is this analysis an independent or a paired comparison?
b. Enter these data into a SAS data set and perform the appropriate t-test. Here is some code to get you started:

```
DATA TEMP;
INPUT GROUP $ SCORE;
```

```
DATALINES;
A 88
A 89
...etc...
;
PROC TTEST DATA=TEMP;
CLASS _____ ; VAR _____ ;
...etc...
RUN;
```

c. What is your conclusion?

11.2 **Perform a *t*-test on pre- and postdata.**

To test if a memory technique was effective, a researcher provided five people with a list of 10 objects for 45 seconds then tested them to see how many they remembered (pretest). He then taught them a memory technique and then presented them with a list of 10 different (although similar) objects and administered a similar test (posttest). The results follow:

Subject	Pretest	Posttest
AD	6	10
GE	7	7
KL	9	10
MM	4	7
OU	7	9

a. Assuming that the differenced data are approximately normally distributed, what analysis is appropriate to test the hypothesis that training subjects on a memory technique would improve their ability to remember a list of 10 objects?

b. Using code similar to that in the paired *t*-test Hands-on Example, write a SAS program to perform the appropriate test for this analysis. Here is some code to get you started:

```
DATA MEMORY;
INPUT PRETEST _____ ;
DATALINES;
6 10
...etc...
;
PROC TTEST DATA=MEMORY;
...etc...
RUN;
```

c. What are your conclusions?

12

CORRELATION AND REGRESSION

LEARNING OBJECTIVES

- To be able to use SAS® procedures to calculate Pearson and Spearman correlations
- To be able to use SAS procedures to produce a matrix of scatterplots
- To be able to use SAS procedures to perform simple linear regression
- To be able to use SAS procedures to perform multiple linear regression
- To be able to use SAS procedures to calculate predictions using a model
- To be able to use SAS procedures to perform residual analysis

Correlation measures the association between two quantitative variables, and the closely related regression analysis uses the relationship between independent and dependent variables for predicting the dependent (response or outcome) variable using one or more independent (predictor or explanatory) variables. In simple linear regression, there is a single dependent variable and a single independent variable, while in multiple linear regression (MLR) there are two or more independent variables. In this chapter, we discuss the use of SAS to perform correlation and regression analyses.

12.1 CORRELATION ANALYSIS USING PROC CORR

Before proceeding to the use of SAS to perform correlation analysis, we first provide a brief discussion of the basics of correlation analysis.

SAS® Essentials: Mastering SAS for Data Analytics, Second Edition. Alan C. Elliott and Wayne A. Woodward.
© 2016 John Wiley & Sons, Inc. Published 2016 by John Wiley & Sons, Inc.

12.1.1   Correlation Analysis Basics

The correlation coefficient is a measure of the linear relationship between two quantitative variables measured on the same subject (or entity). For example, you might want to study the relationship between height and weight for a sample of teenage boys. For two variables of interest, say X and Y, the correlation, ρ, measures the extent to which a scatterplot of data from the bivariate distribution of X and Y tends to fall along a line. The correlation ρ is a unitless quantity (i.e., it does not depend on the units of measurement) that ranges from -1 to $+1$ where $\rho = -1$ and $\rho = +1$ correspond to perfect negative and positive linear relationships, respectively, and $\rho = 0$ indicates no linear relationship.

In practice, it is often of interest to test the hypotheses:

H_0: $\rho = 0$: There is no linear relationship between the two variables.

H_a: $\rho \neq 0$: There is a linear relationship between the two variables.

The correlation coefficient ρ is typically estimated from data using the Pearson correlation coefficient, usually denoted as r. PROC CORR in SAS provides a test of the above hypotheses designed to determine whether the estimated correlation coefficient, r, is significantly different from zero. This test assumes that the data represent a random sample from some bivariate normal population. If normality is not a good assumption, nonparametric correlation estimates are available, the most popular of which is Spearman's ρ, which PROC CORR also provides.

> To examine the nature of the relationship between two variables, it is always a good practice to look at scatterplots of the variables.

12.1.2   Using SAS PROC CORR for Correlation Analysis

The SAS procedure most often used to calculate correlations is PROC CORR. The syntax for this procedure is as follows:

```
PROC CORR <options>; <statements>;
```

Table 12.1 lists common options and statements used with PROC CORR.

TABLE 12.1   Common Options for PROC CORR

Option	Explanation
DATA = dataset-name	Specifies which data set to use
PEARSON	Requests Pearson correlation (default).
SPEARMAN	Requests Spearman rank correlations
NOSIMPLE	Suppresses display of descriptive statistics
NOPROB	Suppresses the display of p-values
PLOTS=	PLOTS=MATRIX requests a scatterplot matrix and PLOTS=SCATTER requests individual scatterplots. The PLOTS=MATRIX(HISTOGRAM) statement requests a scatterplot matrix with embedded histograms
OUTP=	Specifies an output data set continuing Pearson correlations

(continued)

TABLE 12.1   (*Continued*)

Option	Explanation
Common statements for PROC CORR	

`VAR variable list`	All possible pairwise correlations are calculated for the variables listed and displayed in a table
`WITH variable(s);`	All possible correlations are obtained between the variables in the VAR list and variables in the WITH list
`MODEL`	Specifies the dependent and independent variables for the analysis. More specifically, it takes the form `MODEL dependentvar=independentvar(s);` More explanation follows
`BY, FORMAT, LABEL, WHERE`	These statements are common to most procedures and may be used here

HANDS-ON EXAMPLE

This example illustrates how to calculate Pearson correlations on several variables in a data set.

1. Open the program file ACORR1.SAS.

```
PROC CORR DATA="C:\SASDATA\SOMEDATA";
    VAR AGE TIME1 TIME2;
TITLE "Example correlations using PROC CORR";
RUN;
```

2. Run the program and observe the results given in Table 12.2. The output also includes descriptive statistics not shown here. Table 12.1 contains pairwise Pearson correlations between each of the three variables listed in the VAR statement. For example, the correlation between AGE and TIME1 is $r = 0.50088$, and the p-value associated with the test of H_0: $\rho = 0$ is $p = 0.0002$.

TABLE 12.2   Output from **PROC CORR**

Pearson Correlation Coefficients, N = 50 Prob > |r| under H0: Rho=0			
	AGE	TIME1	TIME2
AGE Age on Jan 1, 2000	1.00000	0.50088 0.0002	0.38082 0.0064
TIME1 Baseline	0.50088 0.0002	1.00000	0.76396 <.0001
TIME2 6 Months	0.38082 0.0064	0.76396 <.0001	1.00000

(continued)

(continued)

3. If normality is questionable, you may want to request that the rank correlations (Spearman) be calculated (either by themselves or in combination with the Pearson correlations). Use the following PROC CORR statement to request both Pearson and Spearman correlations:

```
PROC CORR DATA="C:\SASDATA\SOMEDATA" PEARSON SPEARMAN;
```

Rerun the program and observe that a second table is the output containing Spearman correlations and the associated *p*-values.

4. To simplify the output by suppressing the *p*-values and descriptive univariate statistics, change the PROC CORR statement to

```
PROC CORR DATA="C:\SASDATA\SOMEDATA"
PEARSON SPEARMAN NOPROB NOSIMPLE;
```

Rerun the program and observe the output.

12.1.3   Producing a Matrix of Scatterplots

As indicated earlier, it is important to examine a scatterplot of the relationship between two variables to determine the nature of the relationship (e.g., is it linear?). Use of the ODS GRAPHICS mode provides a method for displaying a matrix of the scatterplots associated with correlation estimates. This is illustrated in the following Hands-on Example.

HANDS-ON EXAMPLE

This example illustrates how to create a matrix of scatterplots.

1. Open the program file ACORR2.SAS.

```
PROC CORR DATA="C:\SASDATA\SOMEDATA" PLOTS=MATRIX;
    VAR AGE TIME1 TIME2;
TITLE 'Example correlations using PROC CORR';
RUN;
```

Note the option PLOTS=MATRIX. This option tells PROC CORR to include a graph that is a matrix of correlations in the output.

2. Run the program and observe the matrix of scatterplots illustrated in Figure 12.1. Note that two scatterplots are produced for each pair of variables, so you need to examine only the upper or lower half of the table.

3. To add more information to the plot, change the PLOTS statement to

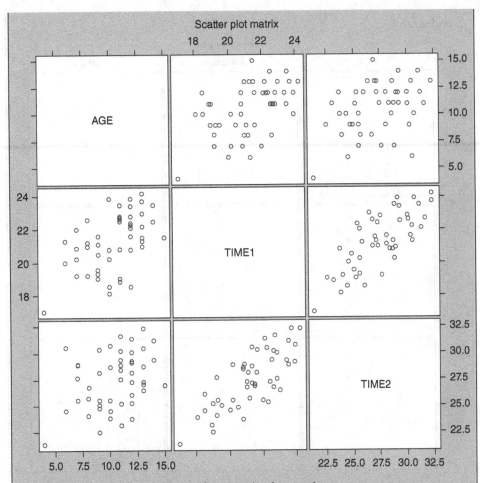

Figure 12.1   Matrix of scatterplots

```
PLOTS=MATRIX(HISTOGRAM);
```

Resubmit the code and observe the results (see Figure 12.2). This time, a histogram is displayed for each variable on the horizontal axis to show the distribution of the data for that variable.

4. To look at scatterplots in more detail, change the PLOTS statement to

```
PLOTS=SCATTER;
```

Resubmit the code and observe the results (see Figure 12.3). This option produces a scatterplot for each pair of variables. It also displays a 95% prediction ellipse. A number of other suboptions are available for the PLOTS= option (see SAS documentation for more information).

(continued)

(continued)

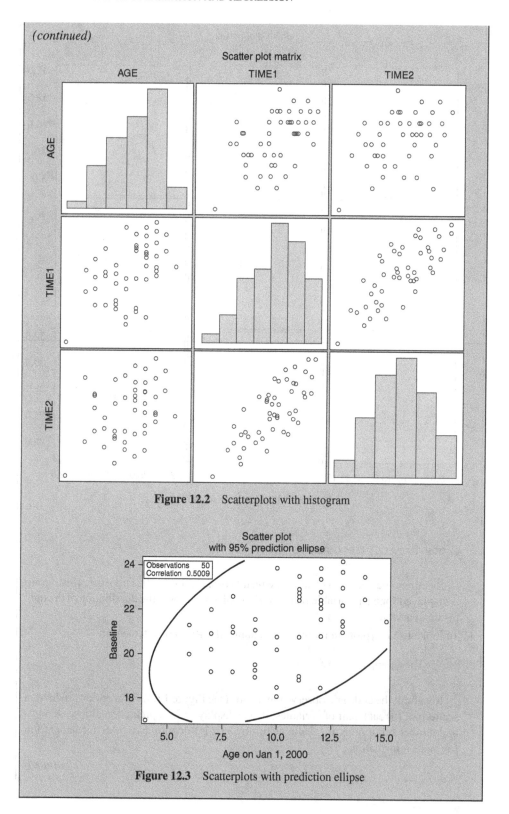

Figure 12.2   Scatterplots with histogram

Figure 12.3   Scatterplots with prediction ellipse

12.1.4   Calculating Correlations Using the WITH Statement

In the previous Hands-on Example, all pairwise correlations were calculated from the list of variables. At times you may want to produce a list of correlations of one or more variables (possibly outcome variables) with several other variables. Use the WITH statement to produce the abbreviated list of correlations, as illustrated in the following Hands-on Example.

HANDS-ON EXAMPLE

This example illustrates how to calculate correlations using a WITH statement.

1. Open the program file ACORR3.SAS.

```
PROC CORR DATA="C:\SASDATA\SOMEDATA";
    VAR TIME1-TIME4;
    WITH AGE;
TITLE "Example correlation calculations using a WITH state-
ment";
RUN;
```

Note that the VAR statement contains TIME1-TIME4, and a WITH statement is included that requests correlations between AGE and the four variables in the VAR statement.

2. Run this example and observe the output given in Table 12.3. Note that the output includes only correlations between AGE and the other variables.

3. Note that a table of simple statistics was included in the output. Put the option NOSIMPLE as an option in the PROC CORR statement (before the semicolon). Resubmit the program and observe the difference.

4. Add the option PLOTS=MATRIX to the PROC CORR statement. Resubmit the program and observe that a single row of scatterplot matrices are displayed.

TABLE 12.3   Correlations Using a WITH Statement

Pearson Correlation Coefficients, N = 50 Prob > |r| under H0: Rho=0				
	TIME1	TIME2	TIME3	TIME4
AGE	0.50088	0.38082	0.44952	0.48846
Age on Jan 1, 2000	0.0002	0.0064	0.0011	0.0003

12.2   SIMPLE LINEAR REGRESSION

Simple linear regression is used to predict the value of a dependent variable from the value of an independent variable. For example, in a study of factory workers, you could use simple linear regression to predict a pulmonary measure, forced vital capacity (FVC), from asbestos exposure (ABS). That is, you could determine whether increased exposure to asbestos is predictive of diminished FVC. The following SAS PROC REG code produces the simple linear regression equation for this analysis:

```
PROC REG;
MODEL FVC=ASB;
RUN;
```

Note that the MODEL statement is used to tell SAS which variables to use in the analysis. As in the ANOVA procedure, which will be discussed in Chapter 13, the MODEL statement has the following form:

```
MODEL dependentvar = independentvar;
```

where the dependent variable (*dependentvar*) is the measure you are trying to predict and the independent variable (*independentvar*) is your predictor.

12.2.1   The Simple Linear Regression Model

The regression line that SAS calculates from the data is an estimate of a theoretical line describing the relationship between the independent variable (X) and the dependent variable (Y). The theoretical line is

$$Y = \alpha + \beta X + \epsilon$$

where α is the y-intercept, β the slope, and ϵ an error term that is normally distributed with zero mean and constant variance. It should be noted that $b = 0$ indicates that there is no linear relationship between X and Y. A simple linear regression analysis is used to develop an equation (a linear regression line) for predicting the dependent variable given a value (x) of the independent variable. The regression line calculated by SAS is given by

$$\hat{Y} = a + bx$$

where a and b are the least squares estimates of a and b.

The null hypothesis states that there is no predictive linear relationship between the two variables. Because $\beta = 0$ indicates that there is no linear relationship between X and Y, the null hypothesis of no linear relationship is tested using

$$H_0: \beta = 0$$
$$H_a: \beta \neq 0$$

A low *p*-value for this test (say, < 0.05) indicates significant evidence to conclude that the slope of the line is not 0 (zero). That is, the knowledge of X would be useful in predicting Y.

The *t*-test for slope is mathematically equivalent to the *t*-test of $H_0: \rho = 0$ in a correlation analysis.

12.2.2   Using SAS PROC REG for Simple Linear Regression

The general syntax for PROC REG is as follows:

```
PROC REG <options>; <statements>;
```

Table 12.4 includes common options and statements used with PROC REG.

TABLE 12.4   Common Options for PROC REG

Option	Explanation
DATA = dataname	Specifies which data set to use
SIMPLE	Displays descriptive statistics
CORR	Displays a correlation matrix for variables listed in the MODEL and VAR statements
PLOTS=option	PLOTS =NONE suppresses graphs. Otherwise, several diagnostic graphs are produced by default
NOPRINT	Suppresses output when you want to capture results but not display them
ALPHA=p	Sets significance levels for confidence and prediction intervals

Common statements for **PROC REG**	
MODEL dependentvar = independentvar </ options >;	Specifies the variable to be predicted (*dependentvar*) and the variable that is the predictor (*independentvar*)
OUTPUT OUT=dataname	Specifies output data set information. For example, MODEL Y=A1 B1; OUTPUT OUT=OUTREG P=YHAT R=YRESID; creates the variables YHAT for predicted values (P) and YRESID for residual values. Other handy variables include LCL and UCL (confidence limits on individual values) and LCLM and UCLM (confidence limits on the mean)
PLOTS=option(s)	Requests plots. Some options include COOKD, LCL, UCLM, UCL, UCLM, and RESIDUALS see SAS documentation for others
BY, FORMAT, LABEL, WHERE	These statements are common to most procedures and may be used here

The MODEL statement in PROC REG is used to specify which variable is to be used to predict the outcome. For example,

```
MODEL TASK=CREATE;
```

indicates that you want to predict TASK (called the dependent variable or outcome variable) from the value of CREATE (called the independent variable or predictor). Similar model statements are used for a number of SAS procedures, so it is helpful to understand fully how this MODEL statement works. You can think of it this way; the variable(s) on the left side of the equal sign are what you want to predict, and the variable(s) on the right side of the equal sign are the predictors. (In more complicated cases, there may be more than one variable on either side of the equal sign.) This is illustrated in Figure 12.4.

Figure 12.4   The SAS model statement

HANDS-ON EXAMPLE

In this example, a random sample of 14 elementary school students is selected from a school, and each student is measured on a creativity score (X) using a new testing instrument and on a task score (Y) using a standard instrument. The task score is the mean time taken to perform several hand–eye coordination tasks. Because administering the creativity test is much cheaper, the researcher wants to know if the CREATE score is a good substitute for the more expensive TASK score (i.e., whether the TASK score can be well predicted from the CREATE score). The data are shown in the code where the CREATE column are the scores on that test, and the TASK scores on the same data lines are the scores for the same individual for that test.

1. Open the program file AREG1.SAS.

```
DATA ART;
INPUT SUBJECT $ CREATE TASK;
DATALINES;
AE      28      4.5
FR      35      3.9
HT      37      3.9
IO      50      6.1
DP      69      4.3
YR      84      8.8
QD      40      2.1
SW      65      5.5
DF      29      5.7
ER      42      3.0
RR      51      7.1
TG      45      7.3
EF      31      3.3
TJ      40      5.2
;
```

```
PROC REG;
MODEL TASK=CREATE;
TITLE "Example simple linear regression using PROC REG";
RUN;
QUIT;
```

2. Examine the code for PROC REG. The MODEL statement indicates that you want to predict the TASK score (the old test) from the CREATE score (the new test). Run the program and observe the output, some of which is given in Table 12.5.

TABLE 12.5   Output from PROG REG for a Simple Linear Regression

Root MSE	1.60348	R-Square	0.3075
Dependent Mean	5.05000	Adj R-Sq	0.2498
Coeff Var	31.75213		

		Parameter Estimates			
Variable	DF	Parameter Estimate	Standard Error	t Value	Pr > |t|
Intercept	1	2.16452	1.32141	1.64	0.1273
CREATE	1	0.06253	0.02709	2.31	0.0396

Information of particular interest in these two tables includes the following:

- **R-Square:** This value is indicated in the first table. It is a measure of the strength of the association between the dependent and independent variables. (It is the square of the Pearson correlation coefficient.) The closer this value is to 1, the stronger the association. In this case, R-Square $= 0.31$ indicates that 31% of the variability in TASK is explained by the regression with CREATE.
- **Slope:** In the Parameter Estimates table, the statistical test on the "CREATE" row is for a test of $H_0: \beta = 0$, and $p = 0.0396$ provides evidence to reject the null hypothesis and conclude that the slope is not zero. (The statistical test on the intercept is generally of little importance.)
- **Estimates:** The column labeled "Parameter Estimate" gives the least squares estimates of the slope and intercept (A and B) of the regression equation

```
TASK = A + B * CREATE;
```

which in this case, is

```
TASK = 2.16452 + 0.06235 * CREATE;
```

Thus, from this equation you can gain some information from the CREATE score for predicting the TASK score.

(continued)

(continued)

However, before making any predictions using this equation, you should analyze the linear relationship further. Some additional output provides visual information on how well this linear relationship might be predictive of TASK. Examine the plots in Figures 12.5 and 12.6, which are included in the output for this analysis.

Figure 12.5   A scatterplot of CREATE * TASK with a regression fit

The scatterplot in Figure 12.5 for CREATE by TASK provides a visual inspection of the relationship between the two variables. In it you can see that as CREATE increases, TASK tends to increase. The dotted bands show prediction limits for individual values. That is, for a given value of CREATE say CREATE=40, then about 95% of the corresponding values for TASK will fall between these two dotted lines. For CREATE=40, these values are approximately 1.0 and 8.3, that is, about 95% of the TASK scores will fall between 1.0 and 8.3 when the CREATE score is 40. (Not too reassuring remembering that the goal was to predict TASK from CREATE.) The shaded area represents a 95% confidence interval for the average TASK score for a given CREATE score. Again, when CREATE=40, then we are 95% confident that the average value of TASK is approximately between 3.5 and 5.5.

The diagnostic plots in Figure 12.6 provide additional information related to the ability of CREATE to predict TASK. Here are brief explanations of these plots:

- In the **Residual by Predicted Value** plot (upper left), we want to see a random scatter of points above and below the 0 line, which is the case here. A nonrandom pattern of dots could indicate an inadequate model.

- The **RStudent by Predicted Value** plot indicates whether any Studentized residuals fall beyond two standard deviations, which would indicate unusual values. In this case, none fall outside the ±2 limits.

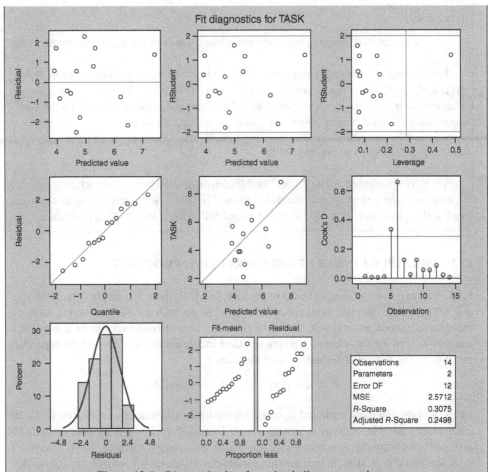

Figure 12.6   Diagnostic plots for a simple linear regression

- The **RStudent by Leverage** plot attempts to locate observations that might have unusual influence (leverage) on the calculation of the regression coefficients. In this case, there is possibly one observation that has undue influence. We'll identify this observation later.

- In the **Residual by Quartile** plot, a tight and random scatter along the diagonal line indicates an adequate fit to the model.

- The **Dependent Variable (TASK) by Predicted Value** plot visualizes variability in the prediction, so if there is a pattern (e.g., variability increases as the predicted value increases) it indicates a nonconstant variance of the error.

- The **Cook's D** plot is designed to identify outliers or leverage points. In this case, it appears that observations 5 and 6 are suspect.

- **Residuals by Percent** plot assesses the normality of the residuals.

- The **Proportion Less** (Spread plot) plots the proportion of the data by the rank for two or more categories. If the vertical spread (base on ranked data) is about the same,

(continued)

(continued)

it means that there is about the same variance in both the fitted and residual values.

For this model, you might conclude that there is a moderate linear fit between CRE-ATE and TASK, but it is not impressive ($R^2 = 30.31$) or about 31% of the variation is accounted for by the regression using CREATE. Using the information in the regression equation, you could predict a value of TASK from CREATE=40.

```
4.67 = 2.16452 + 0.06235 * 40;
```

The QUIT Statement in the PROC REG Examples is used because the REG procedure continues running even after the RUN statement. The QUIT; statement causes a complete end to this procedure. It should always be used following a PROC REG procedure.

12.3   MULTIPLE LINEAR REGRESSION USING PROC REG

MLR is an extension of simple linear regression. In MLR, there is a single dependent variable (Y) and more than one independent (X_i) variable. As with simple linear regression, the multiple regression equation calculated by SAS is a sample-based version of a theoretical equation describing the relationship between the k independent variables and the dependent variable Y. The theoretical equation is of the form

$$Y = \alpha + \beta_1 x_1 + \beta_2 x_2 + \cdots + \beta_k x_k + \epsilon$$

where α is the intercept term and β_i is the regression coefficient corresponding to the ith independent variable. Moreover, as with simple linear regression, ϵ is an error term that is assumed to be normally distributed with zero mean and constant variance. From this model, it is clear that if $\beta_i = 0$ the ith independent variable is not useful in predicting the dependent variable. The multiple regression equation calculated by SAS for predicting the dependent variable from the k independent variables is

$$\hat{Y} = a + b_1 x_1 + b_2 x_2 + \cdots + b_k x_k$$

whereas with simple linear regression, the coefficients $a, b_1, b_2, \ldots,$ and b_k are least squares estimates of the corresponding coefficients in the theoretical model.

As part of the analysis, the statistical significance of each of the coefficients is tested using a Student's t-test to determine whether it contributes significant information to the predictor. These are tests of the hypotheses:

$$H_0: \beta_i = 0$$

$$H_a: \beta_i \neq 0$$

For these tests, if the p-value is low (say, <0.05), the conclusion is that the ith independent variable contributes significant information to the equation. Care must be taken because each variable in the equation may be related to other variables, so decisions about the inclusion or exclusion of a particular variable must take these interrelationships into consideration.

As in the simple linear regression model, the R^2 (R-squared) statistic is used to measure the strength of the relationship between the set of independent variables and the dependent variable. The overall significance of the regression is tested using an analysis of variance approach. This is an overall test that all β_i's are equal to zero. The test statistic and the p-value are reported by SAS. If the p-value is low (say, <0.05), the conclusion is that some β_i's are not equal to zero, and thus the equation will have some predictive value for Y.

When there are several possible independent variables, you may want to determine what subset of them provides the best model. A number of model selection techniques, some manual and some automated (e.g., forward selection, backward elimination) can help you arrive at a parsimonious set of predictors (i.e., those that provide good prediction with few predictors).

12.3.1   Using SAS PROC REG for Multiple Linear Regression

As mentioned in the section on simple linear regression, the general syntax for PROC REG is

```
PROC REG <options>; <statements>;
```

Table 12.6 lists common options and statements used when analyzing a multiple regression model using PROC REG. Some of these are repeats for use in a simple linear regression but are mentioned here for completeness.

When using PROC REG for multiple regression, there are a number of options associated with the MODEL statements. These follow the slash in the statement

```
MODEL dependentvar = independentvar <\ options >;
```

Typical MODEL statement options are given in Table 12.7.

TABLE 12.6   Common Options for PROC REG for Multiple Regression

Option	Explanation
DATA = dataname	Specifies which data set to use
SIMPLE	Displays descriptive statistics
ID variable	The variable specified here is displayed beside each observation in certain output tables to identify observations
CORR	Displays a correlation matrix for variables listed in the MODEL and VAR statements
PLOTS=option	PLOTS =NONE suppresses graphs. Otherwise, several diagnostic graphs are produced by default
NOPRINT	Suppresses output when you want to capture results but not to display them
ALPHA=p	Sets significance levels for confidence and prediction intervals
MODEL dependentvar = independentvar <\ options >;	Specifies the variable to be predicted (*dependentvar*) and the variables that are the predictors (*independentvar*). Model options are listed below
BY variable list;	Produces separate regression analyses for each value of the BY variable

(continued)

TABLE 12.6   (Continued)

Option	Explanation

Common statements for PROC REG for multiple regression

Option	Explanation

OUTPUT
OUT=*dataname*
	Specifies output data set information. For example,
	    MODEL Y=A1 B1;
	    OUTPUT OUT=OUTREG P=YHAT R=YRESID;
	creates the variables YHAT for predicted values (P) and YRESID
	for residual values. Other handy variables include LCL and UCL
	(confidence limits on individual values) and LCLM and UCLM
	(confidence limits on the mean)

PLOTS=*options*	Requests plots. Some options include COOKD, LCL, UCLM, UCL, UCLM, and RESIDUALS (see SAS documentation for others)

TABLE 12.7   Common Statement Options for the PROC REG MODEL statement (Options Follow /)

Option	Explanation
P	Requests a table containing predicted values from the model
R	Requests that the residuals be analyzed
CLM	Prints the 95% upper and lower confidence limits for the expected value of the dependent variable (mean) for each observation
CLI	Requests the 95% upper and lower confidence limits for an individual value of the dependent variable
INCLUDE=*k*	Includes the first *k* variables in the variable list in the model (for automated selection procedures)
SELECTION=*option*	Specifies an automated variable selection procedure. Options include BACKWARD, FORWARD, and STEPWISE (see below)
SLSTAY=*p*	Specifies the maximum *p*-value for a variable to stay in a model during automated model selection. Default values are 0.10 for BACKWARD and 0.15 for STEPWISE
SLENTRY=*p*	Minimum *p*-value for a variable to enter a model for forward or stepwise selection. Default values are 0.50 for FORWARD and 0.15 for STEPWISE

In particular, the SELECTION= options specify how variables will be considered for inclusion in the model. The BACKWARD method considers all predictor variables and eliminates the ones that do not meet the minimal SLSTAY criterion until only those meeting the criterion remain. The FORWARD method brings in the most significant variable that meets the SLENTRY criterion and continues entering variables until none meets the criterion. STEPWISE is a mixture of the two; it begins like the FORWARD method but reevaluates variables at each step and may eliminate a variable if it does not meet the SLSTAY criterion. Additional model selection criteria are also available in SAS.

HANDS-ON EXAMPLE

In this example, an employer wants to be able to predict how well applicants will do on the job once they are hired. He devises four tests that he thinks will measure the skills required for the job. Ten prospects are selected at random from a group of applicants and given the four tests. Then they are given an on-the-job proficiency score (JOBSCORE) by a supervisor who observes their work.

1. Open the program file AREG2.SAS.

```
DATA JOB;
INPUT SUBJECT $ TEST1 TEST2 TEST3 TEST4 JOBSCORE;
CARDS;
    1          75        100         90         88         78
    2          51         85         88         89         71
    3          99         96         94         93         85
    4          92        106         84         84         67
    5          90         89         83         77         69
    6          67         77         83         73         65
    7         109         67         71         65         50
    8          94        112        105         91        107
    9         105        110         99         95         96
   10          74        102         88         69         63
;
PROC REG;
MODEL JOBSCORE=TEST1 TEST2 TEST3 TEST4;
TITLE 'Job Score Analysis using PROC REG';
RUN;
QUIT;
```

Note that the dependent variable in the MODEL statement is JOBSCORE and that the TEST variables, listed on the right side of the equal sign, are the independent variables.

2. Run the program and observe the analysis of variance given in Table 12.8. This table includes an overall test of significance of the model. Because $p = 0.0003$, you would reject the null hypothesis that all $\beta_i = 0$ and conclude that the model is predictive of JOBSCORE. In fact, because R-Square $= 0.9754$, you have evidence that the model is a good fit and should provide a good prediction of JOBSCORE.

TABLE 12.8   Analysis of Variance Output for PROC REG

Analysis of Variance					
Source	DF	Sum of Squares	Mean Square	F Value	Pr > F
Model	4	2495.96648	623.99162	49.58	0.0003
Error	5	62.93352	12.58670		
Corrected Total	9	2558.90000			

Root MSE	3.54777	R-Square	0.9754
Dependent Mean	75.10000	Adj R-Sq	0.9557
Coeff Var	4.72407		

(continued)

(continued)

3. To continue examining the model, look at the parameter estimates in Table 12.9. These estimates show results for tests of the significance (Pr > |t|) of the intercept and each coefficient. In this case, TEST1 ($p = 0.0446$) and TEST3 ($p = 0.0015$) seem to be the best predictors.

TABLE 12.9 Parameter Estimates

		Parameter Estimates			
Variable	DF	Parameter Estimate	Standard Error	t Value	Pr > |t|
Intercept	1	-95.55939	12.82483	-7.45	0.0007
TEST1	1	0.17631	0.06616	2.66	0.0446
TEST2	1	-0.22344	0.14354	-1.56	0.1803
TEST3	1	1.74602	0.27770	6.29	0.0015
TEST4	1	0.26865	0.18424	1.46	0.2046

Examine the diagnostic plots for this analysis in Figure 12.7. General explanations for these plots were given in the previous example using simple linear regression. In this instance, note that issues with the model include a possible outlier identified by the Cook's plot (observation 10). Otherwise, the residual plots look reasonable. There are also some possible issues related to variability identified in the bottom plots. For now, we'll ignore these possible issues.

Figure 12.7 Visualizing a prediction interval

Figure 12.7   (*Continued*)

4. As in this case, the p-values for TEST2 and TEST4 are not significant ($p > 0.05$), a typical strategy is dropping them from the model and rerunning the program to see how the reduced model fits the data. Take TEST2 and TEST4 out of the model statement and resubmit the code.

(a) How does this change the model? Does the R-Square still indicate a good fit?

(b) Are the same issues present in terms of the residual plots?

(c) If each test costs $20 to administer, and you intend to give it to a 100 applicants, do you think the reduced model is still an adequate predictor of JOBSCORE?

12.3.2   Automated Model Selection

It is often the case in multiple regression analysis that one of your goals is to arrive at a model that gives you an optimal regression equation with the fewest parameters. In the previous Hands-on Example, the predictors TEST2 and TEST4 are not significant. As mentioned, following the listing of MODEL options, a variety of automated model selection procedures are available in SAS. You can choose to select variables using manual or automated methods, or a combination of both. The various model selection techniques will not always result in the same final model, and the decision concerning which variables to include in the final model should not be based entirely on the results of any automated procedure. The researcher's knowledge of the data should always be used to guide the model selection process even when automated procedures are used.

The following Hands-on Example illustrates the BACKWARD elimination technique for model selection. In this technique, the full model is examined, and in successive steps the least predictive variable is eliminated from the model until all remaining variables show at least a $p < 0.10$ significance level.

HANDS-ON EXAMPLE

This example illustrates how to use automated model selection techniques.

1. Open the program file AREG3.SAS. This code is similar to the previous example, but includes a SELECTION Statement:

(continued)

(continued)

```
MODEL JOBSCORE=TEST1 TEST2 TEST3 TEST4
       /SELECTION=BACKWARD;
```

2. Submit this program. Because the model contains `BACKWARD` selection criteria, it examines the coefficients in a full model first, and then systematically drops independent variables that are not predictive. In the output, not shown here, you will see that at Step 1, variable `TEST4` is removed from the model and at Step 3, `TEST2` is removed. The remaining two variables (`TEST1` and `TEST3`) are not removed from the model based on the `SLSTAY=.1` criterion. Examine the parameter estimates in Table 12.10. Note that the variables `TEST1` and `TEST3` remain in the model, while `TEST2` and `TEST4` were removed. In this table, `TEST3` is highly significant ($p < 0.0001$) and `TEST1` is marginally significant ($p = 0.0779$). Moreover, note that $R^2 = 0.9528$, which indicates a good predictive model.

TABLE 12.10   Parameter Estimates for Revised Model

Variable	Parameter Estimate	Standard Error	Type II SS	F Value	Pr > F
Intercept	-89.08684	14.33880	666.44871	38.60	0.0004
TEST1	0.15607	0.07562	73.55164	4.26	0.0779
TEST3	1.70426	0.14680	2327.04675	134.78	<.0001

3. Because `TEST1` is only marginally significant (and not significant at the 0.05 level) and if each test is expensive, then you might want to use a more stringent rule to retain variables (e.g., use a smaller value for `SLSTAY`). Change the `MODEL` statement to read

```
MODEL JOBSCORE=TEST1 TEST2 TEST3 TEST4/
      SELECTION=BACKWARD
      SLSTAY=0.05;
```

`SLSTAY=0.05` tells SAS to remove variables whose significance level is 0.05 or larger (the default is 0.10). Run the revised program and observe the parameter estimates in Table 12.11, which now includes only the predictor variable `TEST3`. Also note that $R^2 = 0.924$. Thus, this model is still highly significant and appears to be strongly predictive of JOBSCORE.

TABLE 12.11   Parameter Estimates for Final Model

Variable	Parameter Estimate	Standard Error	Type II SS	F Value	Pr > F
Intercept	-76.81121	15.47905	598.38485	24.62	0.0011
TEST3	1.71651	0.17402	2364.49377	97.30	<.0001

4. Examine the diagnostic plots for the final model. Note that there continue to be a few points (identified by Cook's *D*) that may be outliers, but the Fit Plot indicates a fairly tight fit for predicting JOBSCORE from TEST3 (see Figure 12.8).

Figure 12.8 Fit plot for JOBSCORE model

12.4   GOING DEEPER: CALCULATING PREDICTIONS

Once you decide on a "final" model, you may want to predict values from new subjects using this model. In the JOBSCORE example, you could use the model given in Table 12.10 to predict how well a new job prospect will do on the job. The prediction equation is based on the parameter estimates shown in that table and given by

```
JOBSCORE = -76.81121 +1.71651*TEST3;
```

Using this equation, you can easily manually calculate a JOBSCORE for new applicants. However, you can program SAS to do the calculations for you. This becomes particularly helpful if your final model contains several predictor variables or if you want to make a lot of predictions. The following procedures can be used to predict new values:

- Create a new data set containing new values for the independent variable(s).
- Merge (append) the new data set with the old data set.
- Calculate the regression equation and request predictions.
- Use the ID option to display the new values in the output.

The following Hands-on Example shows how to program SAS to predict JOBSCORE for 10 applicants who received the following scores on TEST3: 79, 87, 98, 100, 49, 88, 91, 79, 84, and 87.

HANDS-ON EXAMPLE

This example illustrates how to calculate predictions for data following the development of a regression model.

(continued)

(continued)

1. Open the program file AREG4.SAS.

```
DATA JOB;
    INPUT SUBJECT $ TEST1 TEST2 TEST3 TEST4 JOBSCORE;
DATALINES;
    1        75      100      90      88      78
    2        51       85      88      89      71
    3        99       96      94      93      85
    4        92      106      84      84      67
    5        90       89      83      77      69
    6        67       77      83      73      65
    7       109       67      71      65      50
    8        94      112     105      91     107
    9       105      110      99      95      96
   10        74      102      88      69      63
;
PROC REG;
MODEL JOBSCORE=TEST3;
TITLE 'Job Score Final Model';
RUN;
DATA NEWAPPS;
      INPUT SUBJECT $ TEST3;
DATALINES;
101 79
102 87
103 98
104 100
105 49
106 88
107 91
108 79
109 84
110 87
;
DATA REPORT; SET JOB NEWAPPS;
PREDICT_ID=CATS(SUBJECT,": ",TEST3);
RUN;
PROC REG DATA=REPORT;
    ID PREDICT_ID;
    MODEL JOBSCORE=TEST3 /P CLI;
RUN;
QUIT;
```

In the first DATA step we recreate the data set JOB that was used in the previous Hands-on Example. The code then uses PROC REG to recalculate the final regression model that selected only TEST3 to predict JOBSCORE. In the second DATA step a data set NEWAPPS is created that contains the TEST3 scores for the 10 new applicants which have been given SUBJECT numbers 101-110. In the third DATA step, the data set NEWAPPS is appended to the JOB data set to create a data set named REPORT. In addition, a new variable is created named PREDICT_ID using a CATS function that concatenates the two variables SUBJECT and TEST3 (see Appendix D). This variable is used as the ID variable in the output so that the predicted scores can be matched to a particular subject. The /P CLI options tell SAS to output a table containing the predicted values and confidence limits on the actual JOBSCORE values. (Actually, simply using CLI will also produce both predictions and confidence limits.)

2. Run this example, and observe the (abbreviated) output in Table 12.12. The first 10 rows of the output table report information about the 10 subjects in the original data set from which the regression model is obtained. Starting with observation 11, the information relates to the new data that did not include a dependent variable (JOB-SCORE). The new data were not used to calculate the regression equation, but their predicted values were calculated. Thus, for observation 11 (i.e., subject 101), you can see that this subject had a score on TEST3 of 79, which is used to calculate a predicted JOBSCORE of 58.79.

TABLE 12.12 Predictions Using Final Model

				Output Statistics			
Obs	PREDICT_ID	Dependent Variable	Predicted Value	Std Error Mean Predict	95% CL Predict		Residual
1	1:90	78.0000	77.6748	1.5806	65.7371	89.6124	0.3252
2	2:88	71.0000	74.2417	1.5613	62.3176	86.1659	-3.2417
3	3:94	85.0000	84.5408	1.8292	72.4158	96.6658	0.4592
4	4:84	67.0000	67.3757	1.7445	55.3172	79.4342	-0.3757
5	5:83	69.0000	65.6592	1.8292	53.5342	77.7842	3.3408
6	6:83	65.0000	65.6592	1.8292	53.5342	77.7842	-0.6592
7	7:71	50.0000	45.0611	3.4211	31.2242	58.8980	4.9389
8	8:105	107.0000	103.4224	3.2671	89.7848	117.0601	3.5776
9	9:99	96.0000	93.1234	2.4018	80.4783	105.7685	2.8766
10	10:88	63.0000	74.2417	1.5613	62.3176	86.1659	-11.2417
11	101:79	.	58.7931	2.2722	46.2760	71.3103	.
12	102:87	.	72.5252	1.5806	60.5876	84.4629	.
13	103:98	.	91.4069	2.2722	78.8897	103.9240	.
14	104:100	.	94.8399	2.5367	82.0555	107.6243	.
15	105:49	.	7.2978	7.0482	-12.5361	27.1318	.
16	106:88	.	74.2417	1.5613	62.3176	86.1659	.
17	107:91	.	79.3913	1.6184	67.4267	91.3559	.
18	108:79	.	58.7931	2.2722	46.2760	71.3103	.
19	109:84	.	67.3757	1.7445	55.3172	79.4342	.
20	110:87	.	72.5252	1.5806	60.5876	84.4629	.

(continued)

(continued)

The "95% CL Predict" column indicates confidence limits for the actual value of JOBSCORE for the TEST3 values. For example, JOBSCORE for subject 101 could plausibly be as low as 46.2760 or as high as 71.3103.

12.5   GOING DEEPER: RESIDUAL ANALYSIS

In the case of the simple linear regression model, scatterplots such as the scatterplot matrix shown in Figures 12.1 and 12.2 are useful graphs for visually inspecting the nature of the association. The following Hands-on Example provides related residual analysis techniques for assessing the appropriateness of a linear regression fit to a set of data that are appropriate for simple and MLRs.

HANDS-ON EXAMPLE

This example illustrates how to examine model residuals as a part of model verification.

1. Open the program file AREG5.SAS. A portion of the code is shown here:

```
DATA JOB;
INPUT SUBJECT $ TEST1 TEST2 TEST3 TEST4 JOBSCORE;
CARDS;
    1        75       100       90       88       78
    2        51        85       88       89       71
    3        99        96       94       93       85
    4        92       106       84       84       67
    5        90        89       83       77       69
    6        67        77       83       73       65
    7       109        67       71       65       50
    8        94       112      105       91      107
    9       105       110       99       95       96
   10        74       102       88       69       63
;
RUN;
TITLE ' Residual Analysis';
PROC REG DATA=JOB;
MODEL JOBSCORE=TEST3/R;
RUN;
QUIT;
```

This program is based on the JOBSCORE example, with the following statements used for the model using TEST3 to predict JOBSCORE. The /R option requests graphs and diagnostics that assist with a residual analysis for this model.

2. Run the program and observe the output statistics in Table 12.13. The "Residual" column gives the difference between the observed dependent variable and the predicted

value using the regression equation. You can inspect this column to find out whether there are certain subjects whose scores were not as well predicted as others'. For example, subject 10's residual score is −11.24, the difference between the observed score from the JOBSCORE (63.0) and the predicted score (74.24). If a residual is much larger for one subject than for the others, examine the data for miscoding or to otherwise understand why the score for that subject is so different from its predicted value.

TABLE 12.13   Output Statistics for PROC REG

							Output Statistics		
Obs	Dependent Variable	Predicted Value	Std Error Mean Predict	Residual	Std Error Residual	Student Residual	−2−1 0 1 2		Cook's D
1	78.0000	77.6748	1.5806	0.3252	4.669	0.0697	I I I		0.000
2	71.0000	74.2417	1.5613	-3.2417	4.676	-0.693	I *I I		0.027
3	85.0000	84.5408	1.8292	0.4592	4.578	0.100	I I I		0.001
4	67.0000	67.3757	1.7445	-0.3757	4.611	-0.0815	I I I		0.000
5	69.0000	65.6592	1.8292	3.3408	4.578	0.730	I I* I		0.043
6	65.0000	65.6592	1.8292	-0.6592	4.578	-0.144	I I I		0.002
7	50.0000	45.0611	3.4211	4.9389	3.549	1.392	I I** I		0.900
8	107.0000	103.4224	3.2671	3.5776	3.691	0.969	I I* I		0.368
9	96.0000	93.1234	2.4018	2.8766	4.305	0.668	I I* I		0.069
10	63.0000	74.2417	1.5613	-11.2417	4.676	-2.404	I ****I I		0.322

The "Student Residual" column contains z-scores for residuals (called Studentized residuals) that provide a measure of the magnitude of the difference. Generally, a residual >2 or <-2 can be seen as statistically significant and may need further investigation. Because the Studentized residual for subject 10 is −2.404, this indicates that the prediction for this subject's JOBSCORE was substantially smaller than expected. The columns labeled "−2 −1 0 1 2" are a crude graph of the Studentized residuals. The "****" in that column for subject 10 provides a visual indication that the prediction is substantially smaller than expected.

The Cook's D statistic gives an indication of the "influence" of a particular data point. A value close to 0 indicates no influence; and the higher the value, the greater the influence. Note that subject 7 had a larger influence on the estimates of the regression coefficients than did most other subjects.

Based on this residual analysis, you should examine why subject 7 had such a high Cook's D score and why the prediction for subject 10 was so much less than expected. Sometimes, such an examination of the data turns up miscoded values or may indicate something different about some subjects that affect whether they should be included in the analysis. This analysis can also help you understand the visual output in the residuals plots also contained in the output (described previously but not shown here).

(continued)

(continued)

In particular, examine the plot of the regression line with mean and individual prediction limits (see Figure 12.8). The smaller, dark bands are 95% confidence limits for the mean of JOBSCORE given values of TEST3, and the larger dashed bands are 95% prediction limits for actual JOBSCORE values for given values of TEST3. The point that is farthest from the line is ID=10 (TEST3=88, JOBSCORE=63) and the lowest point, and one that is far away from other point is ID=7 (TEST3=71, JOBSCORE=50). Understanding the nature of these two subjects and their scores may provide greater insight into the model.

12.6   SUMMARY

This chapter shows you how to measure the association between two quantitative variables (correlation analysis). It also discusses how to calculate a prediction equation using simple or multiple linear regression.

EXERCISES

12.1 **Run a regression analysis involving US crime data.**

This exercise uses crime statistics for Washington, DC, from the *United States Uniform Crime Report* to examine the rise in assaults in the years 1978–1993 (Figure 12.9). In the early 1990s, there was a national concern about a

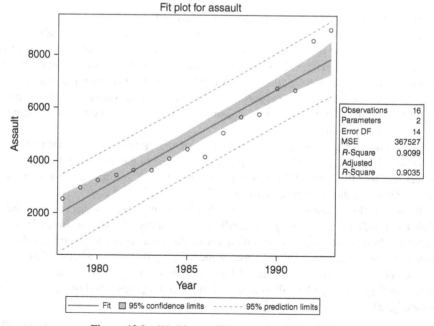

Figure 12.9   Washington, DC, assaults, 1978–1993

greater-than-expected rise in crime. The media predicted that crime was spiraling up out of control and that cities would soon become war zones of violent crimes. They had the statistics to back them up.

a. Open the program file EX_12.1.SAS, which performs a simple linear regression model. Run the program and observe the results, which are summarized in Figure 12.9.

b. If your job was to predict future crimes in order to budget for police personnel, how would these results influence your decision?

c. Based on the results, fill in the blanks in the prediction equation below (Table 12.14):

ASSAULTS = _____ + _____ * YEAR

TABLE 12.14   Regression Estimates for Washington, DC, Crime Data 1978–1993

Parameter Estimates						
Variable	Label	DF	Parameter Estimate	Standard Error	t Value	Pr > |t|
Intercept	Intercept	1	-771153	65279	-11.81	<.0001
Year	Year	1	390.90441	32.87797	11.89	<.0001

d. Using your prediction equation, predict the number of assaults for the years 1990, 1995, 2000, and 2007.

e. How good do you think predictions will be, given the fact that the result shows an impressive fit ($R^2 = 0.91$)?

f. Fill in the table below:

Year	Actual Number of Assaults	Estimated Number of Assaults
1990	7365	
1995	7228	
2000	4582	
2007	3686	

g. Open the program file EX_12.1B.SAS. This contains the same regression model but with data through 2007. Run the model and observe the results.

   I. What is R^2?

   II. Examine the scatterplot of year by number of assaults. How does it differ from the earlier version (Figure 12.9)?

   III. Using the data from 1978 to 1993 to predict number of assaults for 2000 and 2007 is called extrapolation. Based on these results, do you think extrapolation is a wise practice?

12.2 **Perform variable selection in a MLR.**

In this problem we use SAS to predict CITYMPG using the four variables AUTO-MATIC, ENGINESIZE, CYLINDERS, and HYBRID. In this exercise, you will find a "best" model.

a. Open the program file EX_12.2.SAS.

b. Run the program and note which variables are selected for the BACKWARD selection procedure.

c. Change the selection option to FORWARD. Run the program and note which variables are in the final model.

d. Change the selection option to STEPWISE. Run the program and note which variables are in the final model.

e. Are the results the same? What criteria would you use to select the "best" model?

12.3 **Using the WITH statement.**

a. Open the program file ACORR4.SAS.

```
PROC CORR DATA="C:\SASDATA\SOMEDATA" NOSIMPLE;
    VAR _____; WITH _____;
TITLE "Example correlation calculations using a WITH state-
ment";
RUN;
```

Fill in the missing code so the VAR statement contains TIME1-TIME4, and a WITH statement is included that requests correlations between AGE and the four variables in the VAR statement.

b. Run this code and verify that the correlations listed are only between AGE and the TIME variables.

c. Add code that will print a series of scatterplots for AGE by the TIME variables.

13

ANALYSIS OF VARIANCE

LEARNING OBJECTIVES

- To be able to compare three or more means using one-way ANOVA with multiple comparisons
- To be able to perform a repeated measures (dependent samples) analysis of variance with multiple comparisons
- To be able to graph mean comparisons

This chapter illustrates how to perform an analysis of variance (ANOVA) for several common designs. These procedures are used to compare means across groups or to compare three or more repeated measures (dependent samples). SAS® provides three major procedures for performing ANOVA: PROC ANOVA, PROC GLM, and PROC MIXED. We will discuss PROC MIXED in Chapter 14.

In this chapter, we use both PROC ANOVA and PROC GLM in our analysis of a one-way ANOVA. PROC ANOVA is a basic procedure that is useful for one-way ANOVA or for multiway factorial designs with fixed factors and an equal number of observations per cell.

PROC GLM is a SAS procedure that is similar to but more advanced than PROC ANOVA. (GLM stands for General Linear Model.) We also use PROC GLM for the one-way repeated measures analysis, because it involves techniques not supported by PROC ANOVA. In Chapter 14, we illustrate the use of PROC MIXED to analyze a model with both fixed and random factors and for a repeated measures design with a grouping factor.

SAS® Essentials: Mastering SAS for Data Analytics, Second Edition. Alan C. Elliott and Wayne A. Woodward.
© 2016 John Wiley & Sons, Inc. Published 2016 by John Wiley & Sons, Inc.

The "Going Deeper" section in this chapter describes how to perform *posthoc* comparisons for a one-way ANOVA.

13.1   COMPARING THREE OR MORE MEANS USING ONE-WAY ANALYSIS OF VARIANCE

A one-way ANOVA is an extension of the independent group t-test where there are more than two groups. Assumptions for this test are similar to those for the t-test: Data within groups are normally distributed with equal variances across groups. Another key assumption is that of independent samples. That is, not only do the observations within a group represent a random sample, but also there is no matching or pairing of observations among groups. This is analogous to the requirement of independent samples in the two-sample t-test. As with the t-test, the ANOVA is robust against moderate departures from the assumptions of normality and equal variance (especially for larger sample sizes). However, the assumption of independence is critical. The hypotheses for the comparison of independent groups are as follows (k is the number of groups):

H_0: $\mu_1 = \mu_2 = \ldots = \mu_k$: Means of all the groups are equal.

H_a: $\mu_i \neq \mu_j$ for some $i \neq j$: At least two means are not equal.

The test statistic used to test these hypotheses is an F with $k-1$ and $N-k$ degrees of freedom, where N is the number of subjects. A low p-value for the F-test is evidence for rejecting the null hypothesis. In other words, there is evidence that at least one pair of means are not equal. These tests can be performed in SAS using PROC ANOVA. The syntax for the statement is as follows:

```
PROC ANOVA <options>;
    CLASS variable;
    MODEL dependentvar = independentvars;
    MEANS independentvars / typecomparison <meansoptions>;
```

Table 13.1 lists common options and statements used with PROC ANOVA and PROC GLM. Some options for GLM only are listed as (GLM only). Not every option listed here is illustrated in the chapter's examples.

The model statement is a key part of the PROC ANOVA procedures. It is similar to the MODEL statement described in the previous chapter for PROC REG. The form of the statement is

```
MODEL dependentvariable=independentvariable;
```

The dependent variable is the quantitative variable of interest (your outcome variable), and the independent variable (one independent variable in the one-way ANOVA case) is the grouping variable for the analysis (the variable listed in the CLASS statement). For example, if you have measured FEV (pulmonary forced expiratory volume) and want to determine if there is a weight difference by group, your model statement would be

```
MODEL FEV=GROUP;
```

TABLE 13.1   Common Options for PROC ANOVA and PROC GLM for Performing a One-Way ANOVA or Simple Repeated Measures

Option	Explanation
DATA = *dataname*	Specifies which data set to use
NOPRINT	Suppresses output. This is used when you want to extract information from ANOVA results but don't want SAS to produce output in the Results Viewer
OUTSTAT=*dataname*	Names an output data set that saves a number of the results from the ANOVA calculation
PLOTS=*options*	Specifies PLOTS=NONE to suppress plots that are generated by default
ORDER=*option*	Specifies order in which to display the CLASS variable (similar to what was covered in Chapter 10: Analyzing Counts and Tables). Options are DATA, FORMATTED, FREQ, or INTERNAL
ALPHA=*p*	Specifies alpha level for a confidence interval (GLM only)

Common statements for PROC ANOVA and PROC GLM (for one-way analyses)

CLASS *variable list;*	This statement is required and specifies the grouping variable(s) for the analysis
MODEL *specificaion*	Specifies the dependent and independent variables for the analysis. More specifically, it takes the form
	MODEL *dependentvariable=independent variable(s)*; More explanation follows
FREQ *var*	Specifies that a variable represents the count of values for an observation. Similar to the WEIGHT statement for PROC FREQ
MEANS *vars*	Calculates means for dependent variables and may include comparisons. This is illustrated in an example below
LSMEANS *vars*	Calculates least square means for a dependent variable and can be used to request comparisons (GLM only). This is illustrated in an example below
REPEATED *vars*	Used to specify repeated measure variables. This is described in a latter example
TEST *specificaion*	Used to specify a hypothesis test value
CONTRAST *specification*	Allows you to create customized *posthoc* comparisons (GLM only)
BY, FORMAT, LABEL, WHERE	These statements are common to most procedures and may be used here

That is, if you know the value for group, you know something about the value of FEV. If they are related, you have some way to "predict" FEV by knowing GROUP.

You will see the MODEL statement in a number of SAS procedures. In general, the information on the left side of the equal sign is the dependent variable or the variable you are trying to predict, and the variable or variables on the right side of the equal sign are independent (predictor) variables.

13.1.1   Using the MEANS or LSMEANS Statement

When you perform a one-way ANOVA, typically there is a two-step procedure: (1) test H_0 : $\mu_1 = \mu_2 = \ldots = \mu_k$ to determine whether any significant differences exist, and (2) if H_0 is rejected, then run subsequent multiple comparison tests to determine which differences are significantly different. Pairwise comparison of means can be performed using one of several multiple comparison tests specified using the MEANS statement, which has the following format (where independantvar is a CLASS variable):

```
MEANS in dependentvar / typecomparison <meansoptions>;
```

For PROC GLM, use the LSMEANS statement:

```
LSMEANS in dependentvar / typecomparison <meansoptions>;
```

Table 13.2 lists comparison options for both ANOVA and GLM.

For example, suppose you are comparing the time to relief of three headache medicines – brands 1, 2, and 3. The time-to-relief data are reported in minutes. For this experiment, 15 subjects were randomly placed on one of the three medications. Which medicine (if any) is the most effective? The data for this example are as follows:

Brand 1	Brand 2	Brand 3
24.5	28.4	26.1
23.5	34.2	28.3
26.4	29.5	24.3
27.1	32.2	26.2
29.9	30.1	27.8

TABLE 13.2   Common *type comparison* Options for the PROC ANOVA or GLM MEANS Statement (Options Following the Slash /)

Option	Explanation
BON	Bonferroni *t*-tests of difference
DUNCAN	Duncan's multiple range test
SCHEFFE	Scheffe multiple comparison procedure
SNK	Student Newman–Keuls multiple range test
LSD	Fisher's least significant difference test
TUKEY	Tukey's Studentized range test
DUNNETT ('x')	Dunnett's test – compares to a single control, where 'x' is the category value of the control group MEANS
ALPHA=*pvalue*	Specifies the significance level for comparisons (default: 0.05)
CLDIFF	Requests that confidence limits be included in the output

Common *typecomparison* options for the PROC GLM LSMEANS Statement
(options following the slash /)

ADJUST=*option*	Specifies type of multiple comparison. Examples are BON, DUNCAN, SCHFEE, SNK, LSD, and DUNNETT
PDIFF=	Calculates *p*-values base (default is T). You can also specify TUKEY or DUNNETT options

HANDS-ON EXAMPLE

This example illustrates how to compare the means of three or more independent groups using PROC ANOVA. We also illustrate here a technique for performing multiple comparisons.

1. Open the program file AANOVA1.SAS.

```
DATA ACHE;
INPUT BRAND RELIEF;
CARDS;
1 24.5
1 23.5
1 26.4
1 27.1
1 29.9
2 28.4
2 34.2
2 29.5
2 32.2
2 30.1
3 26.1
3 28.3
3 24.3
3 26.2
3 27.8
;

PROC ANOVA DATA=ACHE;
    CLASS BRAND;
    MODEL RELIEF=BRAND;
    MEANS BRAND/TUKEY;
TITLE 'COMPARE RELIEF ACROSS MEDICINES - ANOVA EXAMPLE';
RUN;
```

Examine the PROC ANOVA statement:

- BRAND is the CLASS or grouping variable (containing three levels). The CLASS variable can be either a numeric or character type.
- The MODEL statement indicates that RELIEF is the dependent variable, whose means across groups are to be compared. The grouping factor is BRAND.
- The MEANS statement requests a multiple comparison test for BRAND using the Tukey method.
- Note how the data are set up in the DATA step, with one subject per line, where the grouping variable BRAND indicates the group membership for each subject to SAS.

(continued)

(continued)

2. Run this analysis and observe the results. The ANOVA (partial) results are given in Table 13.3.

   The first ANOVA table is a test of the full model, which in this case is the same as the test of the BRAND effect shown in the second table because only one factor is in the model. This is a test of the null hypothesis shown earlier that the means of all groups are equal. The small p-value ($p = 0.009$) provides evidence for rejecting the null hypothesis that the means are equal.

   If the p-value for the model is not significant ($p > 0.05$), end your analysis here and conclude that you cannot reject the null hypothesis that all means are equal. If, as in this case, the p-value is small, you can perform multiple comparisons to determine which means are different.

TABLE 13.3   ANOVA Results

Source	DF	Sum of Squares	Mean Square	F Value	Pr > F
Model	2	66.7720000	33.3860000	7.14	0.0091
Error	12	56.1280000	4.6773333		
Corrected Total	14	122.9000000			

Source	DF	Type III SS	Mean Square	F Value	Pr > F
BRAND	2	66.77200000	33.38600000	7.14	0.0091

TABLE 13.4   Tukey Multiple Comparisons Results

Means with the same letter are not significantly different.			
Tukey Grouping	Mean	N	BRAND
A	30.880	5	2
B	26.540	5	3
B			
B	26.280	5	1

3. Observe the multiple comparison results given in Table 13.4. This table graphically displays significant mean differences using Tukey's multiple comparison test. Groups that *are not* significantly different from each other are included in the same Tukey grouping. From Table 13.4, we see that there are two groupings, A and B. Note that BRAND 2 is in a group by itself. This indicates that the mean for BRAND 2 (30.88) is

significantly higher than (different from) the means of BRAND 1 (26.28) and BRAND 3 (26.54). Because BRAND 1 and BRAND 3 are in the same grouping, there is no significant difference between these two brands. Because a shorter time to relief is desirable, the conclusion would be that BRANDs 1 and 3 are preferable to BRAND 2.

A comparative boxplot is also included in the output as shown in Figure 13.1. These comparative box plots help you visualize the distribution of observations in the three groups. Fifty percent of the data is in the highlighted box, and the mean is represented by a diamond. You can see that groups 1 and 3 have a lot of overlap, whereas group 2 has a substantially larger mean than both of them.

Figure 13.1   Box plots for one-way ANOVA

4. Another method for displaying the Tukey's results is provided by including the option CLDIFF in the MEANS statement. Change the MEANS statement to read:

```
MEANS BRAND/TUKEY CLDIFF;
```

Rerun the program and observe the output in Table 13.5, showing simultaneous confidence limits on the difference between means.

The asterisks (***) in the multiple comparisons table indicate paired comparisons that are significant at the 0.05 level. In this case, all comparisons except means 1 versus 3 are different. This indicates that mean time to relief for BRAND 3 is not significantly different from that of BRAND 1, but that the mean time to relief for BRAND 2 is significantly different from those for BRAND 1 and BRAND 3. The simultaneous 95% confidence limits provide an estimate of how small or large the difference between the means is likely to be. You can use this information to assess the (clinical) importance of the difference. For example, the difference between BRANDs 2 and 3 could plausibly be as small as 0.69 minutes to relief and as large as 7.99 minutes to relief. If such differences are determined to be of clinical significance, then the conclusions are the same as those obtained from Table 13.4 – that is, BRANDs 1 and 3 are preferable to BRAND 2.

(continued)

(continued)

TABLE 13.5   Simultaneous Confidence Limits

		Comparisons significant at the 0.05 level are indicated by ***.		
BRAND Comparison	Difference Between Means	Simultaneous 95% Confidence Limits		
2 - 3	4.340	0.691	7.989	***
2 - 1	4.600	0.951	8.249	***
3 - 2	-4.340	-7.989	-0.691	***
3 - 1	0.260	-3.389	3.909	
1 - 2	-4.600	-8.249	-0.951	***
1 - 3	-0.260	-3.909	3.389	

5. Change PROC ANOVA to PROC GLM, the GLM procedure. This procedure produces the same output (in this case). It is more generalized and has more features, but for very large data sets it takes more computer time. Add the statement

```
LSMEANS BRAND/PDIFF;
```

Resubmit the program and observe the additional table "Least Squares Means for effect BRAND." This is another way to show pairwise differences. (This technique works in PROC GLM but not PROC ANOVA.) The LSMEANS statement requests a comparison of least square means, which calculates an adjusted probability for each paired difference. This output is given in Table 13.6. These results also indicate no difference between groups 1 and 3 means ($p = 0.8523$) while all other paired comparisons are statistically significant at $p < 0.05$.

LSMEANS will be discussed in more detail later. For this one-way example, the least square means are no different than the unadjusted means. However, you must use the LSMEANS statement rather than a MEANS statement to use the PDIFF option and get the pairwise p-values in GLM.

TABLE 13.6   Analysis of Variance Results

i/j	1	2	3
	Least Squares Means for effect BRAND Pr > |t| for H0: LSMean(i)=LSMean(j) Dependent Variable: RELIEF		
1		0.0056	0.8524
2	0.0056		0.0080
3	0.8524	0.0080	

Some people choose to always use GLM in cases that either GLM or ANOVA would have applied. In the GLM output, you will see results in tables labeled TYPE I and TYPE III sums of squares. In this example, the results in the two tables will be the same. In some more complex settings – for example, multiway ANOVA designs with an unequal number of observations per cell – the TYPE I and TYPE III sums of squares will differ. When this occurs, the typical recommendation is to use the TYPE III sums of squares (see Elliott and Woodward, 1986).

13.2   COMPARING THREE OR MORE REPEATED MEASURES

Repeated measures are observations taken from the same or related subjects over time or in differing circumstances. Examples include weight loss or reaction to a drug over time. When there are two repeated measures, the analysis of the data becomes a paired t-test (as discussed in Chapter 11). When there are three or more repeated measures, the corresponding analysis is a repeated measures ANOVA.

Assumptions for the repeated measures ANOVA are that the dependent variable is normally distributed, and that the variances across the repeated measures are equal. Moreover, as in the one-way ANOVA case, the test is robust against moderate departures from the normality and equal variance assumptions. As in the one-way ANOVA, you will usually perform the analysis in two steps. First, an ANOVA will determine if there is a difference in means across time. If a difference is found, then multiple comparisons can be performed to determine where the differences lie.

The hypotheses being tested with repeated measures ANOVA are as follows:

H_0: There is no difference among the group means (repeated measures).

H_a: There is a difference among the group means.

For this analysis, the PROC GLM procedure will be used because the complexity of this procedure is not supported in PROC ANOVA. The abbreviated syntax for PROC GLM is similar to that for PROC ANOVA:

```
PROC GLM <options>;
     CLASS variable;
     MODEL dependentvar = independentvars/options;
     MEANS independentvars / typecomparison
     <meansoptions>;
```

The CLASS, MODEL, and MEANS statements are essentially the same as for PROC ANOVA. These are not all of the options available in PROC GLM, but this list is sufficient for performing the analysis in this section. Also note that GLM output contains TYPE I and TYPE III sums of squares. In the Hands-on Example that follows, these will be the same. However, in more complex settings they may differ, in which case the typical advice is to use the TYPE III sums of squares.

The repeated measures ANOVA is also called a within-subjects or treatment-by-subject design. Some call it a "Single-factor" experiment having repeated measures on the same element.

The data in the following Hands-on Example are repeated measures of reaction times (OBS) of five persons after being treated with four drugs in randomized order. (These types of data may come from a crossover experimental design.) The data are as follows where it is important to understand that, for example, the first row of results (i.e., 31, 29, 17, and 35) consists of results observed on Subject 1. The data must be entered into SAS in such a way that this relationship is identified. You will note that in the SAS code to follow, each reading on the dependent variable (RESULT) is identified with respect to its corresponding SUBJ and DRUG.

Subj	Drug1	Drug2	Drug3	Drug4
1	31	29	17	35
2	15	17	11	23
3	25	21	19	31
4	35	35	21	45
5	27	27	15	31

HANDS-ON EXAMPLE

This example illustrates how to compare three or more repeated measures (dependent samples) and perform pairwise comparisons using the DUNCAN procedure.

1. Open the program file AGLM1.SAS.

```
DATA STUDY;
INPUT SUBJ DRUG RESULT;
DATALINES;
1    1    31
1    2    29
1    3    17
1    4    35
2    1    15
...etc
5    3    15
5    4    31
;
run;
PROC GLM DATA=STUDY;
     CLASS SUBJ DRUG;
     MODEL RESULT= SUBJ DRUG;
     MEANS DRUG/DUNCAN;
     TITLE 'Repeated Measures ANOVA';
RUN;
```

2. Run the program and observe the results. Several tables are included in the output. Table 13.7 shows the overall ANOVA table and the "Type III SS" table. The test in the first table is an overall test to determine whether there are any significant differences

across subjects or drugs. If this test is not significant, you can end your analysis and conclude that there is insufficient evidence to show a difference among subjects or drugs. In this case, $p < 0.0001$, so you continue to the Type III results table. In the Type III results table, the DRUG row reports a p-value of $p < 0.0001$. This is the test of the null hypothesis of interest, which is that there is no difference among the drugs. Because $p < 0.05$, you reject the null hypothesis and conclude that there is a difference among the drugs. Although SUBJ is included as a factor in the model statement, you will generally not be interested in a subject (SUBJ) effect.

TABLE 13.7   Analysis of Variance Results

Source	DF	Sum of Squares	Mean Square	F Value	Pr > F
Model	7	1331.800000	190.257143	25.03	<.0001
Error	12	91.200000	7.600000		
Corrected Total	19	1423.000000			

Source	DF	Type III SS	Mean Square	F Value	Pr > F
SUBJ	4	648.0000000	162.0000000	21.32	<.0001
DRUG	3	683.8000000	227.9333333	29.99	<.0001

TABLE 13.8   Duncan's Multiple Comparison Results

Means with the same letter are not significantly different.			
Duncan Grouping	Mean	N	DRUG
A	33.000	5	4
B	26.600	5	1
B			
B	25.800	5	2
C	16.600	5	3

3. The multiple comparison test results are given in Table 13.8. This table is similar to the multiple comparisons discussed in the one-way ANOVA example given in Table 13.4 except that in this example we have used the Duncan multiple range test rather than

(continued)

(continued)

the Tukey test for multiple comparisons. The Duncan multiple range test for DRUG indicates that the time to relief for drug 3 is significantly lower than that for all other drugs. There is no statistical difference between drugs 2 and 1; drug 4 has the highest time to relief for all drugs tested. Thus, on this basis, drug 3 would be the preferred drug.

The interaction plot shown in Figure 13.2 visually shows that lines 1 and 2 are very close, but all other lines are far apart. Several other plots are also included in the output that can help you visualize the results. (The plots are by default in color, but we have created them here using an ODS STYLE=JOURNAL statement so the lines can be distinguished in black and white. For ODS STYLE information, see Chapter 8.)

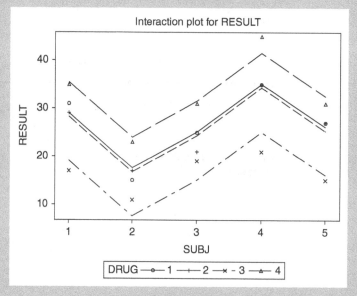

Figure 13.2   Interaction plot for repeated measures

4. Change the MEANS DRUG/DUNCAN line to

```
LSMEANS DRUG/PDIFF ADJUST=TUKEY
```

The LSMEANS statement requests a comparison of least square means with PDIFF ADJUST=TUKEY, which calculates Tukey-type adjusted probability for each paired difference. (Other common ADJUST= options are BON, DUNNETT, and SCHEFFE.) Resubmit the program and observe the results, particularly the LSMEANS results, as given in Table 13.9. The results from this analysis are similar to the DUNCAN comparison. DRUGs 1 and 2 are not different ($p = 0.966$) and all other comparisons are significant at the 0.05 level.

TABLE 13.9   LSMEANS Multiple Comparison Results

Least Squares Means for effect DRUG Pr > |t| for H0: LSMean(i)=LSMean(j) Dependent Variable: RESULT				
i/j	1	2	3	4
1		0.9666	0.0005	0.0147
2	0.9666		0.0010	0.0066
3	0.0005	0.0010		<.0001
4	0.0147	0.0066	<.0001	

13.3   GOING DEEPER: CONTRASTS

At times when you are comparing means across groups in a one-way ANOVA, you may be interested in specific posthoc comparisons. For example, suppose you have a data set consisting of four groups. For some hypothesized reason, you wonder if the average of means 1 and 2 is different from mean 4. Using a CONTRAST statement, you can specify such a comparison. A CONTRAST statement is set up using the following syntax:

CONTRAST 'label' *indvar effectvalues*

where the label is a display label for the contrast, *indvar* is an independent variable from the MODEL statement and *effectvalues* are a set of coefficients that specify the contrast. The tricky part of this statement is the *effectvalues*. The *effectvalues* are a series of numbers in the positional order of the classification variable that corresponds to the effect to be tested. For example, to create a CONTRAST statement to compare GROUP 1 versus the combined mean of GROUP 3 and 4, you could use this statement:

CONTRAST '1 vs 3+4' GROUP -1 0 .5 .5;

Note that the *effectvalues* (-1, 0, 0.5, and 0.5) sum up to zero. You can read them in the following way. The -1 represents the mean of GROUP 1. GROUP 2 is not included in the contrast as its coefficient is 0. GROUPS 3 and 4 both have coefficients of 0.5, which indicate that their means are combined equally, each contributing a half (0.5) to the value. The signs indicate the comparison. In this case, the mean represented by the negative (-1) is contrasted to the positive combination of the means represented by 0.5 and 0.5. The contrast statement

CONTRAST '1 vs 3+4' GROUP -2 0 1 1;

produces the same result although it compares twice the mean of GROUP 1 to the sum of the means of GROUPS 3 and 4. The following example illustrates how this works in SAS.

HANDS-ON EXAMPLE

1. Open the program file AGLM CONTRAST.SAS. A portion of this code is given below. In this data set, there are four groups and an observation for each record. The PROC GLM performs a one-way ANOVA analysis. The LSMEANS statement produces a pairwise comparison for all pairs.

```
DATA CONTRAST;
INPUT GROUP OBSERVATION;
DATALINES;
1 9.81
1 8.92
...Data continues...
4 5.41
4 3.94
;
PROC GLM DATA=CONTRAST;
CLASS GROUP;
MODEL OBSERVATION=GROUP;
CONTRAST '1 vs 3+4' GROUP -1 0 .5 .5;
RUN;
quit;
```

The CONTRAST statement requests a specific comparison of group 1 versus the mean of groups 3 and 4. Submit this code and observe the results. Of particular interest are the results given in Table 13.10. The result indicates that there is a statistically significant difference between the mean of DRUG1 and the average of the means of DRUG3 and DRUG4.

TABLE 13.10   CONTRAST Results from PROC GLM

Contrast	DF	Contrast SS	Mean Square	F Value	Pr > F
Groups 1 vs 3&4	1	156.3497143	156.3497143	55.96	<.0001

2. Add the following CONTRAST statements and resubmit the code.

```
CONTRAST 'Drugs 1 vs 3&4 Again' GROUP -2 0 1 1;
CONTRAST 'Drugs 1&2 vs 3&4' GROUP -.5 -.5 .5 .5;
```

The first statement is an example of another way to specify the original CONTRAST statement and gives the same results. The second statement compares the average of DRUGS 1 and 2 to the average of GROUPS 3 and 4. The results are given in Table 13.11. Note that the results for the first two contrasts are identical. Moreover, there is a significant difference between the average of the means of DRUG1 and DRUG2 versus DRUG3 and DRUG4.

TABLE 13.11   Additional CONTRAST Results

Contrast	DF	Contrast SS	Mean Square	F Value	Pr > F
Groups 1 vs 3&4	1	156.3497143	156.3497143	55.96	<.0001
Groups 1 vs 3&4 Again	1	156.3497143	156.3497143	55.96	<.0001
Groups 1&2 vs 3&4	1	376.5753572	376.5753572	134.79	<.0001

13.4   SUMMARY

This chapter illustrates SAS procedures for comparing three or more means in both an independent group setting and for repeated measures. In both cases, the chapter includes examples illustrating how to perform posthoc multiple comparisons analysis.

EXERCISES

13.1 **Perform multiple comparisons.**

a. Modify the PROC ANOVA program (AANOVA1.SAS) by replacing the Tukey comparison code to perform the Scheffe, LSD, and Dunnett's tests. Use the following statements:

```
MEANS BRAND/SCHEFFE;
MEANS BRAND/LSD;
MEANS BRAND/DUNNETT ('1');
```

Compare the results.

b. Replace PROC ANOVA with PROC GLM in this program and rerun it. Note that the answers are the same. PROC GLM is a more advanced procedure that can do the same analysis as PROC ANOVA as well as more complex analyses.

13.2 **Run a one-way ANOVA.**

A researcher is considering three training videos on how to operate a medical device. To determine which training video is the most effective, he randomly selects students from a class and organizes them into three groups. Each group is shown the video and then is tested on the device. Scores range from 0 to 100. The data are in a snippet of SAS code (EX_13.2.SAS):

```
DATA DEVICE;
INPUT SUBJ $ GROUP SCORE;
DATALINES;
AE 1 99
DF 2 99
ED 1 82
FR 3 79
EE 1 89
```

```
EG 2 87
IS 3 69
OE 2 77
KY 1 100
WD 3 82
AD 2 89
TR 1 99
SS 2 83
WE 3 81
;
TITLE 'Exercise 13.2';
```

a. Which type of ANOVA is appropriate for this analysis?

b. Complete the code to perform the correct analysis.

c. Perform a multiple comparison test.

d. Produce box plots.

e. What are your conclusions?

13.3 **Run a repeated measures ANOVA.**

Complete the code in the program file EX_13.3.SAS to perform a repeated measures ANOVA where SID is the subject ID, TIME includes three (repeated) times of interest observed on each subject (Baseline, Time1, and Time2), and OBS is an observed result from each subject at each time. Use AGLM1.SAS as a model. How would you interpret the results of this analysis?

14

ANALYSIS OF VARIANCE, PART II

LEARNING OBJECTIVES

- To be able to use SAS® procedures to perform analysis of covariance
- To be able to use SAS procedures to perform two-factor ANOVA using PROC GLM
- To be able to perform two-factor ANOVA using PROC MIXED
- To be able to use SAS procedures to perform repeated measures with a grouping factor

SAS provides procedures that can analyze data from a wide range of experimental designs. This chapter illustrates three designs not previously discussed in Chapter 13 and provides you with a brief introduction to PROC MIXED.

14.1 ANALYSIS OF COVARIANCE

An analysis of covariance (ANCOVA) is a combination of analysis of variance and regression. The covariate is a quantitative variable that is related to the dependent variable. However, the covariate is not controlled by the investigator but is some value intrinsic to the subject (or entity). In ANCOVA, the group means are adjusted by the covariate, and these adjusted means are compared with each other. Including this covariate variable in the model may explain some of the variability, resulting in a more powerful statistical test.

Consider an experiment designed to compare three medications for lowering systolic blood pressure (SBP). A potentially useful covariate would be age because it is known that

SAS® Essentials: Mastering SAS for Data Analytics, Second Edition. Alan C. Elliott and Wayne A. Woodward.
© 2016 John Wiley & Sons, Inc. Published 2016 by John Wiley & Sons, Inc.

there is a relationship between SBP and age. If SBP is the dependent variable in a model, it might be helpful to adjust SBP by the covariate age. Thus, in an ANCOVA, the means adjusted for age are compared rather than the raw means.

In the first Hands-on Example, we consider a data set in which a fifth-grade math teacher randomly assigns the 18 students in her class to three different teaching methods for individualized instruction of a certain concept. The outcome of interest is the score on an exam over the concept after the instruction period. An exam of basic math skills (EXAM) is given to the students before beginning the instruction. The data are given in Table 14.1. The variable FINAL is compared across the three teaching methods. The covariate EXAM is assumed to be linearly related to FINAL. Note that if there were no EXAM used to adjust FINAL scores, the analysis would be a standard one-way analysis of variance comparing FINAL scores across the three teaching methods. However, with the addition of the EXAM information, the analysis is potentially more powerful. The ANCOVA tests the null hypothesis that the FINAL means for the three methods adjusted by EXAM are not different.

The procedure requires a multistep approach.

1. Perform a test to determine if the FINAL-by-EXAM linear relationships by METHOD are parallel. That is, when you compare the regression lines for each of the three METHODs, the lines should theoretically be parallel. If the lines are sufficiently non-parallel, ANCOVA is not the appropriate analysis to perform. The statistical test used for parallelism is an F-test.

2. If the F-test in step 1 does not reject parallelism, then another F-test is used to compare the adjusted means across METHOD.

3. If there are differences in means, then appropriate multiple comparisons can be performed to determine which groups differ.

TABLE 14.1 Data from Math Course Analysis

Method	EXAM	FINAL
1	16	38
1	17	39
1	15	41
1	23	47
1	12	33
1	13	37
2	22	41
2	10	30
2	19	45
2	6	28
2	2	25
2	17	39
3	3	30
3	20	49
3	14	43
3	10	38
3	5	32
3	11	37

HANDS-ON EXAMPLE

This example performs an ANCOVA to compare three methods of teaching a fifth-grade math concept.

1. Open the program file AGLM ANCOVA.SAS.

```
DATA ANCOVA;
INPUT METHOD EXAM FINAL @@;
DATALINES;
1   36   38   1   37   39   1   35   41
1   43   47   1   32   33   1   33   37
2   42   41   2   30   30   2   39   45
2   26   28   2   22   25   2   37   39
3   23   30   3   40   49   3   34   43
3   30   38   3   25   32   3   31   37
;
RUN;
* CHECK THE ASSUMPTION THAT SLOPES ARE PARALLEL;
PROC GLM;
   CLASS METHOD;
    MODEL FINAL=EXAM METHOD EXAM*METHOD;
       TITLE 'Analysis of Covariance Example';
RUN;
* IF SLOPES ARE PARALLEL, DROP THE INTERACTION TERM;
PROC GLM;
   CLASS METHOD;
    MODEL FINAL=EXAM METHOD;
       LSMEANS METHOD/STDERR PDIFF ADJUST=SCHEFFE;
RUN;
QUIT;
```

   Note that PROC GLM is run twice. The first instance is to test that the slopes are parallel. This is tested with the following MODEL statement:

```
MODEL FINAL=EXAM METHOD EXAM*METHOD;
```

   The EXAM*METHOD factor in the model is the interaction (or parallel slopes) factor. When the test for this factor is not significant, it suggests that the slopes among types of METHOD can be treated as parallel.

2. Run the program. As mentioned in Chapter 13, we recommend using the Type III sums-of-squares. Observe these sums-of-squares in the output given in Table 14.2. The row for the test of the interaction term (EXAM*METHOD) is nonsignificant ($p = 0.6835$). This provides evidence that the slopes can be treated as parallel and that the ANCOVA is an appropriate analysis.

3. Because the slopes are not significantly nonparallel, the second PROC GLM analysis is appropriate. Note that the interaction term has been removed from the MODEL statement.

(continued)

(continued)

TABLE 14.2 Test of Slopes for Analysis of Covariance

Source	DF	Type III SS	Mean Square	F Value	Pr > F
EXAM	1	476.4504266	476.4504266	114.76	<.0001
METHOD	2	0.8199072	0.4099536	0.10	0.9067
EXAM*METHOD	2	3.2623239	1.6311619	0.39	0.6835

TABLE 14.3 Analysis of Covariance Test of Main Effects

Source	DF	Type III SS	Mean Square	F Value	Pr > F
EXAM	1	627.9168352	627.9168352	165.60	<.0001
METHOD	2	105.9808664	52.9904332	13.98	0.0005

```
MODEL FINAL=EXAM METHOD;
forcing the model to assume equal regression lines
```

Table 14.3 shows the Type III SS output table for the second PROC GLM. The factor of interest in this table is METHOD, and the corresponding F is a statistical test comparing the three methods adjusting for EXAM. Because $p = 0.0005$, we reject the null hypothesis that the adjusted means are equal and conclude that at least one pair of adjusted means are different from each other.

4. Because we found a difference in adjusted means, pairwise comparisons can be used to identify which adjusted means are different from each other. The statement that provides that comparison is

```
LSMEANS METHOD/STDERR PDIFF ADJUST=SCHEFFE;
```

In this case, we have chosen to use the Scheffe multiple comparisons, and the results are given in Table 14.4. (Ignore the Pr > |t| column, it is testing that the mean is different from zero, which is of no interest in this analysis.)

The Scheffe results provide p-values for each pairwise comparison. In this case, the comparisons of METHODs 1 and 3 ($p = 0.0056$) and 2 and 3 ($p = 0.0007$) indicate significant differences. METHODs 1 and 2 are not significantly different ($p = 0.68$).

Because a high FINAL score is the goal, there is evidence to support the contention that the adjusted mean of 40.82 for METHOD 3 is a significantly higher score than for METHODs 1 and 2, and thus that METHOD 3 is the preferred method.

5. Along with the tabled output, SAS includes several graphs. For the first PROC GLM (that included the interaction term) you get the plot shown in Figure 14.1. It shows the three regression lines by METHOD. Note that the lines are near parallel, which confirms the findings in the first PROC GLM procedure. (We show these plots as created using

the ODS STYLE=JOURNAL option. See Chapter 8 for more on ODS. Your plots may appear in color.)

TABLE 14.4   Scheffe Multiple Comparisons for ANCOVA

METHOD	FINAL LSMEAN	Standard Error	Pr > |t|	LSMEAN Number
1	36.0946098	0.8300185	<.0001	1
2	35.0724100	0.7955731	<.0001	2
3	40.8329802	0.8215055	<.0001	3

Least Squares Means for effect METHOD **Pr > |t| for H0: LSMean(i)=LSMean(j)** **Dependent Variable: FINAL**			
i/j	1	2	3
1		0.6837	0.0056
2	0.6837		0.0007
3	0.0056	0.0007	

Analysis of covariance for FINAL

Figure 14.1   Regression lines for ANCOVA data

For the model without the interaction term, we assume that the lines are parallel. Thus, the plot associated with the second PROC GLM uses a common slope estimate, and the lines in Figure 14.2 represent the adjusted means by METHOD.

These plots support our overall finding that the adjusted mean for METHOD 3 is higher than the means for the other methods. In addition, SAS provides a graphical display of the Scheffe results, as shown in Figure 14.3. This plot shows confidence intervals for the adjusted means indicated by lines at the intersection of the three methods. This graph

(continued)

(continued)

indicates that the comparisons of 3 versus 2 and 3 versus 1 are both significant because their lines do not cross the diagonal line. The comparison of 1 versus 2 is not significant.

6. Replace the Scheffe test in the LSMEANS line with a Bonferroni or Tukey test and compare the output and results.

Figure 14.2 Parallel lines for ANCOVA data, for second model assuming parallel lines

Figure 14.3 Graphical representation of Scheffe results

14.1.1   Two-Factor ANOVA Using PROC GLM

A two-way ANOVA is an analysis that allows you to simultaneously evaluate the effects of two experimental variables (factors). Each factor is a "grouping" variable such as type of treatment, gender, brand, and so on. The two-way ANOVA tests determine whether the factors are important (significant) either separately (called main effects) or in combination (via an interaction), which is the combined effect of the two factors.

As an example of interaction effects, suppose you are observing annual salary where the two factors are gender and job category. Figure 14.4 illustrates the difference between an interaction effect and no interaction effect. Figure 14.4(a) indicates that female salaried workers have a different pattern of income from males across hourly and salary categories from males. Figure 14.4b indicates that the mean incomes for hourly and salaried personnel are parallel (noninteracting) across gender. When an interaction effect is present (Figure 14.4a), you cannot easily compare means between male and female workers because they have different patterns. When there is no interaction effect (Figure 14.4b), it makes sense to compare overall means between male and female workers. In Figure 14.4a, it appears that while there is no gender difference in salaries for hourly employees, male salaries are higher for salaried employees.

The dimensions of a factorial design depend on how many levels of each factor are used. For example, a design in which the first factor has two categories and the second has three categories is called a 2×3 (2 by 3) factorial design. Generally, the two-way ANOVA is called a $p \times q$ factorial design.

14.1.2   Understanding Fixed and Random Factors

Factors in an ANOVA are classified as fixed or random. When the factor levels completely define all the classifications of interest, we have what is called a **fixed factor**. For example, GENDER (classified as male or female) is a fixed factor. (The ANOVA examples in Chapter 13 all involve fixed factors.) When the levels used in the experiment are randomly selected from the population of possible levels, the factor is called a **random factor**. For example, a chemist interested in understanding the differences among laboratories that perform a certain assay may randomly select a sample of laboratories from among the large population

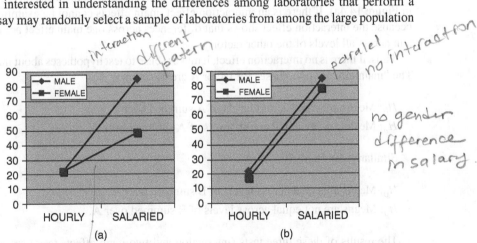

Figure 14.4   (a, b) Example of an interaction effect

of laboratories for his experiment. In this case, LAB would be a random effect. Two-way ANOVA models are classified with the following scheme:

- Both factors fixed: Model I ANOVA
- Both factors random: Model II ANOVA
- One random, one fixed: Model III ANOVA

In this section, we will assume that both factors (A and B) are fixed, and we illustrate an analysis for a Model I ANOVA. We will not provide an example of a Model II analysis, but a Model III ANOVA will be described in the following section.

When gathering data for this fixed-factor ANOVA design, within the $p \times q$ possible combinations of factors (cells), subjects should be randomly assigned to a treatment in such a way as to balance the number of subjects per cell. However, if the data are not balanced, an analysis can still be performed with PROC GLM (but not with PROC ANOVA).

There are some additional calculation issues involved with the unbalanced case that are not discussed here. Generally, in the unbalanced case, the Type III sums-of-squares from the PROC GLM output are recommended. Moreover, the dependent variable should be a quantitative variable whose distribution within each of the $p \times q$ (p by q) combinations is approximately normal with equal variances among combinations. (Some of these issues are relaxed when you are using PROC MIXED.)

There are two types of hypotheses used in a two-factor Model I design: hypotheses about interaction effects and main effects. The interaction effect should be examined first as follows:

H_0: There is no interaction effect.
H_a: There is an interaction effect.

Interaction implies that the pattern of means across groups is inconsistent (as illustrated in Figure 14.4a). If there is an interaction effect, main effects cannot be examined directly because the interaction effect shows that differences across one main effect are not consistent across all levels of the other factor.

Thus, if there is no interaction effect, it makes sense to test hypotheses about main effects. The "main effects" hypotheses for factor A are as follows:

H_0: Means are equal across levels of A summed over B.
H_a: Means are not equal across levels of A summed over B.

Similarly, for factor B:

H_0: Means are equal across levels of B summed over A.
H_a: Means are not equal across levels of B summed over A.

The results of these three tests (interaction and two main effects tests) are given in an analysis of variance table as F-tests. A low p-value (usually <0.05) for a test indicates evidence to reject the null hypothesis in favor of the alternative.

HANDS-ON EXAMPLE

This example (adapted from data set 404 in Hand, Daly, McConway, Lunn, and Ostrowski [1994]) concerns a study on weight loss for those attending meetings about dieting. A variable called CONDITION indicates whether the patient received a weight loss manual (CONDITION=1) or not (CONDITION=2). The STATUS variable indicates whether the patient had already been trying to lose weight before the series of meetings (STATUS=1) or not (STATUS=2).

Both factors are assumed to be fixed effects for this example, and there are an unequal number of subjects in each category. For this case, PROC GLM can be used.

1. Open the program file AGLM 2FACTOR.SAS.

```
DATA SLIM;
INPUT CONDITION STATUS RESPONSE @@;
DATALINES;
1 1 -13.67 1 1 -12.85 1 1 -9.55 1 1 -17.03 1 1 13.61
1 2 .91 1 2 2.48 1 2 2.84 1 2 3.46 1 2 2.20 1 2 -.73
1 2 -3.05 1 2 -5.68 1 2 -3.44 1 2 -7.18 1 2 -3.40 1 2 -.74
2 1 -3.29 2 1 -4 2 1 -2.31 2 1 -3.4 2 1 -7.49 2 1 -13.62
2 1 -7.34 2 1 -7.39 2 1 -1.32 2 1 -12.01 2 1 -8.35
2 2 5.94 2 2 1.91 2 2 -4.0 2 2 -5.19 2 2 0 2 2 -2.8
;
RUN;
TITLE "Two-Way ANOVA Example";
PROC GLM;
CLASS CONDITION STATUS;
    MODEL RESPONSE=CONDITION STATUS CONDITION*STATUS;
        MEANS CONDITION STATUS CONDITION*STATUS;
RUN;
QUIT;
```

Recall that in the MODEL statement, the dependent variable (RESPONSE) appears to the left of the equal sign and the independent variables (CONDITION and STATUS) appear to the right. The CONDITION*STATUS component of the MODEL statement is the interaction term. The two factors, CONDITION and STATUS, are listed in the CLASS statement because they are categorical variables.

2. Run this program and observe the output, partially illustrated in Table 14.5. This is output from the first PROC GLM statement in the code. Note that the overall model is significant ($p = 0.04$), indicating the presence of some differences in means. Note also that because of the unequal number of observations per cell, the Type I and Type III sums-of-squares (SS) give different results. It is recommended that Type III SS be used, and only that SS table is given in Table 14.5.

3. For this analysis, first examine the interaction effect (the CONDITION*STATUS row) in the Type III ANOVA table. Because $p = 0.7872$, there is no evidence of interaction. As mentioned previously:
   - If there is no interaction, examine the main effects tests in the ANOVA table by comparing marginal means.

(continued)

(continued)

TABLE 14.5 ANOVA Results from a Two-Factor Analysis Using PROC GLM

Source	DF	Sum of Squares	Mean Square	F Value	Pr > F
Model	3	309.009404	103.003135	3.13	0.0402
Error	30	987.604196	32.920140		
Corrected Total	33	1296.613600			

Source	DF	Type III SS	Mean Square	F Value	Pr > F
CONDITION	1	6.1546978	6.1546978	0.19	0.6686
STATUS	1	293.1057835	293.1057835	8.90	0.0056
CONDITION*STATUS	1	2.4432188	2.4432188	0.07	0.7872

- If there are interaction effects, the factor effects should not be interpreted in isolation from each other. It is usually more appropriate to compare effects of the first factor within levels of the second factor, and vice versa. That is, compare cell means rather than the marginal means using a posthoc analysis. Because there is no significant interaction in this example, it is appropriate to examine the main effects tests (STATUS and CONDITION):
- The test for the CONDITION main effect, $p = 0.6686$.
- The test for STATUS, $p = 0.0056$.

Thus, you can reject the null hypothesis that there is no STATUS effect and conclude that there is evidence to support the hypothesis that STATUS (i.e., whether the subject was already trying to lose weight) is a statistically significant factor in realized weight loss. Table 14.6 shows the marginal means for the two levels of STATUS. Because $p = 0.67$ for the CONDITION factor, we conclude that there is no significant CONDITION effect (i.e., the manual seemed to have no effect).

Because there are only two categories of STATUS, we do not need to perform multiple comparisons, and the clear conclusion is that STATUS=1 (i.e., those who had previously been trying to lose weight) had significantly more weight loss on average than those in STATUS=2.

It is often helpful to use graphs to help visualize the results of a two-factor analysis. Along with the tabled output, SAS produces the plot shown in Figure 14.5. This plot gives dot plots of the data for the four combinations of STATUS and CONDITION. The solid line connects the mean RESPONSE for subjects in STATUS=1 across CONDITION. The dashed line provides the same information for those in STATUS=2.

It can be seen that the lines are approximately parallel, supporting the finding of no significant interaction and indicating that RESPONSE scores are consistently higher for STATUS=2 across levels of CONDITION. Because RESPONSE is weight loss, this graphical representation supports the finding above that those who had previously been trying to lose weight (STATUS=1) had more success on the weight loss program.

Also included in the output are boxplots by STATUS and CONDITION (not shown here) that provide a visual look at the distribution and location for those variables.

TABLE 14.6 Marginal Means for Levels of STATUS

| Level of STATUS | N | RESPONSE | |
		Mean	Std Dev
1	16	-6.87562500	7.17206058
2	18	-0.91500000	3.63062829

Figure 14.5 Interaction plot for the two-factor ANOVA example

14.2 GOING DEEPER: TWO-FACTOR ANOVA USING PROC MIXED

PROC MIXED performs mixed-model analysis of variance and repeated measures analysis of variance with covariance structure modeling. PROC MIXED has features not available in PROC GLM. Briefly, here are some of the major differences between PROC GLM and PROC MIXED in relation to two-factor ANOVA analysis:

PROC GLM

- Is designed primarily for fixed effects models.
- Calculates based on ordinary least squares and method of moments.
- Defines all effects as fixed and adjusts for random effects after estimation.
- Can perform mixed model analysis, but some results are not optimally calculated.

PROC MIXED

- Is designed for mixed effects models.
- Uses generalized least squares for fixed effects and Restricted Maximum-Likelihood Estimation (RMLE) to estimate variance components.
- Allows selection of correlation models.

Both PROC GLM and PROC MIXED can analyze fixed effects and mixed models. When all factors are fixed, the two approaches produce the same results. However, for mixed models (and some repeated measures models), the two different approaches can lead to differing answers. Because PROC MIXED uses a more general approach that is less restrictive (in terms of assumptions), its results are considered more reliable (Littell, Milliken, Stroup, and Wolfinger, 1996).

The following example is adapted from Chapter 41 of the *SAS/STAT User's Guide*. The data include the response variable HEIGHT (in inches) of 18 individuals. The individuals are classified according to FAMILY and GENDER. Because FAMILY consists of some selection of families, it is reasonable to consider FAMILY to be a random effect. Moreover, the interaction FAMILY*GENDER is a random effect. With this information in mind, we illustrate the use of PROC MIXED to analyze this Model III ANOVA in the following Hands-on Example. In this example, the researcher wants to know if there is a difference in HEIGHT by GENDER and FAMILY.

HANDS-ON EXAMPLE

This example illustrates the use of PROC MIXED and assumes that FAMILY and FAMILY*GENDER are random factors.

1. Open the program file AMIXED1.SAS.

```
DATA HEIGHTS;
INPUT FAMILY GENDER$ HEIGHT @@;
DATALINES;
1 F 67   1 F 66   1 F 64   1 M 71   1 M 72   2 F 63
2 F 63   2 F 67   2 M 69   2 M 68   2 M 70   3 F 63
3 M 64   4 F 67   4 F 66   4 M 67   4 M 67   4 M 69
;
RUN;
PROC MEANS MAXDEC=2 MEAN DATA=HEIGHTS;
   CLASS FAMILY GENDER;
   VAR HEIGHT;
PROC MIXED;
    CLASS FAMILY GENDER;
    MODEL HEIGHT = GENDER;
      RANDOM FAMILY FAMILY*GENDER;
RUN;
```

Run this program and observe the output given in Table 14.7. A table of means is created first using PROC MEANS. Note that the number of observations (N Obs) that go into calculating the means is not balanced. They range from 1 observation to 3.

TABLE 14.7   PROC MEANS Output

Analysis Variable : HEIGHT			
FAMILY	GENDER	N Obs	Mean
1	F	3	65.67
	M	2	71.50
2	F	3	64.33
	M	3	69.00
3	F	1	63.00
	M	1	64.00
4	F	2	66.50
	M	3	67.67

2. Examine how the following PROC MIXED statement is constructed:

```
CLASS FAMILY GENDER;
MODEL HEIGHT = GENDER;
RANDOM FAMILY FAMILY*GENDER;
```

- FAMILY and GENDER appear in the CLASS statement because they are both grouping-type factors.
- The MODEL statement includes only the fixed factor GENDER.
- The RANDOM statement includes the random factors FAMILY and FAMILY*GENDER.

Observe the output table titled "Type 3 Text of Fixed Effects" shown in Table 14.8. This shows the results of a hypothesis test that there is no difference in means by GENDER, which is marginally nonsignificant ($p = 0.07$). SAS reports no test involving FAMILY.

TABLE 14.8   PROC MIXED Output Testing the Fixed Factor

Type 3 Tests of Fixed Effects				
Effect	Num DF	Den DF	F Value	Pr > F
GENDER	1	3	7.95	0.0667

3. To illustrate why it is important to properly classify a random factor as random, change the MODEL to where there are only fixed effects:

```
MODEL HEIGHT = GENDER FAMILY GENDER*FAMILY;
```

Run the changed program and observe the (abbreviated) output given in Table 14.9. Note that in this case the test for a GENDER effect is significant ($p = 0.0018$). How-

(continued)

(continued)

ever, in the fixed effects model, the `FAMILY` effect applies only to the families in the study (fixed effect). When `FAMILY` is classified as a random factor, the test results are applicable to families in general, not just to the ones in the study.

TABLE 14.9   Model Run As If All Factors Were Fixed

Type 3 Tests of Fixed Effects				
Effect	Num DF	Den DF	F Value	Pr > F
GENDER	1	10	17.63	0.0018
FAMILY	3	10	5.90	0.0139
FAMILY*GENDER	3	10	2.89	0.0889

14.3   GOING DEEPER: REPEATED MEASURES WITH A GROUPING FACTOR

A common design in medical research and other settings is to observe data for the same subject under different circumstances or over time (longitudinal). The one-way repeated measures design is illustrated in Chapter 13. When the design also includes a grouping variable, the analysis becomes a little more complicated. The "repeated measures design with a grouping factor" can be analyzed in SAS using `PROC MIXED`. Although it is also possible to perform this analysis using `PROC GLM`, the approach used in `PROC MIXED` is preferred. In addition, a distinct advantage of using `PROC MIXED` is that it allows missing values in the design, whereas `PROC GLM` deletes an entire record from analysis if there is one missing observation.

Suppose you observe a response to a drug over 4 hours for seven subjects, three male and four female. In this case, the repeated measure, `HOUR`, is longitudinal. The effect across hours, because it is a measurement on the same individual four times, is called a within-subject factor. `GENDER` is a between-subject factor because it a measurement between independent groups. In this example, we'll assume that both `GENDER` and `HOUR` are fixed factors because they include all levels of interest. The observed data are given in Table 14.10. Note that there is one missing value and an unequal number of subjects by `GENDER`.

TABLE 14.10   Original Data Set of Repeated Measures Data

SUB	GENDER	HOUR1	HOUR2	HOUR3	HOUR4
1	M	1	1.5	6	5.1
2	M	4	2.2	6.1	5.2
3	M	5.2	4.1	6.8	3.2
4	F	5.1	3.3	4.2	4.8
5	F	6.3	4.9	6.9	6.9
6	F	8.2	5.9	9.5	9.1
7	F	8.3	6.1	Missing	9.2

The data set for this analysis is initially set up as in Table 14.10 (similar to most data sets in this book) with one subject's data per record. However, for repeated measures, the SAS PROC MIXED procedure requires that the data be set up with one observation per record. The following Hands-on Example illustrates how to rearrange the data and perform the repeated measures analysis using PROC MIXED.

HANDS-ON EXAMPLE

This example uses PROC MIXED to analyze a repeated measures design that includes one grouping factor.

1. Open the program file AREPEAT1.SAS. The SAS code used to read in and rearrange the data set for the analysis is shown here:

```
DATA REPMIXED(KEEP= SUBJECT GENDER TIME OUTCOME);
INPUT SUBJECT GENDER $ HOUR1-HOUR4 ;
OUTCOME = HOUR1;   TIME = 1; OUTPUT;
OUTCOME = HOUR2;   TIME = 2; OUTPUT;
OUTCOME = HOUR3;   TIME = 3; OUTPUT;
OUTCOME = HOUR4;   TIME = 4; OUTPUT;
DATALINES;
1  M  1    1.5  6    5.1
2  M  4    2.2  6.1  5.2
3  M  5.2  4.1  5.8  3.2
4  F  5.1  3.3  5.2  4.8
5  F  6.3  4.9  7.9  6.9
6  F  8.2  5.9  9.5  9.1
7  F  8.3  6.1  .    9.2
;
```

The data set is initially set up with one subject per line. However, PROC MIXED requires there to be only one record per data line. That is, there should be one record per line with four records per subject. This necessary rearrangement is accomplished in the SAS code by

(a) assigning each of the four HOUR values to the variable OUTCOME
(b) creating a variable called TIME that contains the time marker (1–4)
(c) for each of these assignments, outputting the variables to the new data set REPMIXED using the OUTPUT statement.

The KEEP statement in parentheses after REPMIXED in the DATA statement tells SAS which variables to include in the final data set. The resulting data set is in the form given in Table 14.11. Compare this data set to the original data setup given in Table 14.10. Note that for each row in the original data set, there are four rows in the REPMIXED data set.

(continued)

(continued)

TABLE 14.11   REPMIXED Data for Use in PROC MIXED

SUBJECT	GENDER	TIME	OUTCOME
1	M	1	1
1	M	2	1.5
1	M	3	6
1	M	4	5.1
2	M	1	4
2	M	2	2.2
2	M	3	6.1
etc	etc	etc	etc

2. The following code is used to perform three repeated measures analyses using PROC MIXED:

```
PROC MIXED DATA=REPMIXED;
      CLASS GENDER TIME SUBJECT;
      MODEL OUTCOME=GENDER TIME GENDER*TIME;
      REPEATED / TYPE=UN SUB=SUBJECT;
RUN;
PROC MIXED DATA=REPMIXED;
      CLASS GENDER TIME SUBJECT;
      MODEL OUTCOME=GENDER TIME GENDER*TIME;
      REPEATED / TYPE=CS SUB=SUBJECT;
RUN;
PROC MIXED DATA=REPMIXED;
      CLASS GENDER TIME SUBJECT;
      MODEL OUTCOME=GENDER TIME GENDER*TIME;
      REPEATED / TYPE=AR(1) SUB=SUBJECT;
RUN;
```

These three PROC MIXED analyses are identical except for the TYPE= statement. Each TYPE statement includes a different specification for the within-subject covariance matrix. A few commonly used structures include the following:

VC (Variance components) is the default and simplest structure with all off-diagonal variances equal to 0.

- AR(1) (Autoregressive) assumes that nearby measurements are correlated and decline exponentially with time. That is, measurements at TIME1 and TIME2 are more highly correlated than are measurements at TIME1 and TIME3.

- CS (Compound symmetry) assumes homogeneous variances that are constant regardless of how far apart the measurements are.

- UN (Unstructured) allows all variances to be different.

See the SAS/STAT Manual (PROC MIXED chapter) for more options and details regarding covariance specifications.

The CLASS option indicates that the three factor variables are all classification (categorical) variables. Categorical variables can be discrete numeric or character.

(We include SUBJECT here even though we are not generally interested in a SUBJECT effect, in order to fully define the model.) The MODEL statement indicates that OUTCOME is the dependent variable and GENDER, TIME, and the interaction term GENDER*TIME are independent variables used to predict outcome.

The REPEATED statement indicates the TYPE of covariance structure to use in the analysis. As mentioned, the TYPE of covariance structures is the only difference among the three calls to PROC MIXED. SUB=SUBJECT indicates the name of the subject variable.

3. Run the program. A lot of output is created by SAS for this analysis, much of it dealing with the iterations required to fit the model. This output will not be discussed here. Initially, take note of the value of AIC (Akaike Information Criterion) in the Fit Statistics output table. This is a measure of the fit of the model, with smaller AIC values considered best. (There are other criteria you could also use, such as BIC and AICC, but we'll limit our discussion to AIC.)

You can fit any number of covariance structures to the data with the TYPE= statement and you then typically select the best-fitting model. In this example, based on the AIC criterion, the AR(1) specification best fits the data. For these three models, the AIC results from the Fit Statistics tables associated with each covariance structure considered are as follows:

- AIC(unstructured) = 71.0
- AIC(compound symmetry) = 77.6
- AIC(autoregressive) = 70.2

4. The primary tests for this model are found in the table titled "Type 3 Test of Fixed Effects." Because the AIC for the AR(1) model is lowest, we'll examine the results in that table, as given in Table 14.12.

TABLE 14.12   Results from PROC MIXED for AR(1) Structure

Type 3 Tests of Fixed Effects				
Effect	Num DF	Den DF	F Value	Pr > F
GENDER	1	5	5.22	0.0710
TIME	3	14	29.67	<.0001
GENDER*TIME	3	14	1.48	0.2637

In this case, the results indicate that there is no interaction (GENDER*TIME, $p = 0.26$) effect. In the presence of no interaction, it is appropriate to examine the main effects tests for TIME and GENDER. For these results, there is a significant TIME ($p < 0.0001$) effect and a nonsignificant (but marginal) GENDER ($p = 0.071$) effect.

The other two models (unstructured and compound symmetry) report a significant GENDER effect (both $p < 0.05$). Thus, the structure selected can affect the outcome of the statistical tests.

(continued)

(continued)

Using the AR(1) results, we conclude that there is at most marginal evidence of a GENDER effect. There is (in all models) evidence of a significant TIME effect. To examine these results more closely, we'll look at plots of the means.

5. Open the program file AREPEAT2.SAS. This program is based on the same data set analyzed previously in this example using the AREPEAT1.SAS code, and it produced two useful graphs. (SAS Graph procedures are discussed more thoroughly in Chapter 18.)

```
*-----------------PRODUCE GRAPHS OF MEANS;
PROC SORT DATA=REPMIXED;BY GENDER TIME;
PROC MEANS noprint; BY GENDER TIME;
    OUTPUT OUT=FORPLOT MEAN=;
RUN;
PROC GPLOT;
PLOT OUTCOME*GENDER=TIME;
SYMBOL1 V=CIRCLE I=JOIN L=1 C=BLACK;
SYMBOL2 V=DOT I=JOIN L=2 C=BLUE;
SYMBOL3 V=STAR I=JOIN L=2 C=RED;
SYMBOL4 V=SQUARE I=JOIN L=2 C=GREEN;
RUN;
PROC SORT DATA=REPMIXED;BY TIME GENDER;
PROC MEANS noprint; BY TIME GENDER;
    OUTPUT OUT=FORPLOT MEAN=;
RUN;
PROC GPLOT;
PLOT OUTCOME*TIME=GENDER;
SYMBOL1 V=CIRCLE I=JOIN L=1 C=BLACK;
SYMBOL2 V=DOT I=JOIN L=2 C=BLUE;
RUN;
```

This code calculates the means by GENDER and TIME (then TIME and GENDER) and plots the results. For more information about PROC GPLOT, see Chapter 18. Run the program and observe the plots, shown in Figure 14.6(a, b).

Although there (visually) appears to be a difference in means across GENDER, it is at most marginally significant (probably because of the small sample size). From the graph, observe that the mean at TIME3 is the highest and the mean at TIME2 is lowest.

6. To determine which TIMEs are significantly different, include the following option in the section of PROC MIXED code related to the AR(1) covariance structure.

```
LSMEANS TIME/PDIFF;
```

This statement produces confidence limits on the differences in the (least square) means. Open and run the SAS program AREPEAT3.SAS. This program is similar to the original but includes only the AR(1) model (and the LSMEANS statement). Observe the results in Table 14.13. As we observed in Figure 14.6(a, b), the difference between TIME2 and TIME3 is the greatest difference ($p < 0.0001$) from the Pr

>|t| column. Note also that there are significant differences between all other TIMEs except between TIME1 and TIME4 ($p = 0.17$).

This example illustrates the iterative nature of repeated measures analyses. It requires that you determine which variance structure best fits the model. It is also advantageous to plot the means and, when there are more than two means in a significant factor, to compare means using the LSMEANS statement.

Figure 14.6   (a, b) Custom plots for repeated measures analysis

(continued)

(continued)

TABLE 14.13   **Comparing Pairwise Times**

			Differences of Least Squares Means				
Effect	TIME	_TIME	Estimate	Standard Error	DF	t Value	Pr > |t|
TIME	1	2	1.3625	0.3507	14	3.89	0.0016
TIME	1	3	-1.7890	0.4879	14	-3.67	0.0025
TIME	1	4	-0.8125	0.5651	14	-1.44	0.1725
TIME	2	3	-3.1515	0.3638	14	-8.66	<.0001
TIME	2	4	-2.1750	0.4781	14	-4.55	0.0005
TIME	3	4	0.9765	0.3638	14	2.68	0.0178

14.4   SUMMARY

This chapter discusses the use of PROC GLM to perform ANCOVA and two-factor ANOVA with fixed effects. We also introduce PROC MIXED and discuss its use on the two-factor mixed model and a repeated measures analysis with a grouping variable.

EXERCISES

14.1   **Use multiple comparisons in** PROC MIXED.

Another way to determine differences in means in a PROC MIXED model such as in AREPEAT3.SAS is to request multiple comparison tests using a statement such as

```
LSMEANS/ADJUST=TUKEY;
```

(You can optionally use BON, SCHEFFE, or SIDAK as the comparison method.) Replace the PDIFF command in AREPEAT3.SAS with one of these options and rerun the analysis.

14.2   **Use** PROC MIXED **with missing data.**

Note that the analysis using PROC MIXED was able to handle a missing value in the data as well as unbalanced data (more females than males). To perform this analysis in PROC GLM, use the program EX_14.2.SAS. Run this program and observe the interaction and main effects tests for GENDER and TIME in the Type III GLM results tables ($P > F$ column). Although the results are similar to those of PROC MIXED, note that one entire subject was eliminated from the analysis because it contained a missing value. The loss of subjects with missing values plus the fact that PROC GLM uses a less sophisticated calculation for random effects makes it desirable to use PROC MIXED.

15

NONPARAMETRIC ANALYSIS

LEARNING OBJECTIVES

- To be able to use SAS® procedures to compare two independent samples (Wilcoxon–Mann–Whitney)
- To be able to use SAS procedures to compare k independent samples (Kruskal–Wallis)
- To be able to use SAS procedures to compare two dependent (paired) samples
- To be able to use SAS procedures to compare k dependent samples (Friedman's test)
- To be able to use SAS procedures to perform multiple comparisons following a significant Kruskal–Wallis test (macro)

An assumption for many statistical tests, such as the t-tests and ANOVA, is that the data are normally distributed. When this normality assumption is suspect or cannot be met, there are alternative techniques for analyzing the data.

Statistical techniques based on an assumption that data are distributed according to some parameterized distribution (such as the normal distribution) are referred to as parametric analyses. Statistical techniques that do not rely on this assumption are called nonparametric procedures. This chapter illustrates several nonparametric techniques. One nonparametric procedure, Spearman's rank correlation, has been discussed earlier in Chapter 12.

15.1 COMPARING TWO INDEPENDENT SAMPLES USING NPAR1WAY

A nonparametric test can be used to compare two independent groups when you cannot make the assumptions associated with the t-test. Using a nonparametric test is also a useful

SAS® Essentials: Mastering SAS for Data Analytics, Second Edition. Alan C. Elliott and Wayne A. Woodward.
© 2016 John Wiley & Sons, Inc. Published 2016 by John Wiley & Sons, Inc.

technique if you do not have exact data values for the observations but you do have order statistics – that is, you don't know the actual response values, but you know which is the largest, the next largest, and so forth, to the smallest. In this case, the smallest value is recoded as 1 and the next to the smallest is recoded as 2, and so forth. Many nonparametric procedures are based on these ranks.

The primary nonparametric test for comparing two groups discussed in this chapter is the Wilcoxon (sometimes called the Wilcoxon–Mann–Whitney) test. The hypothesis tested is as follows:

H_0: The two groups have the same distribution (they come from the same population).

H_a: The two groups do not have the same distributions (they come from different populations).

The SAS procedure for testing these hypotheses is PROC NPAR1WAY. The procedure outputs several statistical test results, but the focus will be on the Wilcoxon test. The syntax for NPAR1WAY is as follows:

```
PROC NPAR1WAY <options>;
```

Table 15.1 lists common options and statements used with PROC NPAR1WAY.

TABLE 15.1   Common Options for PROC NPAR1WAY

Option	Explanation
DATA = dataname	Specifies which data set to use
WILCOXON	Limits output to Wilcoxon-type tests
MEDIAN	Requests median test
VW	Requests Van der Waerden test
NOPRINT	Suppresses output
Common statements for PROC NPAR1WAY	
CLASS vars;	Specifies grouping variable(s)
VAR vars;	Specifies dependent variable(s)
EXACT	Requests exact tests
BY, FORMAT, LABEL, WHERE	These statements are common to most procedures and may be used here

HANDS-ON EXAMPLE

This example illustrates how to compare two independent groups using nonparametric methods. In it, observations from two brands of fertilizers are compared to determine if one provides better overall growth (measured by height) than the other. (This is the same data used in ATTEST2.SAS, which was discussed in the Hands-on Example in the section "Running the Two-sample *t*-test in SAS" in Chapter 11.

1. Open the program file ANPAR1.SAS.

```
DATA FERTILIZER;
INPUT BRAND $ HEIGHT;
DATALINES;
```

```
A    20.00
A    23.00
A    32.00
A    24.00
A    25.00
A    28.00
A    27.50
B    25.00
B    46.00
B    56.00
B    45.00
B    46.00
B    51.00
B    34.00
B    47.50
;
PROC NPAR1WAY WILCOXON;
    CLASS BRAND;
    VAR HEIGHT;
      EXACT;
    Title 'Compare two groups using NPAR1WAY';
RUN;
```

The `WILCOXON` option is included in the `PROC NPAR1WAY` statement to limit the output to Wilcoxon-type analyses. The `EXACT` statement produces additional Exact tests.

2. Run the program and observe the output in Table 15.2.

The "Wilcoxon Scores" table provides summary statistics for the data. The "Wilcoxon Two-Sample Test" table reports a variety of approximate p-values for the Wilcoxon test (both one-sided and two-sided). The Kruskal–Wallis (KW) test is an extension of the Wilcoxon–Mann–Whitney test that is applicable to two or more independent samples. The Kruskal–Wallis p-value reported in this table is a result of a chi-square approximation.

We recommend using the Exact test p-values obtained as a result of the information statement `EXACT`. The two-sided p-value (appropriate for testing the hypotheses as stated earlier) is 0.0025, suggesting a difference between the two distributions (i.e., that the effects of the fertilizers are different). SAS also produces side-by-side boxplots (not shown here) that illustrate the difference between the two distributions.

3. Also note the boxplots produced by this analyses (not shown here) provide visual evidence that the distribution of observations in Group B tend to be higher than those of group A. (Since this is a nonparametric test, the comparison is not of means, but rather a comparison of the distribution of observations.)

Note for comparison that a parametric two-sample test was performed on the same data in Chapter 11. The results were similar, with a reported p-value of 0.0005 for that test.

(continued)

(continued)

TABLE 15.2   Output from NPAR1WAY for a Two-Group Analysis

Wilcoxon Two-Sample Test	
Statistic (S)	31.5000
Normal Approximation	
Z	-2.7824
One-Sided Pr < Z	0.0027
Two-Sided Pr > |Z|	0.0054
t Approximation	
One-Sided Pr < Z	0.0073
Two-Sided Pr > |Z|	0.0147
Exact Test	
One-Sided Pr <= S	0.0012
Two-Sided Pr >= |S - Mean|	0.0025
Z includes a continuity correction of 0.5.	

Kruskal-Wallis Test	
Chi-Square	8.0679
DF	1
Pr > Chi-Square	0.0045

A number of other tests are reported in the SAS output (when the WILCOXON option is not used), which are not described here. They include a median test and a Van der Waerden two-sample test. Which test is appropriate? Different disciplines often favor one test over another, or you may find that the type of analysis you are performing is commonly reported using one or another of these tests.

15.2   COMPARING *k* INDEPENDENT SAMPLES (KRUSKAL–WALLIS)

If more than two independent groups are being compared using nonparametric methods, SAS uses the Kruskal-Wallis (KW) test to compare groups. The hypotheses being tested are as follows:

H_0: There is no difference among the distributions of the groups.

H_a: There are differences among the distributions of the groups.

This test is an extension of the Wilcoxon–Mann–Whitney test described earlier. It uses the WILCOXON procedure to calculate mean ranks for the data and uses that information to calculate the test statistic for the KW test.

HANDS-ON EXAMPLE

This example illustrates how to compare three or more independent groups using nonparametric procedures. The data are weight gains of 28 animals that are randomly assigned to four feed treatments with seven animals to a treatment type. Suppose you want to test whether there are differences among the effects of the different treatments. If you have reason to believe that the normality assumptions associated with the one-way ANOVA are not met, then the KW test would be appropriate. The data for this example are as follows:

Group 1	Group 2	Group 3	Group 4
50.8	68.7	82.6	76.9
57.0	67.7	74.1	72.2
44.6	66.3	80.5	73.7
51.7	69.8	80.3	74.2
48.2	66.9	81.5	70.6
51.3	65.2	78.6	75.3
49.0	62.0	76.1	69.8

1. Open the program file ANPAR2.SAS. (Note that the DATA step uses the compact data entry technique; see the "@@" in the INPUT line.)

```
DATA NPAR;
INPUT GROUP WEIGHT @@;
DATALINES;
1 50.8 1 57.0 1 44.6 1 51.7 1 48.2 1 51.3 1 49.0
2 68.7 2 67.7 2 66.3 2 69.8 2 66.9 2 65.2 2 62.0
3 82.6 3 74.1 3 80.5 3 80.3 3 81.5 3 78.6 3 76.1
4 76.9 4 72.2 4 73.7 4 74.2 4 70.6 4 75.3 4 69.8
;
PROC NPAR1WAY WILCOXON;
    CLASS GROUP;
    VAR WEIGHT;
    Title 'Four group analysis using NPAR1WAY';
RUN;
```

The SAS code for this program is very similar to that for the Wilcoxon–Mann–Whitney test in the previous Hands-on Example. Note that you request the KW test using the WILCOXON option. KW is a *k*-group version of the Wilcoxon–Mann–Whitney test based on Wilcoxon rank sums. The only real difference is that this data set includes four categories for the grouping variable. Also note that again, the WILCOXON option in the NPAR1WAY statement limits the amount of output.

(continued)

(continued)

2. Run the program and observe the output in Table 15.3. The first table provides summary information for the mean scores based on the ranks. The KW test reports $p < 0.0001$, indicating that there is a significant difference in the distribution of the groups. (Note that because in this case there are four groups, NPAR1WAY does not produce output for the two-group Wilcoxon Rank Sums test as in Table 15.1.) Moreover, you can request exact p-values using an EXACT statement, but the computing time involved will be extensive even in the current case of four groups of seven.

Unlike in the PROC ANOVA procedure, there are no multiple comparison tests provided with NPAR1WAY. However, in the Going Deeper section later in this chapter, a method is provided to perform this follow-up procedure.

If you prefer not to use the method for multiple comparisons shown in the Going Deeper section, and the test for k-samples is significant, an acceptable procedure is to perform multiple pairwise comparisons across the groups and adjust the significance level from 0.05 using the Bonferroni technique of dividing the significance level by the total number of comparisons. For example, in the case with four groups, there are six pairwise comparisons, so you would perform six Wilcoxon–Mann–Whitney comparisons. For each test, you would use the significance level adjusted to $(0.05/6 = 0.0083)$ as your criterion for rejecting the null hypothesis.

TABLE 15.3   Output from NPAR1WAY for a Four-Sample Group Comparison

			Wilcoxon Scores (Rank Sums) for Variable WEIGHT Classified by Variable GROUP		
GROUP	N	Sum of Scores	Expected Under H0	Std Dev Under H0	Mean Score
1	7	28.00	101.50	18.845498	4.000000
2	7	77.50	101.50	18.845498	11.071429
3	7	171.00	101.50	18.845498	24.428571
4	7	129.50	101.50	18.845498	18.500000

Average scores were used for ties.

Kruskal-Wallis Test	
Chi-Square	24.4807
DF	3
Pr > Chi-Square	<.0001

SAS displays comparative box plots in the output that provide a visual comparison of the groups (see Figure 15.1). Results of multiple comparison tests for these data will be given in the Hands-on Example in Section 15.5.

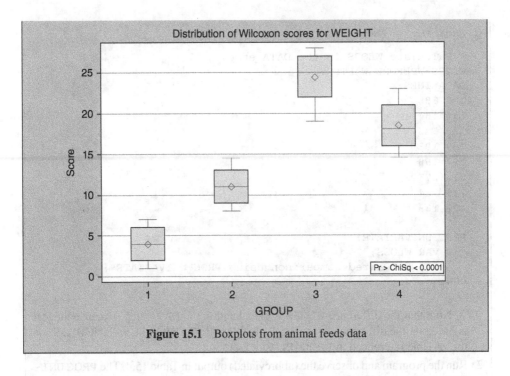

Figure 15.1   Boxplots from animal feeds data

15.3   COMPARING TWO DEPENDENT (PAIRED) SAMPLES

Two nonparametric tests for paired data are available in the PROC UNIVARIATE procedure: the sign test and the signed-rank test. These tests are nonparametric counterparts to
the paired t-test. The sign test is simple. It counts the number of positive and negative differences and calculates a p-value based on this information. The (Wilcoxon) signed-rank
test bases its decision on the magnitude of the ranked differences. The hypotheses for these
tests are as follows:

H_0: The probability of a positive difference is the same as that of a negative difference.
H_a: The probability of a positive difference is different from that of a negative difference.

The following Hands-on Example illustrates how to perform these tests in SAS.

HANDS-ON EXAMPLE

This example illustrates how to compare paired observations using nonparametric techniques.

1. In the Editor window, open the program AUNIPAIRED.SAS.

```
DATA WEIGHT;
INPUT WBEFORE WAFTER;
```

(continued)

(continued)

```
* Calculate WLOSS in the DATA step *;
WLOSS=WBEFORE-WAFTER;
DATALINES;
200 185
175 154
188 176
198 193
197 198
310 275
245 224
202 188
;
PROC UNIVARIATE;
    VAR WLOSS;
    TITLE "Paired comparison using PROC UNIVARIATE";
RUN;
```

Note that the difference `WLOSS` is calculated in the `DATA` step. Because the test is based on the difference between `WBEFORE` and `WAFTER`, the variable `WLOSS` is the variable referenced in `PROC UNIVARIATE`.

2. Run the program and observe the (abbreviated) output in Table 15.4. The `PROC UNI-VARIATE` procedure produces more output, but this is the table we are interested in for the paired comparison.

TABLE 15.4   PROC UNIVARIATE to Test Paired Difference

Tests for Location: Mu0=0				
Test		Statistic	p Value	
Student's t	t	2.788474	Pr > |t|	0.0270
Sign	M	3	Pr >= |M|	0.0703
Signed Rank	S	17	Pr >= |S|	0.0156

In the "Tests for Location" table, three test results are given. The p-value for the Student's t-test is the same that is given in the `PROC MEANS` example in Chapter 11($p = 0.0156$). The two nonparametric tests reported are the sign and signed-rank tests. The sign test reports a p-value of 0.0703 and the signed-rank test reports a p-value of 0.0156. All of the p-values are two-sided. The higher p-value associated with the sign test is typical based on the fact that it tends to be less powerful than the signed-rank test. Note that since the test is one-sided and the results support the alternative hypothesis (of positive weight gain), all the p-values in the table should be divided by 2, and consequently they all lead to rejection of H_0.

15.4 COMPARING *k*-DEPENDENT SAMPLES (FRIEDMAN'S TEST)

When your data include more than two repeated measures and the normality assumption is questioned, you can perform a Friedman procedure to test the following hypotheses:

H_0: The distributions are the same across the repeated measures.

H_a: There are some differences in distributions across the repeated measures.

Although no procedure in SAS performs a Friedman's test directly, you can calculate the statistic needed to perform the test using PROC FREQ.

Recall the repeated measures example in Chapter 13, in which four drugs were given to five patients in random order. In this repeated measures design, the observed value is a reaction to the drug, where a larger value is beneficial. The data are as follows:

Subj	Drug1	Drug2	Drug3	Drug4
1	31	29	17	35
2	15	17	11	23
3	25	21	19	31
4	35	35	21	45
5	27	27	15	31

The following Hands-on Example shows how these data are coded for input so that the Friedman's test may be performed, and how to perform the Friedman's test using PROC FREQ.

HANDS-ON EXAMPLE

This example illustrates how to compare three or more repeated measures using non-parametric techniques.

1. Open the program file AFRIEDMAN.SAS.

```
DATA TIME;
INPUT SUBJ DRUG OBS;
DATALINES;
1    1    31
1    2    29
1    3    17
1    4    35
2    1    15
...ETC...
5    2    27
5    3    15
5    4    31
;
Title "Friedman Analysis";
```

(continued)

(continued)

```
PROC FREQ;
  TABLES SUBJ*DRUG*OBS / CMH2 SCORES=RANK NOPRINT;
RUN;
```

Note that in this analysis, the data set is structured differently from most data sets in this book, although it is set up the same here as for the repeated measures ANOVA analysis in Chapter 13. In a repeated measures analysis, each line contains the observed reading for a single experimental condition, in this case for each subject and each drug administered. Therefore, because each subject received the four drugs (in random order and with a washout period between drugs), there are four lines for each subject.

The PROC FREQ statement requests a three-way table. Statement options include CMH2, which requests Cochran–Mantel–Haenszel Statistics, and the SCORES=RANK option indicates that the analysis is to be performed on ranks. The NOPRINT option is used to suppress the output of the actual summary table because it is quite large and provides nothing needed for this analysis.

2. Run the analysis and observe the output given in Table 15.5.

The test statistic for a Friedman's test is found in the "Row Mean Scores Differ" row, where the Friedman chi-square $= 14.125$ with three degrees of freedom and $p = 0.0027$. Because the p-value is <0.05, you would conclude that there is a difference in the distributions across DRUGs.

As with the KW test, SAS provides no built-in follow-up multiple comparison test for this procedure. If you reject the null hypothesis, you can perform comparisons for each drug pair using the Wilcoxon test on the differences as discussed in the earlier section on paired comparisons. As in the KW multiple comparisons discussed earlier, you should adjust your significance level using the Bonferroni technique. For example, in this case with four groups (measured in repeated readings) you would perform six pairwise comparisons, and for an overall 0.05 level test you would use the $0.05/6 = 0.0083$ level of significance for each individual pairwise comparison.

TABLE 15.5   Results for Friedman's Test

Cochran-Mantel-Haenszel Statistics (Based on Rank Scores)				
Statistic	Alternative Hypothesis	DF	Value	Prob
1	Nonzero Correlation	1	1.2250	0.2684
2	Row Mean Scores Differ	3	14.1250	0.0027

15.5   GOING DEEPER: NONPARAMETRIC MULTIPLE COMPARISONS

Because SAS is a flexible language, SAS programmers often create their own procedures for performing analyses that are not already in the SAS language. For the KW nonparametric analysis of variance described earlier in this chapter, SAS provides no specific posthoc pairwise comparisons when the overall KW test is significant, indicating some difference among groups.

The following Hands-on Example illustrates how a procedure written in SAS code (called a macro) can be used to perform an analysis not included in the SAS program. This example utilizes a SAS macro implementation of a multiple comparison test (Nemenyi [Tukey-type] or Dunn's test) to be used along with SAS NPAR1WAY (see Elliott and Hynan, 2007).

HANDS-ON EXAMPLE

This example shows how you can use a macro to calculate multiple comparisons following a KW test.

This example is based on the previous independent four-group comparison earlier in the chapter, with the addition of code to run a macro procedure performing multiple comparisons.

1. Open the program file ANPAR3.SAS.

```
%INCLUDE C:\SASDATA\KW_MC.SAS;
DATA NPAR;
INPUT GROUP WEIGHT @@;
DATALINES;
1 50.8 1 57.0 1 44.6 1 51.7 1 48.2 1 51.3 1 49.0
2 68.7 2 67.7 2 66.3 2 69.8 2 66.9 2 65.2 2 62.0
3 82.6 3 74.1 3 80.5 3 80.3 3 81.5 3 78.6 3 76.1
4 76.9 4 72.2 4 73.7 4 74.2 4 70.6 4 75.3 4 69.8
;
* BEGIN INFORMATION FOR USING THE SAS MACRO KW>MC;
%LET NUMGROUPS=4;
%LET DATANAME=NPAR;
%LET OBSVAR=WEIGHT;
%LET GROUP=GROUP;
%LET ALPHA=0.05;
Title "Kruskal-Wallis Multiple Comparisons";
***********************************************************
*invoke the KW_MC macro
***********************************************************;
   %KW_MC(source=&DATANAME, groups=&NUMGROUPS,
   obsname=&OBSVAR, gpname=&GROUP, sig=&alpha);
```

Note the %INCLUDE statement at the top of the program. This statement tells SAS to get additional SAS code that is stored in a file in the indicated location. Thus, the file C:\SASDATA\KW_MC.SAS must be at the designated location, or you must change the file name to match the appropriate location.

The data set used in this program is the same as the one used in the previous KW example on weight gains of animals assigned randomly to four treatments.

(continued)

(continued)

The series of %LET statements are used to tell the SAS macro the values of certain parameters needed by the macro. In this case, the number of groups (NUM-GROUPS) is 4. The name of the data set containing the data for analysis is NPAR. The variable containing the dependent variable is WEIGHT, and the grouping variable is named GROUP. The significance level used to perform the test is indicated by ALPHA=0.05.

The statement that begins with %KW_MC(source= is the statement that "calls" the SAS macro. You do not need to change anything about this statement to use the macro for any other data set. If you use this procedure for another analysis, the only items you must change are the four values in the %LET statements.

2. Run the program and observe the results. The KW results are the same as those in the previous example. The multiple comparison test results are given in Table 15.5.

Table 15.6 displays the results of a series of multiple comparison tests. (This test is named the Dunn's test and it is similar to the Tukey multiple comparison procedure illustrated in Chapter 13: Analysis of Variance.) The test is performed at the overall 0.05 significance level. For example, the test indicates that for the comparison of groups 3 and 1, you reject the null hypothesis that the two groups are from the same distribution. The same conclusion is reached for the comparison of groups 3 and 2. Thus, your conclusion based on this test would be that weight gain for group 3 is different from that for groups 1 and 2, but not different from that for group 4. Weight gain for group 4 is significantly different from that for group 1 but not from that for group 2. Finally, weight gain for group 2 is not different from that for group 1. SAS also displays side-by-side boxplots that are the same as shown in Figure 15.1. This graph provides a visual confirmation that treatment 3 is preferred to treatments 1 and 2, which was the finding based on the Hand-on Example in Chapter 13 using the same data set.

TABLE 15.6   Multiple Comparison Test for a Kruskal–Wallis Analysis

Compare		Diff	SE	q	q(0.05)	Conclude
3 vs	1	20.43	4.4	4.64	2.638	Reject
3 vs	2	13.36	4.4	3.04	2.638	Reject
3 vs	4	5.93	4.4	1.35	2.638	Do not reject
4 vs	1	14.5	4.4	3.3	2.638	Reject
4 vs	2	7.43	4.4	1.69	2.638	Do not reject
2 vs	1	7.07	4.4	1.61	2.638	Do not reject

Group sample sizes not equal, or some ranks tied. Performed Dunns test, alpha = 0.05; comparison group = GROUP.
Reference: Biostatistical analysis, 4th Edition, J. Zar, 2010.

15.6   SUMMARY

This chapter introduces several nonparametric alternatives to standard parametric analyses. These procedures are useful when the normality assumption is questionable and particularly important when sample sizes are small.

EXERCISES

15.1 **Run a median test.**

   a. Using the SAS program in ANPAR2.SAS, change the selection from the Wilcoxon (KW) test to the median test, as shown here:

```
PROC NPAR1WAY MEDIAN;
```

   b. Run the program and observe the results. Do the results differ?

15.2 **Run a nonparametric analysis.**

   A retail franchise is interested in stopping shrinkage (the loss of merchandise through theft) in its 11 stores in Denver, Colorado. The management believes that the presence of a uniformed police officer near the entrance will deter theft. Six of the 11 stores are randomly selected to have an officer present for a month. On the following month, the officers are assigned to the other five stores for a month. Shrinkage is determined at the end of each month, yielding the data given in Table 15.7. (Note: The two months selected have historically had about the same sales volume per month.)

   a. Write a SAS program to analyze these data using an appropriate nonparametric procedure. Start with the following code:

```
DATA STORES;
INPUT STORE $ WITHOUT WITH;
LOSSDIFF=WITH-WITHOUT;
DATALINES;
001 1.3 .9
002  .9 .46
...etc
;
PROC _____
VAR _____
RUN;
```

   b. Observe the output and make a decision. Is there evidence that shrinkage is lower when an officer is present?

TABLE 15.7   Store Shrinkage, in Thousands

Store Number	Without Officer	With Officer
001	1.3	0.9
002	0.9	0.46
003	2.6	2.5
004	8.2	4.1
005	2.2	2.1
006	0.89	0.9
007	1.6	1.5
008	2.4	2.2
009	3.2	1.1
010	0.5	0.4
011	1.1	0.5

16

LOGISTIC REGRESSION

LEARNING OBJECTIVES

- To be able to perform a logistic analysis using PROC LOGISTIC
- To be able to create a SAS® program that will perform a simple logistic analysis
- To be able to create a SAS program that will perform multiple logistic analyses
- To be able to use SAS to assess a model's fit and predictive ability

Binary logistic regression models are based on a dependent variable that can take on only one of two values, such as presence or absence of a disease, deceased or not deceased, married or unmarried, and so on. In this setting, the independent (sometimes called explanatory or predictor) variables are used for predicting the probability of occurrence of an outcome (such as mortality).

The logistic regression model is sometimes called a logit model. Logistic analysis methods are available for cases in which the dependent variable takes on more than two values, but this topic is beyond the scope of this book and we will discuss only the binary logistic model. Logistic analysis is used to create an equation that can be used to predict the probability of occurrence of the outcome of interest, to assess the relative importance of independent variables, and to calculate odds ratios (OR) that measure the importance of an independent variable relative to the response. The independent variables can be either continuous or categorical.

SAS® Essentials: Mastering SAS for Data Analytics, Second Edition. Alan C. Elliott and Wayne A. Woodward.
© 2016 John Wiley & Sons, Inc. Published 2016 by John Wiley & Sons, Inc.

16.1   LOGISTIC ANALYSIS BASICS

Before describing the SAS implementation of logistic regression, we briefly discuss some of the basic ideas underlying logistic analysis. We show the actual logistic regression equations here because we believe they provide insights into how logistic regression works.

16.1.1   The Logistic Regression Model

The basic form of the logistic equation is

$$p = \frac{e^{\beta_0 + \beta_1 X_1 + \beta_2 X_2 + \cdots + \beta_k X_k}}{1 + e^{\beta_0 + \beta_1 X_1 + \beta_2 X_2 + \cdots + \beta_k X_k}}$$

where $X_1, \ldots, X_k$ are the k independent variables, p is the probability of occurrence of the outcome of interest (which lies between 0 and 1), β_i is the coefficient on the independent variable X_i, and β_0 is a constant term. As in linear regression, the parameters of this theoretical model are estimated from the data, resulting in the prediction equation

$$\hat{p} = \frac{e^{b_0 + b_1 X_1 + b_2 X_2 + \cdots + b_k X_k}}{1 + e^{b_0 + b_1 X_1 + b_2 X_2 + \cdots + b_k X_k}}$$

where the b_i's are maximum-likelihood estimates of the β_i's (calculated by SAS) and $\hat{p}$ is the estimated probability of occurrence of the outcome of interest. Of course, any variable with a zero coefficient in the theoretical model is not useful in predicting the probability of occurrence. SAS reports tests of the null hypothesis that all of the β_i's, $i = 1, \ldots, k$ are zero.

If this null hypothesis is not rejected, then there is no statistical evidence that the independent variables as a group are useful in the prediction. If the overall test is rejected, then we conclude that at least some of the variables are useful in the prediction. SAS reports individual tests of the importance of each of the independent variables. That is, for each $i = 1, \ldots, k$, SAS reports the results of the tests.

$H_0: \beta_i = 0$: The ith independent variable is not predictive of the probability of occurrence.

$H_a: \beta_i \neq 0$: The ith independent variable is predictive of the probability of occurrence.

16.1.2   Understanding Odds and Odds Ratios

Another use of the logistic model is the calculation of OR for each independent variable. The odds of an event measures the expected number of times an event will occur relative to the number of times it will not occur. Thus, if the odds ratio of an event is 5, this indicates that we expect five times as many occurrences as nonoccurrences. An odds of 0.2 (=1/5) would indicate that we expect five times as many nonoccurrences as occurrences.

Suppose you have a dichotomous-dependent variable such as mortality that is predicted using an independent variable that measures whether or not a person had a penetrating wound in an automobile accident. If you calculate that the odds of dying given a penetrating wound is 0.088 and the odds of dying given a nonpenetrating wound is 0.024, then the OR of dying given a penetrating wound is OR = 0.088/0.0247 = 3.56. Thus, the odds of dying given a penetrating wound relative to a nonpenetrating wound is about four times greater than if one does not have a penetrating wound. ORs for quantitative-independent variables (AGE, SBP, WEIGHT, etc.) are interpreted differently, and this interpretation is discussed in an upcoming example in the section "Using Simple Logistic Analysis."

16.2   PERFORMING A LOGISTIC ANALYSIS USING PROC LOGISTIC

PROC LOGISTIC is the SAS procedure that allows you to analyze the data using a binary logistic model. An abbreviated syntax for this statement is as follows:

```
PROC LOGISTIC < options >;
CLASS variables;
MODEL dependentvar < (variable_options) > =
< independentvars> < / options >;
```

The PROC LOGISTIC and MODEL statements are required, and only one MODEL statement can be specified. The CLASS statement (if used) must precede the MODEL statement. Note that the dependent variable must be binary. For simplicity, all of the examples in this chapter use a response variable that takes on the values 0 or 1.

By default, SAS assumes that the outcome predicted (with p) in the logistic regression equation corresponds to the case in which the dependent variable is 0. If, for example, you have a variable such as DISEASE with DISEASE=0 indicating the disease is absent and DISEASE=1 indicating the disease is present, then SAS will predict the probability of "disease absent" by default.

Table 16.1 lists common options and statements used with PROC LOGISTIC.

The MODEL statement is the heart of the logistic procedure. It specifies the dependent (outcome) variable as well as the independent variables. For example,

```
MODEL DEPVAR = INDVAR1 INDVAR2 etc/options;
```

As noted earlier, in this chapter the dependent variable will always be binary (dichotomous). This dependent variable is often coded 0 and 1 (typically 0 means No, and 1 means Yes) but the variable may take on any two values such as 1 and 2, A and B, Alive and Dead, and so on.

Because the logistic model is based on predicting an event, care must be taken as to how the DEPVAR is set up. By default, SAS bases its prediction on the smallest value of the dependent variable. Therefore, if your dependent variable is FAIL (where 0 means not failed and 1 means failed), then by default SAS will model the prediction for FAIL=0 (not failed). To reverse the default prediction, use the DESCENDING option. When that option is included in the PROC LOGISTIC statement, FAIL=1 will be modeled instead of FAIL=0. Another way to choose the value modeled is to explicitly define it in the MODEL statement. For example,

```
MODEL FAIL(EVENT='1') = independentvars;
```

will cause SAS to use 1 as the value to model for the dependent variable FAIL. The EVENT= option is designated a "Response Variable option." When the response variable is binary, EVENT= FIRST or LAST specifies either the first- or last-ordered value be used as the prediction event. Or you can indicate a value in quotes (as in the example code above). (We recommend that you choose to use either the DESCENDING option (see Table 16.1) or the EVENT= option to specify a value of the response variable to predict, if needed.)

As in the model statements in previous chapters, the dependent variable appears on the left of the equal sign, and independent variables appear on the right side. MODEL statement

TABLE 16.1   Common Options for PROC LOGISTIC

Option	Explanation
DATA = *dataname*	Specifies which data set to use
DESCENDING	Reverses the sorting order for the levels of the response variable. By default, the procedure will predict the outcome corresponding to the lower value of the dichotomous-dependent variable. So, if the dependent variable takes on the values 0 and 1, then by default SAS predicts the probability that the dependent variable is 0 unless you use the DESCENDING option. (See information about the (EVENT=) option below.)
EVENT='option'	Specifies which value of a binary response variable is treated as the one modeled. For example, to the left of the equal sign in a MODEL statement DEATH(Event='1').
ALPHA= *value*	Specifies significance level for confidence limits
NOPRINT	Suppresses output
SIMPLE	Displays descriptive statistics
PLOTS= *option*	In current versions of SAS, the Odds Ratio plot is displayed by default. Use PLOTS=NONE; to suppress this plot. PLOTS=ALL produces a number of plots including receiver-operating characteristic (ROC) and influencing diagnostics

Common statements for PROC LOGISTIC

MODEL *depvar=indvar(s);*	Specifies the dependent and independent variables for the analysis. More specifically, it takes the form MODEL *dependentvariable=independentvariable(s);* More explanation follows
CLASS *variable list;*	Specifies classification (either categorical character or discrete numeric) variables for the analysis. They can be numeric or character. You can specify a reference value for a class variable by including the option (REF='value'). For example, CLASS RACE (REF='HISPANIC') URBAN; Specifies HISPANIC as the reference value to RACE. For URBAN the reference value will be the last ordered (alphabetic or numbered) value
ODDSRATIO 'label' *var;*	Creates a separate table with odds ratio estimates and Wald confidence intervals. For example, ODDSRATIO 'Injury Severity' ISS; ODDSRATIO 'Age' AGE;
OUTPUT *out=NAME;*	Creates an output data set with all predictors and response probabilities. For example, OUTPUT OUT=MYFILE P=PRED; where MYFILE is the name of the resulting data and the predictions are named PRED
BY, FORMAT, LABEL, WHERE	These statements are common to most procedures and may be used here

TABLE 16.2   Common MODEL Statement options for PROC Logistic

Option	Explanation
EXPB	Displays the exponentiated values of parameter. These exponentiated values are the estimated odds ratios for the parameters corresponding to the explanatory variables
SELECTION=*type*	Specifies variable selection method (examples are STEPWISE, BACKWARD, and FORWARD). More explanation below
SLENTRY=*value*	Specifies significance level for entering variables. Default is 0.05
SLSTAY=*value*	Specifies significance level for removing variables. Default is 0.05
LACKFIT	Requests Hosmer–Lemeshow goodness-of-fit test
RISKLIMITS	Requests confidence limits for odds ratios
CTABLE PPROB= *(list)*	CTABLE requests a classification table that reports how data are predicted under the model. Usually used with PPROB to specify a list of cutoff points to display in the table. For example, CTABLE PPROB= (0.2, 0.4 to 0.8 by 0.1)
INCLUDE=*n*	Includes first *n* independent variables in the model
OUTROC=*name*	Outputs ROC values to a data set. Also causes the ROC curve to be included in the output

options appear after a slash (/). Table 16.2 lists some of the common MODEL statement options.

The SELECTION options specify how variables will be considered for inclusion in the model. The BACKWARD method considers all predictor variables and eliminates the ones that do not meet the minimal SLSTAY criterion until only those meeting the criterion remain. The FORWARD method brings in the most significant variable that meets the SLENTRY criterion and continues entering variables until none of the remaining unused variables meets the criterion. STEPWISE is a mixture of the two. It begins like the FORWARD method and uses the SLENTRY criterion to enter variables but reevaluates variables at each step and may eliminate a variable if it no longer meets the SLSTAY criterion. A typical model statement utilizing an automated selection technique would be as follows:

```
MODEL Y = X1 X2 ... Xk
                / EXPB
                  SELECTION=STEPWISE
                  SLENTRY=0.05
                  SLSTAY=0.1
RISKLIMITS;
```

where X1, X2,..., Xk are the *k* candidate-independent variables and Y is the binary-dependent variable. In this example, the STEPWISE procedure is used for variable selection. The *p*-value for variable entry is 0.05. Once variables are considered for the model, they must have a *p*-value of 0.1 or less to remain in the model. RISKLIMITS specifies that an OR table is to be included in the output for the final model.

If a model includes independent variables that are categorical, they must be indicated in a CLASS statement. (However, if a dichotomous-independent (predictor) variable is coded as 0 and 1, it does not need to be included in the CLASS statement.) For example, the following model is the same, except it includes two categorical variables CAT1 and CAT2. CAT1 and CAT2 can be numeric (i.e., 1, 2, 3) or of character type (i.e., A, B, C). Because

CAT1 and CAT2 are categorical, they must appear in the CLASS statement if you put them in the MODEL statement.

```
CLASS CAT1 CAT2;
MODEL Y = X1 X2 ... Xk CAT1 CAT2
                / EXPB
                  SELECTION=STEPWISE
                  SLENTRY=0.05
                  SLSTAY=0.1
                  RISKLIMITS;
```

When a variable is defined as a classification variable, SAS sets up a default parameterization of $N-1$ comparisons (where N is the number of categories). The default reference value to which the other categories are compared is based on the last ordered (alphabetic or numeric) value. For example, if RACE categories are AA (African-American), H (Hispanic), C (Caucasian), and O (Other), then ORs will be reported for AA, H, and C, where the OR is based on the reference to O as O is the last ordered (alphabetic) value. If RACE is defined using discrete numeric codes such as 1, 2, 3, 4, and 5, then the last ordered (numeric) value is 5. You can change the reference category by including the options (REF= "value") after the name in the CLASS statement. For example, the statement CLASS RACE (REF="AA") would make AA the reference value rather than "O". For the discrete numeric coding version of RACE, the designation (REF="1") would make 1 the reference value. (You can also use REF=FIRST or REF=LAST to define a reference value.)

Another way to handle categorical variables with three or more categories is to recode them into a series of dichotomous variables (sometimes called indicator or dummy variables). One reason to do this is that it may make ORs easier to interpret. For example, with the character category coding of RACE, you could create three 0/1 variables. In the DATA step, you could define

```
IF RACE="AA" then RACEA=1; ELSE RACEA= 0;
IF RACE="H" then RACEH=1; ELSE RACEH= 0;
IF RACE="C" then RACEC=1; ELSE RACEC= 0;
```

You need one less than the number of categories. Therefore, if RACEA, RACEH, and RACEC are all 0, the race must be OTHER.

16.3   USING SIMPLE LOGISTIC ANALYSIS

A simple logistic model is one that has only one predictor (independent) variable. This predictor variable can be either a binary or a quantitative measure. The following Hands-on Example illustrates the simple logistic model.

HANDS-ON EXAMPLE

This example uses a simulated trauma data set named ACCIDENTS to find a model to predict death (DEAD=1) using the variable PENETRATE (where a value of 1 represents

(continued)

(continued)

a penetrating wound and 0 represents a nonpenetrating wound) observed at the trauma incident.

1. Open the program file `ALOG1.SAS`.

```
PROC LOGISTIC DATA="C:\SASDATA\ACCIDENTS" DESCENDING;
   MODEL DEAD=PENETRATE / RISKLIMITS;
   TITLE 'Trauma Data Model Death by Penetration Wound';
RUN;
```

In this example, the independent variable `PENETRATE`, which is a 0,1 variable, is used to predict death (`DEAD=1`), so the `DESCENDING` option is used.

2. Run this program. In the output, note the statement that reads

```
Probability modeled is dead=1.
```

This statement tells you what value of the dependent variable for which the predicted probabilities are based. Observe the abbreviated output as given in Table 16.3.

TABLE 16.3   Output from Logistic Regression

Response Profile		
Ordered Value	dead	Total Frequency
1	1	103
2	0	3580

Probability modeled is dead=1.

Analysis of Maximum Likelihood Estimates					
Parameter	DF	Estimate	Standard Error	Wald Chi-Square	Pr > ChiSq
Intercept	1	-3.6988	0.1111	1108.0853	<.0001
penetrate	1	1.2697	0.2584	24.1519	<.0001

Odds Ratio Estimates and Wald Confidence Intervals			
Effect	Unit	Estimate	95% Confidence Limits
penetrate	1.0000	3.560	2.145 5.906

The Response Profile table indicates that there are 103 subjects with `DEAD=1` (which is indicated as the modeled outcome) and 3580 subjects who did not die (`DEAD=0`). The Maximum-Likelihood Estimates table indicates that the variable

PENETRATE is significantly associated with the outcome variable ($p < 0.0001$) and
the OR Estimates table reports that the OR for PENETRATE is 3.56. This indicates
that the odds of a person's dying who had a penetrating wound is 3.56 times greater
than that for a person who did not suffer this type of wound.

3. Change the binary variable PENETRATE to the quantitative variable ISS (injury
severity score) using the following statement:

```
MODEL DEAD=ISS/ RISKLIMITS;
```

Rerun the program and observe the output as given in Table 16.4. In Table 16.4, the
variable ISS is shown to be predictive of mortality ($p < 0.0001$) with an OR = 1.111.
However, this OR is interpreted differently for PENETRATE than for ISS as ISS is
a quantitative measure and PENETRATE is a binary measure. Interpret OR = 1.111
in this way: The odds of dying is estimated to be 1.111 times greater for *each unit
increase* in ISS.

4. Change the PROC LOGISTIC statement by removing the DESCENDING option.
Rerun the code. Observe the results. What is the probability modeled for this version
of the program? Note that the new OR = 0.9 that equals 1/1.111 obtained when we
used DESCENDING.

**TABLE 16.4   Output for a Continuous Measure from Logistic
Regression**

Analysis of Maximum Likelihood Estimates					
Parameter	DF	Estimate	Standard Error	Wald Chi-Square	Pr > ChiSq
Intercept	1	-5.4444	0.2105	668.7126	<.0001
ISS	1	0.1056	0.00721	214.5334	<.0001

Odds Ratio Estimates and Wald Confidence Intervals				
Effect	Unit	Estimate	95% Confidence Limits	
ISS	1.0000	1.111	1.096	1.127

16.3.1 Graphing Simple Logistic Results

It is informative to examine a graph of the simple logistic regression analysis to understand
how predictions are made using the logistic equation. (More details about SAS graphs will
be discussed in Chapter 18.)

HANDS-ON EXAMPLE

This example illustrates a simple logistic regression using a quantitative measure as the independent variable.

1. Open the program file ALOG2.SAS.

```
PROC LOGISTIC DATA="C:\SASDATA\ACCIDENTS" DESCENDING;
   MODEL DEAD=ISS / RISKLIMITS;
   OUTPUT OUT=LOGOUT PREDICTED=PROB;
   TITLE "Simple binary logistic regession with plot.";
RUN;
*- - - - - - - - - - - - - - - - - - - - - - - - - - - - -LOGISTIC PLOT;
PROC SORT DATA=LOGOUT;BY ISS;
TITLE 'LOGISTIC PLOT';
PROC GPLOT DATA=LOGOUT;
   PLOT PROB*ISS;
RUN;
QUIT;
```

   The DESCENDING option is used because death (i.e., DEAD=1) is the outcome of interest in the predictive model. Otherwise, the OR would by default be based on predicting DEAD=0. The OUTPUT statement

```
OUTPUT OUT=LOGOUT PREDICTED=PROB;
```

creates a SAS data set named LOGOUT that contains the predicted values calculated by the logistic regression equation. The logistic equation based on estimates given in the Maximum-Likelihood Estimates tables (Table 16.4) is

$$\hat{p} = \frac{e^{-5.444+0.1056\times ISS}}{1 + e^{-5.444+0.1056\times ISS}}$$

   The variable PROB contains predictions $\hat{p}$ for each subject in the data set ACCIDENTS.

2. Run the program and observe the output. In particular, examine the "S-shaped" plot shown in Figure 16.1. The graph provides a method for estimating the probability of death for each ISS. For example, locate ISS = 50 on the horizontal axis. Draw a vertical line to the plotted curve and from there draw a horizontal line to the vertical axis. This shows that for an ISS = 50, the probability of death is about 0.45 (or 45%). Note that by substituting ISS = 50 in the prediction equation, we obtain

$$\hat{p} = \frac{e^{-5.444+0.1056\times50}}{1 + e^{-5.444+0.1056\times50}} = 0.459$$

which is consistent with the graphical estimate. It is typical that when $\hat{p} < 0.5$ you would predict nonoccurrence of the event of interest (i.e., survival) and if $\hat{p} > 0.5$ you would predict occurrence (i.e., death). In this case, we are pleased to predict that the subject would survive.

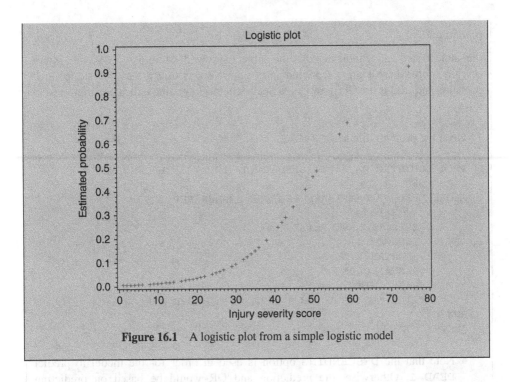

Figure 16.1   A logistic plot from a simple logistic model

16.4   MULTIPLE BINARY LOGISTIC ANALYSIS

A multiple binary logistic regression model has more than one independent variable. As such, it is analogous to a multiple regression model in the case in which the dependent variable is binary. It is common to have several potential predictor variables. One of the tasks of the investigator is to select the best set of predictors to create a parsimonious and effective prediction equation.

16.4.1   Selecting Variables for Multiple Logistic Analysis

The procedure used to select the best independent variables is similar to the one used in multiple linear regression. You can choose to select variables using manual or automated methods, or a combination of both. It is often desirable for the investigator to use his or her knowledge to perform a preliminary selection of the most logically (plausibly) important variables. Automated procedures can then be used to select other potential variables.

The importance of each variable as a predictor in the final model depends on the other variables in the model. Confounding and interaction effects may need to be addressed in certain models, but these topics are beyond the scope of this book.

HANDS-ON EXAMPLE

This example considers several potential predictors for mortality from the simulated ACCIDENTS data set. Subjects range in age from very young to 18 years old. Recall that in this data set, the variable DEAD is coded as a 0/1 variable where 1 indicates that

(continued)

(continued)

the subject died and 0 indicates that the subject survived. Moreover, `ISS` is an injury severity score where a larger score indicates a more severe injury, `SBP` is systolic blood pressure, and `GCS` is the Glasgow Coma Scale where a low value indicates a more severe injury.

1. Open the program file `ALOG3.SAS`.

```
PROC LOGISTIC DATA="C:\SASDATA\ACCIDENTS" DESCENDING;
CLASS GENDER ;
MODEL DEAD =  PENETRATE ISS AGE GENDER SBP GCS
        / EXPB
        SELECTION=STEPWISE
        INCLUDE=1
        SLENTRY=0.05
        SLSTAY=0.05
        RISKLIMITS;
        TITLE 'LOGISTIC ON TRAUMA DATA WHERE AGE LE 18';
RUN;
QUIT;
```

- Note that the `DESCENDING` option is used in order for the model to predict `DEAD=1`. Otherwise, the prediction and OR would be based on predicting `DEAD=0` (survival).
- Seven possible independent variables are included in the `MODEL` statement: `PENETRATE`, `ISS`, `AGE`, `RACE`, `GENDER`, `SBP`, and `GCS`.
- Because `GENDER` is a text variable, it is indicated in a `CLASS` statement before the `MODEL` statement. SAS uses this information to create a design variable so `GENDER` can be used in the model. (Another option would be to recode `GENDER` into a 0/1 variable and use the recoded variable in the model.)
- Stepwise selection is requested with entry into the model set at 0.05 (`SLENTRY`) and removal from the model also set at 0.05 (`SLSTAY`).
- The `INCLUDE=1` option indicates that the first variable in the independent variable list (`PENETRATE`) should always be in the model.
- `RISKLIMITS` requests ORs to be output.

2. Run this program. Note that Table 16.5 shows how the `CLASS` variable `GENDER` has been transformed to allow it to be used in the model.

TABLE 16.5   CLASS Variables

Class Level Information		
Class	Value	Design Variables
GENDER	Female	1
	Male	-1

3. In the output given in Table 16.6, we see that the variables GCS, ISS, and AGE are entered into the model and then no other variables meet the entry criterion. The final model and OR values are shown. Note that the OR for PENETRATE is different than it was in the simple logistic model because it is adjusted for the other variables in the model. The ORs for AGE and GCS indicate that, in general, older children and children with higher GCS scores are more likely to survive an injury.

Other model selection options include BACKWARD and FORWARD selections. These options do not always result in the same "final" model, and the decision concerning variables to be included in the final model should not be entirely based on the results of any automated procedure. The researcher's knowledge of the data should always be used to guide the model selection process even when automated procedures are used.

TABLE 16.6   Final Model

Analysis of Maximum Likelihood Estimates						
Parameter	DF	Estimate	Standard Error	Wald Chi-Square	Pr > ChiSq	Exp(Est)
Intercept	1	-0.4850	0.4661	1.0827	0.2981	0.616
penetrate	1	2.4072	0.4053	35.2776	<.0001	11.103
ISS	1	0.0673	0.00974	47.7172	<.0001	1.070
AGE	1	-0.1092	0.0245	19.9400	<.0001	0.897
GCS	1	-0.4193	0.0453	85.7115	<.0001	0.657

Odds Ratio Estimates and Wald Confidence Intervals			
Effect	Unit	Estimate	95% Confidence Limits
penetrate	1.0000	11.103	5.017 24.570
ISS	1.0000	1.070	1.049 1.090
AGE	1.0000	0.897	0.855 0.941
GCS	1.0000	0.657	0.602 0.719

16.5   GOING DEEPER: ASSESSING A MODEL'S FIT AND PREDICTIVE ABILITY

Once you decide on a final model, you should analyze that model for its predictive ability. One method of analyzing the predictive capabilities of the logistic equation is to use the Hosmer and Lemeshow test. This test is based on dividing subjects into deciles on the basis of predicted probabilities (see Hosmer and Lemeshow, 2000). SAS reports chi-square statistics based on the observed and expected frequencies for subjects within these 10 categories.

The Hosmer and Lemeshow test is requested using the LACKFIT option in the MODEL statement. Another measure used to assess the fit is a receiver operating characteristic curve (ROC), which provides a measure of how well the model predicts outcomes.

HANDS-ON EXAMPLE

This example illustrates the Hosmer and Lemeshow test and an ROC curve.

1. Open the program file ALOG4.SAS.

```
PROC LOGISTIC DATA="C:\SASDATA\ACCIDENTS" DESCENDING;
CLASS GENDER RACE;
MODEL DEAD = PENETRATE ISS AGE GCS
        / EXPB
          LACKFIT
          RISKLIMITS
          CTABLE
          OUTROC=ROC1;
TITLE 'Assess models predictive ability';
RUN;
QUIT;
```

- The LACKFIT option requests a Hosmer and Lemeshow analysis.
- CTABLE requests predictions for various probability cutoff points.
- The OUTROC=ROC1 statement along with the ODS GRAPHICS ON and ODS GRAPHICS OFF statements produces an ROC curve.

2. Run the program. Observe the Hosmer and Lemeshow tables given in Table 16.7. SAS computes a chi-square from observed and expected frequencies in the table.

   Large chi-square values (and correspondingly small p-values) indicate a lack of fit for the model. In this case, we see that the Hosmer and Lemeshow chi-square test for the final model yields a p-value of 0.2532, thus suggesting a model with satisfactory predictive value. Note that the Hosmer and Lemeshow chi-square test is not a test of importance of specific model parameters. It is a separate posthoc test performed to evaluate an entire model.

3. Examine the Classification table (partially) given in Table 16.8. As mentioned earlier, it is a common practice to use 0.5 as the cutoff for predicting occurrence. That is, to predict nonoccurrence of the event of interest whenever $\hat{p} < 0.5$ and to predict occurrence if $\hat{p} > 0.5$. The Classification table indicates how many correct and incorrect predictions would be made for a wide range of probability cutoff points used for the model. In this case, 98% of the cases are correctly classified using the 0.50 cutoff point.

   Also note that at the 0.50 cutoff point, there is 38.8% sensitivity and 99.7% specificity. (Sensitivity is the probability of a correct prediction among subjects with the outcome of interest, and specificity is the probability of a correct prediction among subjects who do not exhibit the outcome.) If you desire to gain sensitivity, you can move the cutoff point to a lower probability level (at the sacrifice of specificity). Similarly, you can increase specificity by raising the cutoff probability. (For more information about selecting a cutoff point, see Cohen, Cohen, West, and Aiken (2002), p. 516 or Hosmer and Lemeshow (2000), pp. 160ff.)

TABLE 16.7   Hosmer and Lemeshow Results

		Partition for the Hosmer and Lemeshow Test			
		dead = 1		dead = 0	
Group	Total	Observed	Expected	Observed	Expected
1	366	0	0.08	366	365.92
2	370	0	0.11	370	369.89
3	369	0	0.13	369	368.87
4	369	0	0.17	369	368.83
5	369	1	0.22	368	368.78
6	369	0	0.29	369	368.71
7	368	0	0.40	368	367.60
8	368	0	0.71	368	367.29
9	368	10	4.94	358	363.06
10	367	92	95.96	275	271.04

Hosmer and Lemeshow Goodness-of-Fit Test		
Chi-Square	DF	Pr > ChiSq
10.1716	8	0.2532

TABLE 16.8   Classification Table for Logistic Regression

	Classification Table								
	Correct		Incorrect		Percentages				
Prob Level	Event	Non-Event	Event	Non-Event	Correct	Sensi-tivity	Speci-ficity	False POS	False NEG
0.000	103	0	3580	0	2.8	100.0	0.0	97.2	.
0.020	97	3226	354	6	90.2	94.2	90.1	78.5	0.2
...etc...									
0.460	43	3567	13	60	98.0	41.7	99.6	23.2	1.7
0.480	41	3569	11	62	98.0	39.8	99.7	21.2	1.7
0.500	40	3569	11	63	98.0	38.8	99.7	21.6	1.7
0.520	38	3570	10	65	98.0	36.9	99.7	20.8	1.8
...etc...									
0.940	5	3580	0	98	97.3	4.9	100.0	0.0	2.7
0.960	1	3580	0	102	97.2	1.0	100.0	0.0	2.8
0.980	1	3580	0	102	97.2	1.0	100.0	0.0	2.8
1.000	0	3580	0	103	97.2	0.0	100.0	.	2.8

(continued)

(continued)

4. Examine the ROC curve, shown in Figure 16.2. This curve, which is a plot of 1-Specificity versus Sensitivity, measures the predictive ability of the model. Note that the "area under the curve" (AUC) is 0.9718. When the AUC is close to 1.0, a good fit is indicated. The closer the curve extends to the upper left corner, the closer the AUC is to 1. AUC approaches 0.50 as the curve gets closer to the diagonal line and would indicate a poor fit. The AUC statistic is often reported as an indicator of the predictive strength of the model. When you are considering competing "final" models, the Hosmer and Lemeshow test and AUC (larger is better) are criteria often used.

Figure 16.2 ROC curve

Another way to assess the model is to use the information in the Model Fit Statistics table (not shown). For example, note that in the example, the value of -2 times the log likelihood for the model is given by $-2\log L = 417.470$ where 417.470 is given in the last row, second column of the "Model Fit Statistics" table (not shown) (for intercept and covariates). In general, when comparing models, the lower the $-2\log L$ value, the better the fit. To determine whether the inclusion of an additional variable in a model gives a *significantly* better fit, you can use the difference in the $-2\log L$ values for the two models to compute a chi-square test statistic.

For example, for this model $-2\log L$ is 417.470 (on the SAS output). By removing the AGE variable from the equation and rerunning the analysis, we get $-2\log L = 438.094$ (try it). The difference has a chi-squared distribution with one degree of freedom, and if this value is larger than the α-level critical value for a chi-square with one degree of freedom, then this is evidence at the α-level of significance that the variable AGE should be included in the model. For this example, the difference is 20.61, and thus at the $\alpha = 0.05$ level (critical value is 3.84) we conclude that AGE should be included in the model. Other criteria that can be used to assess competing models are the AIC (Akaike information criterion) or SC (Schwarz criterion) values in the Model Fit Statistics table (smaller values indicate a better model in both cases).

16.6   SUMMARY

This chapter provides examples of the use of SAS for running simple and multivariate logistic regression analyses. Also techniques for selecting a model and for assessing its predictive ability are illustrated.

EXERCISES

16.1 **Run a multiple logistic regression.**

Data were collected on 200 males. All had no evidence of coronary disease. After 10 years, the subjects were examined for evidence of coronary disease. The researcher wants to know if the demographic information collected at the beginning of the study is helping in predicting if the subjects will develop coronary disease.

a. Using the following code as a beginning, use all three methods of model fitting to see what model looks the most promising.

```
PROC LOGISTIC DATA='C:\SASDATA\CORONARY' DESCENDING;
MODEL CORONARY= SBP DBP AGE BMI INSURANCE
    /_____;
RUN;
```

b. What variables are in your final model?

c. Use SAS code to produce an ROC curve for the final model. What is the AUC for this model? How do you interpret this?

d. Use SAS code to produce a Hosmer and Lemeshow test on the final model. How do you interpret the results?

e. What are the ORs for the variables in the final model? How are they interpreted?

f. How well do you think this model predicts coronary disease in 10 years?

g. If a 60-year-old man has a body mass index (BMI) of 25, what is your best guess of his probability of having coronary disease in 10 years? Hint: Use the following formula:

$$\hat{p} = \frac{e^{b_0 + b_1 X_1 + b_2 X_2}}{1 + e^{b_0 + b_1 X_1 + b_2 X_2}}$$

16.2 **The appliance department in a big "box store" wants to know what helps them sell big ticket items. A portion of the data they've collected on past sales is given in Table 16.9.**

TABLE 16.9 Big Box Store Sales

Obs	Age	Price100	RACE	FREEBIE	GENDER	SOLD
1	45	75.0	AA	Yes	M	1
2	34	125.0	C	No	M	0
3	26	150.0	H	Yes	M	1
4	54	38.5	C	Yes	F	1
5	44	17.0	AA	No	F	0
6	19	28.0	C	Yes	M	0
7	82	44.5	H	No	M	1

1. Open the program file EX_16.1.SAS.

    a. Using this preliminary code below, perform a logistic analysis with BACK-WARD selection to find a model for predicting whether an appliance is sold to a potential customer.

```
PROC LOGISTIC DATA=mysaslib.boxstore ;
CLASS GENDER FREEBIE RACE;
MODEL SOLD= GENDER FREEBIE  RACE AGE PRICE100
        / EXPB
            SELECTION=BACKWARD;
TITLE 'What helps sales?';
RUN;
QUIT;
```

    What probability is modeled? Sales=Yes or No?

    b. Change the probability modeled to Sales=Yes by adding a DESCENDING option to the PROC LOGISTIC statement. Examine the OR for FREEBIE. Because its reference is "No," the OR is interpreted as the OR for getting a sale given no freebie is given. You want the reference to be "Yes." Add a (REF="Yes") after FREEBIE in the CLASS statement. Rerun and note the change in OR for FREEBIE. What is it now? How would you interpret this OR?

    c. Add these options after the / to perform diagnostics for the fit.

```
            LACKFIT
            RISKLIMITS
            OUTROC=ROC1
```

Rerun the code.

    1. What does the Hosmer–Lemeshow test (LACKFIT) indicate?
    2. What additional information does the RISKLIMITS provide?
    3. What does the OUTROC option provide in the output? How does it help you assess how well this model fits the data?

    d. Run this model using FORWARD instead of BACKWARD selection. How does this change the outcome?

17

FACTOR ANALYSIS

LEARNING OBJECTIVES

- To be able to perform an exploratory factor analysis using PROC FACTOR
- To be able to use PROC FACTOR to identify underlying factors or latent variables in a data set
- To be able to use PROC FACTOR to rotate factors for improved interpretation)
- To be able to use PROC FACTOR to compute factor scores

Factor analysis is a dimension reduction technique designed to express the actual observed variables (possibly many in number) using a smaller number of underlying latent (unobserved) variables. In this chapter, we shall discuss the SAS® implementation of exploratory factor analysis, which involves identifying factors, determining which factors are needed to satisfactorily describe the original data, interpreting the meaning of these factors, and so on. Confirmatory factor analysis goes further and involves techniques for testing hypotheses to confirm theories, and so on. Although SAS contains procedures for running confirmatory factor analysis, we shall only discuss exploratory factor analysis in this chapter.

17.1 FACTOR ANALYSIS BASICS

The typical steps in performing an exploratory factor analysis are the following:

(a) Compute a correlation (or covariance) matrix for the observed variables.

SAS® Essentials: Mastering SAS for Data Analytics, Second Edition. Alan C. Elliott and Wayne A. Woodward.
© 2016 John Wiley & Sons, Inc. Published 2016 by John Wiley & Sons, Inc.

(b) Extract the factors (this involves deciding how many factors to extract, the method to use, and the values to use for the prior communality estimates).

(c) Rotate the factors to improve interpretation.

(d) Compute factor scores (if needed).

Before proceeding, we mention that an exploratory factor analysis can be quite subjective without unique solutions. Consequently, there is a certain amount of "art" involved in any factor analysis solution. This fact has caused the subject to be somewhat controversial. We believe that factor analysis methods can be useful in helping to understand the data, but that interpretations and conclusions should be made with caution.

17.1.1   Using PROC Factor

The SAS procedure used to perform exploratory factor analysis is PROC FACTOR. A simplified syntax for this procedure is as follows:

```
PROC FACTOR <options> ;
     VAR variables ;
     PRIORS communalities ;
```

There are many options available for PROC FACTOR. A few common of these along with some useful statements are listed in Table 17.1.

If the Methods=Principal option is used, then principal component analysis is performed when the PRIORS= option is not used or is set to ONE (the default). If you specify

TABLE 17.1   Common Options for PROC FACTOR

Option	Explanation
DATA = *dataname*	Specifies which data set to use
METHOD=*option*	Specifies the estimation method. Options include ML and PRINCIPAL
MINEIGEN=n	Specifies the smallest eigenvalue for retaining a factor
NFACTORS=n	Specifies the maximum number of factors to retain
NOPRINT	Suppresses output
PRIORS= *option*	Specifies the method for obtaining prior communalities
ROTATE = *name*	Specifies the rotation method. The default is ROTATE=NONE. Common rotation methods are VARIMAX, QUARTIMAX, EQUAMAX, and PROMAX. All of the above are orthogonal rotations except PROMAX
SCREE	Displays a Scree plot of the eigenvalues
SIMPLE	Displays means, standard deviations, and number of observations
CORR	Displays the correlation matrix

Common statements for PROC FACTOR

VAR *variable list;*	Specifies the numeric variables to be analyzed. Default is to use all numeric variables
BY, FORMAT, LABEL, WHERE	These statements are common to most procedures and may be used here

a `PRIORS=` value other than `PRIORS=ONE`, then a principal factor analysis is performed. A common usage is `PRIORS=SMC` in which case the prior communality for each variable is the squared multiple correlation of it with all other variables. After extracting the factors, the communalities represent the proportion of the variance in each of the original variables retained after extracting the factors.

Unless you are highly skilled at using factor analysis, we recommend that you check out references such as Stevens (2002), Johnson and Wichern (2007), and Johnson (1998) for more discussion of these concepts and the issues involved.

HANDS-ON EXAMPLE

Intelligence is a multifaceted quality. For example, some people may be good at reasoning with numbers, others may have outstanding memories, while others may have the ability to express themselves well, may be very adept at dealing with other people, and so on Researchers, see, for example, Gardiner (2006), have studied the issue of identifying types of intelligence. Two of the types of intelligence identified by Gardiner are Logical–Mathematical Intelligence (Math Intelligence) and Linguistic Intelligence. In addition to the existence of several types of intelligence, there are also a variety of aspects related to each type of intelligence. In this example, we examine a hypothetical data set that contains six variables, each measured on a 0–10 scale and designed to measure an aspect of either Linguistic or Math Intelligence. The variables are as follows:

`COMPUTATION` – Test on mathematical computations

`VOCABULARY` – A vocabulary test

`INFERENCE` – A test of the use of inductive and deductive inference

`REASONING` – A test of sequential reasoning

`WRITING` – A score on a writing sample

`GRAMMAR` – A test measuring proper grammar usage.

Clearly, the variables are designed so that `COMP`, `INFER`, and `REASON` measure Math Intelligence while `VOCAB`, `WRITING`, and `GRAMMAR` seem to measure Linguistic Intelligence. We will use the techniques of factor analysis to determine the extent to which these two components of intelligence can be extracted from the data.

1. Open the program file `AFACTOR1.SAS`.

```
PROC FACTOR DATA=MYSASLIB.INTEL SIMPLE CORR SCORE
METHOD=PRINICPAL
ROTATE=VARIMAX
OUT=FS
PRIORS=SMC
PLOTS=SCREE;
RUN;
```

2. Run the program and observe the several tables and plots of results. As we did not specify variables in a `VAR` statement, the analysis will be based on all numeric variables in the data set, that is, `COMPUTATION` through `GRAMMAR`. Table 17.2

(continued)

(continued)

shows the descriptive statistics and Table 17.3 shows the correlation matrix for the six variables. This output is obtained as a result of including SIMPLE and CORR as PROC FACTOR options. The high pairwise correlations among COMPUTATION, INFERENCE, and REASONING (to a lesser extent) seem to indicate some tendency to measure Math Intelligence while the variables VOCABULARY, WRITING, and GRAMMAR that seem to be measuring Linguistic Intelligence are also positively pairwise correlated. These observations and the discussion related to the construction of the hypothetical example suggest the possibility of detecting two underlying factors.

TABLE 17.2   Descriptive Statistics for Intelligence Data

Means and Standard Deviations from 200 Observations		
Variable	Mean	Std Dev
COMPUTATION	5.0300000	1.7874774
VOCABULARY	5.2450000	1.6909380
INFERENCE	4.3400000	1.6758407
REASONING	4.6300000	1.9395643
WRITING	5.0000000	1.9949685
GRAMMAR	4.3800000	1.8446173

TABLE 17.3   Correlations for Intelligence Data

Correlations						
	COMPUTATION	VOCABULARY	INFERENCE	REASONING	WRITING	GRAMMAR
COMPUTATION	1.00000	0.13222	0.84374	0.53082	0.10569	0.10473
VOCABULARY	0.13222	1.00000	0.03962	0.09826	0.75227	0.67726
INFERENCE	0.84374	0.03962	1.00000	0.49961	0.05712	0.03765
REASONING	0.53082	0.09826	0.49961	1.00000	0.14805	0.15467
WRITING	0.10569	0.75227	0.05712	0.14805	1.00000	0.78519
GRAMMAR	0.10473	0.67726	0.03765	0.15467	0.78519	1.00000

3. Because we specified METHOD=PRINCIPAL and PRIORS=SMC, SAS uses the principal factors method where the prior communality estimate for each variable is the squared multiple correlation of it with all other variables. These prior communality estimates are given in Table 17.4.

Table 17.5 displays eigenvalues associated with the factors based on the reduced correlation matrix. It is clear from the table that there are two dominant eigenvalues (2.319 and 1.725). Based on any reasonable criterion, it is clear that a two-factor solution should be used.

The Scree plot in Figure 17.1 (obtained via the option PLOTS=SCREE) gives a visual illustration of the sizes of the eigenvalues. Again, it is clear that there are two dominant eigenvalues.

TABLE 17.4   Prior Communalities Estimates using PRIORS=SMC

Prior Communality Estimates: SMC					
COMPUTATION	VOCABULARY	INFERENCE	REASONING	WRITING	GRAMMAR
0.73727417	0.59614561	0.72279682	0.30703390	0.70916506	0.63690981

TABLE 17.5   Eigenvalues of the Reduced Correlation Matrix

Eigenvalues of the Reduced Correlation Matrix: Total = 3.70932538 Average = 0.6182209				
	Eigenvalue	Difference	Proportion	Cumulative
1	2.31945916	0.59413444	0.6253	0.6253
2	1.72532473	1.72851659	0.4651	1.0904
3	-.00319186	0.07536140	-0.0009	1.0896
4	-.07855326	0.02936223	-0.0212	1.0684
5	-.10791548	0.03788243	-0.0291	1.0393
6	-.14579792		-0.0393	1.0000

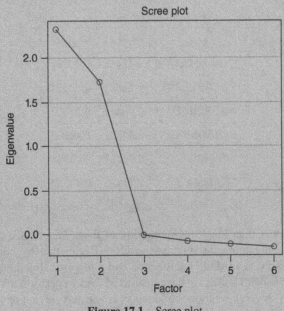

Figure 17.1   Scree plot

(continued)

(continued)

4. The communalities in Table 17.6 are the proportion of the variance in each of the original variables retained after extracting the factors. It seems that all six variables are sufficiently well represented by the two factors, with variable REASONING having the smallest communality, 0.335.

TABLE 17.6   Communalities Associated with the Two-Factor Solution

Final Communality Estimates: Total = 4.044784					
COMPUTATION	VOCABULARY	INFERENCE	REASONING	WRITING	GRAMMAR
0.80308734	0.64531015	0.77920274	0.33460577	0.78740819	0.69516970

5. Next we examine the two factors that are obtained and are described by the Factor Pattern Matrix given in Table 17.7.

   In the table, it can be seen that for Factor 1, each variable has a positive coefficient ranging from .41 for REASONING to .77 for WRITING. A reasonable interpretation of this factor is that it is an overall measure of intelligence. The second factor has negative loadings on the variables measuring Linguistic Intelligence and positive coefficients on the others.

**TABLE 17.7   Factor Pattern Matrix
Associated with the Two-Factor Solution**

Factor Pattern		
	Factor1	Factor2
COMPUTATION	0.55465	0.70389
VOCABULARY	0.69841	-0.39691
INFERENCE	0.48432	0.73800
REASONING	0.41302	0.40500
WRITING	0.77097	-0.43934
GRAMMAR	0.72423	-0.41310

6. Based on the less than ideal interpretability of these factors, we use a rotation in hope of producing more interpretable results. (Recall that by construction, there should be two factors: Math Intelligence and Linguistic Intelligence.) Using the option ROTATE=VARIMAX, we have instructed SAS to perform a Varimax rotation. SAS provides several rotation options, and Varimax is a popular "orthogonal rotation," which produces two orthogonal factors that are potentially easier to interpret. The resulting Factor Pattern Matrix after Varimax rotation is given in Table 17.8.

The rotated factor pattern matrix in Table 17.7 is much easier to interpret. For example, the coefficients for COMPUTATION are the correlations of the variable COMPUTATION with each of the two factors. In this case, there is a large positive correlation between COMPUTATION and Factor 2 and a very small correlation between COMPUTATION and Factor 1. Similar interpretations show that Factor 1 is highly correlated with the three variables measuring Linguistic Intelligence and Factor 2 tends to correspond to Math Intelligence. Consequently, the two rotated factors are consistent with the way in which the data were generated.

TABLE 17.8   Rotated Factor Pattern Matrix Using VARIMAX Rotation

Rotated Factor Pattern		
	Factor1	Factor2
COMPUTATION	0.06278	0.89395
VOCABULARY	0.80071	0.06457
INFERENCE	-0.01456	0.88260
REASONING	0.11376	0.56716
WRITING	0.88457	0.07029
GRAMMAR	0.83118	0.06570

7. Suppose you want to calculate factor scores and save them in a temporary working file FSCORES. In order to accomplish this, add the following PROC FACTOR options before PLOTS=SCREE;

```
SCORE
     NFACTOR=2
     OUT=FSCORE
```

Then, after the RUN; statement add the code

```
PROC PRINT DATA=FSCORE;
     VAR FACTOR1 FACTOR2;
     RUN;
```

The first few lines of the output from PROC PRINT are given in Table 17.9. The two-factor scores are given the default names FACTOR1 and FACTOR2 (the prefix "FACTOR" can be changed using the PREFIX= option). Recalling that Factor 1 is a measure of Linguistic Intelligence and Factor 2 measures Math Intelligence, from the factor scores it can be seen that Subject 1 has a higher Linguistic Intelligence score, Subject 2 seems to have High Math Intelligence, and Subject 3 unfortunately doesn't seem to have strength in either dimension.

(continued)

(continued)

TABLE 17.9 Output from PROC PRINT Showing the First 8 Factor Scores

Obs	Factor1	Factor2
1	0.51223	0.14558
2	-1.22246	1.92068
3	-1.31092	-0.80015
4	1.58737	0.78032
5	0.03969	2.64229
6	0.29565	-0.54992
7	-1.51494	1.09095
8	0.77701	-0.40789

HANDS-ON EXAMPLE

We consider a data set containing scores of 193 athletes who completed all 10 decathlon events in the 1988 through 2012 Olympic Games. The 10 events in the decathlon are 100-m run, long jump, shot put, high jump, 400-m run, 100-m hurdles, discus, pole vault, javelin, and 1500-m run. These events measure a wide variety of athletic ability, and in this example we use this decathlon data set to explore whether there are some underlying dimensions of athletic ability. It should be noted that the "times" in the running events are given negative signs so that "larger" values are better than "smaller" values as is the case in the distance measurements. Moreover, the 1500-m results are given in (negative) seconds rather than the usual reporting of minutes and seconds. Additional variables in the data set include YEAR (the year of the Olympic Games) and PTOTAL (the total number of points for that athlete based on the decathlon scoring system).

We use the procedure outlined in the previous example to run the factor analysis for the Olympic Athlete Data.

1. Open the program file AFACTOR2.SAS.

```
PROC FACTOR SIMPLE CORR DATA MYSASLIB.OLYMPIC
METHOD=PRINCIPAL MSA
    PRIORS=SMC
    ROTATE=VARIMAX
    OUTSTAT=FACT_ALL
    PLOTS=SCREE;
    VAR RUN100 LONGJUMP SHOTPUT HIGHJUMP RUN400
        HURDLES DISCUS POLEVAULT JAVELIN RUN1500S;
RUN;
```

2. Run the program and again there are several pages of tables and plots. Because we want to run only the factor analysis on the 10-event results (and not YEAR or PTO-TAL), we have included a VAR statement listing the variables related to the 10 events. Tables 17.10 and 17.11 show the descriptive statistics and correlation matrix obtained as a result of the options SIMPLE and CORR.

Note the negative values in Table 17.9 for the running events: RUN100, RUN400, HURDLES, RUN1500S. In Table 17.10, note that as would be expected, there are positive correlations between speed events such as the 100-m run (RUN100) and 100-m hurdles (HURDLES) (0.692) and between strength events SHOTPUT and DIS-CUS (0.748). Also note that the 1500-m run (RUN1500S) is not highly correlated with any of the other events with the strongest correlation being with the medium distance 400-m run (0.368).

TABLE 17.10 Descriptive Statistics for Olympic Athlete Data

Means and Standard Deviations from 193 Observations		
Variable	Mean	Std Dev
RUN100	-11.02399	0.280812
LONGJUMP	7.22306	0.350490
SHOTPUT	14.32907	1.236130
HIGHJUMP	1.98575	0.085869
RUN400	-49.33124	1.283435
HURDLES	-14.69803	0.555085
DISCUS	43.58699	4.201578
POLEVAULT	4.73575	0.342200
JAVELIN	59.03295	6.378388
RUN1500S	-278.74715	13.178349

3. Since, as in the previous Hands-on Example, we specified METHOD=PRINCIPAL and PRIORS=SMC, SAS uses the principal factors method where the prior commu-nality estimate for each variable is the squared multiple correlation of it with all other variables. These prior communality estimates are given in Table 17.12.

Table 17.13 displays eigenvalues associated with the factors based on the reduced correlation matrix. PROC FACTOR selected three factors. It is clear from Table 17.13 and the Scree plot in Figure 17.2 that there are three dominant eigenvalues. Conse-quently, SAS selects three factors.

(continued)

(continued)

TABLE 17.11   Correlations for Olympic Athlete Data

Correlations

	RUN100	LONGJUMP	SHOTPUT	HIGHJUMP	RUN400	HURDLES	DISCUS	POLEVAULT	JAVELIN	RUN1500S
RUN100	1.00000	0.62456	0.46900	0.22067	0.62085	0.69179	0.36482	0.32626	0.15162	-0.00871
LONGJUMP	0.62456	1.00000	0.37162	0.46107	0.54245	0.54579	0.32381	0.43859	0.31312	0.23859
SHOTPUT	0.46900	0.37162	1.00000	0.36760	0.19800	0.46851	0.74831	0.38049	0.40673	-0.11159
HIGHJUMP	0.22067	0.46107	0.36760	1.00000	0.21265	0.32034	0.33854	0.33966	0.30340	0.21658
RUN400	0.62085	0.54245	0.19800	0.21265	1.00000	0.51803	0.14483	0.31663	0.12819	0.36825
HURDLES	0.69179	0.54579	0.46851	0.32034	0.51803	1.00000	0.37030	0.43456	0.28326	0.04951
DISCUS	0.36482	0.32381	0.74831	0.33854	0.14483	0.37030	1.00000	0.26674	0.35354	-0.10200
POLEVAULT	0.32626	0.43859	0.38049	0.33966	0.31663	0.43456	0.26674	1.00000	0.35950	0.15728
JAVELIN	0.15162	0.31312	0.40673	0.30340	0.12819	0.28326	0.35354	0.35950	1.00000	0.16692
RUN1500S	-0.00871	0.23859	-0.11159	0.21658	0.36825	0.04951	-0.10200	0.15728	0.16692	1.00000

TABLE 17.12 Prior Communalities Estimates Using PRIORS=SMC for Olympic Athlete Data

	Prior Communality Estimates: SMC								
RUN100	LONGJUMP	SHOTPUT	HIGHJUMP	RUN400	HURDLES	DISCUS	POLEVAULT	JAVELIN	RUN1500S
0.68603651	0.56671045	0.65394191	0.32430313	0.55219465	0.56191691	0.57223097	0.32024561	0.28455354	0.31622257

(continued)

(continued)

TABLE 17.13   Eigenvalues of the Reduced Correlation Matrix for Olympic Athlete Data

Eigenvalues of the Reduced Correlation Matrix: Total = 4.83835625 Average = 0.48383562			
	Eigenvalue	Difference	Proportion	Cumulative
1	3.67980012	2.63192235	0.7605	0.7605
2	1.04787777	0.40825292	0.2166	0.9771
3	0.63962484	0.52785571	0.1322	1.1093
4	0.11176913	0.04690376	0.0231	1.1324
5	0.06486537	0.12766893	0.0134	1.1458
6	-.06280356	0.02819416	-0.0130	1.1329
7	-.09099772	0.05539013	-0.0188	1.1140
8	-.14638785	0.04594770	-0.0303	1.0838
9	-.19233555	0.02072076	-0.0398	1.0440
10	-.21305631		-0.0440	1.0000

Figure 17.2   Scree plot for Olympic Athlete Data

4. The communalities in Table 17.14 are the proportion of the variance in each of the original variables retained after extracting the factors. It seems that all 10 events are fairly well represented by the three factors, with all communalities above 0.33. However, HIGHJUMP, POLEVALULT, JAVELIN, and RUN1500S all having communalities below 0.4.

TABLE 17.14   Communalities Associated with the Three-Factor Solution for the Olympic Athlete Data

			Final Communality Estimates: Total = 5.367303					
RUN100	LONGJUMP	SHOTPUT	HIGHJUMP	RUN400	HURDLES	DISCUSS	POLEVAULT	JAVELIN	RUN1500S
0.77536218	0.61125386	0.73515987	0.36009667	0.60920635	0.60227652	0.61756653	0.34739171	0.33404144	0.37494760

(continued)

(continued)

5. Next, we examine the three factors that are obtained and are described by the Factor Pattern Matrix given in Table 17.15.

   As was the case for the unrotated solution for the Intelligence Data, it can be seen that Factor 1 has a positive coefficient, all of which are above 0.4 except for RUN1500S, which has a coefficient of 0.17. A reasonable interpretation is that Factor 1 measures overall athletic ability, primarily related to the first nine events. Factors 2 and 3 are more difficult to interpret.

TABLE 17.15   Factor Pattern Matrix Associated with the Three-Factor Solution for the Olympic Athlete Data

Factor Pattern		Factor1	Factor2	Factor3
run100	100 meters	0.75484	0.16862	-0.42089
longjump	long jump	0.74377	0.23169	0.06613
shotput	shot put	0.69665	-0.49932	-0.02274
highjump	high jump	0.50550	-0.03943	0.32095
run400	400 meter run	0.60300	0.48624	-0.09575
hurdles	110 meter hurdles	0.74637	0.09212	-0.19164
discus	discus	0.59898	-0.50870	0.00398
polevault	pole vault	0.55685	0.02540	0.19149
javelin	javelin	0.44551	-0.16759	0.32783
run1500s	1500 meter run	0.16723	0.42715	0.40562

6. Based on the confusing interpretations associated with the Three-Factor solutions given in Table 17.15, we use a rotation to produce more interpretable results. Using the option ROTATE=VARIMAX results in the Rotated Factor Pattern Matrix given in Table 17.16.

The first rotated factor seems to focus on events 100-m long jump, 400-m run, and 110-m hurdles that involve the legs (speed and spring). Factor 2 seems to be primarily an arm strength factor with high coefficients for shot put and long jump and to a lesser extent javelin, pole vault, and (surprisingly) high jump. Finally, the only event with a large coefficient in Factor 3 is the 1500-m hurdles. This is consistent with our initial look at the correlation matrix that suggested the 1500-m run was "different" from the other events.

TABLE 17.16   Rotated Factor Pattern Matrix for the Olympic Athlete Data Using VARIMAX Rotation

	Rotated Factor Pattern			
		Factor1	Factor2	Factor3
run100	100 meters	0.84580	0.23258	-0.07671
longjump	long jump	0.60647	0.36590	0.33100
shotput	shot put	0.30160	0.77719	-0.20041
highjump	high jump	0.17997	0.47975	0.31233
run400	400 meter run	0.70075	0.04678	0.34054
hurdles	110 meter hurdles	0.68461	0.36227	0.04849
discus	discus	0.21230	0.72866	-0.20384
polevault	pole vault	0.31426	0.42324	0.26363
javelin	javelin	0.07697	0.52602	0.22676
run1500s	1500 meter run	0.09184	-0.01599	0.60519

17.2   SUMMARY

In this chapter, we have discussed methods for using PROC FACTOR to perform exploratory factor analysis. In the Hands-on Example, we have illustrated the use of rotation to obtain more understandable results.

EXERCISES

17.1 **Run a factor analysis on the intelligence data using principal components.**

a. Modify the file AFACTOR1.SAS to run a principal component analysis by removing the PRIORS=SMC option.

b. What are the initial communalities?

c. Compare and contrast the results with those obtained using principal factors method used in the first Hands-on Example. Do you arrive at similar factors?

d. Find the correlation between new variables Factor1 and Factor2? Do the rotated factors appear to be uncorrelated (orthogonal)?

17.2 **Run a factor analysis on the Olympic Athlete Data using maximum likelihood.**

a. Modify the file AFACTOR2.SAS to perform factor analysis on the Olympic Athlete Data using maximum likelihood.

b. Compare and contrast the results with those obtained using principal factors method used in the first Hands-on Example. Are the interpretations the same?

c. Change the rotation method to PROMAX and rerun the analysis. Has this changed the basic interpretations of the factors?

d. Modify the SAS program to print out factor scores for the three factors after PRO-MAX rotation. Name the factor scores ML1, ML2, and ML3. Find the correlation between new variables Factor1 and Factor2? Do the rotated factors appear to be uncorrelated (orthogonal)?

18

CREATING CUSTOM GRAPHS

LEARNING OBJECTIVES

- To be able to use SAS® to create scatterplots and line graphs using GPLOT
- To be able to use SAS to create charts using PROC GCHART
- To be able to use SAS to create boxplots (box-and-whiskers plots) using PROC BOXPLOT
- To be able to create basic plots using SGPLOT

SAS provides several procedures for creating graphs, which are an essential part of data analysis. In this chapter, graphs that are often used to complement the data analyses discussed in this book are illustrated by example. Some of these were discussed in earlier chapters. This chapter provides more details and introduces graphs that have not been discussed earlier.

In fact, SAS provides a number of other sophisticated techniques for creating a variety of graphs that are not discussed in this chapter. However, you should be able to take what you learn here and adapt it to other SAS graphs.

18.1 CREATING SCATTERPLOTS AND LINE GRAPHS USING GPLOT

PROC GPLOT is the basic routine used to obtain several types of graphs in SAS. This section illustrates how to create scatterplots and line graphs using PROC GPLOT, with an

---

SAS® Essentials: Mastering SAS for Data Analytics, Second Edition. Alan C. Elliott and Wayne A. Woodward.
© 2016 John Wiley & Sons, Inc. Published 2016 by John Wiley & Sons, Inc.

emphasis on creating graphs that are useful for data analysis. The abbreviated syntax for this procedure is as follows:

```
PROC GPLOT <options>; <PLOT plot-request(s)/ option(s)>;
```

It is a good idea to include the following command to reset all SAS graphics options before you use `PROC GPLOT` or other SAS graph procedures:

```
GOPTIONS RESET=ALL;
```

Moreover, it is a good practice to include a `QUIT` statement after a plot to tell the SAS program that the graph is complete. Otherwise, you may note a "PROC GPLOT Running" warning in the Editor window, indicating that SAS is waiting for more information about the plot. Some of these options are illustrated in this chapter's Hands-on Examples.

Table 18.1 lists some of the common options used with `PROC GPLOT` and Table 18.2 lists some of the common statements used with `PROC GPLOT`.

The `PLOT` statement is the heart of `PROC GPLOT`. Using this statement, you request an X–Y plot from the `PROC GPLOT` procedure using code such as the following:

```
PROC GPLOT DATA=sasdatafile;
    PLOT yvariable*xvariable/options;
RUN;
```

TABLE 18.1   Common Options for PROC GPLOT

Option	Explanation
DATA = dataname	Specifies which data set to use
ANNOTATE=	Allows you to change default graphical elements or add new elements to the graph. (This feature is not demonstrated in this chapter.)
UNIFORM	Specifies that the same axes be used in all of the graphs produced by the procedure

TABLE 18.2   Common Statements for PROC GPLOT

Statement	Explanation
PLOT (and PLOT2)	Specifies information about vertical and horizontal axes in a scatter/line plot, along with statement options that customize the look of the plot. These statements are discussed below. (PLOT2 is not discussed in this chapter.)
BUBBLE (and BUBBLE2)	Similar to the PLOT statement but specifies information that creates a bubble plot. (An example BUBBLE is given in the SGGRAPH section in this chapter.)
AXIS, FOOTNOTE, PATTERN, TITLE	These are statements that can be used to enhance graphs. Examples in this chapter illustrate these options
BY, FORMAT, LABEL, WHERE	These statements are common to most procedures, and may be used here

Note: At least one PLOT or BUBBLE statement is required.

The *yvariable* is the variable that defines the (left) vertical axis and the *xvariable* defines the horizontal axis. These can be either numeric or character variables. If you specify

```
PLOT yvariable*xvariable=n;
```

The *n* indicates which symbol to use for the points on the plot. These symbols are described in Appendix A in the section "Using SAS Plotting Symbols." You can also request multiple plots by including more than one variable within parentheses, such as in

```
PLOT (yvar1 yvar2)*xvariable;
```

This statement would produce two plots, one that is *yvar1*xvariable* and the other that is *yvar2*xvariable*. You could specify the same series of plots using

```
PLOT yvar1*xvariable yvar2*xvariable;
```

Another form of the PLOT statement allows you to use a third variable that is a grouping (classification) variable. For example,

```
PLOT yvariable*xvariable=group;
```

where *group* is some grouping variable. This will cause the points on the plot to be styled differently for each value of the grouping variable. (You can specify the symbol to use with the SYMBOL option.)

Options that appear after the PLOT specification are used to enhance the plot. For example,

```
PLOT yvariable*xvariable/CAXIS=color;
```

would cause the axes in the plot to be display in the specified color. Table 18.3 lists some of the most common statement options for the PLOT statement including those used in the examples in this chapter. (For more options, refer to SAS documentation.)

18.1.1 Creating a Simple Scatterplot

The basic plot generated by PROC GPLOT is a scatterplot. The other plots are based on this framework, so the first example shows how to create a simple *x–y* scatterplot.

HANDS-ON EXAMPLE

This example illustrates how to produce a simple scatterplot using PROC GPLOT.

1. Open the program file AGRAPH1.SAS.

```
GOPTIONS RESET=ALL;
Title ''Simple Scatterplot";
PROC GPLOT DATA="C:\SASDATA\CARS";
```

(continued)

(continued)

```
        PLOT HWYMPG*ENGINESIZE;
RUN;
QUIT;
```

This simple program requests a scatterplot of the variables HWYMPG (highway miles per gallon) by ENGINESIZE in the CARS data set.

2. Run the program and observe (in the Graph window) the results shown in Figure 18.1. This graph shows a decrease in HWYMPG as engine size increases. Note that the variable names are displayed on the *x*- and *y*-axes, and that the limits for each axis are selected by the program.

3. To make a simple change in the plot, for example, the color of the text, add the statement CTEXT=RED so the PLOT statement reads

```
PLOT HWYMPG*ENGINESIZE/CTEXT=RED;
```

Resubmit the code and observe the results. Note what text the CTEXT= option changes.

Figure 18.1   Default scatterplot using PROC GPLOT

18.1.2   Managing Your SAS Graph

As mentioned earlier, when you create a graph in SAS, the results are placed in the Results Viewer window. Here are some handy tips for working in the Results Viewer window.

TABLE 18.3 Common Options for PROC GPLOT's PLOT Statement

Option	Explanation
CAXIS=*color*	Specifies a color to use for the axis line and tick marks. Colors are described in Appendix A. For example, CAXIS=BLUE
CFRAME= *color*	Specifies color for the background frame. Colors are described in Appendix A
CTEXT= *color*	Specifies color for text. Colors are described in Appendix A
HAXIS= or VAXIS=	Specifies information about the horizontal or vertical axis including values and spacing of tick marks. For example, HAXIS=AXISk – Indicates which AXISk definition to apply to the horizontal axis. For example, HAXIS=AXIS1 indicates that the AXIS1 definition is to be applied VAXIS=AXISk – Indicates which AXISk definition to apply to the vertical axis. For example, VAXIS=AXIS2 indicates that the AXIS2 definition is to be applied
HREF=*value list* or VREF= *value list*	Draws a horizontal or vertical line at the indicated axis value or values
LEGEND=*legend<n>*	Specifies which legend definition to use for a plot. An example is given in the chapter
NOLEGEND	Suppresses the standard plot legend
SYMBOL<n>	Allows you to specify which symbol to use for points, and attributes of that symbol such as color and size. See Appendix A for a list of symbols. See the section "Enhancing a GPLOT Using the SYMBOL statement" below
NOFRAME	Suppresses the (default) frame around the plot
GRID	Draws grid line at major tick marks

These options appear after a /.

Copy Graph: To copy the graph to the Clipboard, it can be pasted into Word, PowerPoint, or some other program, click on the graph and select Edit → Copy from the menu bar (or right-click on the graph and select copy).

Export Graph: To export the graph to a standard graphics format file right-click on the graph, select Save Picture as ... , and select Files of Type according to the output type you need. Options are PNG and BIT (bitmapped). See the section on Saving Graphs later in this section for information on how to programmatically save the plot in other formats.

Print: Use the File → Print menu option to print a hard copy of the graph. (or select right-click Print Picture ...)

18.1.3 Enhancing a GPLOT Using the SYMBOL statement

Often, the purpose of displaying a scatterplot is to illustrate an association between two variables. You may also want to include a regression line through the scatter of points to emphasize the relationship, or you may want to make improvements to the plot that are also available. The following example shows how to use the SYMBOL statement to enhance your plot. This statement may appear before or within the PROC GPLOT statement. The abbreviated syntax for the SYMBOL statement is as follows:

```
SYMBOL<1...255>
<COLOR=symbol-color>
<appearance-option(s)>
<INTERPOLATION=interpolation-option>;
```

An example statement is

```
SYMBOL1 V=STAR I=RL C=BLUE L=2;
```

The symbol number indicates the plot to which the options will be applied. Some commonly used appearance options for SYMBOL are given in Table 18.4.

The following example illustrates how to use the SYMBOL statement and some of its options.

TABLE 18.4   Common Options for PROC GPLOT's SYMBOL Statement

Option	Explanation
COLOR= color (or C=)	Indicates the color used for the dot in the plot. For example, C=BLUE causes the dots in the graph to be blue. Other common color options are RED, GREEN, and BLACK. See Appendix A for a more extensive list of available colors
INTERPOLATION=type (or I=)	Instructs SAS to include an interpolation curve in the plot. Several types of interpolation curves are available. A commonly used option is the RL or "regression, linear" fit. Common options are as follows: RL – Linear Regression RQ - Quadratic regression RC - Cubic regression STDk - Standard error bars of length k STDEV (add J [join at mean], B [include error bars], and T [include tops on error bars]). For example, STDkJ to join the bars STDM - Same as STDk but uses standard error of the mean JOIN - Joins dots BOXT - Indicates the pattern of the line drawn in the graph. For example, 1 is a solid line, 2 is small dots, 3 is larger dots, and so on. See Appendix A for other options
LINE=n (or L=)	Indicates the pattern of the line drawn in the graph. For example, LINE=1 produces a solid line. A value 2 produces small dots, 3 is larger dots, and so on. See Appendix A for other options
VALUE=n (or V=)	Indicates the symbol to be used for the dots on the plot. For example, V=STAR displays a star instead of the default character (+). Some commonly used symbols are SQUARE, STAR, CIRCLE, PLUS, and DOT. See Appendix A for other options

HANDS-ON EXAMPLE

This example illustrates how to change the style of a plot's points and regression line.

1. Open the program file AGRAPH2.SAS.

```
GOPTIONS RESET=ALL;
Title "Simple Scatterplot, Change symbol";
PROC GPLOT DATA=MYSASLIB.CARS
    PLOT HWYMPG*CITYMPG;
    SYMBOL1 V=STAR I=RL C=BLUE L=2;
RUN;
QUIT;
```

2. Run this program and observe the output shown in Figure 18.2.

    Note on your screen that the following items are specified for this plot (see Appendix A for more information).
    - The displayed symbol is a star (V=STAR).
    - The displayed symbol is blue (C=BLUE).
    - A linear regression line is displayed (I=RL).
    - The displayed line is dotted (L=2).

3. Change the C, V, and L options by choosing other values from the definitions listed in Appendix A and rerun the plot to observe how changing these options modifies the plot.

Figure 18.2   PROC GPLOT with dots and line specified

18.1.4 Customizing Axes in a Plot

If you are preparing a plot for use in a project presentation or publication, you may want to change the characteristics of the plot axes. The following Hands-on Example illustrates some of the basic techniques. The syntax for the AXIS statement is

```
AXIS<n> <options>;
```

where n defines options for a specific axis such as AXIS1, AXIS2, and so on. Applying an axis definition to a plot requires the following two steps:

Step 1: Define the axis using an AXIS<n> statement.

Step 2: Associate the defined axis to a specific axis in the plot. GPLOT and GCHART (discussed in an upcoming section) have different names for the plot axes. Axis names for GPLOT and GCHART are listed in Table 18.5.

Axis options define the "look" of the axis: its scale, appearance, tick marks, and text. As an example for the GPLOT procedure, the following code defines AXIS1. This is step 1 in using an axis.

```
AXIS1 C=RED ORDER=(0 TO 80 BY 5)
LABEL=('City Miles Per Gallon' FONT=SWISS)
OFFSET=(5) WIDTH=2 VALUE=(H=2);
```

To apply this axis to a plot (step 2 in using an axis), you would use code such as this example:

```
PROC GPLOT DATA=CARS;
    PLOT HWYMPG*CITYMPG/HAXIS=AXIS1;
```

TABLE 18.5   AXIS Names for GPLOT and GCHART

Axis Name for GPLOT	Refers to Which Axis?
HAXIS	HAXIS=AXIS<n> applies the specifications defined by axis<n> to the *horizontal* axis, also called the *X*-axis in a standard *X*–*Y* plot
VAXIS	VAXIS=AXIS<n> applies the specifications defined by axis<n> to the *vertical* axis, also called the *Y*-axis in a standard *X*–*Y* plot

Axis Name for GCHART	Refers to
MAXIS=	MAXIS=AXIS<n> applies the specifications defined by axis<n> to the *midpoint* axis, which is the axis associated with a group (categorical) specification
GAXIS=	GAXIS=AXIS<n> applies the specifications defined by axis<n> to the *group* axis, when you use a GROUP= statement (see example below)
RAXIS=	RAXIS=AXIS<n> applies the specifications defined by axis<n> to the *response* axis, which is the axis associated with the count, percent, or frequency

TABLE 18.6   Common Options for PROC GPLOT's AXIS Statement

Option	Explanation
COLOR=*color* (or C=)	Indicates the color used for the axis in the plot. For example, C=BLUE causes the axis to be blue. Other common color options are RED, GREEN, and BLACK. See Appendix A for a comprehensive list of available colors
LABEL=(*specifications*)	Specifies characteristics of an axis label. The text arguments define specific parts of the label's appearance. These include angle, color, font, justification, and rotation angle (A=), where A=90 means to display the label at a 90° angle (vertical). LABEL=NONE suppresses a label. An example of a label statement is LABEL=(H=4 J=C C=BLUE "My Axis"); where H= 4 specifies Height of the text J=C means Justify Center C=BLUE specifies color of label text
ORDER=*(list)*	Specifies the order of the values on the axis. For example, ORDER=(1 to 100 by 5) specifies that the axis will contain the numbers 1–100 with axis label increments of 5
VALUE=(*options*)	Specifies the height of text (among other items) – for example, VALUE=(H=4)
WIDTH=*thickness*	Specifies the width of the axis (affects the width of the entire frame unless a NOFRAME option is used as defined below)
OFFSET=*(x,y) <UNITS>*	Moves the axis away from the edge by a certain amount. For example, OFFSET=(3,4) moves the x-axis 3% horizontally, and the y-axis 4% vertically. You can also specify percent (3,4)pct, cm (3,4)cm, or in (for inches) (3,4)in. Percent is the default
A=*n*	Specifies text angle. For example, use A=90 to place a horizontal axis at a 90° angle so it aligns with the axis
MAJOR=(*options*)	Controls major tick marks. For example, MAJOR=(COLOR=BLUE HEIGHT=3 WIDTH=2)
MINOR=(*options*)	Controls minor axis tick mark. MINOR=NONE causes no minor ticks to be displayed. For example, MINOR=(NUMBER=4 COLOR=RED HEIGHT=1)
JUSTIFICATION=*type* (J=)	Justification, L=Left, C=Center, R=Right

The AXIS1 statement creates a horizontal axis (HAXIS) that is red, whose tick marks are from 0 to 80 and labeled by 5's. The label for the axis is "City Miles Per Gallon" and is displayed in a Swiss font. Table 18.6 lists common AXIS statement options:

> For Windows SAS version 9.3 and later, you may need to turn off automatic Output Delivery System ODS HTML type graphics (which is the default in those versions) in order for some of the upcoming graph examples to work (particularly the colors). To turn off ODS graphics, put this statement at the beginning of your code:

```
ODS GRAPHICS OFF;
```

To turn ODS graphics back on, use the code

```
ODS GRAPHICS ON;
```

Another way to return ODS graphics back to their normal default state in SAS versions 9.3 and later is

```
ODS PREFERENCES;
```

HANDS-ON EXAMPLE

This example illustrates how to format axes using PROC GPLOT.

1. Open the program file AGRAPH2A.SAS.

```
GOPTIONS RESET=ALL;
AXIS1 C=RED ORDER=(0 TO 80 BY 5)
      LABEL=('City Miles Per Gallon' FONT=SWISS)
      OFFSET=(5) WIDTH=2 VALUE=(H=2);
AXIS2 C=GREEN ORDER=(0 TO 80 BY 5)
      LABEL=(A=90 'Highway Miles Per Gallon' FONT=SWISS)
      OFFSET=(5,5)PCT WIDTH=4 VALUE=(H=1);
TITLE "Enhanced Scatterplot";
PROC GPLOT DATA=MYSASLIB.CARS;
    PLOT HWYMPG*CITYMPG/HAXIS=AXIS1 VAXIS=AXIS2 NOFRAME;
    SYMBOL1 V=DOT I=RL C=PURPLE L=2;
RUN;
QUIT;
```

   This program obviously creates a plot with strange color combination, but it illustrates the possibilities. Note that there are two axis definitions (AXIS1 and AXIS2) and that these axis definitions are applied in the PLOT statement where VAXIS=AXIS2 and HAXIS=AXIS1.

2. Run the program and observe the color version shown on your screen. A black and white version is illustrated in Figure 18.3.

   Because of the NOFRAME option, there is no frame around the entire plot (the frame is the default border that surrounds the plot as in Figure 18.2), but the colors of the axes are defined in the AXIS statements.

3. Clean up this plot by doing the following:

   - Remove the definition for axis color in the AXIS1 and AXIS2 statements.
   - Remove the NOFRAME option.
   - Change the COLOR for the dots to GRAY.
   - Change the LINE style (L=) to 5 (long dashes).
   - Change the OFFSET to 2.
   - Make the WIDTHs 4 for each axis in both cases.
   - Specify HEIGHT (H=1) for AXIS1.
   - Rerun the program and observe the changes in the graph.

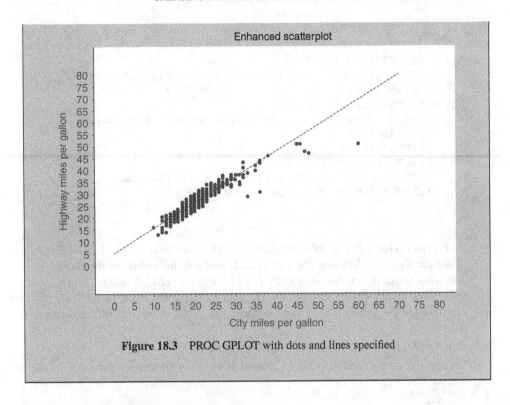

Figure 18.3   PROC GPLOT with dots and lines specified

18.1.5   Displaying Error Bars in GPLOT

For some data presentations, it is helpful to display data by groups with error bars on the graph to indicate the variability of data within a group. Displaying error bars (and other types of bars) is accomplished with the I= option in the SYMBOL statement (see Table 18.4 for more options). For example,

```
SYMBOL<n> INTERPOLATION=specification (or I=)
```

To employ this option to display error bars, use one of the following techniques:

- I=STD1JT produces error bars that are 1 standard deviation (STD1) and that are joined (J) at the means with tops (T) on each bar. STD also supports values of 2 and 3.
- I=BOXT includes boxplots with tops (T) on each whisker.

HANDS-ON EXAMPLE

In this example, you will create a graph that plots means and error bars.

1. Open the program file AGRAPH3.SAS.

```
GOPTIONS RESET=ALL;
```

(continued)

(continued)

```
AXIS1 ORDER=(4 TO 12 BY 1)
      LABEL=('Number of Cylinders' FONT=SWISS HEIGHT=4)
      OFFSET=(5);
AXIS2 ORDER=(0 TO 50 BY 5)
      LABEL=(A=90 'Highway Miles Per Gallon' FONT=SWISS
      HEIGHT=4)
      OFFSET=(5);
PROC GPLOT DATA=MYSASLIB.CARS
      PLOT HWYMPG*CYLINDERS/HAXIS=AXIS1 VAXIS=AXIS2;
      SYMBOL1 I=STD1JT H=1 LINE=1 VALUE=NONE;
RUN;
QUIT;
```

This plot is for highway miles per gallon (HWYMPG) by the number of CYLINDERs in the car's motor. Note that the I=STD1JT interpolation option in the SYMBOL1 statement requests 1 standard deviation error bars. The VALUE=NONE option suppresses the graph of individual points. The AXIS1 statement requests that the *x*-axis contain only the values from 4 to 12 because that is the number of CYLINDERs in the data set.

2. Run the program and observe the output in Figure 18.4.
3. Change the interpolation option to request boxplots with tops on the ends of the whiskers:

```
I=BOXT
```

Run the revised program and observe the output.

Figure 18.4   PROC GPLOT showing error bars

There are several other methods for customizing a SAS GPLOT. Refer to Appendix A and the SAS documentation for additional options.

18.2   CREATING BAR CHARTS AND PIE CHARTS

You can produce bar and pie charts to display counts or percentages for frequency data. These charts are created with the SAS GCHART procedure. The abbreviated syntax is as follows:

```
PROC GCHART <DATA=dataset>;
HBAR|HBAR3D|VBAR|VBAR3D chartvar(s) </ chartoption(s)>;
PIE|PIE3D|DONUT|STAR chartvar(s) </ chartoption(s)>;
```

Chart-type specifications such as HBAR and VBAR refer to horizontal and vertical bar charts, pie charts, and three-dimensional (3D) versions of the charts. An example is

```
PROC GCHART DATA=MYDATA;
HBAR STATUS/DISCRETE COUTLINE=BLUE WOUTLINE=3;
```

Some common GCHART statements are listed in Table 18.7. Common option for the bar chart options are listed in Table 18.8. Refer to SAS documentation for other statements and options.

A simple example of PROC GCHART is a horizontal bar chart (HBAR), shown in the following Hands-on Example.

TABLE 18.7   Common Options for PROC GCHART

Options	Explanation
DATA=dataname	Specifies which data set to use
HBAR, HBAR3D, VBAR, VBAR3D, PIE, PIE3D, DONUT, or STAR	Specify which type of plot to create. The option /HTML=variable specifies a variable that contains an HTML link address.
AXIS, FOOTNOTE, PATTERN, TITLE	These are statements that can be used to enhance graphs. Examples in this chapter illustrate these options
BY, FORMAT, LABEL, WHERE	These statements are common to most procedures, and may be used here

TABLE 18.8   Common GCHART Options for Bar Charts

Option	Explanation
CAXIS=color CFRAME=color CTEXT=color	Specifies a color to use for the axis, frame, or text. For example, CAXIS=BLUE
COUTLINE=color WOUTLINE=n	COUTLINE specifies color for bar outline (or SAME) and WOUTLINE specifies outline width. Default width is 1. For example, COUTLINE=BLUE WOUTLINE=3
DISCRETE	Treats numeric values as discrete (categorical)
GROUP variable	Splits bars into groups using specified classification variable

(continued)

TABLE 18.8   *(Continued)*

Option	Explanation
SUBGROUP *variable*	Specifies qualities of bars according to subgroups within the group defined by the GROUP variable (i.e., displays a different color for each subgroup)
WIDTH=*n* SPACE=*n*	WIDTH specifies BAR WIDTH and SPACE= specifies the space *between bars*
INSIDE=*statistic* OUTSIDE=*statistic*	Determines where a statistic will be displayed in a chart. Statistics are MEAN, SUM, PERCENT (PCT), or FREQ
TYPE=*statistic*	Defines the statistic to be computed (to display on the chart). Options include SUM, MEAN, PERCENT (PCT), and FREQ(default)
SUMVAR=*varname*	Defines the response variable. When you use this option TYPE= should be MEAN or SUM
NOLEGEND	Suppresses chart legend
CLM=*p*	Specifies the level for a confidence interval to be displayed on the bars. For example, CLM=95
ERRORBAR=*type*	Specifies TOP, BARS, or BOTH
HTML=	Defines an HTML link for a displayed category. When the graph image representing the group (represented by a bar, pie slice, etc) is clicked, the HTML address defined for that group is activated. For example HTML="http://www.cnn.com";

These options appear after the /.

HANDS-ON EXAMPLE

This example illustrates how to create a horizontal bar chart.

1. Open the program file AGRAPH4.SAS.

```
GOPTIONS RESET=ALL;
Title "Horizontal Bar Chart";
PROC GCHART DATA="C:\SASDATA\SOMEDATA";
HBAR STATUS/DISCRETE;
RUN;
QUIT;
```

   This code requests a horizontal bar chart on the variable STATUS. The /DIS-CRETE option tells SAS that the numeric values for the STATUS variable should be treated as discrete values. Otherwise, SAS may assume that the numeric values are a range and create a bar chart using midpoints instead of the actual values.
2. Run the program and observe the output in Figure 18.5.
3. Change HBAR to VBAR and rerun the program and observe the output.
4. Change the statement by adding WIDTH=10,

```
VBAR STATUS/DISCRETE WIDTH=10;
```

Rerun the program and observe the output. How did the WIDTH statement change the chart?

5. Remove the WIDTH=10 statement and change VBAR to PIE and rerun the program. Observe the output. Experiment with HBAR3D and PIE3D.

Figure 18.5   Horizontal bar chart using PROC GCHART

6. Change back to HBAR and include a PATTERN and COLOR statement to change the look of the graph. For example,

```
HBAR STATUS/DISCRETE;
PATTERN1 VALUE=R1 COLOR=GREEN;
```

Run the revised program and observe the output.

7. Remove the /DISCRETE option and rerun the program. How does that change the output?

18.3   DEFINING GRAPH PATTERNS

As illustrated in the above example, the PATTERN statement allows you to change the color and pattern of a bar in a bar chart. A simplified syntax for the statement is

```
PATTERN<n> <COLOR=color> <VALUE= pattern >;
For example,
PATTERN1 VALUE=R1 COLOR=GREEN;
```

Patterns are discussed further in Appendix A. Colors are standard SAS colors. The <n> in the statement determines which category the pattern will be defined for, where the categories are the order in which categories are displayed for the chart. These are listed in Table 18.9.

For example, the statement

```
PATTERN1 VALUE=SOLID C=LIGHTBLUE;
```

TABLE 18.9   Pattern Definitions for the PATTERN Value Statement

Option	Explanation
COLOR=*color*	Specifies color for a pattern. See color options in Appendix A
EMPTY (E)	Defines EMPTY bar
SOLID (S)	Defines a SOLID bar
R1 to R5	Defines right 45° stripes. Thickness is specified by R1 (lightest) to R5 (heaviest)
X1 to X5	Defines crosshatch pattern. Thickness is specified by X1 (lightest) to X5 (heaviest)
L1 to L5	Defines left 45° stripes. Thickness is specified by R1 (lightest) to R5 (heaviest)

results in a solid light blue bar related to the first category in the chart.

In the following Hands-on Example, we create a bar chart using two grouping variables. This is accomplished with a /GROUP option as illustrated here:

```
VBAR INJTYPE/GROUP=GENDER;
```

HANDS-ON EXAMPLE

This example illustrates how to modify axes in a bar chart.

1. Open the program file AGRAPH5.SAS.

```
GOPTIONS RESET=ALL;
AXIS1 LABEL=NONE VALUE=(H=1.2);
AXIS2 LABEL=(A=90 "Count");
TITLE "Vertical Bar Chart";
PROC GCHART DATA=MYSASLIB.SOMEDATA;
VBAR GENDER/GROUP=GP MAXIS=AXIS1 RAXIS=AXIS2;
PATTERN1 VALUE=R1 COLOR=GREEN;
RUN;
QUIT;
```

   Note that AXIS= controls the frequency (vertical) axis for GCHART and MAXIS= controls the appearance of the midpoint (horizontal) axis.
2. Run the program and observe the output in Figure 18.6. This type of plot can be used to display cross-tabulation analyses.
3. The visual impact of this graph might be more dramatic if the Female and Male bars were in different colors. To accomplish this, we could use a SUBGROUP=GENDER command and define the second bar color using a PATTERN2 statement.

   Open the program file AGRAPH6.SAS.

```
GOPTIONS RESET=ALL;
TITLE 'Bar Chart by Group with different bar colors';
PROC GCHART DATA="C:\SASDATA\SOMEDATA";
VBAR GENDER/GROUP=GP SUBGROUP=GENDER;
PATTERN1 VALUE=R1 COLOR=RED;
```

```
PATTERN2 VALUE=R1 COLOR=BLUE;
RUN;
QUIT;
```

Note the added SUBGROUP= statement. This tells SAS to color the bars for each subgroup using a different color. The PATTERN2 statement specifies the color for males because the patterns are assigned in alphabetical order.

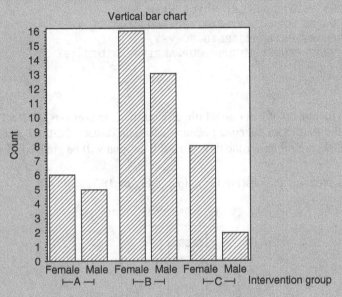

Figure 18.6   PROC GCHART showing groups bars

4. Run the program and observe the output. Note that the bars for each GENDER are now in different colors. The PATTERN remains the same because of the VALUE=R1 specification in both PATTERN statements.

5. Change the statement in PATTERN1 to VALUE=X4 and rerun the program to see how that change alters the output.

6. Change VBAR to VBAR3D. Note that the colors for the bars remain, but the PATTERN option no longer has any effect.

   If you want the bars to appear in an order other than alphabetical, you can create a format for the variable and apply that format to the variable for the PROC GCHART statement.

18.4   CREATING STACKED BAR CHARTS

Another often-used type of bar chart is a stacked bar chart. To create stacked bar charts, you *do not* use the GROUP option. This is illustrated in the following Hands-on Example.

HANDS-ON EXAMPLE

This example illustrates how to create stacked bar charts using PROC GCHART.

1. Open the program file AGRAPH7.SAS.

```
GOPTIONS RESET=ALL;
PATTERN1 V=R1 C=RED; * FOR BUS;
PATTERN2 V=R2 C=BLUE; * FOR CAR;
PATTERN3 V=R3 C=BLACK; * FOR WALK;
TITLE C=RED 'Stacked Bars, Method of Arrival';
PROC GCHART DATA=MYSASLIB.SURVEY;
     VBAR GENDER / SUBGROUP=ARRIVE  WIDTH=15;
RUN;
QUIT;
```

    Note that this plot is set up a little differently from previous GCHART examples, in that the PATTERN statement occurs before the PROC GCHART statement. The PATTERNs are set up for the three arrival types that will be graphed: Bus, Car, and Walk.

2. Run this program and observe the output in Figure 18.7.

Figure 18.7   Stacked bar chart

3. Suppose that for a publication that doesn't print in more than one color, you want the bars to be in different shades of gray. Change the PATTERN and V statements to read as follows:

```
PATTERN1 V=S C=GRAYAA; * FOR BUS(Dark Gray);
PATTERN2 V=S C=GRAYCC; * FOR CAR (Medium Gray);
PATTERN3 V=S C=GRAYEE; * FOR WALK (Light GRAY);
```

    V=S indicates solid, and the various shades of gray are given as GRAYAA, GRAYCC, and so on to GRAYFF, which is white.

4. Change the GCHART code to

```
PROC GCHART DATA=MYSASLIB.SURVEY;
       VBAR GENDER / GROUP=ARRIVE SUBGROUP=GENDER WIDTH=10;
RUN;
```

Rerun the program and observe the difference.

5. For further enhancement to the bar chart, open the program file AGRAPH7A.SAS and observe the additional code defining a plot key and an enhancement to the vertical axis.

```
GOPTIONS RESET=ALL;
PATTERN1 V=R1 C=RED; * FOR BUS;
PATTERN2 V=R2 C=BLUE; * FOR CAR;
PATTERN3 V=R3 C=BLACK; * FOR WALK;
LEGEND1
 ACROSS=1 LABEL=("Gender")
 POSITION=(top inside left)
 VALUE=(H=1 'Male' 'Female');
AXIS1 label=(a=90 Color=RED H=2 f="Swiss/Bold" "Count");
TITLE C=RED 'Example Bar Chart';
PROC GCHART DATA=MYSASLIB.SURVEY;
       VBAR GENDER / GROUP=ARRIVE SUBGROUP=GENDER WIDTH=10
                     LEGEND=LEGEND1 RAXIS=AXIS1
                     OUTSIDE=FREQ ;
RUN;
QUIT;
```

- The LEGEND1 and AXIS1 statements. The LEGEND1 statement creates a key named "Gender" that appears at the top, inside left in the graph frame, with the key items "Male" and "Female" listed. The ACROSS option specifies that the key has items listed one across.

- The AXIS1 statement defines an axis to be used as the vertical axis where the name "Count" will be displayed at a 90° angle using the Swiss font, in red, with a height of 2 units (default is 1).

- In the PROC GCHART statements, note the LEGEND=LEGEND1 and RAXIS=AXIS1 statements. These statements apply the legend and axis to the chart.

- Note the statement OUTSIDE=FREQ. This tells the program to display the count (FREQ) for each bar, and to display it outside the bar.

  a. Run this program and observe the results shown in Figure 18.8.

  b. Take out the ACROSS=1 option and rerun. How does this change the legend?

  c. Change the legend position to the top inside right. Rerun the program to see if your change worked.

(continued)

(continued)

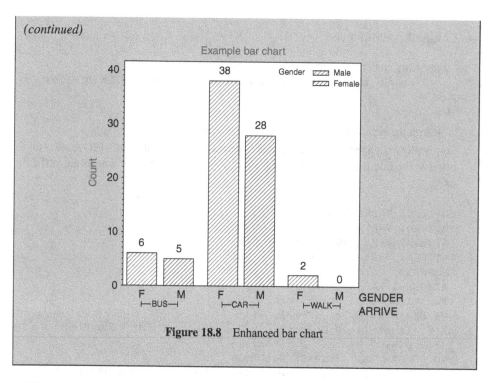

Figure 18.8   Enhanced bar chart

There are many options for customizing these plots, only a few of which have been discussed here. Several of the options (e.g., `AXIS` and `LEGEND`) are similar to those used in `PROC GPLOT`.

18.5   CREATING MEAN BARS USING GCHART

An often-used analysis graphic is one that displays means as bars with error bars around the mean indicating a level of variability. `PROC GCHART` can produce this graph with a little help. The following Hands-on Example shows how this is accomplished.

HANDS-ON EXAMPLE

In this example, you will produce a bar chart with error bars representing means by group.

1. Open the program file `AGRAPH8.SAS`.

```
PATTERN1 V=L3 COLOR=LIGHTBLUE;
AXIS1 LABEL=(A=90 H=1.5 F="SWISS" "OBSERVATION" C=BLUE);
AXIS2 LABEL=(H=1.5 F="SWISS" "GROUP");
TITLE1 'Mean Displayed with Error Bars';
PROC GCHART DATA=MYSASLIB.SOMEDATA;
VBAR GP /
WIDTH=10
```

```
TYPE=MEAN
SUMVAR=TIME1
INSIDE=MEAN
CLM=99
ERRORBAR=TOP
RAXIS=AXIS1 MAXIS=AXIS2
COUTLINE=SAME WOUTLINE=2;
RUN;
QUIT;
```

Note the following statements and how they are used in this code:

- The PATTERN statement makes the bars light blue with an L3 (left stripe pattern).
- The AXIS1 statement is used to specify the RAXIS (which is the Response axis), and the AXIS2 statement is used to specify the MAXIS (Midpoint Axis). The RAXIS is displayed rotated by 90°. Both are displayed with a height of 1.5.
- The SUMVAR tells SAS which variable is used to calculate the mean (as specified by INSIDE=).

Figure 18.9   Means with error bars

- INSIDE=MEAN causes the mean values to be displayed within the bars.

(continued)

(continued)

- The `CLM=99` specifies a 99% confidence interval on the mean.
- The `TYPE=` option specifies the type of statistic used in the `ERRORBAR` option.
- The `ERRORBAR=TOP` causes the CI error bars to be displayed on the top of the bars.
- `COUTLINE` and `WOUTLINE` specify a black outline with width 1.

  Run this program and observe the output, as shown in Figure 18.9.

2. Change the `AXIS1` statement to control attributes of the major and minor axes on the response scale.

```
AXIS1 LABEL=(A=90 H=1.5 F="SWISS" "OBSERVATION" C=BLUE)
MAJOR=(COLOR=BLUE HEIGHT=3 WIDTH=2)
MINOR=(NUMBER=4 COLOR=RED HEIGHT=1);
```

3. Change the `ERRORBAR` specification to `BOTH`, rerun and observe the changes.
4. Take off the `ERRORBAR`, `TYPE`, and `CLM` statements and change `INSIDE=MEAN` to `OUTSIDE=FREQ` (`ERRORBAR`, `TYPE`, and `CLM` do not work with `FREQ`), rerun and observe the changes.

18.6 CREATING BOXPLOTS

Examples in earlier chapters have shown how default SAS output creates boxplots in some cases. This section provides information on methods for creating and enhancing boxplots. The abbreviated syntax for this procedure is as follows:

```
PROC BOXPLOT <DATA=datasetname>; <options>;
          PLOT <depvar*>groupvar(s)</options>;
<statements>;
```

The `PLOT` statement is required. For example, a typical simple use (group must first be sorted):

```
PROC BOXPLOT DATA = MYDATA;
   PLOT HEIGHT*GROUP;
RUN;
```

There are numerous options for `PROC BOXPLOT`. Some commonly used statements are listed in Table 18.10.

Options for the `PLOT` statement appear after a slash. For example,

```
PROC BOXPLOT DATA=CARDATA;
   PLOT HWYMPG*CYLINDERS/CBOXFILL=LIGHTGREEN;
```

Some common options for the `PLOT` statement associated with `PROC BOXPLOT` are listed in Table 18.11.

A number of other options are available, many similar to those listed for `PROC GPLOT` (see SAS documentation for more details).

TABLE 18.10   Common Statements for PROC BOXPLOT

Statement	Explanation
`DATA=dataname`	Specifies which data set to use
`PLOT <depvar*>groupvar(s);`	Specifies the variables to use in the plot. Typically, a dependent variable and grouping variable such as `PLOT AGE*GROUP;`
`INSET`	Specifies an inset key similar to those previously described for histograms. See Chapter 9
`ID variables;`	Specifies which variables will be used to identify observations
`BY, FORMAT, LABEL, WHERE`	These statements are common to most procedures and may be used here

TABLE 18.11   Common Options the BOXPLOT PLOT Statement (Follows a Slash (/) in PLOT Statement)

Option	Explanation
`CBOXES=color`	Specifies outline color for boxes. For example, `CBOXES=RED`
`CBOXFILL=color`	Specifies the fill pattern for boxes. For example, `CBOXFILL=LIGHTBLUE`
`NOCHES`	Species that boxes will be notches. For an explanation for notches, see McGill, Tukey, and Larsen (1978)
`BOXSTYLE=`	Specifies the style of the boxplot. Options include `SCHEMATIC`, `SCHEMATICID`, `SKELETAL` (default). `SCHEMATIC` displays outliers. `SCHEMATICID` displays labels for outliers according to the `ID` variable specified in the `ID` statement. `SKELETAL` does not display outliers. (See example that follows for more explanation.)

18.6.1   Creating a Simple Boxplot

The basic plot request consists of indicating the variables used for the analysis and grouping in the statement:

`PLOT analysisvariable*groupingvariable;`

HANDS-ON EXAMPLE

This example illustrates a simple use of `PROC BOXPLOT`.

1. In the Editor window, open the file AGRAPH9.SAS.

```
GOPTIONS RESET=ALL;
Title "Simple Box Plot";
* You must sort the data on the grouping variable;
PROC SORT DATA=MYSASLIB.CARS
```

(continued)

(continued)

```
        OUT=CARDATA;BY CYLINDERS;
 PROC BOXPLOT DATA=CARDATA;
        PLOT HWYMPG*CYLINDERS/CBOXFILL=LIGHTGREEN;
        WHERE CYLINDERS GT 1;
 RUN;
```

Note that when creating side-by-side boxplots, you must sort the data on the grouping variable before running the PROC BOXPLOT procedure. Also note that the WHERE statement is necessary because one car (the Mazda RX-8) is listed as −1 cylinders as it uses a rotary engine. You could have also recoded the −1 as a missing value to obtain the same result.

2. Run this program and observe the output in Figure 18.10.

Figure 18.10   Boxplots showing highway MPG by cylinders

3. Change the PLOT statement to include the following:

```
    PLOT HWYMPG*CYLINDERS/
            CBOXFILL=VLIGB
            CBOXES=BLACK
            BOXSTYLE=SCHEMATIC
            NOTCHES;
```

The CBOXFILL and CBOXES options specify the fill color and outline color of the boxes, respectively. BOXSTYLE requests the SCHEMATIC style plot, which specifies the type of outliers displayed in the plot. The SCHEMATIC option defines outliers as those values greater than the absolute value of 1.5*(interquartile range) from the top or bottom of the box. Run the program and observe the output in Figure 18.11. Note that outliers are marked at the top of two of the boxplots.

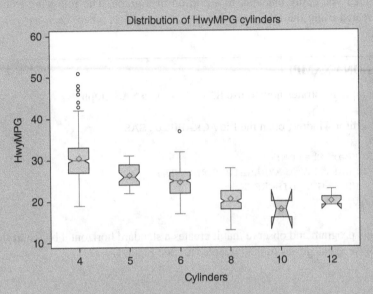

Figure 18.11   Boxplots with enhancements

4. To display the IDs of outliers, change the style to SCHEMATICID and include the statement ID MODEL using the code shown here. Rerun and observe the results. (In this case, some of the ID text overlaps so that it is hard to read some of the results.)

```
PLOT HWYMPG*CYLINDERS/
        CBOXFILL=VLIGB
        CBOXES=BLACK
        BOXSTYLE=SCHEMATICID
        NOTCHES;
        ID MODEL;
```

5. To display summary statistics on the graph, include an INSETGROUP statement as in the code shown here. Rerun and observe the results.

```
INSETGROUP MEAN (5.1) MIN MAX /
        header = 'Mean and Extremes';
```

The notches are a way to measure the difference between two medians. If there is no overlap in the corresponding notches for two plots, it indicates a significantly different in the group medians at approximately the 0.95 confidence level.

18.7   GOING DEEPER: CREATING AN INTERACTIVE BAR USING ODS

A useful feature of the ODS introduced in Chapter 8 is its ability to create interactive links within graphs in HTML mode. To do this you create a variable that creates a hypertext link, and then you apply that link to a portion of a graph. The following example uses a graph created using the SAS procedure PROC GCHART, where each bar is a link to a report.

HANDS-ON EXAMPLE

This example illustrates how to use HTML links in a SAS graph.

1. In the Editor window, open the file AGRAPH10.SAS.

```
TITLE "Bar Chart";
PROC GCHART DATA=MYSASLIB.SOMEDATA;
     HBAR GP/ DISCRETE;
RUN; QUIT;
```

2. Run this program and observe that it creates a standard horizontal bar chart that consists of three categories of the variable GP. See Figure 18.12.

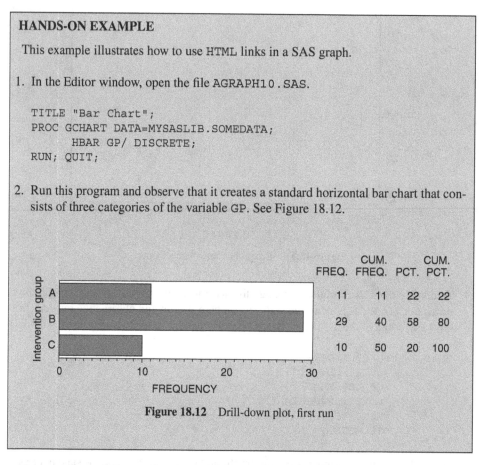

Figure 18.12   Drill-down plot, first run

Suppose for each "group," represented by one of the bars on the plot, you want to make available a set of background statistics. You can associate a link for each bar on the graph to a separate Web page. Thus, each bar becomes a Web page link, and when you click on a bar on the graph, you open an HTML page. The code shown in Figure 18.13 creates an HTML file that contains the report (from PROC MEANS) you wish to associate with Group A. (We'll see this code again in an upcoming example.) Note that the HTML report is saved in the file named GPA.HTM, and that it contains information about GP="A". (Remember that the format to specify the file in ODS HTML is BODY=.)

The report created by the code in Figure 18.13 is given in Table 18.12. We'll create this and other tables in an upcoming example.

To define the link that will take the user to this report, use a standard IF statement in a DATA step such as the following:

The ODS code specifies the HTML file where the output will be saved.

```
ODS HTML BODY="C: \SASDATA\GPA.HTM";
PROC MEANS DATA=  "C: \SASDATA\SOMEDATA" MAXDEC=2 N MEAN STD;
VAR AGE TIME1-TIME4;
WHERE GP="A";
TITLE  'Summary for GROUP A' ;
RUN;
```

The PROC MEANS code creates the report we want to save.

Figure 18.13   Code to create an HTML report file

TABLE 18.12   Report for Group A

Summary for GROUP A

The MEANS Procedure

Variable	Label	N	Mean	Std Dev
AGE	Age on Jan 1, 2000	11	10.36	2.87
TIME1	Baseline	11	20.90	2.08
TIME2	6 Months	11	27.00	2.93
TIME3	12 Months	11	30.35	3.20
TIME4	24 Months	11	30.44	3.96

```
IF GP="A" THEN HTMLLINK='HREF="GPA.HTM"';
```

This IF statement assigns the text 'HREF="GPA.HTM"' to a variable named HTMLLINK. The HREF statement is a standard HTML statement used in pages on the web to create links to other pages. (Note how the HREF is included in single quotation marks and the file name is in double quotation marks.) In this example, a link is defined when the group (GP) is "A." Once a link variable (HTMLLINK) is created, it can be applied to a portion of a graph as illustrated in the following Hands-on Example.

HANDS-ON EXAMPLE

1. Open the program file AGRAPH11.SAS. In Part 1 of the code, note that there are three PROC MEANS procedures that create three files containing reports for Groups A, B, and C. These three PROC MEAN calls are all similar to the code shown in Figure 18.13 and each create an HTML report file.

```
*......PART 1: CREATE REPORTS FOR GROUPS A, B, and C;
ODS HTML BODY ="C:\SASDATA\GPA.HTM";
PROC MEANS DATA= "C:\SASDATA\SOMEDATA" MAXDEC=2 N MEAN STD;
VAR AGE TIME1-TIME4;
WHERE GP="A";
TITLE 'Summary for GROUP A';
RUN;
ODS HTML BODY="C:\SASDATA\GPB.HTM";
PROC MEANS DATA= "C:\SASDATA\SOMEDATA" MAXDEC=2 N MEAN STD;
VAR AGE TIME1-TIME4;
WHERE GP="B";
```

(continued)

(continued)

```
TITLE 'Summary for GROUP B';
RUN;
ODS HTML BODY ="C:\SASDATA\GPC.HTM";
PROC MEANS DATA= "C:\SASDATA\SOMEDATA" MAXDEC=2 N MEAN STD;
VAR AGE TIME1-TIME4;
WHERE GP="C";
TITLE 'Summary for GROUP C';
RUN;
*.......PART 2: CREATE THE LINKS IN  A DATA STEP;
DATA BARCHART;SET "C:\SASDATA\SOMEDATA";
LENGTH HTMLLINK $40;
IF GP="A" THEN HTMLLINK='HREF="GPA.HTM"';
IF GP="B" THEN HTMLLINK='HREF="GPB.HTM"';
IF GP="C" THEN HTMLLINK='HREF="GPC.HTM"';
ODS HTML FILE="C:\SASDATA\GCHART.HTM" GPATH="C:\SASDATA\";
*.......PART 3: CREATE THE GRAPH;
PROC GCHART;
      HBAR GP/ HTML=HTMLLINK;
      TITLE 'Summary information for each GP.';
RUN; QUIT;
ODS HTML CLOSE;
ODS PREFERENCES; *Reset HTML output;
```

Part 2 of the code creates a data set called BARCHART that includes a new variable named HTMLLINK that is defined for each of the three groups. The third section of the code creates the bar chart using GCHART. In PROC GCHART, the statement option /HTML= in the line

```
HBAR GP/ HTML=HTMLLINK;
```

relates the HTML link (HTMLLINK) to each category of GP. Part 3 of the code creates the bar chart.

Run the program and observe the output in the Results Viewer (or view GCHART.HTM in a Browser). The graph is virtually identical to the one illustrated in Figure 18.12. However, there is a difference.

2. Place your cursor on one of the bars. The icon turns to a pointing hand indicating a link. Click on the bar for group A and the information given earlier in Table 18.12 appears.

3. To return to the graph, locate the left arrow at the top of the window and click it once. Try the links for the other two bars. Using this technique, you can create graphs with drill-down capabilities that allow you to display background information for each category in a graph.

4. Change the last IF statement in the code to

```
IF GP="C" THEN HTMLLINK='HREF="http://www.cnn.com"';
```

or to some other Web page. (Be careful to include the quote marks correctly in the HTMLLINK statement. Resubmit the program and click on the third bar. If you specified a correct http page address, the contents of the indicated Web page should be displayed when you click on the bottom bar.)

18.8   GOING DEEPER: SGPLOTS

Starting with SAS 9.2, a new way of creating high-quality graphs was introduced. These are called Statistical Graphics Procedures. These include SGPLOT, SGSCATTER, and SGPANEL. We'll illustrate the use of SGPLOT in this section. One advantage of these "SG" plots is that they can easily be created in standard graphical file types such as JPG (JPEG) or TIF. The basic syntax for SGPLOT is

```
PROC SGPLOT <DATA=dataname> ;
plotstatements/options;
```

At least one plot type statement is required. For example,

```
PROC SGPLOT;
 HISTOGRAM AGE;
 DENSITY AGE/TYPE=NORMAL;
```

A simplified list of these statements appears in Table 18.13:

TABLE 18.13   Common Plot Statements for PROC SGPLOT

Plot Statement	Explanation
HBAR vname or VBAR vname	Specifies horizontal or vertical bar chart. For example, HBAR AGE; Options /GROUP= specifies group and GROUPDISPLAY=CLUSTER displays groups as clusters. (Default is stacked.)
HISTOGRAM vname	Specifies histogram. For example, HISTOGRAM AGE;
SCATTERPLOT	Specifies scatterplot. For example, SCATTER X=AGE Y=SBP;
DENISTY vname	Displays density plot. For example, DENSITY AGE </TYPE=Kernel or Normal) Normal is default
KEYLEGEND/options;	LOCATION= specifies location of legend (INSIDE or OUTSIDE) POSITION specifies position of legend (topleft , topright, bottomleft, bottomright)
XAXIS options; and YAXIS options;	Common options: LABEL='Label name' MAX=, MIN=, VALUES=(Min to Max by interval) OFFSETMIN= OFFSETMAX= (from 0 to 1)
REG X=xvar Y=yvar/ options	Specify regression line for scatterplot, where options include ALPHA=, CLI and CLM and GROUP=
FILLATTRS=	Can be used to specify a fill color for elements in a plot. For example FILLATTRS=(COLORS=GREEN); See additional color choices in Appendix A, section A.2.
TRANSPARENCY=pct	Specifies transparency for bubbles in a BUBBLE plot where pct ranges from 0 to 1. For example TRANSPARANCY=0.50.

Creating an SGPLOT HISTOGRAM: One of the main differences in using SGPLOT (as opposed to GPLOT) is that you can more easily overlay various components in the same plot. For example, to create a histogram, you could use the code

```
PROC SGPLOT;
 HISTOGRAM AGE;
RUN;
```

To add a density plot (default is a normal plot), you simply add another plot statement:

```
PROC SGPLOT;
 HISTOGRAM AGE;
 DENSITY AGE;
RUN;
```

HANDS-ON EXAMPLE

1. Open the program file SGPLOT1.SAS.

```
PROC SGPLOT DATA=MYSASLIB.WOUND;
HISTOGRAM sbp;
TITLE "SGPLOT Histogram";
RUN;
```

Run this code and observe the output shown in Figure 18.14.

Figure 18.14   Histogram created using SGPLOTS

2. Add the following code after the HISTOGRAM line:

```
DENSITY SBP/TYPE=KERNEL;
```

Rerun the code and observe that a normal curve is overlaid on the plot.

3. Add the following code after the DENSITY line:

```
DENSITY SBP/TYPE=NORMAL;
```

Figure 18.15   Histogram with normal and kernel curves

Rerun this code and observe that it contains all three plots – the histogram, the normal curve, and a kernel density curve as shown in Figure 18.15.

Creating an SGPLOT BAR CHART: You can also use PROC SGPLOT to create a Bar Chart. The code for a horizontal bar chart is

```
PROC SGPLOT;
    HBAR AGE;
RUN;
```

The following example illustrates some of the options for bar charts.

HANDS-ON EXAMPLE

1. Open the program file SGPLOT2.SAS. Submit this code and observe the output shown in Figure 18.16.

```
PROC SGPLOT DATA=MYSASLIB.WOUND;
  HBAR RACE_CAT;
  TITLE "SGPLOT Bar Chart";
RUN;
```

(continued)

(continued)

2. Change HBAR to VBAR and rerun the analysis to see a vertical bar chart version of this plot.
3. Change the bar code to read

```
VBAR RACE_CAT/ GROUP=GENDER;
```

   Resubmit the code and observe the stacked vertical bar chart created.
4. Change the code again to read

```
VBAR RACE_CAT/ GROUP=GENDER GROUPDISPLAY=CLUSTER;
```

Figure 18.16   Horizontal bar chart

   Submit this code and observe the vertical bar chart with bars clustered.
5. To illustrate manipulating the legend and axis labels add this code:

```
KEYLEGEND / LOCATION=INSIDE POSITION=TOPLEFT;
XAXIS LABEL="Race";
```

   Resubmit this code and observe the results.
6. To produce a grayscale version of this plot, place the code.

```
ODS RTF STYLE=GRAYSCALEPRINTER;
```

   Before PROC SGPLOT, and

```
ODS RTF CLOSE;
```

   after the RUN; statement, run the revised code. Observe the results as shown in Figure 18.17.

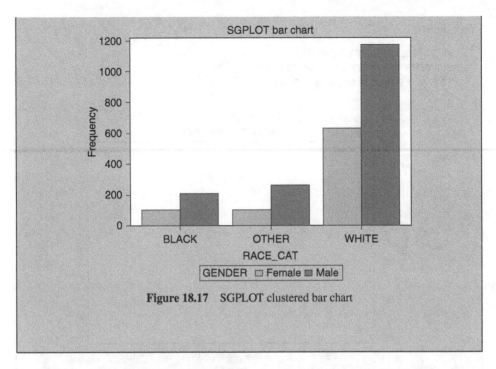

Figure 18.17 SGPLOT clustered bar chart

Creating a Scatterplot Using SGPLOT: Another way to use SGPLOT is to create a scatterplot. The code for a scatterplot is:

```
PROC SGPLOT DATA =sasfilename;
     SCATTER X=varname1 Y=varname2;
RUN;
```

An option that is helpful for the `SCATTER` plot type is `MARKERAT-TRS=(specifications)`. This option allows you to specify the type of symbol displayed at each point, along with size and color. For example,

```
MARKERATTRS=(symbol=trianglefilled size=10px color=red);
```

Specifies a red filled triangle of size 10 pixels. Other common ODS marker symbols (as these are called) include triangle (not filled), circle (filled or not), square (filled or not), and star (filled or not.) Color options are listed in Appendix A. Refer to SAS documentation for other ODS marker symbols.

The following example illustrates some of the options for scatterplots.

HANDS-ON EXAMPLE

1. Open the program file `SGPLOT3.SAS`. These data are pretest- and posttest for two different teaching methods. To look at the entire data at once, submit this code and observe the output shown in Figure 18.18.

(continued)

(continued)

```
PROC SGPLOT DATA =ANCOVA;
 SCATTER X=PRETEST Y=POSTTEST;
 TITLE "SGPLOT Scatter Plot";
RUN;
```

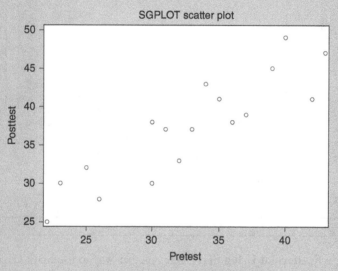

Figure 18.18 SGPLOT scatterplot

2. Change the SCATTER statement by adding a GROUP option:

```
SCATTER X=PRETEST Y=POSTTEST/GROUP=METHOD;
```

Resubmit the code and observe that the groups are displayed in different colors.

3. Change the SCATTER statement by adding Marker Attributes using the following code:

```
SCATTER X=PRETEST Y=POSTTEST/GROUP=METHOD
        MARKERATTRS=(symbol=trianglefilled size=10px);
```

(Other symbol types for SGPLOT are listed in Appendix A, Section A.6.)

Note that no color option is used here as we want each group to be represented by a unique color. Resubmit this code and note how the "dots" are changed to triangles.

4. Add these lines just before the RUN; statement to control the legend and labels:

```
KEYLEGEND / LOCATION=INSIDE POSITION=TOPLEFT ;
XAXIS LABEL="Pre Test Results";
YAXIS LABEL="Post Test Results";
```

Submit this code and observe the results.

5. Finally, add this code (just before the RUN; statement) to display a regression line for each group:

```
REG X=PRETEST Y=POSTTEST/ GROUP=METHOD;
```

Submit the code and observe the results shown in Figure 18.19. The three lines represent three linear regression lines, each fit through the data for one of the three groups.

Figure 18.19   SGPLOT scatterplot with regression lines

Using SGPLOT to create a Bubble Plot: A bubble plot is similar to a scatterplot, but where a third variable determines the size of the point (bubble). For example,

```
PROC SGPLOT DATA = MYDATA;
    BUBBLE X = AGE Y = SBP SIZE = WEIGHT;
RUN;
```

This example makes use of an option TRANSPARENCY=value, which is also available when creating bar graphs. Values range from 0 (opaque) to 1 (clear). The following example illustrates some of the options for SPPLOT bubble plots.

HANDS-ON EXAMPLE

1. Open the program file SGPLOT4.SAS. Observe the BUBBLE statement and the option following the slash. Run this program and observe the output shown in Figure 18.20.

(continued)

(continued)

```
PROC SGPLOT DATA =MYSASLIB.CORONARY;
   TITLE 'BUBBLE PLOT USING CORONARY DATA';
   TITLE2 'Bubble is BMI';
   BUBBLE X = AGE Y = SBP SIZE = BMI
        / TRANSPARENCY = 0.5;
   YAXIS GRID;
RUN;
```

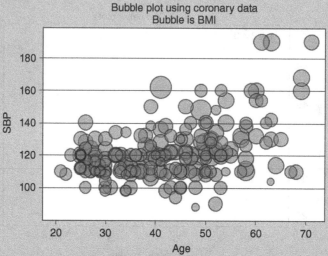

Figure 18.20   Bubble plot created using SGPLOT

Information you might learn from this graph other than that SBP tends to increase with AGE is that the bubbles get bigger towards the right and top meaning that BMI might be associated with older subjects and higher SBP (which makes medical sense).

2. Change the transparency to 0.9 and run the code. Change it to 0.1 and run the code. Note how transparency changes the appearance of the plot.

3. Change the transparency back to 0.5. Add the option GROUP=INSURANCE after the TRANSPARENCY statement (and before the semicolon). Rerun and note the different colors by group. Does this provide any additional information about how people with insurance might differ from those who don't have it?

4. Change the option in the BUBBLE statement to /TRANSPARENCY=0.5 FILLATTRS=(COLORS=GREEN) to change the color of the bubbles to green. Other possible colors are listed in Appendix A, Section A.2.

18.9   OTHER WAYS TO CUSTOMIZE PLOTS

There are at least two other techniques you can use to customize plots: Annotation Data Sets and the Graph Template Language (GTL).

The Annotation technique can be used to customize plots that are created with GPLOT, GCHART, and other similar procedures. In this technique, you create an Annotation Data Set containing graphic commands that you then apply to an existing plot (or create an entirely custom plot).

The GTL is the SAS sublanguage used to specify the details of how an ODS graph is created. Each ODS graph has a default template, where these GTL commands are located. You can edit this template language to customize the graphs to meet specific needs.

Both of these techniques are beyond the scope of this book, but if you want to go deeper into the capabilities of SAS graphs, you can find more information about these techniques in SAS documentation.

18.10   SUMMARY

This chapter described a small portion of the many graphical options available in SAS. However, the discussion of graphs in this chapter (and elsewhere in the book) covered many of the common graphs used in data analysis.

EXERCISES

18.1 **Graph a comparison of means.**

Using the data in the file AANOVA1.SAS and the example illustrated by AGRAPH8.SAS, create a graph that displays means as bars and standard error markers.

18.2 **Display comparative box plots.**

Using AGRAPH9.SAS as a guide, create a plot of comparative box plots by CYLINDERS (where CYLINDERS > 1) for CITYMPG in the CARS data set.

```
GOPTIONS RESET=ALL;
PROC SORT DATA="C:\SASDATA\CARS" OUT=MPGFILE;
     BY _____ ;
PROC _____ DATA=MPGFILE;
     PLOT _____*CYLINDERS;
     WHERE CYLINDERS GT _____;
RUN;
QUIT;
```

18.3 **Use an interactive ODS graph.**

a. Open AGRAPH11.SAS. Change the type of chart from HBAR to PIE and run the program. Test to verify that the HTML links work.

b. Change the type of chart to VBAR and run the program. Test to verify that the HTML links work.

c. Change the type of chart to a VBAR3D and run the program. Test to verify that the HTML links work.

d. Similarly, try the graph types BLOCK, HBAR3D, PIE3D, and STAR.

18.4 **Use SGPLOT to create a scatterplot.**

Using the skeleton SGPLOT code below, display a scatterplot of X=CITYMPG and Y=HWYMPG and fit a regression line through the scatter with an individual confidence limit (CLI).

```
PROC SGPLOT DATA ="C:\SASDATA\CARS";
SCATTER X=CITYMPG Y=_____;
XAXIS LABEL="City _____";
YAXIS _____;
REG X=_____ Y=HWYMPG / CLI;
TITLE "SGPLOT Scatter Plot for Miles Per Gallon";
RUN;
```

19

CREATING CUSTOM REPORTS

LEARNING OBJECTIVES

- To be able to create custom reports using PROC TABULATE
- To be able to create custom reports using PROC REPORT
- To be able to create a custom report using the DATA step

Throughout the book, procedures such as PROC PRINT and PROC FREQ have been used to produce simple summaries of data. However, these procedures are limited. This chapter introduces two advanced reporting procedures that are designed to help you create professional reports.

19.1 USING PROC TABULATE

PROC TABULATE is used to make summary data tables. Unlike PROC FREQ, it can handle multiple levels in rows and columns. You can use PROC TABULATE to create professional reports and publication ready tables. An abbreviated syntax for PROC TABULATE is as follows:

```
PROC TABULATE <options>;
CLASS variables < / options>;
VAR variables < / options>;
TABLE <page> ,
```

SAS® Essentials: Mastering SAS for Data Analytics, Second Edition. Alan C. Elliott and Wayne A. Woodward.
© 2016 John Wiley & Sons, Inc. Published 2016 by John Wiley & Sons, Inc.

```
<row> ,
column
< / options> ;
... other statements ... ;
RUN;
```

Table 19.1 lists commonly used options for PROC TABULATE. Moreover, Table 19.2 lists useful statements for PROC TABULATE.

The basic building blocks for PROC TABULATE are the TABLE, CLASS, and VAR statements:

The TABLE Statement: This statement is the most important component in PROC TABULATE. It is used to define what information will be displayed in the table. For example, this simple PROC TABULATE statement defines a class variable (GP) and a table.

```
PROC TABULATE DATA=sasdataset;
  CLASS GP;
  TABLE GP;
RUN;
```

The CLASS Statement: This statement identifies a categorical variable to be used in a table. You must identify the variables you are going to use before you use them in a TABLE statement. The TABLE statement above tells the procedure to create a table using the GP variable. For example,

TABLE 19.1   Common Options for PROC TABULATE

Option	Explanation
DATA=*dataname*	Specifies which data set to use
OUT=*dataname*	Specifies an output data set
STYLE=*styletype*	Specifies an ODS style format for the table
FORMAT=	Specifies a default overall format for each cell, Best 12.2 is the default
ORDER=*option*	Specifies order that categories are displayed. Options are UNFORMATTED, DATA, FORMATTED, and FREQ
MISSING	Specifies that missing values are to be treated as a category

TABLE 19.2   Common Statements in PROC TABULATE

Statements	Explanation
VAR *variables*;	Specifies which variables you will use to calculate statistics. Must be numeric
CLASS *variables*;	Specifies categorical variables
TABLE *specification*;	Identifies the dimensions and other components of the table to create
BY, FORMAT, LABEL, WHERE	These statements are common to most procedures and may be used here

```
CLASS VNAME1 VNAME2;
TABLE VNAME1, VNAME2;
```

Commas separate table dimensions. In the TABLE statement commas separate rows from columns. Therefore, the code creates a table, where the categories of VNAME1 define rows, and VNAME2 defines columns. An asterisk (*) crosses two variables, where categories of the second variable are expanded within the first one. Thus,

```
CLASS VNAME1 VNAME2 VNAME3;
TABLE VNAME1, VNAME2*VNAME3;
```

creates a table where the categories of VAR1 define rows, VAR2 defines columns, and VAR3 defines columns within the categories of VAR2.

The VAR Statement: The VAR statement identifies quantitative (numeric) data. This variable may be used to indicate summary statistics in table cells, such as means, sums, or medians. For example,

```
CLASS VNAME1 VNAME2;
VAR OBS;
TABLE VNAME1, VNAME2*MEAN*OBS;
```

The MEAN*OBS addition to this code tells the procedure to place the mean of OBS, broken down by VNAME1 and VNAME2 variables, in each cell. These building blocks for PROC TABULATE are illustrated in a series of upcoming Hand-on Examples.

Before doing the upcoming exercises, it is helpful to know something about the data set that will be used, MYSASLIB.REGION. To see the first few records of this SAS® data set, run the following PROC PRINT code.

```
PROC PRINT DATA=MYSASLIB.REGION (FIRSTOBS=1 OBS=20); RUN;
```

The results are given in Table 19.3. Note that there are several categorical variables and one quantitative variable (SALES_K).

TABLE 19.3 The Regions Data Set

Obs	REGION	AREA	SITE	TYPE	MONTH	SALES_K
1	1	N	DOWNSTAIRS	KIOSK	NOV	33
2	1	N	DOWNSTAIRS	STORE	NOV	57
3	1	N	DOWNSTAIRS	STORE	NOV	41
4	1	S	DOWNSTAIRS	STORE	NOV	66
5	1	S	UPSTAIRS	STORE	NOV	72
6	1	S	DOWNSTAIRS	KIOSK	NOV	33
7	1	S	UPSTAIRS	KIOSK	NOV	34
8	1	E	DOWNSTAIRS	KIOSK	NOV	31
9	1	E	DOWNSTAIRS	STORE	NOV	49
10	1	W	UPSTAIRS	KIOSK	NOV	40

(continued)

TABLE 19.3   *(Continued)*

Obs	REGION	AREA	SITE	TYPE	MONTH	SALES_K
11	1	W	UPSTAIRS	STORE	NOV	47
12	1	W	UPSTAIRS	STORE	NOV	73
13	1	N	UPSTAIRS	KIOSK	NOV	35
14	1	N	DOWNSTAIRS	STORE	NOV	43
15	1	N	UPSTAIRS	KIOSK	NOV	26
16	1	S	DOWNSTAIRS	KIOSK	NOV	40
17	1	S	DOWNSTAIRS	STORE	NOV	61
18	1	S	UPSTAIRS	KIOSK	NOV	32
19	1	E	UPSTAIRS	STORE	NOV	52
20	1	E	DOWNSTAIRS	KIOSK	NOV	26

HANDS-ON EXAMPLE

1. Open the program file ATAB1.SAS. Observe that the variable TYPE is identified as a categorical variable (CLASS), and that a table is constructed using that variable. As TYPE has two categories, we expect the table to consist of two cells, each with a count (N) that represents the number of items for that group. Submit the code and observe the output given in Table 19.4.

```
PROC TABULATE DATA=MYSASLIB.REGION;
  CLASS TYPE;
  TABLE TYPE;
RUN;
```

TABLE 19.4   Simple PROC TABULATE Table

TYPE	
KIOSK	STORE
N	N
27	45

2. Add another variable by modifying the CLASS and TABLE statements:

```
CLASS TYPE AREA;
TABLE TYPE*AREA;
```

where AREA values are the compass points N, S, E, and W. Submit this code and observe the results given in Table 19.5. Note that the first variable TYPE appears as the top categories for the table followed by the next division specified by the AREA variable.

TABLE 19.5   PROC TABULATE Table Using Two Variables

TYPE							
KIOSK				STORE			
AREA				AREA			
E	N	S	W	E	N	S	W
N	N	N	N	N	N	N	N
9	5	8	5	9	17	8	11

3. Switch the variables in the TABLE statement so the statement reads

```
CLASS TYPE AREA;
TABLE AREA*TYPE;
```

   Submit this code and observe the results. Note that this time AREA is the top (first) variable with TYPE below.

4. Add a third variable to the class statement (SITE) and to the TABLE statement, so they read

```
CLASS TYPE AREA SITE;
TABLE SITE*AREA*TYPE;
```

   where site takes on the values "Upstairs" and "Downstairs."

   Submit this code and observe the results in Table 19.6. Note that another layer is added to the table (and the table is very busy and hard to read).

TABLE 19.6   A PROC TABULATE Table with Rows and Columns

	AREA							
	E		N		S		W	
	TYPE		TYPE		TYPE		TYPE	
	KIOSK	STORE	KIOSK	STORE	KIOSK	STORE	KIOSK	STORE
	N	N	N	N	N	N	N	N
SITE								
DOWNSTAIRS	5	5	2	9	3	2	1	3
UPSTAIRS	4	4	3	8	5	6	4	8

5. Change the TABLE statement to the following. Note that the difference is in the comma between SITE and AREA (instead of an asterisk (*)).

(continued)

(continued)

```
CLASS TYPE AREA SITE;
TABLE SITE,AREA*TYPE;
```

Submit this code and observe the results. Note what the comma did. A comma separates row dimensions from column dimensions. In this case, `SITE` defines a row and `AREA*TYPE` defines columns.

Adding Labels and Formats to Variables: A label can be added to any variable by using an equal sign (=) followed by a quoted string. For example,

```
TABLE SITE="Store Site", AREA="Area"*TYPE="Type Store";
```

If you also want to format variables, you can create a format definition for N, S, E, and W using

```
PROC FORMAT;
VALUE $FMTCOMPASS "N"="1.North" "S"="2.South" "E"="3.East"
"W"="4.West";
RUN;
```

Note that you have indicated the order in which you want the compass points to appear. Using the format plus an `ORDER=` statement will make the category labels appear in the preferred order as illustrated in the next example:

HANDS-ON EXAMPLE

1. Open the program file `ATAB2.SAS`. Observe how the format `$FMTCOMPASS` along with the `ORDER=FORMATTED` statement cause the `AREA`s to appear in a preferred order. Labels are also assigned to each of the variables in the table. Submit this code and observe the results given in Table 19.7.

```
PROC FORMAT;
VALUE $FMTCOMPASS "N"="1.North" "S"="2.South" "E"="3.East"
"W"="4.West";
RUN;
PROC TABULATE DATA=MYSASLIB.REGION ORDER=FORMATTED;
  CLASS TYPE AREA SITE;
  TABLE SITE="Store Site", AREA="Area"*TYPE="Type Store";
  FORMAT AREA $FMTCOMPASS.;
RUN;
```

2. Take away the `ORDER=FORMATTED` statement and rerun the code. Note the order in which the `AREA` categories appear – in alphabetic order according to original values E N S W.

TABLE 19.7   A PROC TABULATE Table with Labels and Formats

	Area							
	1.North		2.South		3.East		4.West	
	Type Store		Type Store		Type Store		Type Store	
	KIOSK	STORE	KIOSK	STORE	KIOSK	STORE	KIOSK	STORE
	N	N	N	N	N	N	N	N
Store Site								
DOWNSTAIRS	2	9	3	2	5	5	1	3
UPSTAIRS	3	8	5	6	4	4	4	8

Reporting SUMS and MEANS: Currently, the table shows the number of stores for each breakdown of Area, Type Store, and Store Site. The data set also includes sales figures (SALES_K) in thousands. To report the total sales, indicate the variable to sum using a VAR statement and cross that value with a category variable in the TABLES statement. For example,

```
VAR SALES_K;
TABLE SITE="Store Site", AREA="Area"*TYPE="Type Store"*SALES_K;
SUM is the default statistic calculated for this
method, but you can request other statistics. For example to
request the mean of SALES_K, change the statement to
VAR SALES_K;
TABLE SITE="Store Site", AREA="Area"*TYPE="Type Store"
*SALES_K*MEAN;
```

Statistics you can request are listed in Table 19.8.

TABLE 19.8   Statistics Available in PROC Tabulate

PCTSUM	NMISS	P5
COLPCTSUM	SUM	P10
MAX	PAGEPCTSUM	P99
ROWPCTN	PCTN	Q1 | P25
MEAN	VAR	QRANGE
ROWPCTSUM	MEDIAN | P50	P5
MIN	P1	PROBT
STDDEV / STD	Q3 | P75	T
N	P90	
STDERR	P95	

HANDS-ON EXAMPLE

1. Open the program file ATAB3.SAS. Note the new VAR SALES_K statement to define the numeric variable, and how it is crossed with the TYPE variable in the TABLE statement. Submit this code and observe the results given in Table 19.9. Note the value for Downstairs, North, Kiosk is 63, meaning that the sum of sales for that cell is $63,000.

```
PROC FORMAT;
VALUE $FMTCOMPASS "N"="1.North" "S"="2.South" "E"="3.East"
"W"="4.West";
RUN;
PROC TABULATE DATA=MYSASLIB.REGION ORDER=FORMATTED;
  CLASS TYPE AREA SITE;
  VAR SALES_K;
  TABLE SITE="Store Site",
    AREA="Area"*
    TYPE="Type Store"*
    SALES_K;
  FORMAT AREA $FMTCOMPASS.;
RUN;
```

TABLE 19.9   A PROC TABULATE Table with Sum

	Area							
	1.North		2.South		3.East		4.West	
	Type Store		Type Store		Type Store		Type Store	
	KIOSK	STORE	KIOSK	STORE	KIOSK	STORE	KIOSK	STORE
	SALES_K	SALES_K	SALES_K	SALES_K	SALES_K	SALES_K	SALES_K	SALES_K
	Sum	Sum	Sum	Sum	Sum	Sum	Sum	Sum
Store Site								
DOWNSTAIRS	63.00	495.00	110.00	127.00	139.00	256.00	32.00	211.00
UPSTAIRS	93.00	436.00	173.00	374.00	123.00	205.00	139.00	445.00

2. Provide a label for sales by using SALES_K="Mean Sales $1000" in the Table Statement. Suppose you're interested in average sales per store. Change the TABLE statement to

```
    TABLE SITE="Store Site",
        AREA="Area"*
        TYPE="Type Store"*
        MEAN="Mean Sales $1000"*SALES_K;
```

Resubmit the code and observe the results.

3. To add a format to a numeric value, use F=format. For example, `MEAN="Sales $1000"*SALES_K *F=DOLLAR6.2`. Change the `TABLE` statement to

```
TABLE SITE="Store Site",
     AREA="Area"*
     TYPE="Type Store"*
     MEAN="Mean Sales $1000"*SALES_K*F=DOLLAR6.2;
```

Resubmit the code. The results are shown in Table 19.10. The dollar values now include a dollar sign because of the format.

TABLE 19.10   A PROC TABULATE Table with Means

	Area							
	1.North		2.South		3.East		4.West	
	Type Store		Type Store		Type Store		Type Store	
	KIOSK	STORE	KIOSK	STORE	KIOSK	STORE	KIOSK	STORE
	Mean Sales $1000	Mean Sales $1000	Mean Sales $1000	Mean Sales $1000	Mean Sales $1000	Mean Sales $1000	Mean Sales $1000	Mean Sales $1000
	SALES_K	SALES_K	SALES_K	SALES_K	SALES_K	SALES_K	SALES_K	SALES_K
Store Site								
DOWNSTAIRS	$31.50	$55.00	$36.67	$63.50	$27.80	$51.20	$32.00	$70.33
UPSTAIRS	$31.00	$54.50	$34.60	$62.33	$30.75	$51.25	$34.75	$55.63

Dress up the Table: As seen in the previous example, you can dress up a value using a label, a statistic, and a format. For example,

```
*MEAN="Mean Sales $1000"*SALES_K*F=DOLLAR6.2;
```

Here is a breakdown of these components:
1. `*MEAN` - Report the Mean statistic
2. `="Mean Sales $1000"` – Apply a label
3. `*SALES_K` – Variable to use (must be in the `VAR` Statement)
4. `*F=DOLLAR6.2` – Apply a format

The table as created still looks busy and has unneeded information such as the actual names of the variables. For example, there are six lines of labels before the actual numbers in Table 19.10. To get rid of unwanted labels, change the labels in the `TABLE` statement to two quotation marks ("") as in `MEAN=""` . Add the same kind of label to `SALES_K`. The revised `TABLE` statement is

```
TABLE SITE="",
     AREA=""*
     TYPE=""*
     MEAN="Mean Sales $1000"*SALES_K=""*F=DOLLAR6.2;
```

Moreover, we want to add new cells that reflect averages by SITE and by AREA. To add these cells, we use the ALL keyword. For example, we replace AREA with

```
(AREA ALL)
```

Or if we don't want the label used for AREA, we'd use

```
(AREA="" ALL)
```

HANDS-ON EXAMPLE

1. Open the program file ATAB4.SAS. The TABULATE portion of this code is as follows. Note that most variable labels have been replaced with "" and that a request for ALL means has been added to AREA. Submit this code and observe the results in Table 19.11.

1.
```
PROC TABULATE DATA=MYSASLIB.REGION ORDER=FORMATTED;
   CLASS TYPE AREA SITE;
   VAR SALES_K;
   TABLE SITE="",
      AREA=""*
      TYPE=""*
      MEAN="Mean Sales $1000"*SALES_K=""*F=DOLLAR6.2;
   FORMAT AREA $FMTCOMPASS.;
RUN;
```

Note the "All" columns at the right of the table. These are the overall means by store type. Also the blank labels eliminated some of the labels and made the table less busy.

2. Flip the table by exchanging the SITE and AREA variables.

```
TABLE(AREA="" ALL),
   SITE=""*
   TYPE=""*
   MEAN="Sales $1000"*SALES_K*F=DOLLAR6.2;
```

Resubmit the code and note the changes. If you want to print the output in portrait orientation, this version would fit better.

3. Change SALES_K to a blank label with SALES_K="" and change the SITE variables to include means by group (SITE="" ALL).

```
TABLE(AREA="" ALL),
   (SITE="" ALL)*
   TYPE=""*
   MEAN="Sales $1000"*SALES_K=""*F=DOLLAR6.2;
```

Resubmit the code and note the differences.

TABLE 19.11   A PROC TABULATE with ALL

	1.North		2.South		3.East		4.West		All	
	KIOSK	STORE	KIOSK	STORE	KIOSK	STORE	KIOSK	STORE	KIOSK	STORE
	Sales $1000	Sales $1000	Sales $1000	Sales $1000	Sales $1000	Sales $1000	Sales $1000	Sales $1000	Sales $1000	Sales $1000
DOWNSTAIRS	$31.50	$55.00	$36.67	$63.50	$27.80	$51.20	$32.00	$70.33	$31.27	$57.32
UPSTAIRS	$31.00	$54.50	$34.60	$62.33	$30.75	$51.25	$34.75	$55.63	$33.00	$56.15

Enhancing Your Table: It is fairly easy to add information to your table. For example, suppose you want to report more than one statistic, say N and MEAN. You can combine statistics by placing them in parentheses such as

```
(N MEAN)
```

Or to eliminate the label being put into the table, you could use

```
(N="" MEAN="")
```

Another enhancement is to put some information in the box that appears at the upper left of your table. You can do this by including a /BOX= "label" option. For example,

```
TABLE(AREA="" ALL="By Area"),(SITE="" ALL="By Site")*TYPE=""
        *(N="" MEAN="")*SALES_K=""*F=DOLLAR6.2
    / BOX="Fall Sales";
```

HANDS-ON EXAMPLE

1. Open the program file ATAB5.SAS. Submit this code and see that it contains all of the options discussed so far.

```
PROC TABULATE DATA=MYSASLIB.REGION ORDER=FORMATTED;
  CLASS TYPE AREA SITE;
  VAR SALES_K;
  TABLE(AREA="" ALL),(SITE="" ALL)*TYPE=""
        *MEAN=""*SALES_K=""*F=DOLLAR6.2;
  FORMAT AREA $FMTCOMPASS.;
RUN;
```

2. Add the N statistic to the table by changing the MEAN="" statement to (N=""
   MEAN=""). Submit the code. Observe how both the count and mean are now
   reported.

3. Put a text in the upper-left box by adding the code

```
/ BOX="Fall Sales";
```

Make sure the code is within the semicolon of the TABLE statement. Submit the code. Observe how the text appears in the box.

4. To save the table as a Word document using ODS, add the following lines. Before the TABULATE statement add the line

```
ODS RTF STYLE=BANKER;
    Your PROC TABULATE;
RUN;
ODS RTF CLOSE;
```

Resubmit the code. The final table with these changes is given in Table 19.12.

TABLE 19.12   A PROC TABULATE with ALL

| Fall Sales | DOWNSTAIRS | | UPSTAIRS | | All | |
	KIOSK	STORE	KIOSK	STORE	KIOSK	STORE
1.North	2.00 / 31.50	9.00 / 55.00	3.00 / 31.00	8.00 / 54.50	5.00 / 31.20	17.00 / 54.76
2.South	3.00 / 36.67	2.00 / 63.50	5.00 / 34.60	6.00 / 62.33	8.00 / 35.38	8.00 / 62.63
3.East	5.00 / 27.80	5.00 / 51.20	4.00 / 30.75	4.00 / 51.25	9.00 / 29.11	9.00 / 51.22
4.West	1.00 / 32.00	3.00 / 70.33	4.00 / 34.75	8.00 / 55.63	5.00 / 34.20	11.00 / 59.64
All	11.00 / 31.27	19.00 / 57.32	16.00 / 33.00	26.00 / 56.15	27.00 / 32.30	45.00 / 56.64

Saving Your Table in Excel: Once you create a table using PROC TABULATE, you may want to save it in an Excel format. As in the case of saving it to Word (RTF), you use an ODS procedure. The process is to open the Excel file using an ODS statement such as

```
ODS TAGSETS.EXCELXP BODY='C:SASDATA\TABLE.XLS';
      Your  PROC TABULATE code;
      RUN;
ODS TAGSETS.EXCELXP CLOSE;
```

HANDS-ON EXAMPLE

(For this example, you must have Microsoft Excel installed on your computer to complete the example.)

1. Open the program file ATAB6.SAS. A portion of the code is shown here. Note the ODS statement before and after PROC TABULATE. Note the name of the file to be saved as the BODY= statement. If necessary, change the Windows patch to match an available folder on your computer. Submit the code.

```
ODS TAGSETS.EXCELXP
BODY='C:\SASDATA\TABLE.XLS';
PROC TABULATE DATA=MYSASLIB.REGION ORDER=FORMATTED;
   CLASS TYPE AREA SITE;
   VAR SALES_K;
TABLE(AREA="" ALL="By Area"),(SITE="" ALL="By Site")*TYPE=""
       *(N="" MEAN="")*SALES_K=""*F=6.2
   / BOX="Fall Sales";
   FORMAT AREA $FMTCOMPASS.;
RUN;
ODS TAGSETS.EXCELXP CLOSE;
```

   The results of submitting this code are a series of XML commands in the Results Viewer that begin with a line such as

(continued)

(continued)

```
<?xml version="1.0" encoding="windows-1252" ?>
```

This is the code (created by the SAS procedure) that copied the information to an Excel file. (You don't need to learn or understand this code.) To see the Excel file created by this program, begin Excel and open the file as you have named it. In this case, the resulting file (in Excel) is given in Table 19.13.

TABLE 19.13   A PROC TABULATE as Output to Excel

	A	B	C	D	E	F	G	H	I	J	K	L	M
			DOWNSTAIRS				UPSTAIRS				By Site		
2	Fall Sales	KIOSK		STORE		KIOSK		STORE		KIOSK		STORE	
3	1.North	2	31.5	9	55	3	31	8	54.5	5	31.2	17	54.76
4	2.South	3	36.67	2	63.5	5	34.6	6	62.33	8	35.38	8	62.63
5	3.East	5	27.8	5	51.2	4	30.75	4	51.25	9	29.11	9	51.22
6	4.West	1	32	3	70.33	4	34.75	8	55.63	5	34.2	11	59.64
7	By Area	11	31.27	19	57.32	16	33	26	56.15	27	32.3	45	56.64

We have just scratched the surface regarding the features of PROC TABULATE. Experiment with some of the other statements to see how they can be used to enhance your tabled report even more.

19.2   USING PROC REPORT

PROC REPORT is a procedure in SAS that allows you to create professional data reports and summaries. It is widely used in companies and organizations that need to produce reports on topics such as income, contributions, services rendered, sales, and so on. These reports are highly customizable using the many varied options within PROC REPORT. Although only a few of these options are illustrated here, these examples will help you learn how to use the basics of PROC REPORT.

The syntax for PROC REPORT is a little different from most statistical procedures because it has a particular emphasis on defining the columns of the report. Here is a simplified syntax for PROC REPORT:

```
PROC REPORT DATA= sasdataset <options>;
   COLUMN variables and specifications;
   DEFINE column / attributes;
   COMPUTE column; compute statements; ENDCOMP;
RUN;
```

COLUMN: The COLUMN statement is used to identify variables of interest to be reported in columns and to specify headers and groups. Every column you want to display in the table must be indicated in the COLUMN statement. A simple report would be

```
PROC REPORT DATA=MYSASLIB.CARS NOFS;
COLUMN BRAND CITYMPG HWYMPG;
RUN;
```

TABLE 19.14   PROC REPORT DEFINE Statement Options

Name	Purpose
DISPLAY	Displays the indicated variable in the column. This is the default `DEFINE SBP/DISPLAY;`
ORDER	Sorts data and forms groups
GROUP	Group (consolidate) observations using the specified variable. For example, `DEFINE BRAND/GROUP;` Displays records grouped by BRAND
ANALYSIS	Defines a variable used to calculate a statistic within the cell of a report
COMPUTE and ENDCOMP	Begins and ends a code segments that calculates a data value
ACROSS	Creates groups across page rather than down the page

TABLE 19.15   PROC REPORT DEFINE Statement Option Attributes

Attributes	Example
FORMAT = format	Example FORMAT=6.1
'LABEL'	Example 'Model Type' Or 'Model/Type' to split title
STATISTICNAME	Any statistic that is available in PROC MEANS. For example, N, MEAN, SUM, or STD
ORDER=ordertype	(DATA, FORMATTED, FREQ, or INTERNAL) same as in PROC FREQ. Use DESCENDING option to reverse normal ascending order

which is about the same as a PROC PRINT. To enhance the report requires a DEFINE statement.

DEFINE: The DEFINE statement is used to specify the appearance of the columns. Its syntax is

```
DEFINE report-item / <option(s)>;
```

DEFINE statements allow you to specify attributes that determine how a variable in a column will be displayed. Options for the DEFINE statement follow a slash (/). These options control the appearance of the information in a column. They can be of several types including

- options that describe how to use a variable;
- options that control column headings;
- options that customize a report item;
- other options for a report item.

The options include DISPLAY, GROUP, ANALYSIS, COMPUTED, ORDER, and ACROSS. Table 19.14 includes explanations of each of these options.

Some common attributes you can include with the DEFINE options are listed in Table 19.15. These appear after the slash and statement option named in a DEFINE statement. For example,

```
DEFINE var/DISPLAY statement options;
```

or a more specific example:

```
DEFINE AGE/DISPLAY 'A Label' FORMAT=6.1;
```

Just as the split character / in a label indicates to go to the next line, so the label "Model/Type" is displayed on two lines. Note in the Label example, the default split character is a slash (/). However, it can be defined as a different character in the PROC REPORT statement. For example, SPLIT='*' makes the asterisk the split character. The following Hands-on Examples illustrate several uses of the DEFINE option.

DISPLAY OPTION: The DEFINE var/DISPLAY option in the DEFINE statement allows you to specify attributes for that variable including format and labels. This is illustrated in the following example.

HANDS-ON EXAMPLE

1. Open the program file AREPORT1.SAS.

```
PROC REPORT DATA=MYSASLIB.CARS NOFS;
   COLUMN BRAND MODEL CITYMPG HWYMPG;
   DEFINE CITYMPG/DISPLAY FORMAT=6.1 'CITY/MPG';
RUN;
```

In this instance, CITYMPG is displayed using a 6.1 format and with a column label CITY MGP on two lines. (The NOFS option turns off an older option that is rarely used nowadays. We do not discuss it here.) Submit this code and observe the output given (partially) in Table 19.16. Note how the CITYMPG column label is split, and the numbers are in a 6.1 format.

TABLE 19.16   PROC REPORT DISPLAY Option Example

Brand	Model	CITY MPG	HwyMPG
TOYOTA	Prius	60.0	51
HONDA	Civic Hybrid	48.0	47
HONDA	Civic Hybrid	47.0	48
HONDA	Civic Hybrid	46.0	51
HONDA	Civic Hybrid	45.0	51

2. Create a DISPLAY statement that creates a column for HWYMPG using the 6.1 format and with an appropriate label. Resubmit and observe changes.
3. Add another variable, ENGINESIZE, to the COLUMN statement and create a similar DISPLAY statement for it. Resubmit and observe the changes.

ORDER OPTION: The DEFINE *var* / ORDER option defines a column variable used to sort the data. You can control the ORDER by adding DESCENDING to reverse the order and use an additional ORDER= to specify FORMATTED (default), FREQ, INTERNAL, or DATA order. The following Hands-on Example illustrates this ORDER option.

HANDS-ON EXAMPLE

1. Open the program file AREPORT2.SAS.

```
TITLE "ORDER OPTION EXAMPLE";
PROC REPORT DATA=MYSASLIB.CARS NOFS;
  COLUMN BRAND CITYMPG HWYMPG;
  DEFINE BRAND/ORDER 'BRAND';
  DEFINE CITYMPG/DISPLAY FORMAT=6.1 'CITY MPG';
  DEFINE HWYMPG/DISPLAY FORMAT=6.1 'HIGHWAY MPG';
RUN;
```

In this example, the BRAND/ORDER option in the DEFINE statement causes the report to be ordered by car brand. The other DEFINE statements are similar to the previous example. Submit this code and observe the (partial) output given in Table 19.17.

TABLE 19.17   PROC REPORT Using ORDER Option

Brand	City MPG	Highway MPG
ACURA	27.0	34.0
	25.0	34.0
	23.0	31.0
	22.0	31.0
	21.0	30.0
	20.0	29.0
	20.0	29.0
	18.0	26.0
	17.0	23.0
	17.0	24.0
	17.0	24.0
AUDI	24.0	32.0
	23.0	29.0
	23.0	34.0

(continued)

(continued)

2. Change the order direction by putting DESCENDING after BRAND/ORDER. Rerun and verify that now VOLVO appears as the first brand in the report.
3. Replace the DESCENDING with ORDER=DATA so that it reads

```
DEFINE BRAND/ORDER ORDER=DATA 'Brand'
```

which puts it in the order the brands appear in the data set. Rerun and verify that now TOYOTA (which is the first brand in the data set) appears as the first brand in the report.
4. Add the variable CYLINDER after BRAND in the COLUMN statement so that it reads

```
COLUMN BRAND CYLINDERS CITYMPG HWYMPG;
```

After the BRAND/ORDER statement add a new statement

```
DEFINE CYLINDERS /ORDER 'Cylinders';
```

to specify that you want to sort by number of cylinders within BRAND. Resubmit the code to verify that your changes produced the desired results. The output should show Toyota four cylinder cars first, then six cylinder cars, then Honda, and so on. (The CYLINDERS column only lists the new number of cylinders the first time, and the column for the remaining cars with that cylinder count is blank until the next new cylinder count appears.)
5. Remove the =DATA option from the ORDER (for BRAND) statement, rerun, and now the order for brand returns to start with ACURA.

GROUP OPTION: The DEFINE *var*/GROUP option causes the table to be grouped by the specified variable. Here is an example using the GROUP option. This DEFINE GROUP option is illustrated in the following Hands-on Example.

HANDS-ON EXAMPLE

1. Open the program file AREPORT3.SAS.

```
PROC REPORT DATA=MYSASLIB.CARS NOFS;
  COLUMN BRAND (CITYMPG HWYMPG), MEAN;
  DEFINE BRAND/GROUP;
  DEFINE CITYMPG/DISPLAY FORMAT=6.1 'CITY MPG';
RUN;
```

The GROUP option causes the values to be grouped by BRAND. Note that the MEAN statistic is applied to both variables listed in the parentheses. And the format 6.1 is applied to both CITYMPG and HWYMPG because they are grouped within the parentheses. Submit this code and observe the output given (partially) in Table 19.18.

Observe that by using the GROUP option all of the ACURA cars are combined and reported as the mean miles per gallon. If the MEAN option had not been used, the default statistic is SUM.

TABLE 19.18   PROC REPORT by GROUP

Brand	City MGP MEAN	HwyMPG MEAN
ACURA	20.6	28.6
AUDI	19.1	26.7
BMW	18.2	26.2
BUICK	18.0	25.1
CADILLAC	15.7	22.3

2. Redo the COLUMN statement to read

```
COLUMN BRAND CITYMPG,MEAN HWYMPG,MEAN;
```

Resubmit the code and note that the mean for HWYMPG is no longer using the 6.1 format.

3. Write a new DEFINE (with DISPLAY) statement that puts HWYMPG into a 6.1 format, and define an appropriate label for the column.

```
DEFINE HWYMPG/DISPLAY FORMAT=6.1 'Highway MPG';
```

Resubmit the code to verify that your changes produced the expected results.

4. Change BRAND to CYLINDERS in both the COLUMN and DEFINE statements. Rerun and verify that the report is now grouped by number of CYLINDERS. (−1 means a rotary engine).

5. Add the variable N in the COLUMN statement after CYLINDERS and add the option ORDER=FREQ to the DEFINE statement after GROUP.

```
COLUMN CYLINDERS N CITYMPG,MEAN HWYMPG,MEAN;
DEFINE CYLINDERS/GROUP ORDER=FREQ;
```

Rerun the code. The order of the groups should now be in the order or smallest N per group to largest.

ANALYSIS OPTION: The DEFINE *var*/ANALYSIS option allows you to display a statistic for a specified column. This is illustrated in the next Hands-on Example.

HANDS-ON EXAMPLE

1. Open the program file AREPORT4.SAS.

```
PROC REPORT DATA=MYSASLIB.CARS NOFS;
   COLUMN BRAND CITYMPG HWYMPG;
   DEFINE BRAND/GROUP;
   DEFINE CITYMPG/ANALYSIS MEAN FORMAT=6.1 'CITY/MPG';
RUN;
```

Instead of defining MEAN in the COLUMN statement, the ANALYSIS option allows you to indicate MEAN for the CITYMPG variable in a DEFINE statement. (The default is SUM.) (You can leave off the ANALYSIS option in the DEFINE statement and it will still work.) Submit this code and observe the output given (partially) in Table 19.19. Note that the mean is reported for CITYMPG, but the SUM is reported for HWYMPG.

2. Create a DEFINE statement (with ANALYSIS) that causes the mean HWYMPG to be displayed with a 6.1 format and with an appropriate label. Resubmit the code to verify that your changes produced the expected results.

TABLE 19.19   PROC REPORT Using ANALYSIS Option

Brand	City MGP	HwyMPG
ACURA	20.6	315
AUDI	19.1	1094
BMW	18.2	1517
BUICK	18.0	401
CADILLAC	15.7	514

3. Add the ENGINESIZE variable as the last variable in the COLUMN statement and write a DEFINE statement (with ANALYSIS) that displays mean engine size with a 6.1 format and with an appropriate label.

```
DEFINE ENGINESIZE/ANALYSIS FORMAT=6.1 'Engine Size';
```

Resubmit the code to verify that your changes produced the expected results.

COMPUTE OPTION: The COMPUTE and ENDCOMP statements begin and end a segment of SAS code that allows you to calculate values of new variables. The following Hands-on Example illustrates the COMPUTE option.

HANDS-ON EXAMPLE

1. Open the program file AREPORT5.SAS.

```
TITLE "ORDER OPTION EXAMPLE";
PROC REPORT DATA=MYSASLIB.CARS NOFS SPLIT="~";
   COLUMN BRAND CITYMPG, MEAN HWYMPG, MEAN RATIO_MPG;
   DEFINE BRAND/ORDER;
   DEFINE BRAND/GROUP;
   DEFINE CITYMPG/DISPLAY FORMAT=6.1 'CITY MPG';
   DEFINE HWYMPG/DISPLAY FORMAT=6.1 'HIGHWAY MPG';
   DEFINE RATIO_MPG/COMPUTED FORMAT=6.2 'Ratio~CITY/HWY';
   COMPUTE RATIO_MPG;
      RATIO_MPG=_C2_/_C3_;
   ENDCOMP;
RUN;
```

Note the COMPUTE statement, the calculation that follows, and the ending END-COMP statement. In order to use the COMPUTE statement to create a new variable, you also need to

- specify the new variable name in the COLUMN statement,
- include a DEFINE statement with the /COMPUTED option to define the new variable, and
- put the actual computation between COMPUTE and ENDCOMP statements.

The way you calculate variables between COMPUTE and ENDCOMP is the same as you would use in a DATA step. To name variables used for computing, you must refer to the variables by which column they represent as _C2_ (CITYMPG) for the column 2 variable and _C3_ (HWYMPG) for the column 3 variable. The output for this example is given in Table 19.20.

Also note in this example that a SPLIT character is defined in the PROC REPORT statement (SPLIT="~"), so the label for the ratio can be defined as 'Ratio~CITY/HWY', which is split with RATIO on one line and CITY/HWY on the other line of the label in the output. Because the default split character is a slash, a new one had to be defined in order for this label to work correctly.

(continued)

(continued)

TABLE 19.20   PROC REPORT Using COMPUTE Option

	City MPG	Highway MPG	
Brand	MEAN	MEAN	Ratio CITY/HWY
ACURA	20.6	28.6	0.72
AUDI	19.1	26.7	0.71
BMW	18.2	26.2	0.70
BUICK	18.0	25.1	0.72
CADILLAC	15.7	22.3	0.70
CHEVROLET	17.8	23.7	0.75
CHRYSLER	19.5	26.5	0.74

2. Create a new column named City Engine Ratio based on the calculation `CITYMPG/ENGINESIZE`. Resubmit your code to verify that your new column appears correctly.

ACROSS OPTION: The `DEFINE` *var*/`ACROSS` option allows you to create a column for each unique item for a categorical variable. The following Hands-on Example illustrates the `ACROSS` option.

HANDS-ON EXAMPLE

1. Open the program file `AREPORT6.SAS`.

```
PROC FORMAT;
VALUE FMTSUV 0="NOT SUV" 1="SUV";
PROC REPORT DATA=MYSASLIB.CARS NOFS;
   COLUMN BRAND CITYMPG,SUV HWYMPG,SUV;
   DEFINE BRAND/ORDER;
   DEFINE BRAND/GROUP;
   DEFINE CITYMPG/ANALYSIS MEAN FORMAT=6.1;
   DEFINE HWYMPG/ANALYSIS MEAN FORMAT=6.1;
   DEFINE SUV/ ACROSS 'BY SUV';
   FORMAT SUV FMTSUV.;
RUN;
```

In this example, the `SUV` variable has values 0 and 1. To display the MPG variables by `SUV` or not, the `SUV` variable is listed with those two variables separated by a comma as in `CITYMPG,SUV`. The `SUV` variable is then defined as an `ACROSS` variable and given a label. For this example, a format is created for the `SUV` variable and applied to that variable within `PROC REPORT`. The results are given in Table 19.21.

Note how the mean MPG is listed across the table as defined by `SUV` or `NOT SUV` for each of the two MPG variables. (Some car brands do not have `SUV`s or have all `SUV`s, so there are some missing values in the table.)

TABLE 19.21   PROC REPORT Using the ACROSS Option

PROC REPORT ACROSS Example

	CityMPG		HwyMPG	
	BY SUV		BY SUV	
Brand	NOT SUV	SUV	NOT SUV	SUV
ACURA	21.0	17.0	29.2	23.0
AUDI	19.3	16.0	27.1	22.0
BMW	18.5	16.3	26.6	22.7
BUICK	19.1	16.9	27.4	22.8
CADILLAC	16.4	14.4	24.2	19.4
CHEVROLET	18.8	15.2	25.2	19.7

2. Create another column for ENGINESIZE were the sizes are listed across the table by SUV.
3. Change all of the SUV references to AUTOMATIC to compare MPG and ENGINE-SIZE for cars with and without automatic transmissions.

ADDITIONAL TECHNIQUES: Beyond the original six DEFINE statement options (options that appear after DEFINE *var/*), there are several other ways you can enhance the output of your report. The next two examples illustrate these additional techniques.

Reporting Multiple Statistics: In the COLUMN statement, you can request multiple statistics for a variable by placing a request in parenthesis. For example,

```
COLUMN BRAND CITYMPG,(N MEAN STD);
```

The following Hands-on Example illustrates this technique.

HANDS-ON EXAMPLE

1. Open the program file AREPORT7.SAS.

```
TITLE "PROC REPORT Multiple Statistics Example";
PROC REPORT DATA=MYSASLIB.CARS NOFS;
COLUMN BRAND CITYMPG,(N MEAN STD) HWYMPG ENGINESIZE ;
    DEFINE BRAND/GROUP;
    DEFINE CITYMPG/ FORMAT=6.1 'City MPG';
    DEFINE N / 'N' format=4.;
    DEFINE HWYMPG/ ANALYSIS MEAN FORMAT=6.1;
    DEFINE ENGINESIZE/ ANALYSIS MEAN FORMAT=6.1;
RUN;
```

(continued)

(continued)

Note the COLUMN statement where some statistics are listed with parentheses (N MEAN STD). Submit the code and observe the output given (partial) in Table 19.22. Note the N, MEAN, and STD in the CITYMPG column.

In particular, note the two DEFINE statements all related to CITYMPG. The first statement defined the label and format for CITYMPG. The FORMAT=6.1 applies to all of the statistics in the parentheses (N MEAN STD). However, the second DEFINE specifies a separate format for N, so it appears as an integer.

```
DEFINE CITYMPG/ FORMAT=6.1 'City MPG';
DEFINE N / 'N' format=4.;
```

TABLE 19.22   PROC REPORT with Means

PROC REPORT Multiple Statistics Example

Brand	City MPG			HwyMPG	Engine Size
	N	MEAN	STD		
ACURA	11	20.6	3.4	28.6	2.8
AUDI	41	19.1	2.7	26.7	2.9
BMW	58	18.2	1.8	26.2	3.2
BUICK	16	18.0	1.8	25.1	3.9
CADILLAC	23	15.7	1.6	22.3	4.5
CHEVROLET	95	17.8	3.6	23.7	4.0
CHRYSLER	37	19.5	2.2	26.5	3.3
DODGE	42	17.1	3.7	23.0	4.0

2. Create similar columns for HWYMPG and ENGINESIZE.

Reporting Totals and Subtotals: As in PROC PRINT, you may want to display totals at the bottom of a column of numbers. To do this in PROC REPORT, use the BREAK and RBREAK statements. The BREAK statement produces a summary at a specified break, and RBREAK specifies a summary at the beginning or end of a report. A simplified BREAK statement syntax is

```
BREAK <BEFORE|AFTER> var/SUMMARIZE <SUPPRESS>;
```

For the RBREAK statement, the syntax is

```
RBREAK < BEFORE|AFTER >/SUMMARIZE;
```

HANDS-ON EXAMPLE

1. Open the program file AREPORT8.SAS. This program lists cars by BRAND. Each BRAND is summarized by the number of cars by CYLINDERS. BREAK is used to count the number of cars that are automatic or are SUVs and RBREAK creates a grand total. Submit the code and observe the output given (partial) in Table 19.23.

TABLE 19.23   A Portion of the PROC REPORT Table with Means

PROC REPORT Subtotals

Brand	Cylinders	Automatic	SUV
ACURA	4	2	0
	6	4	1
		6	1
AUDI	4	9	0
	6	11	2
	8	6	1
	12	1	0
		27	3
	12	1	0
		30	2
VOLVO	5	21	3
	6	2	1
	8	1	1
		24	5
		753	279

```
PROC REPORT DATA=MYSASLIB.CARS NOFS;
COLUMN BRAND CYLINDERS AUTOMATIC SUV;
  DEFINE BRAND/GROUP;
  DEFINE CYLINDERS/GROUP;
  BREAK AFTER BRAND/SUMMARIZE SUPPRESS;
  RBREAK AFTER/ SUMMARIZE;
  WHERE CYLINDERS NE -1 ;
RUN;
```

Note the subtotals after the ACURA 6 cylinder line and the grand total after the VOLVO subtotal.

(continued)

(continued)

2. To see what the SUPPRESS option does in the BREAK statement, delete SUPPRESS and rerun the code. Observe that without SUPPRESS, the name of the BRAND is repeated on the subtotal line.

19.2.1   Writing Reports in a Data Statement

Another way to create reports from a SAS data set is to use the PUT statement within a DATA step. Typically, this is done using the following technique:

1. Specify the name _NULL_ as the data set name in a DATA step in order to be able to use the features of the DATA step without creating a SAS data set as output. (Because you are interested in creating a report rather than creating a SAS data set.)
2. Define a destination (output file) for the report using a FILE statement. The statement FILE PRINT sends the report output to the SAS Results Viewer. When you use FILE "file-specification," the report output is sent to the specified text file location.
3. Use PUT statements within the DATA step to create lines of output for the report.

HANDS-ON EXAMPLE

The heart of a DATA statement report is the PUT statement. By default, a PUT statement displays information for each record in a data set in the SAS Log. For example, open the program file APUT_REPORT1.SAS.

```
DATA _NULL_; SET MYSASLIB.SOMEDATA;
     PUT AGE;
RUN;
```

This simple program lists the values of AGE for each record in the specified SAS data set. In this case, when no FILE option is used, the report output is sent to the SAS Log.

1. Run this program and observe the output in the log. Note that there are 50 lines of ages listed there.
2. You typically want to display the results of your report in the SAS Results Viewer or capture the results in a File. To display the output in the Results Viewer, include the statement FILE PRINT; in the code:

```
DATA _NULL_; SET MYSASLIB.SOMEDATA;
     FILE PRINT;
     PUT AGE;
RUN;
```

Rerun the code and observe the output. This time the values of AGE are displayed in the SAS Results Viewer.

3. To make the report more interesting, change the PUT statement to read

```
PUT "The Age for Subject " ID " is " AGE;
```

Run the revised code. This time, the following lines are displayed in the Results Viewer:

```
The Age for Subject 101  is 12
The Age for Subject 102  is 11
The Age for Subject 110  is 12
The Age for Subject 187  is 11
... and so on...
```

Note that text in quotes is output verbatim. However, a variable name in a PUT statement (that is not in quotes) causes the value for that variable for a particular record in the SAS data set to be listed.

4. Alternatively, you can specify an output file as the destination for the report. Change the FILE PRINT statement to

```
FILE "C:\SASDATA\OUTPUT.TXT";
```

Run the revised program. Go to Windows and look in the C:\SASDATA folder. Open the file named OUTPUT.TXT to verify that the report was written to that file.

There are a number of other ways to customize each line of output using the PUT statement. Table 19.24 lists common options for the PUT statement.

The upcoming example uses a small data set containing grades for a class. The goal is to create a summary report that includes a listing of grade, each student's grade average, and an average for the class. The data are the following, which are results of three tests.

```
Alice, Adams   88.4 91   79
Jones, Steve   99   100 88.4
Zabar,Fred     78.6 87   88.4
```

To make student's grades available for the report, AVE is calculated when the data set GRADES is created using the following code:

```
DATA GRADES;
INPUT NAME $15. G1 G2 G3;
AVE=MEAN(of G1-G3);
DATALINES;
Alice, Adams   88.4 91 79
Jones, Steve   99 100 88.4
Zabar,Fred     78.6 87 88.4
;
RUN;
```

Because we also want to include the class average in the report, PROC MEANS is used to calculate that value, using the following code:

```
PROC MEANS DATA=GRADES NOPRINT;OUTPUT OUT=GMEAN;RUN;
```

TABLE 19.24   Options for the PUT Statement

Option	Meaning
`'text'`	Information in quotes is output verbatim (unless macro variables are within the quotes). For example, `PUT 'Some Text';`
`Variablename(s)`	The value of a variable for each record in the data set is output where a variable name is included, not in quotes. For example, `PUT TIME1 TIME2 TIME3;`
`@n`, `@var`, or `@expression`	Moves the pointer to a specified column location. When using `@var` or `@expression`, they must be numeric. For example, `PUT @5 'Age =' AGE;`
`+n`, `+var`, or `+expression`	Moves the pointer to a relative location n columns to the right from its current location. When using `@var` or `@expression`, they must be numeric
`@`	Holds the output on the current output line. The default is to move to the next line of output
`var format.`	A format specification following a variable causes the variable to be displayed with the specified format. For example, `PUT AGE 5.1;` displays the value of `AGE` using a 5.1 format
`n*'char';`	Repeats a character n times. For example, `PUT 50*'-';` creates a dashed line 50 characters wide

TABLE 19.25   Results of PROC MEANS on the GRADE Data

Obs	_TYPE_	_FREQ_	_STAT_	G1	G2	G3	AVE
1	0	3	N	3.0000	3.000	3.0000	3.0000
2	0	3	MIN	78.6000	87.000	79.0000	84.6667
3	0	3	MAX	99.0000	100.000	88.4000	95.8000
4	0	3	MEAN	88.6667	92.667	85.2667	88.8667
5	0	3	STD	10.2026	6.658	5.4271	6.0491

The overall class mean is captured in the output SAS data set named GMEAN. The contents of this data set are given in Table 19.25. To display this table, go to the SAS Explorer, Work Library, and double-click on the table GMEAN to view this information in the VIEWTABLE.

Note that the class mean is 88.8667. It appears in the GMEAN data set on the line where the variable _STAT_ is "MEAN."

A final step before writing the report is to capture the overall average into a macro variable. This is accomplished with a CALL SYMPUT statement (see Appendix B) as shown here:

```
DATA _NULL_;SET GMEAN;
IF _STAT_="MEAN" THEN CALL SYMPUT('CLASSMEAN',ROUND(AVE,.01));
RUN;
```

In this case, DATA _NULL_ is used to create the macro variable named CLASSMEAN, which is assigned the value AVE from the data set GMEAN. The name _NULL_ was used because we did not need to create any SAS data set from the DATA step.

The report created using this information is illustrated in the following Hands-on Example:

HANDS-ON EXAMPLE

1. Open the program file APUT_REPORT.SAS. Examine the code. The preliminary calculations appear at the beginning of the code. Note the section of code that produces the report:

```
TITLE "Grade Report for Course 1234";
DATA _NULL_; SET GRADES END=EOF;
TABLEHEAD="SUMMARY OF GRADES";
FILE PRINT;
IF _N_ = 1 then DO; * PUT HEADER;
      L=5+(60-LENGTH(TABLEHEAD))/2; * CENTER HEAD;
      PUT @L TABLEHEAD;
      PUT @5 60*'=';
      PUT @5 "NAME" @20 "| TEST 1" @30 "| TEST 2 "
          @40 "| TEST 3" @50 "| AVERAGE";
      PUT @5 60*'-';
END;
PUT @5 NAME @20 "|" G1 5.1 @30 "|" G2 5.1
            @40 "|" G3 5.1 @50 "|" AVE 5.1;
IF EOF =1 then do; * PUT BOTTOM OF TABLE;
      PUT @5 60*'-';
      PUT @5 "CLASS AVERAGE " @; * HOLDS LINE FOR NEXT PUT;
      PUT @50 "| %TRIM(&CLASSMEAN) " ;
      PUT @5 60*'=';
END;
RUN;
```

A breakdown of this code is as follows:

- The report is created within a DATA _NULL_ step using the information from the GRADES SAS data set. (The EOF variable is created to mark the last records in the GRADES data set.)
- TABLEHEAD is a title to be displayed in the report.
- FILE PRINT sends the report to the SAS Results Viewer.
- Note the three parts of the program within the DATA step:
  1. The section beginning with IF _N_ =1 is a header that is only displayed when the first record of the data set is read. It centers and PUTs the title (TABLEHEAD) and PUTs several lines that make up the header for the report.

(continued)

(continued)

2. The center of the report is a PUT statement that outputs each grade (G1–G3) in specified columns and with specified formats, and also displayed the student average AVE.

3. The end of the report is output only when the last record is reached (IF EOF=1). PUT statements are used to output footer information that includes the class mean (using the macro variable &CLASSMEAN). The trim statement trims unwanted blanks.

Submit this code and note the output as given in Table 19.26.

TABLE 19.26   Grade Report Created Using PUT Statements

Grade Report for Course 1234

```
                        SUMMARY OF GRADES
    =================================================================
    NAME              | TEST 1  | TEST 2  | TEST 3  | AVERAGE
    - - - - - - - - - - - - - - - - - - - - - - - - - - - - - - - - -
    Alice, Adams      | 88.4    | 91.0    | 79.0    | 86.1
    Jones, Steve      | 99.0    |100.0    | 88.4    | 95.8
    Zabar,Fred        | 78.6    | 87.0    | 88.4    | 84.7
    - - - - - - - - - - - - - - - - - - - - - - - - - - - - - - - - -
    CLASS AVERAGE                                   | 88.87
    =================================================================
```

2. Add a new student to the data, and rerun to see how the table adapts to new information. Rerun the code to verify that your change works correctly. Are the new averages calculated correctly?

3. Change the format for the student averages to 6.2. Rerun the code to verify that your change works correctly.

EXERCISES

19.1 Tabulate procedure

Open the program file EX_19.1.SAS. This file contains a program that creates a table showing average CITYMPG by BRAND and SUV.

```
PROC TABULATE DATA=MYSASLIB.CARS;
  CLASS BRAND SUV;
  VAR CITYMPG;
  TABLE BRAND, SUV*MEAN*CITYMPG;
RUN;
```

a. Add code to clean up this table by removing unnecessary labels.

b. Create a FORMAT for SUV that displays SUV and NON-SUV for labels.

c. Add code to save the table to a Word file (using RTF) and apply a style.

d. Add code to save the table to an Excel file.

19.2 Report procedure

Open the program file EX_19.2.SAS.

```
PROC REPORT DATA=MYSASLIB.SOMEDATA NOFS ;
   COLUMN AGE STATUS TIME1-TIME4 MEANTIME;
   DEFINE AGE/GROUP;
   DEFINE TIME1/ANALYSIS MEAN ;
   DEFINE MEANTIME/COMPUTED  'AVE TIME 1 TO 2';
   COMPUTE MEANTIME;
      MEANTIME=(_C3_+_C4_)/2; *MEAN OF TIME1 AND TIME2;
   ENDCOMP;
RUN;
```

a. Using the code above as a start, create a report using the SOMEDATA data set that groups subjects by AGE, displays columns of means for TIME1 through TIME4, and summarizes the data at the end of the table.

b. Why does MEANTIME=(_C3_+_C4_)/2; calculate the average of TIME1 and TIME2?

c. Add format statements so that each TIME variable and MEANTIME are reported to one decimal place.

19.3 Creating a report using PUT statements

Using example APUT_REPORT2.SAS, make the following changes:

a. Add a standard deviation at the bottom of the table. This value is already in the GMEAN SAS data set. Use the following code:

```
IF _STAT_="STD" THEN CALL SYMPUT('CLASSSTD',ROUND(STD,.01));
```

To create a macro variable named CLASSSTD. (Put the statement below the current CALL SYMPUT statement.)

Add the following statement to the report:

```
PUT @5 "CLASS Standard Deviation" @;
   PUT @50 "| %TRIM(&CLASSSTD) " ;
```

Put this statement immediately following the PUT statement for CLASS AVERAGE. Rerun the revised code to verify that your new information is included in the tabled output.

b. Change the columns so that there is more room for the name by placing the test scores at columns 25, 35, and 45 and the average at column 55. Rerun to verify that your changes worked.

APPENDIX A

OPTIONS REFERENCE

This appendix is a brief reference to a number of SAS® elements used in graphs and other procedures. These elements allow you visual control over many of the graphs produced in SAS procedures. Not all of the options for these elements are listed in this appendix. Refer to the SAS documentation for further information. The elements included in this appendix are as follows:

- Fonts
- Color options
- Graph patterns
- Bar and block patterns
- Line styles
- Plot symbols
- Informats and formats

A.1   USING SAS FONTS

Several standard SAS fonts are illustrated in Figure A.1. These are typical fonts for a Windows computer. The fonts available to you may differ according to your Windows and SAS versions.

Use these fonts in any statement that allows the specification of a font. For example,

```
TITLE1 F="SWISS" "This is an example use of the SWISS font.";
```

SAS® *Essentials: Mastering SAS for Data Analytics*, Second Edition. Alan C. Elliott and Wayne A. Woodward.
© 2016 John Wiley & Sons, Inc. Published 2016 by John Wiley & Sons, Inc.

ABCabc Example Brush Script

ABCabc Example Century

ABCabc Example COURIER

ABCabc Example Hersey

ABCabc Example SWISS font.

ABCabc Example TIMES font.

ABCabc Example ZAPF font.

Figure A.1 Example SAS fonts. (Source: Created with SAS® software, Version 9.4. Copyright 2012, SAS Institute Inc., Cary, NC, USA. All Rights Reserved. Reproduced with permission of SAS Institute Inc., Cary, NC)

In Windows, you can also specify any installed font on your machine. For example, the following statement uses the Times New Roman font.

```
TITLE F="TIMES" "This is an example use of the TIMES font.";
```

You can also specify height and color in such statements. (The default height is usually H=1.) For example,

```
TITLE1 F="COURIER" H=2 C=RED "Specify the height of the font.";
```

There are also bold, italic, and wide versions of some fonts. Refer to the SAS documentation for more information.

A.2 SPECIFYING SAS COLOR CHOICES

Color choices that can be used in SAS procedures include the following:

Black
Blue
Brown
Cream
Cyan
Gold
Gray
Green
Lilac
Lime

Magenta

Maroon

Orange

Pink

Purple

Red

Rose

Salmon

Tan

Violet

White

Yellow

If you do not specifically indicate a color, the SAS default color is BLACK. You can modify these colors with prefixes such as LIGHT to create, for example, LIGHTBLUE. Other prefixes include the following:

Brilliant

Dark

Deep

Light

Medium

Moderate

Pale

Strong

Vivid

Not all combinations work, so you may have to experiment to get the color you want.

Thousands of other SAS colors are available. If you know a standard RGB specification for a color (often, institutions will have a specified RGB color for official documents), you can use that specification in a color option. An example would be CX3230B2 as the RGB code for "Brilliant Blue." Here are two examples (where H is the height option):

```
TITLE H=2 C=RED "This produces a Red title.";
TITLE2 H=1.5 C="CX3230B2" "This title is Brilliant Blue";
```

A.3 SPECIFYING PATTERNS FOR PROCS GPLOT AND PROC UNIVARIATE

To specify a pattern in SAS you use a pattern code as in a histogram, typically in a PFILL statement, in the form

```
PFILL=Mabccc
```

where the definitions of these a, b, and ccc codes are listed in Table A.1. These patterns also apply to the VALUE= option in the PATTERN statement used to fill bars or under a curve for various SAS/GRAPH types.

TABLE A.1   Custom Pattern Codes

Code	Meaning
a	Ranges from 1 to 5 (thickness/density of line, 1=thinnest)
b	X indicates crosshatch and N indicates crosshatch
ccc	ccc is a number ranging from 0 to 360 where 0 indicates no angle, 45 is 45° angle, and so on.
EMPTY or E	Use PFILL=EMPTY to specify no fill
SOLID or S	Use PFILL=SOLID to specify solid fill

For example, open the program file GPATTERN1.SAS. For some versions of SAS, you may need to include the statement

```
ODS GRAPHICS OFF;
```

for this example to work as it applies to standard SAS graphs, and not ODS graphs. The example code

```
PROC UNIVARIATE DATA="C:\SASDATA\SOMEDATA" NOPRINT;
  VAR AGE;
  HISTOGRAM /NORMAL PFILL=M3X45;
RUN;
```

produces (along with a number of tables) a histogram using a crosshatch pattern at a 45° angle as shown in Figure A.2. To control the color of the pattern, include a statement such as the following before the PROC statement:

```
PATTERN COLOR=RED;
```

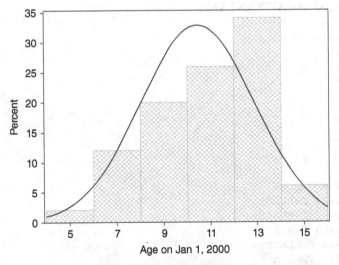

Figure A.2   Example crosshatch pattern

A.4   BAR AND BLOCK PATTERNS FOR BAR CHARTS, PIE CHARTS, AND OTHER GRAPHICS

Pattern choices can be used to specify colors and patterns for graphs in the PROC GCHART, PROC GPLOT, and PROC UNIVARIATE procedures with the PATTERN statement:

PATTERN*n* *options;*

where *n* (ranging from 1 to 30) specifies the graph element in which the pattern is to be used. The following codes in the PATTERN statement allow you to specify colors and patterns.

E

   Empty pattern (empty box)

R1 to R5

   Right 45° stripes (light to heavy lines)

X1 to X5

   Crosshatched patterns (light to heavy lines)

L1 to L5

Left 45° stripes (light to heavy lines)

   For example, open the program file GPATTERN2.SAS. For some versions of SAS, you may need to include the statement

ODS GRAPHICS OFF;

for this example to work because it applies to standard SAS graphs, and not ODS graphs. The example code (GPATTERN2.SAS)

```
GOPTIONS RESET = ALL;
DATA BARS;
INPUT A B;
DATALINES;
1 1
2 2
3 3
4 4
5 5
;
PATTERN1 V=E C=BLUE;
PATTERN2 V=R1 C=BLACK;
PATTERN3 V=X2 C=BLACK;
PATTERN4 V=L3 C=BLACK;
PATTERN5 V=S C=BLACK;
PROC GCHART ;VBAR A
/DISCRETE WIDTH=10
```

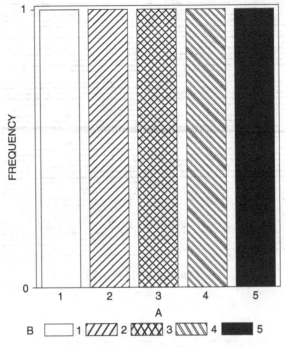

Figure A.3   Example fill patterns

```
SUBGROUP=B;
RUN;
QUIT;
```

produces the graph in Figure A.3, which shows examples of the various patterns. Each PATTERN statement is applied to the bars, `Pattern1` to the first bar, `Pattern2` to the second, and so on.

A.5   SAS LINE STYLES

When drawing lines in a procedure such as `PROC GPLOT`, you can choose from one of the line styles shown in Figure A.4. These are specified within a `SYMBOLn` statement where n refers to lines in the order they are specified in the plot.

For example, open the program file. `GLINE.SAS`. For some versions of SAS, you may need to include the statement

```
ODS GRAPHICS OFF;
```

for this example to work because it applies to standard SAS graphs, and not ODS graphs. The example code

```
GOPTIONS RESET = ALL;
SYMBOL1 V=CIRCLE C=BLUE I=R L=2 W=5;
TITLE 'REGRESSION LINE TYPE SELECTED';
```

Figure A.4   Line styles

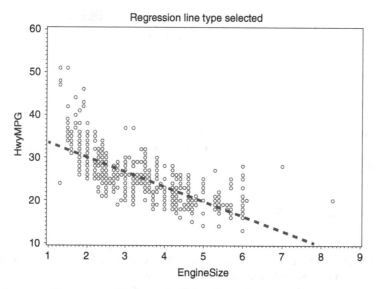

Figure A.5   Select line style

```
PROC GPLOT DATA="C:\SASDATA\CARS";
    PLOT HWYMPG*ENGINESIZE ;
RUN;
QUIT;
```

produces a scatterplot and regression line with line style L=2 and width W=5 for emphasis to illustrate the selected line style, as shown in Figure A.5.

VALUE=	SYMBOL	VALUE=	SYMBOL
PLUS	+	%	♣
X	×	&	♧
STAR	*	'	♣
SQUARE	□	=	☆
DIAMOND	◇	-	☉
TRIANGLE	△	@	☿
HASH	#	*	♀
Y	Y	+	⊕
Z	Z	>	♂
PAW	∴	. (DOT)	♃
POINT	.	<	♄
DOT	●	,	♅
CIRCLE	○	/	♆
	⊟	?	♇
˜	♤	(	☾
#	♡	)	♂
$	◇	:	✳

Figure A.6   Standard SAS symbols

A.6 USING SAS PLOTTING SYMBOLS

The symbol used for displaying a point on a graph such as a scatterplot in PROC GPLOT can be specified in a SYMBOL statement such as the following:

```
SYMBOL1 V=CIRCLE;
```

The standard SAS symbols you can select from are shown in Figure A.6. Similar symbols are used for PROC SGPLOT. They include Arrowdown, Asterisk, Circle, Diamond, GreaterThan, Hash, Homedown, Ibeam, Plus, Square, Star, Tack, Tilde, Triangle, Union, X, Y, Z, CircleFilled, DIamondFilled, HomedownFilled, SquareFilled, StarFilled, and TriangeFilled.

A.7 USING ODS STYLE ATTRIBUTES

ODS style attributes allow you to specify how ODS Traffic Light values are displayed (see ODS9.SAS for an example). Values for these items are given in other sections of this appendix. For example, for all colors, refer to the color descriptions earlier in this appendix. For other attributes, refer to SAS documentation. Table A.2 lists some common options for ODS Styles.

A.8 COMMON (INPUT) INFORMATS

Informats are used to read data. The use of informats is introduced in Chapter 4. Table A.3 lists some common informats.

TABLE A.2   Common ODS Style Options

Style Item	What It Sets
BACKGROUND=	Sets the color of the cell background. For example, BACKGROUND=YELLOW
FLYOVER=	Displays text when the mouse is moved on top of the item. For example, FLYOVER="Summed Value"
FONT=	Defines a font definition for the item. For example, FONT=("SWISS",10pt)
FONT_FACE=	Specifies the font typeface. For example, FONT_FACE=SCRIPT
FONT_SIZE=	Specifies the font size. For example, FONT_SIZE=12
FONT_WEIGHT=	Specifies weight of font. For example, FONT_WEIGHT=BOLD
FOREGROUND=	Specifies the color for text and column labels not otherwise specified. For example, FOREGROUND=LIGHTBLUE
JUST=	Specifies cell justification (horizontal, left, right, or center). For example, JUST=LEFT

TABLE A.3   Common SAS Informats (Input Formats)

Informat	Meaning
5.	Five columns of data as numeric data
$5.	Character variable with width 5, removing leading blanks
$CHAR5.	Character variable with width 5, preserving leading blanks
COMMA6.	Six columns of numeric data and strips out any commas or dollar signs (i.e., $40,000 is read as 40,000)
COMMA10.2	Reads 10 columns of numeric data with two decimal places (strips commas and dollar signs). $19,020.22 is read as 19,020.22
MMDDYY8.	Date as 01/12/16. (Watch out for Y2K issue.)
MMDDYY10.	Date as 04/07/2016
DATE7.	Date as 20JUL016
DATE9.	Date as 12JAN2016. (No Y2K issue.)

A.9   COMMON (OUTPUT) FORMATS

Formats are similar to informats (and there are some overlaps). They are used to write out data values. The use of formats is introduced in Chapter 4. Table A.4 lists some common formats.

TABLE A.4   Common SAS (Output) FORMATs

Format	Meaning
`5.`	Writes data using five columns with no decimal points. For example, 1234
`5.1`	Writes data using five columns with 1 decimal point. For example, 123.4
`DOLLAR10.2`	Writes data with a dollar sign, commas at thousands, and with two decimal places. For example, $1,234.56
`COMMA10.1`	Writes data with commas at thousands, and one decimal place. For example, 1234.5
`MMDDYY10.`	Displays dates in common American usage as in 01/09/2016
`DATE9.`	Display time using a military style format. For example, 09JAN2016
`WORDDATE12.`	Displays dates with abbreviated month names as in January 9, 2016
`WORDDATE18.`	Displays dates with full month names such as in January 9, 2016
`WEEKDATE29.`	Display dates with day of week as in Saturday, January 9, 2016
`DOWNAME.`	Outputs day of week as a name
`MONNAME.`	Outputs month as a name

APPENDIX B

SAS® FUNCTION REFERENCE

SAS functions can be used in a DATA statement to calculate new variables or as a part of a conditional statement. This appendix is more of a reference than a tutorial, but it does illustrate the use of a number of common functions in SAS. It is not an exhaustive list of functions, but it does include commonly used functions that are useful in manipulating data in the preparation for analysis. Some examples are provided for functions, whose use may not be apparent in a simple description. For a more extensive description of this material, please refer to the SAS documentation.

B.1 USING SAS FUNCTIONS

Here are some examples of how SAS functions are used:

```
DATA NEWDATA;SET OLDDATA;
TOTAL=SUM(A,B,C);
GENDER=UPCASE(SEX);
SQRAGE=SQRT(AGE);
RUN;
```

Note that in these cases, the function on the right side of the = sign does something to the argument(s) in the parentheses and returns a value, which is then assigned to the name on the left-hand side of the = sign.

The SUM function returns the total of the variables A, B, and C. The SQRT function returns the square root of the AGE variable. The UPCASE function makes all character values in the SEX variable uppercase. For example, if the SEX variable contains the value f, then the GENDER variable will contain the value F. The syntax for a function is

```
NEWVARIABLE = FUNCTIONNAME(argument1, argument2... argumentk);
```

SAS® Essentials: Mastering SAS for Data Analytics, Second Edition. Alan C. Elliott and Wayne A. Woodward.
© 2016 John Wiley & Sons, Inc. Published 2016 by John Wiley & Sons, Inc.

where arguments can be constants, variables, expressions, or other functions. For functions that are not described in this appendix, refer to the SAS documentation.

B.2   ARITHMETIC/MATHEMATICAL FUNCTIONS

Using arithmetic functions provides a way to obtain common mathematical results using simple code. For example,

```
AVE=MEAN(OF OBS1-OBS5);
```

calculates the average of the variables OBS1 through OBS5. Typically, using the function to calculate certain values is easier than coding the actual arithmetic calculation such as

```
AVE=(OBS1+OBS2+OBS3+OBS4+OBS5)/5;
```

Moreover, in this case, the MEAN function finds an appropriate mean even if there are missing values in the list, whereas the individually added variables will result in the MEAN being set to missing if any one of the OBS values is missing.

Also take note how the various lists of arguments are used in the function. For example, both of these calls to the SUM function calculate the same results:

```
SUMVAL=SUM(PRE,MONTH6,MONTH12,MONTH24);
SUMVAL=SUM(OF PRE—MONTH24);
```

Note that when you use a range such as PRE--MONTH24 or OBS1-OBS50 as arguments in a SAS function, you must precede the list with an OF argument. Otherwise, you may get unexpected results (Table B.1).

TABLE B.1   Arithmetic and Mathematical Functions

Function	Description
ABS (x)	Absolute value. Example: Y=ABS(-9) returns the value 9
EXP (x)	Exponentiation. Example: Y=EXP(1) returns the value 2.71828
LOG (x)	Natural log. Example: Y=LOG(10) returns the value 2.30259
LOG10 (x)	Log base 10. Example: Y=LOG10 returns the value 1.0
FACT (x)	"Factorial. Example: FACT(7) returns the value 5040, which is $(7 \times 6 \times 5 \times 4 \times 3 \times 2 \times 1)$."
MAX $(x1,x2,x3 \dots)$	Returns maximum value in the list
MEAN $(x1,x2,x3 \dots)$	Returns the arithmetic mean of nonmissing values in list. Example: MEAN(2,4,.,6) returns the value 4. (Note that the value dot . in the list represents a missing value.)
MEDIAN $(x1,x2,x3 \dots)$	Returns the median of nonmissing values in the list
MIN $(x1,x2,x3 \dots)$	Returns the minimum in the list

(continued)

TABLE B.1 (*Continued*)

Function	Description
MOD(x, k)	Remainder of x/k. Examples: MOD(5,3)=2, MOD(6,2)=0
N($x1, x2, x3\dots$)	Returns the number of nonmissing values. Example: N(1,2,.,4) returns the value 3
NMISS($x1, x2, x3\dots$)	Returns the number missing. Example: NMISS(1,2,.,4) returns the value 1
ORDINAL($k, x1, x2, x3\dots$)	Finds the kth number in the sorted list. ORDINAL(2,11,6,9,3) = 6 because it is second in the ordered list
RANUNI(0)	A different random number (uniform distribution) each time
RANUNI(x)	Returns the same random sequence (uniform) each time for that particular seed, where x is a seed value you enter
RANNOR($seed$)	A random number from a normal distribution with mean 0 and standard deviation 1. (See seed info for RANUNI.)
SIGN(x)	Returns the sign of x as a 1 or −1 value
SQRT(x)	Square root. Example: Y=SQRT(9) returns the value 3
SUM($x1, x2, x3\dots$)	Returns the sum of nonmissing values in list

---

HANDS-ON EXAMPLE

1. Open the program file FUNC_ARITH.SAS. This code uses several arithmetic functions to summarize data for the time variables PRE to MONTH24. Run the code and observe the results given in Table B.2.

```
DATA ARITH; SET MYSASLIB.HASMISSING;
MAXTIME=MAX(PRE,MONTH6,MONTH12,MONTH24);
MINTIME=MIN(OF PRE--MONTH24);
MISSTIME=NMISS(OF PRE--MONTH24);
MEANTIME=MEAN(OF PRE--MONTH24);
;
TITLE "Use Arithmetic Functions";
PROC PRINT DATA=ARITH; RUN;
```

2. Using the SUM function with the argument list PRE, MONTH6, MONTH12, MONTH24, add code to calculate SUMTIME. Using the MEDIAN function with the argument list OF PRE—MONTH24, add code to calculate MEDIANTIME. Run the code and observe the results.

TABLE B.2   Using of Arithmetic Functions

Use Arithmetic Functions

Obs	ID	PRE	MONTH6	MONTH12	MONTH24	TEMP1	TEMP2	TEMP3	TEMP4	MAXTIME	MINTIME	MISSTIME	MEANTIME
1	00101	22.3	25.3	28.2	30.6	101	95	94	97	30.6	22.3	0	26.6000
2	00102	22.8	27.5	33.3	.	95	103	94	101	33.3	22.8	1	27.8667
3	00110	18.5	26.0	29.0	27.9	98	103	94	101	29.0	18.5	0	25.3500
4	00187	22.5	29.3	32.6	33.7	102	101	96	99	33.7	22.5	0	29.5250
5	00312	17.0	21.3	22.7	21.2	104	95	103	100	22.7	17.0	0	20.5500
6	00390	21.3	30.5	30.7	30.1	95	103	94	97	30.7	21.3	0	28.1500
7	00445	22.1	31.3	31.6	31.6	100	101	100	101	31.6	22.1	0	29.1500
8	00543	20.8	28.6	34.2	30.0	100	101	98	.	34.2	20.8	0	28.4000
9	00544	18.1	23.8	29.0	27.8	98	98	100	95	29.0	18.1	0	24.6750

TABLE B.3   Arithmetic and Trigonometric Functions

Function	Description
ARCOS(x)	Returns the value of arccosine
ARSIN(x)	Returns the value of arcsine
ATAN(x)	Returns the value of arctangent
COS(x)	Returns the value of cosine
COSH(x)	Returns the value of hyperbolic cosine
SIN(x)	Returns the value of sine
SINH(x)	Returns the value of hyperbolic sine
TAN(x)	Returns the value of tangent
TANH(x)	Returns the value of hyperbolic tangent

B.3   TRIGONOMETRIC FUNCTIONS

Each of these functions returns the specified trigonometric value for the value of the argument (in radians) entered into the function. For example,

```
Y=COS(3.14);
```

returns the value −1.000 (Table B.3).

B.4   DATE AND TIME FUNCTIONS

SAS date and time values are stored as integers and indicate the number of days since 1/1/1960. A positive number indicates a date after 1/1/1960, and a negative number indicates a date before 1/1/1960. Date values that contain both date and time are stored in SAS as the number of seconds since midnight on 1/1/1960. Dates are typically displayed using a SAS date format such as MMDDYY10., which displays a date as 03/09/2016.

For these functions, a SAS date is a variable designated as a date value. Here are two examples of how variables can be designated as dates:

- Assign a date value to a fixed date. A d at the end of the value tells SAS to interpret this quoted string as a date. For example (note that case does not matter either for the month abbreviation or for the "d"),

```
BDATE = '12DEC1994'd;
BEGINDATE ="1jan2011"D;
EXAMDATE = '13-APR-2014'd;
```

- Read a value as a date in an INPUT statement. For example,

```
INPUT BDATE MMDDYY10.;
```

In the following examples, a "date" is a SAS value that contains only a date, and a "datetime" value contains both date and time values.

When using date functions, beware of the "Y2K" problem. Any two-digit year lower than 20 is interpreted as being in the twenty-first century (e.g., the two-digit year 15 is interpreted as 2015) and two-digit year 20 or greater are interpreted as being in the twentieth century (e.g., the two-digit year 21 is interpreted as 1921). You can change this default using the statement YEARCUTOFF=19*XX* in your program. For example, if you specify YEARCUTOFF=1925, any two-digit year that is between 00 and 24 will be interpreted as being in the twenty-first century (e.g., 21 will be interpreted as 2021), and years from 25 to 99 will be interpreted as in the twentieth century (e.g., 44 will be interpreted as 1944):

```
DATDIF(sdate,edate,basis)
```

returns the number of days between two dates. Basis is (default) '30/360', 'ACT/ACT', 'ACT/360', or 'ACT/365'. The BASIS option tells SAS what counting method to use to count days. (These are some day-count conventions used in investing, accounting, and other disciplines.)

- '30/360' option means to use a 30-day month and a 360-day year.
- 'ACT/ACT' means to use the actual number of days.
- 'ACT/360' means to use the actual number of days in each month and 360 days in a year.
- 'ACT/365' means to use the actual number of days in each month and 365 days in a year.

For example,

```
DAYS=DATDIF('07JUL1976'd,'01JAN2013'd,'30/360');
```

returns the value (number of days) as 13,134, whereas

```
DAYS=DATDIF('07JUL1976'd,'01JAN2013'd,'ACT/ACT');
```

returns the value (number of days) as 13,327. These integer values can be displayed in a date-readable manner by applying a date format to the variable such as

```
FORMAT DAYS MMDDYY10.;
```

Table B.4 lists some of the common functions used to manage dates in a SAS program.

TABLE B.4 Date and Time Functions

Function	Description
DATDIF(sdate,edate,basis)	Calculates the difference between two dates using the indicated basis method (described earlier)
DATE()	Returns the current date (SAS date value)
DATEPART(datetime)	Extracts and returns only the date from a SAS datetime variable
DATETIME()	Returns the current date and time of day from the computer's date and time values
DAY(date)	Returns the day of month (a value from 1 to 31) from a SAS date
DHMS(date,hour,minute,second)	Returns a SAS datetime value from the argument date, hour, minute, and second in the function

TABLE B.4   *(Continued)*

Function	Description
HMS (*hour, minute, second*)	Creates a SAS time value from hour, minute, and second
HOUR (*<time | datetime>*)	Returns the hour value from a SAS time or datetime variable
INTCK ('*interval*', *from, to*)	Returns the number of time intervals in a given time span, where interval can be as follows: **Datetime intervals:** DTDAY, DTWEEKDAY, DTWEEK, DTTENDAY, DTSEMIMONTH, DTMONTH, DTQTR, DTSEMIYEAR, DTYEAR **Date intervals:** DAY, WEEKDAY, WEEK, TENDAY, SEMIMONTH, MONTH, QTR, SEMIYEAR, YEAR **Time intervals:** HOUR, MINUTE, SECOND For example, WEEKS=INTCK('WEEK','07JUL1976'd, '01JAN2013'd); Returns a value of 1904, indicating the number of weeks between the two indicated dates
INTNX ('*interval*', *start-from, increment<, 'alignment'>*)	Advances a date, time, or datetime value by a given interval, and returns a date, time, or datetime value – see intervals above
MDY (*month, day, year*)	Creates and returns a SAS date from month, day, and year
MINUTE (*<time | datetime>*)	Extracts and returns the minute value (1–60) from a SAS time or datetime variable
MONTH (*date*)	Extracts and returns the month value (1–12) from a SAS date value
QTR (*date*)	Extracts and returns the quarter value (1–4) of the year from a SAS date value
SECOND (*<time | datetime>*)	Extracts and returns the value for seconds (1–60) from a SAS time or datetime value
TIME ()	Returns the current time of day as a datetime value (from the computer's system clock)
TIMEPART (*datetime*)	Extracts and returns the time value from a SAS datetime variable
TODAY ()	Returns the current date as a SAS date (from the computer's system clock)
WEEKDAY (*date*)	Extracts and returns the day of the week (1–7) from a SAS date value
YEAR (*date*)	Extracts and returns the year value (such as 2019) from a SAS date value
YRDIF (*startdate, enddate, basis*)	Returns the difference in years between two dates. Basis is '30/360', 'ACT/CT', 'ACT/360', or 'ACT/365'. (See descriptions of these basis values in the DATDIF function above.)
YYQ (*year, quarter*)	Extracts and returns a SAS date from year and quarter

Vertical bars in the function definitions indicate choose one listed option "or" the other.

HANDS-ON EXAMPLE

1. Open the program file FUNC_DATETIME.SAS. This program reads in a date and time arrived as separate variables and datetime leave as a single variable.

```
DATA TIME;
FORMAT DTARRIVE MMDDYY10. TIMEARRIVE TIME10.
       ARRIVETIME DATETIMELEAVE DATETIME19.;
INPUT @1 DTARRIVE DATE10.
      @12 TIMEARRIVE TIME10.
         @23 DATETIMELEAVE DATETIME19.;
*MERGE DTARRIVE and TIMEARRIVE;
         ARRIVETIME=DHMS(DTARRIVE,0,0,TIMEARRIVE);
         SECONDS1=DATETIMELEAVE-ARRIVETIME;
         SECONDS2=INTCK('seconds',ARRIVETIME,DATETIMELEAVE);
DATALINES;
10NOV2016  1:13 pm     10NOV2016:18:49:19
12DEC2016  9:20 am     12DEC2016:13:23:22
;
PROC PRINT DATA=TIME;RUN;
```

To calculate the difference between the arrive and leave time, we want to first combine the date arrived with the time arrived. Note how this is done using the DHMS function:

```
ARRIVETIME=DHMS(DTARRIVE,0,0,TIMEARRIVE);
```

The first parameter is the date, and as we don't have Hours and Minutes, we put TIMEARRIVE in the Seconds argument. Once we have ARRIVETIME, we can calculate the number of seconds between the two datetimes. This is done both by subtraction and with the INTCK function. Run the program and observe the results given in Table B.5.

2. Calculate minutes and hours using two methods as follows:

```
MINUTES1=SECONDS1/60;
HOURS2=MINUTES1/60;
MINUTES2= INTCK('MINUTE',ARRIVETIME,DATETIMELEAVE);
HOURS2= INTCK('HOUR',ARRIVETIME,DATETIMELEAVE);
```

Resubmit the code and observe the output. Note the difference in the results. INTCK gives the integer portion of the results, whereas a straight calculation preserves the fraction.

3. Extract the month and day of the week from DTARRIVE using the MONTH and DAY functions:

```
MONTH=MONTH(DTARRIVE);
DOM=DAY(DTARRIVE);
```

Run the code and observe the results. The month and day of the month are reported as numbers. See the example in the Special Functions for an example of how to display the month and day of the month in words.

(continued)

(continued)

TABLE B.5   Using Date and Time Functions

Obs	DTARRIVE	TIMEARRIVE	ARRIVETIME	DATETIMELEAVE	SECONDS1	SECONDS2
1	11/10/2016	13:13:00	10NOV2016:13:13:00	10NOV2016:18:49:19	20179	20179
2	12/12/2016	9:20:00	12DEC2016:09:20:00	12DEC2016:13:23:22	14602	14602

B.5   CHARACTER FUNCTIONS

Character functions allow you to manipulate text values. These functions are essential when you must extract information from text values, when you need to create a new text value from several pieces of information, or when you need to "clean up" text values to make them into better data values for analysis.

Table B.6 lists some of the common functions used to manipulate character/text variables.

TABLE B.6   Character Functions

Function	Description
CAT(*text1, text2, ...*) CATS(*text1, text2, ...*) CATT(*text1, text2, ...*)	Concatenates text without removing leading or trailing blanks. CATS removes leading and trailing blanks and CATT removes trailing blanks. For example, RESULT=CAT("GEORGE"," WASHINGTON"); Returns the value GEORGE WASHINGTON, and For example, RESULT=CATS("GEORGE"," WASHINGTON"); Returns the value GEORGEWASHINGTON
CATX (*separator, text1, text2, ...*)	Removes leading and trailing blanks and inserts a separator between concatenated components. For example, RESULT = CATX(":","GEORGE"," WASHINGTON"); Returns the value GEORGE:WASHINGTON
COMPBL(*text*)	Removes multiple blanks between words in a character string
COMPRESS(*text<, characters-to-remove>*)	Removes specified characters from a character string
DEQUOTE(*text*)	Removes quotation marks from text
FIND(*text, text-tofind <,'modifiers'> <,start>*)	Finds an instance of the texttofind within the text. Start is an optional value indicating where in the text to start looking and modifiers are I for ignore case and T for ignore blanks. For example, RESULT=FIND("aBcDef", "DEF","I"); Returns a value of 4 because DEF begins at the fourth character of ABCDEF (and case is ignored). If no match is found, a value of 0 is returned

(continued)

TABLE B.6   *(Continued)*

Function	Description
INDEX(*text*,*texttofind*)	Searches text for specified texttofind string and returns a number where the text begins, or 0
LEFT(*text*)	Left-aligns a character string
LENGTH(*text*)	Returns the length of a text string
LOWCASE(*text*)	Converts all letters to lowercase
QUOTE(*text*)	Adds double quotation marks to text
REPEAT(*text*,*n*)	Repeats text *n* times. For example, R=repeat("ABC",**3**); Results in R="ABCABCABC"
REVERSE(*argument*)	Reverses a text expression
RIGHT(*argument*)	Right-aligns text
SCAN(*text*,*n*<,*delimiters*>)	Returns the *n*th word from a text expression. For example, FIRST=SCAN("JOHN SMITH",1,' '); returns JOHN and LAST=SCAN("JOHN SMITH",2,' '); returns SMITH
SOUNDEX(*text*)	Turns text into a sounds-like argument For example, SOUNDEX("ALLEN")=SOUNDEX("ALAN"); matches and SOUNDEX("ALLEN")=SOUNDEX("MELON"); does not
SUBSTR(*text*,*start*<,*n*>)	Searches for and replaces text. For example, VAR=SUBSTR("LINCOLN",3,2); returns VAR ="NC" and SUBSTR("LINCOLN",3,2)= "XX"; returns LIXX
TRANSLATE(*text*,*to1*,*from1*<, ... *ton*,*fromn*>)	Replaces characters in text with specified new characters. For example, TRANSLATE('LINCOLN',"X","C"); returns LINXOLN
TRANWRD(*source*,*target*,*replacement*)	Replaces or removes all occurrences of a word in a text string. For example, TRANWRD('SPECIAL WED MEAL','WED','MON'); returns 'SPECIAL MON MEAL'
TRIM(*text*)	Removes trailing blanks from the text. (Returns one blank if the expression is missing.)
TRIMN(*text*)	Removes trailing blanks from the text. (Returns a null string if the expression is missing.)
UPCASE(*text*)	Converts text to uppercase
VERIFY(*source*,*excerpt-1*<, ... *excerpt-n*)	Searches text and returns the position of the first nonmatched character in the first argument. VERIFY("12345","54301") returns 2 because the second character doesn't match any character in the second argument

HANDS-ON EXAMPLE

1. Open the program file FUNC_CHAR.SAS. This program illustrates how you could separate two numeric values from a text value. In this case, systolic and diastolic blood pressures were recorded as a single text value such as 120/80. Run this code and observe how the two values are extracted and made into two numeric values SBP and DBP.

```
DATA BP;
INPUT BP $10.;
I=FIND(BP,"/");
SBP=SUBSTR(BP,1,I-1); * get number before the /;
DBP=SUBSTR(BP,I+1); *get number after the /;
DROP I;
DATALINES;
120/80
140/90
110/70
;
PROC PRINT DATA=BP;RUN;
```

2. Note the code I=FIND(BP,"/"). What value is the variable I set to on the first record?
3. What does the code SUBSTR(BP,1,I-1) do?
4. What does the code SUBSTR(BP,I+1) do?

HANDS-ON EXAMPLE

1. Open the program file FUNC_SCAN.SAS. The goal of this program is to separate a series of names into first and last names. In this case, we don't care about middle initials. Run the program and observe the results in Table B.7.

```
DATA NAMES;
FORMAT FIRST LAST MAYBE $20.;
INPUT @1 NAME $30.;
FIRST=SCAN(NAME,1," ");
LAST = SCAN(NAME, -1);
MAYBE=SCAN(NAME,-2);
IF MAYBE=FIRST THEN MAYBE="";
IF LENGTH(MAYBE)=1 THEN MAYBE="";
LASTNAME=CAT(MAYBE, LAST);
FULLNAME=CAT(FIRST,TRIM(LASTNAME));
DATALINES;
Alfred J. Prufrock
Benjamin Harrison
George H. W. Bush
Vincent Van Gogh
A. C. Elliott
;
```

```
RUN;
PROC PRINT DATA=NAMES;RUN;
```

2. Put your name in the data segment as first name, initial, and last name. Run the program to see if it separates your name correctly.

3. Look at the three uses of the SCAN function

```
FIRST=SCAN(NAME,1," ");
LAST = SCAN(NAME, -1);
MAYBE=SCAN(NAME,-2);
```

   What does each do? What do the negative numbers as arguments mean?

4. What does the LENGTH function do? How is it used to tell if there is a middle name?

5. What does the CAT function do? Replace it with a CATS function when creating FULLNAME, rerun the code. What changes? Finally, note the TRIM function used in the FULLNAME statement. It is needed to trim off any extra blanks in LASTNAME.

TABLE B.7   SCAN, LENGTH, and CAT Functions

Obs	FIRST	LAST	MAYBE	NAME	LASTNAME	FULLNAME
1	Alfred	Prufrock		Alfred J. Prufrock	Prufrock	Alfred Prufrock
2	Benjamin	Harrison		Benjamin Harrison	Harrison	Benjamin Harrison
3	George	Bush		George H. W. Bush	Bush	George Bush
4	Vincent	Gogh	Van	Vincent Van Gogh	Van Gogh	Vincent Gogh
5	A.	Elliott		A. C. Elliott	Elliott	A. Elliott

B.6   TRUNCATION FUNCTIONS

Truncation Functions are used to extract certain portions of a number such as the smallest integer, largest integer, nearest integer, and so on. These are described in Table B.8.

B.7   FINANCIAL FUNCTIONS

Financial functions allow you to perform common financial calculations on values. There are over 50 such functions available in SAS, too many to describe here. A few of the most commonly used financial functions are listed in Table B.9.

TABLE B.8   Truncation Functions

Function	Description
CEIL(x)	Returns the smallest integer greater than or equal to the argument
FLOOR(x)	Returns the largest integer less than or equal to the argument
FUZZ(x)	Returns the nearest integer if value is within 1E-12
INT(x)	Returns the decimal portion of the value of the argument
ROUND(x, roundoffunit)	Rounds a value to the nearest round-off unit. For example, ROUND(1.2345,.01) returns the value 1.23

TABLE B.9   Special Use Functions

Function	Description
IRR(*period,cash0,cash1, ...*)	Returns the internal rate of return as a percentage
MORT(*amount,payment,rate, number*)	When you set the PAYMENT variable to missing, this returns the payment for a loan calculation. For example, when you run DPAYMENT.SAS DATA LOAN; PAYMENT= MORT(30000,.,.06/12,48); RUN; PROC PRINT;RUN; the value of (the monthly) PAYMENT is 704.55
NPV(*rate,period,cash0, cash1, ...*)	Returns the net present value expressed as a percentage

HANDS-ON EXAMPLE

1. Open the program file FUNC_MORT.SAS. This program uses the MORT function to calculate the payments for a loan. This example displays payment for different loan, interest, and number of payments. Run the program and observe the results in Table B.10.

```
DATA LOAN;
FORMAT VALUE DOLLAR12.
       INTRATE1-INTRATE3 4.2
         NUMBER 4.;
INPUT VALUE INTRATE1-INTRATE3 NUMBER;
ARRAY INT(3) INTRATE1-INTRATE3;
ARRAY PAY(3);
DO I=1 to 3;
   PAY(I)= MORT(VALUE,.,INT(I)/12,NUMBER);
END;
LABEL MORT="Mortgage Payment";
LABEL INTRATE1="Int. Rate 1 ";
LABEL INTRATE2="Int. Rate 2 ";
LABEL INTRATE3="Int. Rate 3 ";
LABEL PAYMENT= "Amount of Payment";
LABEL VALUE="Loan Amount";
LABEL NUMBER="Num. Payments";
DROP I;
DATALINES;
100000 .05 .04 .03 360
100000 .05 .04 .03 180
150000 .05 .04 .03 360
150000 .05 .04 .03 180
;
RUN;
PROC PRINT LABEL DATA=LOAN ;
RUN;
```

2. Add lines to the data for $200,000 loan for a 30- and 15-year mortgage with 0.05, 0.04, and 0.03 interest rates. Run the program and observe the results.

TABLE B.10   Example of MORT Function

Obs	Loan Amount	Int. Rate 1	Int. Rate 2	Int. Rate 3	Num. Payments	PAY1	PAY2	PAY3
1	$100,000	0.05	0.04	0.03	360	536.82	477.42	421.60
2	$100,000	0.05	0.04	0.03	180	790.79	739.69	690.58
3	$150,000	0.05	0.04	0.03	360	805.23	716.12	632.41
4	$150,000	0.05	0.04	0.03	180	1186.19	1109.53	1035.87

B.8   SPECIAL USE FUNCTIONS

The term "special use function" is a catch-all phrase referring to other functions that are useful in SAS. They include functions that provide ways to convert variables from one type to another, create macro variables, create lag values, and determine differences in distance using zip codes. These functions are listed in Table B.11.

TABLE B.11   Special Use Functions

Function	Description
INPUT(*string,informat*)	The INPUT function converts a character variable to character or numeric

For example,
```
s="1,212";
x=input(s,comma5.);
```
returns x=1212 (a numeric value).

Note: INPUTC(*string1,char-informat*) and INPUTN(string1, num-informat) are similar to INPUT(), but you can assign the format within the code

| PUT(*x1,format*) | The PUT function converts variables from character or numeric to character |

In the function, *x1* is character or numeric. The PUT function returns a character value. For example,
```
x=PUT(1234,comma6.);
```
returns the string value 1,234

Note: PUTC(x1,char-informat) and PUTN(x1,num-informat) are similar to PUT(), but you can assign the format within the code

TABLE B.11 (*Continued*)

Function	Description
CALL SYMPUT and CALL SYMPUTN	Not strictly functions, but these routines assign a value produced in a DATA step to a macro variable. The formats for these routines are as follows: CALL SYMPUT(macro-var,cval); CALL SYMPUTN(macro-var,nval); where cval is some character value or variable and nval is some numeric value or variable name. For example, to store the value of the character variable MYVAR into the macro variable named LEVEL, use the command CALL SYMPUT('LEVEL',MYVAR); You can then reference the variable as &LEVEL elsewhere in your SAS code
LAGn(x)	Returns the value of the nth previous observation. Example: If your data are x=10, 30, 15, then LAG2(x) for the third item would be 10. LAG() is the same as LAG1()
DIFn(x)	Returns the difference in the current value and the nth previous value. Example: If your data are x=10, 30, 15, then DIF2(x) of the third item would be 5 (15 − 10 = 5). DIF() is the same as DIF1()
ZIPCITY(zipcode)	Converts a ZIP code to a city and state. For example, the expression CITY=ZIPCITY(75137); where the *zipcode* (in this case, 75137) is a character or numeric variable returns a value of "Duncanville, TX" for the CITY variable
ZIPCITYDISTANCE(zipcode1, zipcode2)	Returns the distance (in miles) between the two ZIP codes
ZIPSTATE(zipcode)	Converts a ZIP code to a two-letter state code. For example, the expression STATE=ZIPSTATE("75137"); where the *zipcode* (in this case, "75137") is a character or numeric variable returns a value of "TX" for the STATE variable

HANDS-ON EXAMPLE (PUT AND INPUT)

1. Open the program file FUNC_CONVERT.SAS. Run the code and observe the output in Table B.12. This program demonstrates the INPUT and PUT functions and illustrates how you can convert character variables to numeric and numeric variables to character.

```
DATA TEMP;
LENGTH CHAR4 $ 4;
INPUT NUMERIC CHAR4;
* CONVERT CHARACTER VARIABLE TO NUMERIC;
NEW_NUM=INPUT(CHAR4,BEST4.);
```

```
* CONVERT NUMERIC VARIABLE TO CHARACTER;
NEW_CHAR=PUT(NUMERIC,4.0);
DATALINES;
789.1 1234
009.2 0009
1.5 9999
;
PROC PRINT;
FORMAT NEW_NUM 6.1 NEW_CHAR $8.;
RUN;
```

Note that the converted numbers (NEW_CHAR) have been rounded to integers, because they were converted using a 4.0 format in the PUT statement.

TABLE B.12   Output from PUT and INPUT Example

Obs	CHAR4	NUMERIC	NEW_NUM	NEW_CHAR
1	1234	789.1	1234.0	789
2	0009	9.2	9.0	9
3	9999	1.5	9999.0	2

HANDS-ON EXAMPLE (PUT WITH MONNAME AND DONAME)

1. Open the program file FUNC_SPECIAL.SAS. This example shows how to use the PUT function along with the MONNAME and DOWNAME formats to create variables that contain the name of the week and the name of the month. Run this program and observe the results given in Table B.13.

```
DATA DATES;
FORMAT BDATE WEEKDATE17.;
INPUT @1 BDATE MMDDYY8.;
BDATEDOW=PUT(BDATE,DOWNAME.);
BDATEMONTH=PUT(BDATE,MONNAME.);
DATALINES;
08212016
07041776
01011900
;
PROC PRINT DATA=DATES; RUN;
```

(continued)

(continued)

2. Add these lines after the `BDATEMONTH` line. Rerun the program and observe the output.

```
BDAY=DAY(BDATE);
BYEAR=YEAR(BDATE);
```

This illustrates how to extract various components from a date.

TABLE B.13   Convert Dates to Components

Obs	BDATE	BDATEDOW	BDATEMONTH
1	Sun, Aug 21, 2016	Sunday	August
2	Thu, Jul 4, 1776	Thursday	July
3	Mon, Jan 1, 1900	Monday	January

HANDS-ON EXAMPLE (LAG)

1. Open the program file `FUNC_LAG.SAS`. This program uses the `LAG` function to calculate the difference in price of gold from the previous year. Run this program and observe the results in Table B.14.

```
DATA PRICE;
INPUT YEAR PRICE;
 LAG_PRICE = LAG(PRICE);
 DIFF_PRICE = PRICE - LAG_PRICE;
 PCT_INCREASE = (DIFF_PRICE/LAG_PRICE)*100;
DATALINES;
2005 424.15
2006 549.86
2007 631.17
2008 889.60
2009 858.69
2010 1117.96
2011 1356.40
2012 1656.12
2013 1670.95
2014 1244.80
;
RUN;
PROC PRINT;RUN;
```

2. Change the `LAG` function to `LAG2` to find the 2-year changes. Rerun the program and observe the output.

TABLE B.14   January London Fix Gold Prices, Yearly Change

Obs	YEAR	PRICE	LAG_PRICE	DIFF_PRICE	PCT_INCREASE
1	2005	424.15	.	.	.
2	2006	549.86	424.15	125.71	29.6381
3	2007	631.17	549.86	81.31	14.7874
4	2008	889.60	631.17	258.43	40.9446
5	2009	858.69	889.60	-30.91	-3.4746
6	2010	1117.96	858.69	259.27	30.1937
7	2011	1356.40	1117.96	238.44	21.3281
8	2012	1656.12	1356.40	299.72	22.0967
9	2013	1670.95	1656.12	14.83	0.8955
10	2014	1244.80	1670.95	-426.15	-25.5035

HANDS-ON EXAMPLE (ZIP FUNCTIONS)

A hospital is treating people with a rare disease from all over the world. They want to study the distance their patients have to travel for treatment based on the hospital and subject's zip code. The following program calculates that distance using ZIP functions.

1. Open the program file FUNC_ZIP.SAS.

```
DATA ZIP;
INPUT BEGIN $ END $;
HOSPITAL=ZIPCITY(BEGIN);
SUBJECT=ZIPCITY(END);
DISTANCE=ZIPCITYDISTANCE(BEGIN, END);
DATALINES;
75275 75201
75275 10001
75275 96801
75275 96951
;
PROC PRINT;
RUN;
```

   Run this program and the results are given in Table B.15. There you can see, for instance, that the distance from Honolulu to the hospital in Dallas is 3795 miles.

2. You are curious how far it is from the smallest zip code (Holtsville, NY, 00501) to the largest (Ketchikan, AK, 99950). Put those values into the program, run it, and observe the distance. (By the way, the 96951 zip code is for Sonsong (Rota) Mariana Islands (MP) which is northeast of Guam.)

(continued)

(continued)

TABLE B.15 Find Distances Using the ZIP Functions

Obs	BEGIN	END	HOSPITAL	SUBJECT	DISTANCE
1	75275	75201	Dallas, TX	Dallas, TX	4.0
2	75275	10001	Dallas, TX	New York, NY	1371.5
3	75275	96801	Dallas, TX	Honolulu, HI	3794.7
4	75275	96951	Dallas, TX	Rota, MP	7228.3

APPENDIX C

CHOOSING A SAS® PROCEDURE

The guidelines in this appendix help you determine the proper analysis to perform based on your data. In these tables the term *Normal* indicates that the procedure is based on a normality assumption. The term *at least ordinal* indicates that the data have an order.

C.1 DESCRIPTIVE STATISTICS

Make decision by reading from the left to the right (Table C.1).

TABLE C.1 Decision Table for Descriptive Statistics

	What Is the Data Type?	Statistical Procedures/SAS PROC
You want to describe a single variable.	Normal	Descriptive statistics: mean, standard deviation, etc. `PROC MEANS, UNIVARIATE` (Chapter 9)
	Quantitative	Descriptive statistics, median, histogram, boxplots `PROC UNIVARIATE` (Chapters 9 and 18)
	Categorical	Frequencies `PROC FREQ, GCHART` (Chapters 10 and 18)
You want to describe two related or paired variables.	Both are normal	Pearson's correlation and graphs `PROC CORR, REG, GPLOT` (Chapters 12 and 18)
	Both are at least ordinal	Spearman's correlation and graphs `PROC CORR, GPLOT` (Chapters 12 and 18)
	Both are categorical	Cross-tabulation (Chapters 10 and 18)

SAS® Essentials: Mastering SAS for Data Analytics, Second Edition. Alan C. Elliott and Wayne A. Woodward. © 2016 John Wiley & Sons, Inc. Published 2016 by John Wiley & Sons, Inc.

C.2   COMPARISON TESTS

Make decision by reading from the left to the right (Table C.2).

TABLE C.2   Decision Table for Comparison Tests

	What Is the Data Type?	Procedure to Use/SAS PROC
You are comparing a single sample to a norm (gold standard).	Normal	Single-sample t-test PROC MEANS, UNIVARIATE (Chapter 11)
	At least ordinal	Sign test PROC UNIVARIATE (Chapters 9 and 15)
	Categorical	Goodness-of-fit PROC FREQ (Chapter 10)
You are comparing data from two independent groups.	Normal	Two-sample t-test PROC TTEST (Chapter 11)
	At least ordinal	Mann–Whitney PROC NPAR1WAY (Chapter 15)
	Categorical	Test for homogeneity chi-square PROC FREQ (Chapter 10)
You are comparing paired, repeated, or matched data	Normal	Paired t-test PROC TTEST, UNIVARIATE (on difference) (Chapter 9 and 11)
	At least ordinal	Sign test or Wilcoxon signed-rank test PROC NPAR1WAY (Chapter 15)
	Binary (dichotomous)	McNemar PROC FREQ/AGREE (Chapter 10)
More than two groups – INDEPENDENT	Normal	One-way ANOVA PROC ANOVA, GLM (Chapter 13)
	At least ordinal	Kruskal–Wallis PROC NPAR1WAY (Chapter 15)
	Categorical	$r \times c$ test for homogeneity/chi-square, or kappa for interrater reliability PROC FREQ, FREQ/KAPPA (Chapter 10)
More than two groups – REPEATED MEASURES	Normal	Repeated measures PROC GLM (only for one way) or PROC MIXED (Chapter 14)
	At least ordinal	Friedman ANOVA PROC FREQ (Chapter 15)
	Categorical	Cochran Q (not discussed)
Comparing means, model includes covariate adjustment	Normal	Analysis of covariance PROC GLM (Chapter 14)

C.3   RELATIONAL ANALYSES (CORRELATION AND REGRESSION)

Make decision by reading from the left to the right (Table C.3).

TABLE C.3   Decision Table for Relational Analysis

	What Is the Data Type for the Dependent (Response) Variable?	Procedure to Use/SAS PROC
You want to analyze the relationship between two variables (if regression, one variable is classified as a response variable and the other a predictor variable).	Normal	Pearson correlation, simple linear regression PROC CORR, REG (Chapter 12)
	At least ordinal	Spearman correlation PROC CORR (Chapter 12)
	Categorical	$r \times c$ contingency table analysis PROC FREQ (Chapter 10)
	Binary	Logistic regression PROC LOGISTIC (Chapter 16)
You want to analyze the relationship between a response variable and two or more predictor variables.	Normal	Multiple linear regression PROC REG (Chapter 12)
	Binary	Logistic regression PROC LOGISTIC (Chapter 16)

In this table the term "Data type" applies to the dependent variable for regression procedures. For assessment of association (such as correlation or crosstabulation), the data type applies to both variables.

APPENDIX D

QUICK REFERENCE

This appendix provides a series of brief descriptions of basic SAS® tasks. Most of the tasks are listed here without explanation, except for a reference to a chapter.

Ways to name a data set – can be used whenever a dataset is named:

```
DATA SOMEDATA;     * create working/temporary data set;
DATA "C:\SASDATA\SOMEDATA"; *create permanent data set
   in specified location;
LIBNAME MYSASLIB "C:\SASDATA"; * create a temporary SAS library;
DATA MYSASLIB.SOMEDATA;     * create permanent data set in MYSASLIB
   library;
```

Versions of the INPUT statement:

```
* freeform input;
INPUT ID $ GENDER $ SBP DBP WEIGHT;
* column numbers specify location of data;
INPUT ID 1-4 SEX $ 5-5 AGE 6-9;
* specify beginning column, name, informat.
INPUT @1 ID 4. @5 SEX $1. @10 BDATE DATE9.;
```

Read date using format specification (see format table, Appendix A):

```
DATA MYDATA;
INPUT @1 FNAME $11. @12 LNAME $12. @24 BDATE DATE9.;
DATALINES;
```

SAS® Essentials: Mastering SAS for Data Analytics, Second Edition. Alan C. Elliott and Wayne A. Woodward.
© 2016 John Wiley & Sons, Inc. Published 2016 by John Wiley & Sons, Inc.

```
Bill        Smith        08JAN1952
;
RUN;
```

Ways to specify source of data or enter data set:

```
DATALINES;          * data are listed in the code following
   this statement;
INFILE filename;    * data are in an ASCII file on disk;
SET dataset;        * data are in a SAS data file;
PROC IMPORT;        * imports data from a non-SAS filetype;
```

Common ways to manipulate data within the DATA step (Chapters 4–7):

```
* Conditionally specify missing value;
IF AGE LE 0 then AGE = .;
IF SBP GE 140 THEN HIGHBP=1; ELSE HIGHBP=0; * If-Then-Else;
IF GENDER="MALE";              * Subsetting if statement;
* Define label for a variable name;
LABEL ID="Identification";
AREA=LENGTH * WIDTH;           * Calculate a new variable;
```

Titles and footnotes (Chapter 5)

```
TITLE 'First title line';
TITLE2 'Up to 9 title lines';
FOOTNOTE 'First footnote line';
FOOTNOTE9 'Up to 9 footnote lines';
```

ODS – Output Delivery System (Chapter 8)

```
ODS TRACE ON;
ODS GRAPHICS ON;
ODS LISTING; *standard output;
ODS HTML [BODY='FILENAME.HTML'];
ODS PDF [FILE='FILENAME.PDF'];
ODS RTF [FILE='FILENAME.RTF'];
ODS PS [FILE='FILENAME.PS'];
   PROC MEANS * PUT PROCS HERE;
ODS TYPE CLOSE;
ODS TRACE OFF;
ODS GRAPHICS OFF;
```

PROC FORMAT – used to define custom formats for values (Chapter 4)

```
PROC FORMAT;
VALUE $fmtsex 'F' = 'Female'
              'M' = 'Male';
VALUE   fmtyn 1='Yes'
              2='No';
PROC PRINT;     * apply a format to variables;
```

```
FORMAT SEX $fmtsex.
       QUEST fmtyn.;
RUN;
```

PROC SORT – sort a data set (Chapter 4)

```
PROC SORT DATA=dataset;
   BY AGE SBP descending;
RUN;
```

PROC PRINT – create a listing of the data (Chapter 5)

```
PROC PRINT DATA=dataset;
   VAR varlist;
   SUM sumvar;
RUN;
```

PROC MEANS – used to calculate statistics for quantitative data (Chapter 9)

```
PROC MEANS N MEAN MEDIAN MAXDEC=2 DATA=dataset;
   VAR varlist;
RUN;
PROC MEANS DATA=dataset; * Means by group;
   CLASS groupvar;
   VAR varlist);
RUN;
```

PROC UNIVARIATE – calculate detailed statistics on a variable (Chapter 9)

```
PROC UNIVARIATE DATA=dataset NORMAL PLOT;
   VAR SBP;
   HISTOGRAM SBP/NORMAL;
RUN;
```

PROC FREQ – frequencies and crosstabulations (Chapter 10)

```
PROC FREQ DATA=dataset; * basic frequency table;
   TABLES varlist;
RUN;
PROC FREQ DATA=dataset;
   TABLES var1*var2/CHISQ; * crosstabulation with chi-square;
RUN;
```

PROC TTEST – comparing means (Chapter 11)

```
PROC TTEST DATA=dataset H0=30; * Single sample t-test;
   VAR varname;
RUN;
PROC TTEST DATA=dataset; * independent group t-test;
   CLASS groupvar;
   VAR varname;
```

```
RUN;
PROC TTEST DATA=dataset; * paired t-test;
   PAIRED WBEFORE*WAFTER;
RUN;
```

PROC ANOVA, GLM, and MIXED – comparing more than three means (Chapters 13 and 14)

```
PROC ANOVA DATA=dataset; * one-way independent group;
   CLASS groupvar;
   MODEL depvar= groupvar;
   MEANS groupvar /TUKEY;
RUN;
PROC GLM;                * two fixed-factors;
  CLASS factor1var factor2var;
  MODEL RESPONSE= factor1var factor2var factor1var*factor2var;
RUN;
PROC MIXED;              * two-factor, one random;
  CLASS randomfactor fixedfactor;
  MODEL depvar = fixedfactor;
  RANDOM randomfactor randomfactor*fixedfactor;
RUN;
```

PROC CORR – correlations between pairs of variables (Chapter 12)

```
PROC CORR DATA=SOMEDATA Spearman Pearson;
   VAR AGE TIME1-TIME4;
RUN;
```

PROC REG – linear regression analysis (Chapter 12)

```
PROC REG DATA=dataset; * simple linear regression;
    MODEL dependentvar = independentvar/R; * examine residuals;
RUN;
PROC REG DATA=dataset;     * multiple linear regresson;
    MODEL dependentvar = ind1 ind2 ...etc
    /SELECTION=STEPWISE
    SLENTRY=0.05
    SLSTAY=0.05;
RUN;
```

PROC NPAR1WAY – nonparametric comparisons (Chapter 15)

```
PROC NPAR1WAY DATA=dataset;
    CLASS GROUP;            * compare independent groups;
    VAR SALARY;
RUN;
```

PROC LOGISTIC – logistic regression (Chapter 16)

```
PROC LOGISTIC DATA=dataset;
```

```
CLASS variables;
MODEL dependentvar = independentvar(s)
/ EXPB
  SELECTION=SETPWISE
  SLENTRY=0.05
  SLSTAY=0.1
  RISKLIMITS
  CTABLE
  OUTROC=ROC1;
RUN;
```

PROC FACTOR – factor analysis (Chapter 17)

```
PROC FACTOR DATA=dataset;
    METHOD=P PRIORS=SMC
    ROTATE=PROMAX SCREE CORR RES;
RUN;
```

PROC GPLOT – scatterplot with regression line (Chapter 18)

```
GOPTIONS RESET=ALL;
SYMBOL1 V=STAR I=RL;
PROC GPLOT DATA=dataset;
  PLOT yvar*xvar;
RUN;
QUIT;
```

PROC GCHART – barchart (Chapter 18)

```
PROC GCHART DATA=dataset;
  HBAR varname;
RUN;
```

PROC BOXPLOT – boxplot (Chapter 18)

```
PROC SORT DATA=dataset; BY groupvar;
PROC BOXPLOT DATA=dataset;
    PLOT varname*groupvar;
RUN;
```

PROC TABULATE – create tables (Chapter 19)

```
PROC TABULATE DATA=dataset ORDER=FORMATTED;
  CLASS TYPE AREA SITE;
  VAR SALES_K;
  TABLE(AREA="" ALL),(SITE="" ALL)*TYPE=""
        *MEAN=""*SALES_K=""*F=DOLLAR6.2;
  FORMAT AREA $FMTCOMPASS.;
RUN;
```

PROC REPORT – create reports (Chapter 19)

```
PROC REPORT DATA=MYSASLIB.CARS NOFS;
  COLUMN BRAND CITYMPG,SUV HWYMPG,SUV;
  DEFINE BRAND/ORDER;
  DEFINE BRAND/GROUP;
  DEFINE CITYMPG/ANALYSIS MEAN FORMAT=6.1;
  DEFINE HWYMPG/ANALYSIS MEAN FORMAT=6.1;
  DEFINE SUV/ ACROSS 'BY SUV';
  FORMAT SUV FMTSUV.;
RUN;
```

PUT STATEMENTS – create reports (Chapter 19)

```
DATA _NULL; SET GRADES END=EOF;
TABLEHEAD="SUMMARY OF GRADES";
FILE PRINT;
IF _N_ = 1 then DO; * PUT HEADER;
     L=5+(60-LENGTH(TABLEHEAD))/2; * CENTER HEAD;
     PUT @L TABLEHEAD;
     PUT @5 60*'=';
     PUT @5 "NAME" @20 "| TEST 1" @30 "| TEST 2 "
        @40 "| TEST 3" @50 "| AVERAGE";
     PUT @5 60*'-';
END;
PUT @5 NAME @20 "|" G1 5.1 @30 "|" G2 5.1
          @40 "|" G3 5.1 @50 "|" AVE 5.1;
IF EOF =1 then do; * PUT BOTTOM OF TABLE;
     PUT @5 60*'-';
     PUT @5 "CLASS AVERAGE " @; * HOLDS LINE FOR NEXT PUT;
     PUT @50 "| %TRIM(&CLASSMEAN) " ;
     PUT @5 60*'=';
END;
RUN;
```

Sample Complete SAS Program - This sample SAS program illustrates many of the components of the SAS DATA Step covered in this book. (See `SampleProgram.SAS`)

```
***** PROC FORMAT defines formats for categorical variables;
PROC FORMAT;
VALUE $fmtgender 'F' = 'Female'  'M' = 'Male';
VALUE  fmtversion  1='Test Version 1' 2='Test Version 2';
VALUE  fmtyn      1='Yes' 0='No';
RUN;
* Define up to 9 titles and footnotes;
TITLE 'Example SAS Program';
TITLE2 'From SAS Essentials by Elliott and Woodward';
FOOTNOTE 'Uses the SURVEY data Set';
FOOTNOTE3 'Illustrates typical SAS DATA statements';
* Begin a data set by reading a current SAS data set;
DATA NEW; SET MYSASLIB.SAMPLE;
****** apply formats to several variables;
```

```
FORMAT GENDER $fmtgender. VERSION  fmtversion. SATISFIED
MARRIED FMTYN.;
FORMAT SCHOOLING $14.;
****** Create a new variable by calculation;
IF SATISFACTION GT 80 then SATISFIED=1; ELSE SATISFIED=0;
****** Create a new variable using IN statement;
IF ARRIVE IN("BUS" "CAR") then HOW="Arrive by Vehicle"; else
HOW='Arrived by Walking';
****** define labels;
LABEL  GENDER="Gender"
       MARRIED="Married"
       SATISFIED="Satisfied with Service"
       HOW="How Arrived at Clinic?"
       SCHOOLING="How Much School"
       AGE="Age in 2016";
****** set missing values;
IF TEMP GT 110 then TEMP=.;
IF GENDER="X" then GENDER="";
****** Use a subsetting IF to limit records in the dataset;
IF STAYMINUTES GE 20;
****** Recode a value using SELECT;
SELECT;
   WHEN (EDU LT 12 and EDU GT 5) SCHOOLING="Less than 12";
   WHEN (EDU EQ 12) SCHOOLING="High School";
   OTHERWISE SCHOOLING="Some College";
END;
****** DROP (or KEEP) certain variables;
DROP SATISFACTION EDU;
RUN;

PROC PRINT LABEL DATA=NEW;
VAR  GENDER AGE MARRIED HOW SATISFIED SCHOOLING;
RUN;

PROC MEANS MAXDEC=2 DATA=NEW;
CLASS SCHOOLING;
VAR TEMP STAYMINUTES;
RUN;

PROC FREQ DATA=NEW;
TABLES SCHOOLING*HOW/CHISQ NOPERCENT NOCOL;
RUN;
```

APPENDIX E

USING SAS® UNIVERSITY EDITION WITH SAS ESSENTIALS

SAS University Edition (SUE) is a fully functional version of SAS software that includes these components: SAS Studio, Base SAS, SAS/STAT, SAS/IML, and SAS/ACCESS. (These modules are sufficient for performing most of the examples in this book. Exceptions are indicated in the following section named "Limitations.") Although the interface is different from a locally installed version, the program provides the same analytics software provided by the standard SAS version. In addition, the SUE will run on a PC (Windows), Mac, or Linux workstation. The key difference is that in order to run the SUE version, you must have an active Internet connection. When you submit (run) a SAS program using SUE, the code is sent to a server (via the Internet) and the code is processed there and returned to your workstation.

This appendix shows how you can use SUE to run the examples in *SAS Essentials*. The main differences are in the user interface and how you access files. This brief information tells you how to access files for *SAS Essentials* in the SUE.

E.1 INSTALLING SAS UNIVERSITY EDITION

Follow the instructions provided by SAS to install the SUE. It differs according to the type of computer you are using. Here is a summary of the instructions (for installation on Windows).

Step 1: Download Visualization Software To install SUE, go to http://www.sas.com/en_us/software/university-edition/download-software.html and follow the instructions from SAS on installing a virtualization program (free) for your computer. For this example, we'll use the Oracle VM VirtualBox on a Windows platform. (There are several virtual applications to choose from on this web page. Choose the one that matches your computer's operating system.)

SAS® Essentials: Mastering SAS for Data Analytics, Second Edition. Alan C. Elliott and Wayne A. Woodward.
© 2016 John Wiley & Sons, Inc. Published 2016 by John Wiley & Sons, Inc.

Suggestions:

- Accept the defaults for installing the Virtual Box.
- We recommend that you download and print the "Start Guide" for specific instructions on installing the SUE on your computer. Note: You must have a SAS profile (free to set up). You will be prompted to set up a profile during the install process if you don't already have one.
- This download can take 30 minutes or more depending on your computer and network speed.

Step 2: Add SAS to your VirtualBox (Important): We recommend that you download the sample files used in this book before you set up SUE. Go to the http://www. alanelliott.com/sas website and follow instructions for downloading these sample files. This creates a folder on your computer named C:\SASDATA that contains the sample files used for *SAS Essentials.*

As part of the SUE setup, you are instructed to create a folder (in Windows) named C:\SASUniversityEdition\myfolders. To set up the program for *SAS Essentials,* also create a folder named C:\SASUniversityEdition\myfolders\SASDATA. And copy and paste all of the files from the C:\SASDATA folder into C:\SASUniversityEdition\myfolders\SASDATA. (Make note of the case used for myfolders since this will become important later.)

From the same SUE web page, locate the Quick Start Guide link that matches the virtualization program you installed in Step 1. Follow those instructions to add SAS to your virtual machine. (Step 3 uses the instructions named "Oracle VirtualBox Quick Start Guide ".)

Step 3: Begin SAS   Once you have installed the Visualization Software and SUE, these are typical steps to begin SAS:

1. Open the Visualization Software you installed in Step 1. (This example uses Oracle VirtualBox.) The Oracle VM VirtualBox Manager is shown in Figure E.1.

Figure E.1   Oracle VM VirtualBox Manager. (Source: Created with SAS® software, Version 9.4. Copyright 2012, SAS Institute Inc., Cary, NC, USA. All Rights Reserved. Reproduced with permission of SAS Institute Inc., Cary, NC)

Start the SUE "Machine" by double-clicking on the SAS University logo in the left panel. (Or see the SAS instructions "Quick Start Guide" if you are using a different visualization software.)

2. After the virtual machine has started, open a browser. (In our experience, we find that both Internet Explorer and Firefox work fine with the Oracle VirtualBox.)

3. In the browser address box, enter the following address: http://localhost:10080/ and press Enter. A screen similar to Figure E.2 should appear.

4. Click on the Start SAS Studio button. The initial screen for SAS Studio is shown in Figure E.3.

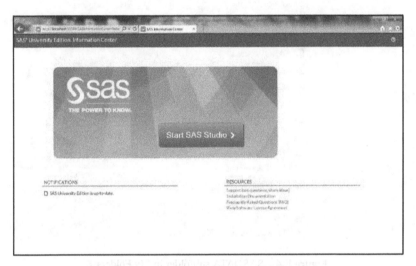

Figure E.2   Initial SAS University Edition Screen.

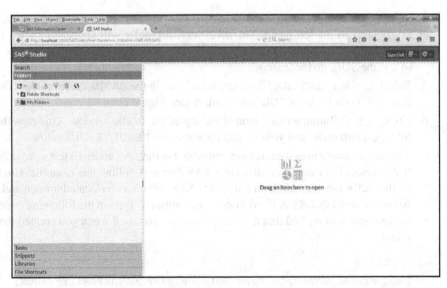

Figure E.3   Initial SAS Studio Screen.

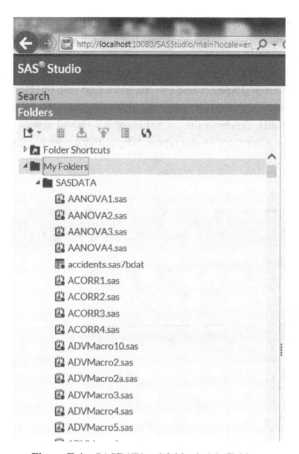

Figure E.4   SASDATA subfolder in My Folders.

Step 4: Using SUE with the SAS Essentials data sets and example code. Double-click on My Folders in the left panel. The SASDATA subfolder will appear as shown in Figure E.4 (if you installed it in Step 2).

To test the SUE, do these steps:

A. Select the file FIRST.SAS from the list of files in the SASDATA subfolder. The code will open in the "CODE" tab window (see Figure E.5).

B. Click on the "Running man" icon at the top of the CODE window. This runs the SAS program code, and your results appear in the RESULTS tab window.

C. This first example uses data that are embedded in the SAS code. To test a program that accesses data stored on disk (in a SAS data set), follow this example. Click on the CODE tab, then click on the New SAS Program icon (located immediately below the word CODE). A blank code screen appears. Type in the following code, making sure that myfolders matches the case you used when you created that folder.

```
PROC MEANS DATA="/folders/myfolders/SASDATA/FAMILY"; RUN;
```

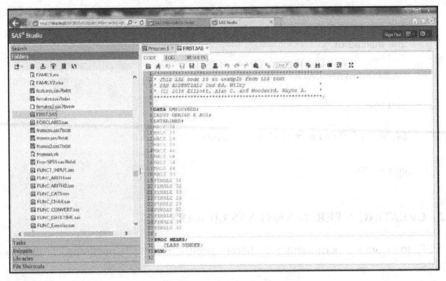

Figure E.5   FIRST.SAS Opened.

TABLE E.1   Output for PROC MEANS

The SAS System					
The MEANS Procedure					
Variable	N	Mean	Std Dev	Minimum	Maximum
FOODEXP	75	7.1293333	5.9533042	2.5000000	51.0000000
INCOME	75	37.9466667	19.4205891	12.0000000	112.0000000
FAMILYSIZE	75	2.7733333	1.5472149	1.0000000	7.0000000
AGE	75	37.5200000	10.9116352	23.0000000	68.0000000
OWNRENT	75	0.5200000	0.5029642	0	1.0000000

After you enter this code, click the running man icon and the output in Table E.1 appears. This verifies that you have access to the SAS files in the SASDATA subfolder. (If you get an error, examine the Log and note the errors reported. Click on the CODE tab again, correct any errors in your code, and resubmit.)

D. Make note that whenever you see a file path in this book such as C:\SASDATA, (and you are using the SUE), you must instead use this path:

```
/folders/myfolders/SASDATA/
```

where myfolders matches the case of the folder you created. For example, instead of

```
PROC MEANS DATA="C:\SASDATA\SOMEDATA";
```

you would use

```
PROC MEANS DATA="/folders/myfolders/SASDATA/SOMEDATA";
```

and instead of

```
DATA "C:\SASDATA\NEWDATA";
```

you use

```
DATA "/folders/myfolders/SASDATA/NEWDATA";
```

and so on.

E.2   CREATING A PERMANENT SAS LIBRARY

In SUE, to create the permanent SAS library similar to those is mentioned in this book, do this:

1. Click on the Libraries Tab at the left of the screen.
2. Click on the leftmost icon (New Library). The dialog box shown in Figure E.6 appears. Enter the information shown in the dialog box to create a library called mysaslib. Make sure case for /folders/myfolders/ matches what you created for that folder.
3. Make sure you check the box "Re-create this library at start-up."
4. Click OK to create the folder.

Figure E.6   Create a SAS Library Dialog Box.

To test your library setup, click on the CODE table and enter

```
PROC MEANS data=mysaslib.family;RUN;
```

If successful, the results of the PROC MEANS will appear in your RESULTS tab. (The same results as shown in Table E.1.)

E.3 LIMITATIONS

A few SAS PROCS are not included in SUE, so examples in this book that use these PROCS will not run. These include PROC that created graphs in GPLOT, GCHART, and BOXPLOT. Graphs in other PROCs such as the normal plot in PROC UNIVARIATE are also not available. However, ODS-type graphs created in analysis PROCs such as PROC TTEST are provided in this edition.

E.4 SUMMARY

The SAS University Edition is available free to all students and educators and can be downloaded from the web. You need an active Internet connection to run this version of SAS. The SAS University Edition is sufficient to do most of the examples in *SAS Essentials*, and can be used to learn basic SAS programming skills.

REFERENCES

Cohen, J., Cohen, P., West, S.G., and Aiken, L.S. (2002). *Applied multiple regression/correlation analysis for the behavioral sciences* (3rd Edition). Mahwah, N.J.: Lawrence Erlbaum.

Elliott, A.C., and Hynan, L.S. (2007). "A SAS Macro Implementation of a Multiple Comparison Post Hoc Test." Proceedings of the Joint Statistical Meetings.

Elliott, A.C., and Woodward, W.A. (1986). "Analysis of an Unbalanced Two-Way ANOVA on the Microcomputer". *Commun Stat*, B15(1):215–25.

Fleiss, J.L. (1981). *Statistical methods for rates and proportions* (2nd Edition). New York: Wiley.

Frigge M., Hoaglin, D.C., and Iglewicz, B. (1989). "Some Implements of the Boxplot". *Am Stat* 43(1):50–54.

Gardiner, H. (2006). *Multiple intelligences: new horizons*. New York: Basic Books.

Hand, D., Daly, F., McConway, K., Lunn, D., and Ostrowski, E. (1994). *A handbook of small data sets*. Boca Raton, F.L.: Chapman and Hall.

Hosmer, D.W., and Lemeshow, S. (2000). *Applied logistic regression* (2nd Edition). New York: Wiley.

Johnson, D.E. (1998). *Applied multivariate methods for data analysis*. Pacific Grove, C.A.: Duxbury Press.

Johnson, R.A., and Wichern, D.W. (2007). *Applied multivariate statistical analysis* (6th Edition). Englewood Cliffs, N.J.: Pearson Prentice Hall.

Landis, J.R., and Koch, G.G. (1977). "The Measurement of Observer Agreement for Categorical Data". *Biometrics* 33:159–74.

Littell, R.C., Milliken, G.A., Stroup, W.W., and Wolfinger, R.D. (1996). *SAS system for mixed models*. Cary, N.C.: SAS Institute, Inc.

McGill, R., Tukey, J.W., and Larsen, W. A. (1978). "Variations of Box Plots". *Am Stat*, 32:12–16.

Moore, D., McCabe, G., and Craig, B. (2014). *Introduction to the practice of statistics* (8th Edition). New York: Freeman.

Stevens, J.P. (2002). *Applied multivariate statistics for the social sciences* (4th Edition), Mahwah, N.J.: Lawrence Erlbaum Associates, Publishers.

SAS$^®$ Essentials: Mastering SAS for Data Analytics, Second Edition. Alan C. Elliott and Wayne A. Woodward.
© 2016 John Wiley & Sons, Inc. Published 2016 by John Wiley & Sons, Inc.

FURTHER READING

District of Columbia's 2005 Cities Crimes and Rates as reported in the FBI's September 2006 release of the "UCR for Metropolitan Statistical Areas," http://www.disastercenter.com/crime/dccrime.htm.

SAS Institute, Inc. (2013). *SAS/STAT software: reference, version 9.3*. Cary, N.C.: SAS Institute, Inc.

INDEX

SAS® *Essentials: Mastering SAS for Data Analytics*, Second Edition. Alan C. Elliott and Wayne A. Woodward.
© 2016 John Wiley & Sons, Inc. Published 2016 by John Wiley & Sons, Inc.